A Tale Within a Tale

A Personal Journey through the 20th Century

by
Maureen Barclay

Researched by
Sheila Carpenter

emp3
books

published by emp3books

Published in October 2010 by emp3books,
Kiln Workshops, Pilcot Road, Crookham Village,
Fleet, Hampshire, GU51 5RY, England

©Maureen Barclay

The author asserts the moral right to be identified as the author of
this work

ISBN-13: 978-1-907140-27-3

Front cover designed by Sheila Carpenter

www.emp3books.com

For Victoria

in memory of the great-grandparents

you have never met

but whose legacy lives on.

CONTENTS

INTRODUCTION

I used to spend many a happy hour listening to my parents' reminiscences about their childhoods in the early 1900's. Even then (from the 1960's onwards) they were talking about a bygone age and already the changes they had witnessed were truly remarkable.

I suppose, at that stage, I had the vague notion that I would someday pass these memories on to my own children, but fate decreed otherwise. Thus, as the century entered its twilight years, I realised the memories would have to be recorded if they were not to be forever lost. So in 1983 Mum, Dad and I sat down and made tape recordings of everything they could remember.

The cassette tapes were then stored for another twenty years, largely ignored but surviving my parents' demise, moves abroad, children becoming parents and grandparents and myself moving, all too rapidly, towards old age.

Then several things conspired to make me re-play the tapes and to push me towards making written records of some kind. For one thing several cousins were amazed that I held so many memories of the family and they all said they would love to hear the stories. Then my sister became a grandmother and we realised that Vicky would never have the joy of knowing our parents. It was Sheila who suggested the memories should be turned into a book. So the blame is entirely hers.

CHAPTER ONE

A New Century Dawns
(1901-1902)

1901 had just begun, and suddenly Britain and its Empire had to imagine a world without their monarch.   The unthinkable had happened.   After a record sixty-three years on the throne, Queen Victoria had died, on 22nd January, at eighty-one years of age.

Her death marked the end of the remarkable "Victorian era", which had seen constitutional government fully develop, the crown's prestige restored, the empire grow, and had been witness to so many innovations in roads, railways, canals, underground trains, electric tramways, steam-ships, wireless telegraphy and the newly-invented internal combustion engine.   The Queen's sense of duty, and strict moral code, had set the pattern for nineteenth-century Britain and now she would be succeeded by her son "Bertie", who took the title Edward VII.   The century was thus about to begin the "Edwardian era" and, with a pleasure-loving King about to be crowned, for the favoured few it must have seemed that a more halcyon time was ahead.

But, despite the many innovations of the "Victorian Age", the vast majority of people still had to live in a world without domestic electricity, and thus without any modern appliances, such as washing machines or television sets, that nowadays we take for granted.   It was a world without cars or aeroplanes.   A world without telephones, computers or even a ballpoint pen.   A world without penicillin, antibiotics or any vaccinations against common diseases such as measles, diphtheria or tetanus.

This was the world at the dawn of the twentieth century, just over one hundred years ago, and this was the world that greeted my parents, Clem and Anne Oakley, née Martin.   This is their story, told within the personal and public events that happened around them, so let me tell you a little about where it all began.

Clement Benjamin Oakley was born on 8th October 1901 and Annie Elizabeth Ellen Martin four years later, on 20th August 1905, and not a lot changed in those four years, but Dad was a country-boy and Mum a town-girl and in many ways their childhoods were very different.   So join me on a nostalgic journey into the heart of rural Sussex, circa 1900, as I relate Clem's story first.

The actual place in which Clem was born was a little village called Duncton, which stands high on the South Downs, 830 feet above sea level. In 1901 it had 140 residents and was surrounded by farms, as it still is today. It has been inhabited for centuries and even has the remains of Roman buildings buried in its fields. It boasted a church, a school, a mill and a public house called *The Cricketers*, in honour of two past residents, Jimmy Dean and Jem Broadbridge, who both played cricket for Sussex in the nineteenth century. The church also has a claim to fame as it has one of the oldest bells in England, dated 1369. Over the centuries, there have been no less than four working mills recorded in the parish of Duncton; a paper mill, a dye mill and two corn mills, testament to the abundant and steady supply of water from the many streams emanating from the chalk strata.

Situated above the valley of the River Rother, Duncton is just one mile south from the medieval market-town of Petworth with its narrow, cobbled streets, old, half-timbered, Tudor houses and perhaps the finest of all the Sussex mansions, Petworth Park, the original seat of the Dukes of Somerset and set in a 700 acre deer park, landscaped by Capabilty Brown and immortalized in Turner's paintings. (Since 1947 the mansion has been in the hands of the National Trust.)

In 1901, the road linking Petworth to Duncton was little more than a glorified cart-track, rough and dusty in summer and rutted and potholed in winter, with a long, steep hill winding onwards and upwards from the village to Duncton Beacon and beyond. In 1901 negotiating the hill would be strenuous and difficult but in bad weather it must have been almost impassable. I remember in the 1970′s, when I was working in an office in the coastal town of Bognor Regis, some twenty miles away, a colleague drove in from Petworth every day and, in the ice and snow of winter, she had trouble getting the car up Duncton Hill.... and this was in a modern car on tarmacadamed roads! In 1901 there would be virtually no cars of course; the traffic then would be foot travellers, people on horse-back, carts and carriages, and dray wagons pulled by huge working-horses: Shires, Suffolk Punches or Clydesdales. The occasional bicycle might be spotted, even an old penny-farthing, but none would be easy to negotiate on the many hills in the area.

On market days, intermingled with the extra travellers, would be drovers, and their working dogs, from the surrounding farms, herding cattle, sheep and pigs before them for sale in the tiny market-square in Petworth. No large-scale factory-farming in 1901 but added to the dust or mud, depending on the season and the vagaries of the weather, would be animal excrement! This was a real problem on all roads when the main mode of transport was the horse and thus some poor soul would be designated to clear the road of the worst of the mess and transport it by dung-cart to a neighbouring farm. There it would be added to a huge pile of manure which, when rotted down,

4

would be ploughed into the fields to add much valued nutrients to the soil. No artificial fertilizers or nitrates in 1901, nor were there artificial pesticides or herbicides, and it would be another ten or twenty years before cars were a regular sight on the road.

Eventually, and inevitably, we too drove along the road occasionally (now the modern A285 Petworth to Chichester road) on our regular, family, Sunday afternoon excursions into the countryside and, whenever we did so, Dad would invariably point to a cottage, just off the main road, and say, "That's where I was born!". We would dutifully turn our heads and peer (yet again!), at a small, very modest dwelling, one of a pair of a "two-rooms-up, two-rooms-down" design, set almost right on the road-side. There was no front garden to speak of but, as was normal in Victorian times when the house was built, there was a large, back garden where the tenant of the day could grow some vegetables, keep a few chicken or ducks, possibly a nanny-goat for milk, or even fatten up a goose as a special treat for Christmas. When Clem was born, most rural families would keep a pig or two at the bottom of the plot, to eat the scraps, devour the vegetable debris, and generally get bigger and fatter until it too could be eaten. Nothing would be wasted.

In 1901, electricity was still in its infancy and it would be thirty years before it became a common amenity in most households. Thus there were no modern, labour-saving devices whatsoever: no washing machines, no vacuum cleaners, and no electric stoves. Not even electric lights. The only indoor artificial lights would be oil-lamps, powered by kerosene, or candles. Outdoors, hurricane lamps would be used, for there were no street lamps in rural Sussex.

Probably there would not have been water piped to the house. Most rural communities were still using a communal pump, or a well sited somewhere in the garden. Most houses would have a water-butt or two collecting rain-water, but all other water would have to be carried to the house in pails and any hot water would have to be heated on the fire, or in the copper. No house in those days would have been without "a copper" unless you were really, really poor. This was like a large barrel, made of copper, with a wooden lid, and raised off the ground so a fire could be lit underneath and thus heat the water. Coal or coke might be used for the fire in towns but the cost of transport would be prohibitive in the countryside, so the more readily available wood would be used instead. The copper was usually stored in an outhouse and came into its own on wash-day when soap, grated from a huge solid bar, would be added to the water and then all the cotton and linen articles (sheets, towels, shirts, underwear and suchlike) would be scrubbed and thrown into it to be boiled up.

The country kitchen of 1901 would be unrecognisable today. It would be the room for cooking, dining, living and probably even washing. If there was a sink, this would double as a kitchen-sink and a wash-basin and would probably not be in this room but in the outhouse, or a separate room called the scullery; if there was no sink then wooden or galvanised pails or buckets would be placed outside on benches instead. There would be no cooking stove as we know it, but there might be something called a "kitchener" in the recess of the fireplace. This can only be likened to a primitive "Aga", made in cast-iron and fuelled by wood, with a compartment with a door where the fuel was placed. There would be hot-plates on the top for pans and kettles and an oven at the side for bread, casseroles etc.

But most countrymen's cottages would not have had this luxury and then all the cooking would have to be done on the open fire, either with a grid across it, on which the cooking pots and pans could be placed, or in pots hanging over the embers and secured by chains to the top of the fireplace. Some of the older cottages might have had a brick oven at the side of the fire-place, a real advantage, otherwise bread would have to be cooked on a simple griddle, which sat on the embers and resembled something like a metal plate with a handle.

The furniture would be minimal; a scrubbed table in the kitchen for food preparation and for use as a dining table, some hard-back chairs, a bench for the children and possibly a rocking-chair or a wooden settle placed near the fire. A wooden dresser might stand against one wall to contain plates, cutlery and the like, and iron saucepans, blackened from the fire, might be hung on the walls or placed under the sink, if there was one! Lines would be strung across the ceiling of the kitchen on which to dry and air the washing on inclement days, and the floor would be bare flagstones. The best furniture would be reserved for the front room, or parlour, which was used to entertain visitors, unless it was a small house with a large family and then it might have to be turned into another bedroom. The bedrooms were generally upstairs: one main room with a double bed for the parents and a cot or crib for the latest baby, and beds in the other room(s) in which the children slept together, with the sexes strictly segregated, even from an early age; boys in one bed, girls in the other.

There would have been no bathroom in 1901. The bath would be a large, portable, oblong tub made of galvanised metal, usually placed in what was called the kitchen, in front of the fire. The water for it would be heated by the copper, or on an open fire, or on the kitchener, if there was one, and then transported to the bath in a kettle, bowl or saucepan. (No plastic products in 1901!) Bath-nights were usually once a week, if you were lucky, the family taking it in turns to share the same water. (Normally parents first, then children in descending age, hence the saying, " *Don't throw out the baby with the bath water!*" as by the time the poor baby got to the water it was so murky you could not see the bottom of the bath!)

So no bathroom and no indoor toilet. The toilet would have been an earth closet in another wood or brick-built outhouse at the bottom of the garden, as far away from the house as possible! It might even have been shared with the house next door and was basically just a pit with a wooden box structure on the top with a lid which had a round hole in the middle, or possibly even had two round holes so you could share the experience with a family member or even your neighbour! Occasionally lime would be thrown into the stinking mass but the smell was still indescribable. But the house and its amenities were typical of its day in the rural areas and the farm workers would be grateful for the solid walls and a weather-proof roof.

There was no television, radio or gramophone for entertainment, all these had yet to be invented, so in the evenings, when it was too dark to work outside, the lady of the house would mend, or darn, knit or sew and the men would smoke their pipes and read (if they were able to read), or perhaps make a piece of furniture or whittle a toy for the children. Occasionally they might play cards together, but the duties of the sexes were clearly defined in 1901, and it would be rare indeed for a husband to cook, or sew, or change a baby, any more than a wife would be expected to chop wood, or drive a cart.

It was a hard life for the rural poor and only the toughest survived. Clem's father, my grandfather, was born in 1878 and had been working since he was eight years old, when he went to work under his father who was a stockman. He could write his name and read simple text but his literacy abilities were very limited. In 1901 he was just 23 years of age and already married with a small daughter, Mabel Louisa. His Christian names were Benjamin Clement (a reversal of his first-born son's names) and, at this time, he was employed by Lord Woolavington, at nearby Graffham, as a carter. (A carter looked after and worked the horses, including ploughing, and maintained and drove the farm-carts.) His Lordship was famous as a race-horse breeder but he also bred shire-horses, so, as part of his carter duties, Ben was responsible for breeding and rearing the working-horses.

Ben was short in stature but as strong as an ox, with broad, calloused hands, giving testament to hard manual labour. Despite an over-large nose and big ears, he was still a good-looking man with twinkling, blue eyes and a ready smile. In the early 1900's he sported the fashionable bushy moustache of the day and invariably had a flat cap perched on his head, gaiters or string tied around his calves and a clay pipe clamped between his teeth, belching out noxious fumes of his favourite *Black Beauty* tobacco. He had a stubborn, selfish streak but he was normally a patient man, a hard worker and with a sense of humour that must have appealed to his wife, May Blanche Pilkington, known to her family by her second name. In later years, the moustache became a long, bushy beard and, with his wizened, shrivelled frame, he always reminded me of an animated garden-gnome! His favourite saying was, "*I'll live to be 100 or die in the attempt!*" In the event he lived to see his 95th birthday, smoking his tobacco right to the end, which, in his case at least, rather made a nonsense of the (much later) Government health warning on the packet. He had lived to see so many changes, including the introduction of the National Health Service, a man on the moon and television in his living room. Of the latter, he truly believed that the young female newsreaders could see him just as well as he could see them, and he used to say, "*She smiled at me, you know!*"

Not much is known about Clem's mother, (May) Blanche Oakley, née Pilkington, born in Islington, London, in 1882, and sadly we have no photograph of her. Cameras had been around since the 1850's but, in the early 1900's, they were generally still cumbersome, box-like objects, mounted on a tripod, and the operator disappeared under a black shroud before he pressed a rubber ball that would activate the mechanism and record the image. They were not that easy to transport and thus they were generally used in a studio and produced very stiff, highly-posed, po-faced portraits. It is possible Ben and Blanche posed for such a photograph to commemorate their wedding in 1899 but, alas, if they did so, it has disappeared with the passage of time. Clem remembered her only as small and slim, worn out with work and worry and bearing too many children, but she was always there to kiss away a hurt, or give a cuddle when things went wrong. Where his father was a rather distant, authoritarian figure, typical of the Victorian age in which he was born, Clem remembered his mother only as gentle and kind. He adored her but in later years he found it hard to forgive his father for saddling his mother with so many children in quick succession. Oakley legend has it that she came from a well-to-do lineage whose family felt she was marrying beneath her. Perhaps she was the much-loved and pampered daughter of a city merchant? But, be that as it may, what IS known, is that she married, at just seventeen years of age, without her parents' blessing and that, after the conjugal knot was tied, she never saw her parents, or her family, again.

Their first child, Mabel Louisa, was born in July 1900, exactly a

8

year after their wedding and, as we know, Clem was born a little over a year later, in October 1901. Marrying Ben, therefore, must have come as a huge culture shock and was not made easier by the fact that Ben liked a pint (or two) of beer after a hard day's work. Apart from the terrible drain this must have placed on the precarious family finances (even if a pint of beer did only cost 3d in those days) if he had rather more than a couple of pints, he became argumentative and unreasonable. Also he changed jobs frequently in these early days of his marriage and, as every change of job meant a change of house, because they invariably lived in the cottage that went with the employment, poor Blanche must have despaired of ever being settled. And by 1902, baby number three was already on its way.

CHAPTER TWO

Food, Fire and Theft!
(1903-1908)

Baby number three was another boy, born in 1903, and christened Edwin but forever known as Ted by the family. By the time Blanche junior came along two years later, in February 1905, Ben had changed jobs (and houses) again and over the years, to my knowledge, would work as a cowman, a shepherd and a thatcher, and probably there were other occupations that he undertook. But this is not as unlikely, or as unusual, as it sounds, as all countrymen were remarkably versatile, turning their calloused hands to a large number of the varied jobs demanded of them. Sometimes he changed employment for more money, or extra perquisites like free milk, or a better house, but at other times just because it suited him so to do.

Moving house normally meant piling your meagre belongings on a hand-cart and slowly, slowly wending your way along country lanes until you reached your new abode. At barely more than walking pace, this could take all day if they were moving any distance, and would have been no joke in the pouring rain. For some of the younger children it might be the first time they had travelled more than a few miles from home.

Finding enough food for them all was a constant headache and often had to be supplemented by rabbiting, preferably using ferrets, and even poaching. As the boys got older, their father showed them how to set snares to catch the rabbits. They would set off early in the morning, before it was properly light, and put a noose of thin wire around the rabbit holes, secured with a peg of wood. The idea was that the rabbit would come out of its burrow, with or without the aid of a ferret put down the hole first, and get trapped in the wire noose as it tried to wriggle to freedom. Then the rabbit would then be quickly despatched by breaking its neck.

Strictly speaking, the taking of a wild rabbit, or any game, without the permission of the land owner was a criminal offence, but generally the farmers did not mind them taking rabbits in this way, and indeed very often encouraged it as a form of pest control, but a land owner was a lot less happy if his pheasants were taken. Pheasants cost a lot of money to rear and they were not for the likes of the rural poor. However, when faced by the prospect of a full belly, or seeing the children go hungry, I am afraid the pheasants and the rabbits were doomed, whatever the risks, although, the land-owner could actually only prosecute for trespass, not theft, if a wild animal or bird was taken. However, it would

10

be almost impossible for a working man to prove a pheasant was a wild bird so the poacher knew he was taking a calculated risk of being charged with trespass and theft by poaching, although punishments were more severe if caught at night and if a firearm, bludgeon or offensive weapon was carried.

In 1723, poaching had been made a capital crime but had ceased to be a hanging offence in 1820. Instead, from 1816, until the practice was discontinued in 1867, some offenders were transported to Australia, and it was not until the 1830's that man-traps (aimed to kill, mutilate or break the legs of the poacher) and spring-guns were made illegal. In the 19th century poachers were treated more harshly than any other persons accused of other kinds of theft. By the time the 20th century dawned, attitudes had changed but nevertheless, if caught, the culprit could still expect a hefty fine; 40s 0d (£2) for the first offence and this was a lot of money, probably at least four weeks wages in 1901. If it was a third offence, the guilty person could expect to receive up to seven years "penal servitude".

But despite the risk of a fine, and when the opportunity arose, Ben and the older boys would set off for a spot of poaching and, if pheasants were the target, then this could be a much more costly undertaking than the "theft" of a rabbit.

Pheasants were reared, nurtured and fiercely protected by the game-keepers, so the number one rule was to avoid game-keepers like the plague! The younger boys would be posted as lookouts, while Ben scattered raisins that had been soaked in a cheap alcohol where the birds came to feed. Then they would hide down-wind and wait for the birds to get drunk on the alcoholic fruit. When the creatures started staggering about, in went Ben, quickly and painlessly, wringing their necks. They would feast on pheasant for days!

Dad told the story that one time they were so busy rounding-up the drunken pheasants that they did not hear the game-keeper approaching until it was too late to take to their heels and run, so they jumped into the nearest bushes and wriggled their way into the centre, out of sight until the game-keeper had gone away. He recalled the incident only too well as it was just his luck that the bush he dived into was a bramble, and he was torn to pieces by the thorns, but at least he was not spotted by the "enemy"!

Another supplement to the larder would be collecting blackberries in the autumn for their mother to make blackberry jelly and picking, or even scrumping apples, cherries and pears, whenever they got the chance. Gathering mushrooms was another task the children would have to do, as was combing the potato fields after the main crop had been harvested, in the hope of picking up a few tubers that had been left behind. They all did whatever it took to keep from starving but, Dad

11

commented, in spite of all their efforts, often they were hungry.

Without the family pig at the bottom of the garden, probably they would have been severely malnourished at best. In fact most families kept two pigs; one to sell and one to eat. Occasionally the farmers gave the poorer families the undersized runt of the litter, known as the dolly pig, so they could fatten it up until it weighed up to 250kgs. Sometimes the boys were given the job of taking the pig to the woods in order that it could eat the acorns. (In some places this is an ancient right dating back many centuries.)

Most countrymen could kill a chicken or a rabbit without too many scruples but not many could kill their own pig, in some cases it had become almost a member of the family. So there would be someone in the village who was regarded as the expert pig dispatcher and he would be paid in pigmeat or money: 1s 6d for killing it and 2s 0d for cutting up the carcase. There was too much to eat in one go of course, so some joints were preserved in a barrel of salt, or a slate tank filled with brine, which most rural cottages had as standard in their back gardens. The rest of the joints were stuffed in a special crevice up the chimney where it was gradually smoked. Even into old age Dad could still remember the taste of the fattened pigs they slaughtered. He maintained that he never tasted smoked ham, salted pork or bacon as good as what they had reared themselves, and that the only bit of the pig that was not used, was the squeak!

The pig provided plenty of lard, so dumplings were a favourite with the family, as was steamed bacon roly-poly pudding. (Dad's particular treat, which he enjoyed even into old age, was pigs' trotters!) A stock made from boiled bones, especially marrow bones, or a chicken carcase, or an oxtail, would be turned into a nutritious vegetable soup, and pigs' brains and lambs' tails turned into brawn or jelly. When no meat or soup was available, they had to make do with just bread and potatoes, or bread and dripping, for their main midday meal but at least it was wholemeal bread and good pork or beef dripping. The chicken and ducks provided eggs as well as meat, of course, but an egg each would be a rare treat.

Most probably, all the food had to be cooked on an open wood fire in the kitchen, which must have been full of smoke and cooking smells, but at least it was warm, and it was on this fire that tragedy struck the Oakley family one cold and wintry morning. The exact circumstances have been lost in the mist of time but Clem was about six years old and baby Blanche was a toddler, aged about twenty-one months. Their mother popped out to the garden to hang out some washing, leaving the children happily engrossed on the floor, when Blanche struggled to her feet, tottered towards the fire, lost her footing and fell towards the flames. Clem reached out and pulled her clear but fell into the fire in her stead.

His left shoulder, the top of his arm, part of his back and part of his chest were severely burned. Blanche suffered bad burns to the top of one arm. The doctor must have been summoned but it is nothing short of a miracle that they both survived and that infection did not set in; they both bore the scars to their dying days.

Calling the doctor in those days was not done lightly. For one thing the doctor would have to be paid for each visit (probably 2s 6d) and, for another, someone would have to physically go and fetch him; there were no telephones. The doctor would arrive eventually on horse-back, or in a small carriage; in the case of an accident, many times it would be too late. Even in childbirth, they would almost never be summoned, unless the baby or the mother was in severe difficulties. All births were, of course, at home, with the local "midwife" in attendance. This was not a trained nurse but a woman from the village who would have had many children herself and who seemed to have a flair in helping to deliver other women's babies.

If a doctor was called, he would dispense his own medicine and then he would charge a few pennies extra. Thus with the cost of the visit, and the cost of the remedy, most country folk turned to their own superstitions and herbal remedies before they called on a doctor's services. Some of these cures are still in use today, such as dock leaves rubbed on the rash from stinging nettles and dandelion root rubbed onto warts, but others would probably not be recommended; blowing tobacco smoke into the ear for ear-ache, for example, or placing a "chew" of tobacco on a wasp or bee sting. When my sister's children had whooping cough, many years later, her mother-in-law told her to make a cough mixture from layers of chopped onion, garlic and brown sugar. She left the mixture overnight, and then fed it to them in the morning, and it worked! A similar remedy for a baby's cold is well documented; mince an onion, add 2-3 teaspoons of sugar and feed it to the baby. Among other folk remedies that proved to be successful was camphorated oil rubbed into the chest for a cold, and the oil warmed-up is said to cure ear-ache. There must have been many remedies, for almost every ailment, but, sadly, most have been lost as we have become dependent on medical science and prescription drugs.

Herbal douches to prevent pregnancy have been around for centuries, as has self-induced abortion, but the lack of reliable and suitable contraception was probably the main reason for having such large families in the early 1900's. Indeed, in many countries, like America for example, to practise any form of contraception was actually illegal. Condoms, made from sheep intestine and tied on with silk ribbon, had been around since the 1700's, but it was not until 1839 that Charles Goodyear developed a process of vulcanising rubber, and rubber condoms that were thin, strong and relatively cheap were mass-produced. However, although people knew these could prevent pregnancy, men generally wore them only to protect themselves against sexually transmitted diseases. So for decades condoms carried the stigma of being associated with disease and prostitution, and thus it was the last thing a "decent" man would use with his "decent" wife!

In fact these early condoms, and other contraceptive products made from rubber, aged quickly and the quality was doubtful. It would be 1919 before Frederick Killian of Ohio, USA, discovered a way of hand-dipping natural rubber latex that produced the forerunner of the thin, reliable, modern condom. It would take the early family planning clinics, such as those run by Marie Stopes in the 1920's, to make birth control, and the condom, intrauterine devices and diaphragms, socially acceptable.

Strange to say, apart from the accident with the fire, Dad could not recall himself, or any of his siblings, suffering any of the childhood illnesses that were so prevalent, and fatal, in those pre-vaccination days. Indeed it was probably the high mortality rate among children and expectant mothers that produced a life expectancy, in 1900, of just forty-seven years. In those days, people were used to hard work, long hours, low wages and accidents and illnesses that were often fatal. They accepted poor housing with few facilities, poor roads and transport. They expected large families. But there was a contentment then that seems sadly lacking now; despite it all they were happy.

CHAPTER THREE

A Rural Childhood
(1909-1910)

By 1909 the family was struggling. Another job, another house and now another two mouths to feed. A girl Ellen, known as Nellie, had been born in 1907 and, in September 1908, a boy, christened John, but known as Jack, was the latest arrival. The older children, Mabel aged ten, Clem aged eight, and Ted aged six were going to school, leaving Blanche aged four, toddler Nellie and baby Jack at home with their mother.

Work was hard for the men, and the hours long, but it was no less arduous for the housewife. Apart from caring for a large family and all that that entailed, there were no refrigerators (or ready meals!) and most women therefore shopped daily if they could, buying small portions of perishable goods, like butter and cheese. (Lack of money dictated this too, of course.) The floors and kitchen table would be scrubbed every day, rugs taken out, hung over the washing-line and banged to get the dust out. The laundry was washed by hand and ironed on the kitchen table with flat-irons heated on the fire. The kitchener, if you had one, would have to be black-leaded at least once a week. There were no scourers or washing-up liquid, so the pots and pans would be scrubbed with a mixture of sand, salt and vinegar. All the chores played havoc with their hands and where the men's were calloused, the women's would be chapped and cracked. No rubber gloves in the early twentieth century, and the only remedy was to rub their hands in foul-smelling tallow fat.

For the children, before trudging off to school, there would be chores to complete; wood and water to collect, chickens and pigs to feed, eggs to gather, and then more of the same on their return. Even the young ones had something to do. And travelling to school was not always an easy task as they had to walk, quite often without boots, across ploughed fields, muddy lanes and through long grass meadows. (Only the upper classes wore shoes in those days.) They were not allowed to be barefoot in class but often their boots were so badly fitting that they carried them until they were within sight of the school and only put them on at the last minute. Dad could remember that at one time they had to walk no less than four miles to school, and then back again at night.

By this time I think Blanche senior must have been fighting a losing battle to keep them all decently clothed and shod as Dad remembered many times going to school not only with no shoes on his feet, but with his clothes torn and dirty. All the clothes got passed down and nothing fitted properly. The boys wore their father's trousers, cut off at the knee

15

when the knees had worn out, and held up with an old, leather belt, or a piece of twine, tied in a knot. On wet days, the only protection for adults and children alike was covering the shoulders with an old sack. Once wet, they stayed wet. There were no mackintoshes, anoraks or even Wellingtons in 1909.

The schools, and the dress standards they dictated, varied from village to village and were subject to the whim of the schoolmaster, or mistress. Corporal punishment was standard and most teachers, male and female alike, had a cane within easy reach which could be employed for something as simple as giggling in class or giving the wrong answer. Some teachers were not averse to using their hands and would give the errant student a clip around the ear instead. But this was considered normal practice and no different to what went on at home. It would be unheard of for a parent to make a complaint about their child's treatment. Indeed if the child was to mention to his father that he had got the cane at school, the chances were that the father would give the miscreant another caning! (Or use his belt which was the normal punishment at home.) Hard though it now seems, there was never any disorder in the classroom and the children learnt good manners and discipline alongside the 3R's.

Most of the village schools consisted of just one large room with a cast-iron, wood-burning stove in the middle, surrounded by a fire-guard. The younger children would be at one end of the room and the older ones at the other. Dad could well remember trying to get as close to the stove as possible when it was cold in the winter, but as they all had the same idea, it meant leaving home extra early! Sometimes, in one particular school, the teacher would cook potatoes on the stove, or bring in a box of apples, and hand these around at lunch-time. For hungry mouths this was nectar from the Gods! Normally if they took anything at all to eat mid-day, it would be a hunk of bread and dripping.

Since 1891, education had been free to all children under the age of thirteen and it is a great credit to the schools that, despite the hardships, all the children were literate and numerate by the time they left. Especially as they had very little access to pencils, paper or books, and most exercises would be completed on slates with chalk. The older children did graduate to pen and ink eventually; this was the old-fashioned pen with a nib on the end of a bit of wood that had to be dipped constantly in the ink-well in order to make it write. Dad could remember one school where the ink-monitor (the person who filled the inkpots) had to arrive earlier than the rest of the class, so the teacher paid him 1d a week. They all took it in turns to earn the penny!

I cannot remember Dad talking about Sunday School, or toys, or Christmas presents, but I can remember him chuckling away as he recalled his unruly band of ragamuffins and the antics they got up to.

16

One great lark was best undertaken at night, preferably when the wind was howling through the trees and clouds obscured the moon. He and his younger brother, Ted, would hide in the bushes at the edge of a dark lane, with a sheet that they had borrowed from home over their heads. Then they would wait for an unsuspecting traveller and jump out at them muttering blood-curdling ghostly screams! They must have been thrashed, not only for scaring the living daylights out of a neighbour but for taking the sheets, but he seemed to have forgotten the punishment, only remembering the deed and what fun it had been.

CHAPTER FOUR

Tragedy Strikes
(1911-1913)

In 1911, when Clem was 10 years old, they were living in Westhampnett, near Chichester, and Blanche was pregnant with her seventh child. She was not yet thirty years of age when, undernourished, exhausted, isolated and only just coping, she went into labour, at home as usual of course, and was delivered of a healthy girl they called Elsie Blanche. There was nothing to indicate that this birth was any different to the six that had gone before, but a few days later Blanche suffered from severe headaches, fever, and pain in her lower abdomen. The symptoms gradually worsened until Blanche was barely conscious and could not even rouse herself to feed the baby. The doctor was summoned and diagnosed puerperal fever. There was nothing he could do except prescribe morphine for the pain and later that day she passed away.

Puerperal sepsis, to give it its proper name, was quite a common killer in these pre-penicillin, pre-antibiotic days. It attacks women who have just given birth, especially when their resistance is low or if bits of the placenta have been left behind in the birth canal. Without treatment it leads to septicaemia and peritonitis and death. There was no effective treatment in 1911 so the end result was inevitable.

The family were in total disbelief. One day their wife, or mother, was alive, all smiles at another safe delivery and a healthy baby, and the next she was gone. That as many as one woman in every one hundred and ten deliveries, would die in childbirth at that time, was no comfort to them. They were absolutely devastated. Many, many years later Dad could still recall the physical pain he felt at his mother's death and he remembered that he cried for days and days. I am sure the feelings of grief and disbelief were no less for the rest of the family.

Somehow Ben managed to find the money for a plain, pine coffin and her body was duly laid out in it in the front parlour, in order that friends and relatives could pay their last respects. As was the custom in those days, the children were filed past so they could kiss their mother goodbye. Then the coffin was sealed and was lifted onto a hand-cart for its journey to the church. Clem was ten years old and he remembered clearly helping his father pull the hand-cart along the lane, crying all the way. His beloved mother was laid to rest in an unmarked grave.

If it was devastating for the children, I cannot imagine what it must have been like for Ben; seven children under the age of twelve and three of them under school-age. I do not suppose he knew which way to turn but, in the event, rightly or wrongly, he decided he could manage with the three eldest; Mabel aged twelve, Clem aged ten and Ted aged eight. However Blanche aged six and Nellie aged four would have to go to the workhouse orphanage; toddler Jack aged two and new-born Elsie would be taken in by his sister Rosina and her husband, Edwin Standage. Thus here began the strong link we have always maintained with the Standage clan.

It can have been no easy decision for Rosina and Edwin (also called Ted but I will call him by his full name to avoid confusion with brother Ted!) as they already had six children. The eldest, Evelyn, was aged about sixteen, and Margaret was aged about fourteen, and probably both of them would have been in domestic service. However, that left Gladys aged ten, Dora aged eight, Hilda Irene (known as Irene) aged four, and baby Edwin (known as Ted, another Ted!) born a few months before Elsie. So at least four children, ranging in age from a few months to ten years, were still at home. Perhaps they thought two more small mouths to feed would make very little difference? Edwin was employed at the time as a brick-maker, which was one of the better paid jobs in those days as it was very skilled, and physically and mentally demanding, but nevertheless, whatever their reasons, no-one could have foreseen that many years after their own demise, the favour would be returned in kind.

Eventually Jack and Elsie were returned to the family but alas that was not to be for Blanche and Nellie. Many years later, Blanche spoke to me briefly about her life in the orphanage. At aged six years, she had thought it was supposed to be only a temporary measure, until her father could sort himself out, find a housekeeper perhaps, but in the event she and Nellie stayed until they were sent into domestic service at aged fourteen. This was just about the only job available to working class girls in the early 1900's and was basically a cleaner cum dogsbody for someone with enough money to pay for the service. The job could be live-in or out. In Blanche and Nellie's case, with nowhere else to go, it would have to be live-in.

Blanche maintained that life in the orphanage was cruel and hard; clothes and shoes never fitted properly; the food was bland and barely adequate; home comforts non-existent and punishments severe. They had to undertake all the cleaning, the scrubbing and the laundry, and every Saturday they were given some foul-tasting medicine "to keep them regular" whether they needed it or not. It seemed she hated every single minute and right into old age she was very, very bitter in the belief that her father had deserted them. She never really forgave him.

Nellie was less scathing but as she was younger, maybe she adapted to orphanage life more easily. Nellie eventually married and had two children but Blanche never did marry. I am sorry to say that both of them grew into cantankerous old know-it-alls, only too ready with a caustic comment or criticism and a sarcastic sense of humour. I think it is fair to say the family did not look forward to their visits with much enthusiasm. Did their experience in the orphanage bring out the worst in them and turn them into clones of one another? Or was it in their genes? Elsie also married but as she lived in London, we saw less of her. At least on these few visits, I have to say that she did not seem as unlikeable as her sisters.

Workhouses had been around since 1722, supposedly to give shelter and sustenance to the local poverty-stricken but, by 1911, the horror stories of the poor-houses were well documented, particularly by writers such as Charles Dickens (his novel *Oliver Twist* for example). Also there was a very popular old music hall song called "*My Old Duch*" (short for "Duchess") which tells the heart-breaking story of an elderly couple who "*have been together now for forty years and it don't seem a day too much,.....*" The song goes on to mourn the fact that, as they enter one of these establishments, they know that they will be separated.

The conditions Blanche described were more or less what had come to be expected but, by 1911, the whole set-up was in the melting-pot. A recent Royal Commission had unanimously condemned the Poor Law System, under which workhouses were administered, and, amongst other improvements, were encouraging further extensions of the boarding out of children to cottage or foster homes, or barrack schools, as a matter of urgency. They wanted children removed from pauper association and to be given a good start in life. So Blanche and Nellie were unlucky in that they were born too soon to benefit from these new reforms. One can only hope that as they grew up in the orphanage, conditions improved.

Thus children were the first to benefit from the recommendations but workhouses for the elderly, infirm or destitute, remained places that sent shivers up the spine of every working-class person who had fallen on hard times. They were not finally abolished until 1929 when County Councils and County Boroughs were charged with caring for their disadvantaged citizens.

So by 1912 the family of eight is cut in half almost overnight. Ben carried on working of course, leaving Mabel to attempt to run the house. It was hopeless. She left school to take on her mother's duties but her father was never there and the boys would not obey her. Everybody was grieving and they all seemed to be pulling in different directions instead of working together. Ben took refuge from the chaos at home in the local public house and things just went from bad to worse. Eventually Mabel gave up the unequal struggle, the boys ran wild and Ben carried on drinking himself into oblivion.

Then one day the public house had a new face; an Irish woman, working in service on a local farm, so Ben bought her a drink. Then another. And another. Now there was an added incentive to go for a drink in the evenings. She was good company. She was on her own and lonely. So was he. He needed a wife and what is more, the children needed a mother. HURRAH! Problem solved! They moved in together with almost indecent haste, but never married, or at least no trace of a marriage certificate can be found, and thus I do not know her name but for the purposes of this story, I will call her "Fanny".

From the first, the children hated her. I do not know what persona she presented to Ben before they lived together but it soon became apparent that she was lazy, cruel, bad tempered, vicious and a drunkard. Neither do I know if Jack and Elsie were returned to the family at this time but I assume so, and I can only think it was some kind of miracle they did not die of neglect or abuse. As soon as she could, Mabel left home and went into service. Nothing more is known about her except that she never married and died in 1935.

Meanwhile Clem and Ted did their best to stay out of their "step-mother's" way, for the slightest misdemeanour would draw a verbal and physical assault. The only peace they got was at school, or when she and Ben disappeared to the pub´ for the evening. When they came home, however, there were the most terrible rows and fights. From a peaceful family with just the usual childish squabbles, home now resembled a war-zone.

In the mornings, when he was sober, Ben must have known that life could not go on like this. From thinking that this woman was the answer to a prayer, she had become an ongoing nightmare.

One night she and Ben came home from the pub´ more drunk than usual and the row that ensued as they came through the door was even more vitriolic and vicious than in the past. The children lay listening in their beds absolutely terrified. The couple came upstairs still arguing and a fight started at the top of the stairs. The children hid under the covers, wishing it would all just go away. Then there was an almighty thud, a scream and a body went tumbling down the stairs. For a few seconds, all was quiet. They hardly dared to breathe. Then they heard their father's drunken slur, "Are ye OK, Fanny? Fanny?" Then louder, "Fanny?" At last they dared to creep out. Their father was at the bottom of the stairs leaning over the twisted body of his common-law wife. Her neck was broken. Clem was instructed to run for the doctor but this was just a formality. There was nothing he could do.

Did she fall or was she pushed? At the coroner's inquest, Ben said she had missed her footing and the court accepted that it had been a tragic accident brought on by drunkenness, but, to his dying day, Clem maintained his father had deliberately pushed her down the stairs and killed her. Whatever the cause, she was dead and, frankly, they all breathed a huge sigh of relief.

Ben decided the more sensible option this time would be to pay for someone to look after the family, so he recruited the services of a neighbour, Ada, who was to cook and clean and keep an eye on the children, just for a few hours each day for a few shillings a week. She was married with a small child and, as it turned out, desperately unhappy. The inevitable happened and Ben and Ada had an affair. Divorce in those days was not an option for a working man; the cost was prohibitive, it took too long and the permitted reason basically limited only to adultery. (Incidentally a wife could divorce her husband only if he committed adultery AND cruelty!) Obviously Ada´s husband had grounds to divorce her but, for whatever reason, this does not appear to have happened for only one marriage (to May Blanche Pilkington) has been recorded for Ben throughout his life-time. At this stage, records for Ben living in West Sussex disappear and re-surface in Bedingham, near Lewes. I think it is safe to assume, therefore, that when Ada moved in with Ben, they decided to make a new life on the other side of the county, away from all the gossip. This time, married or not, Ben chose wisely and it was third time lucky. Ada was a pleasant, good-natured lady who took everything in her stride. She made a happy home that Ben did not feel he had to avoid by drinking to excess. She nurtured her own child, the younger children from his first marriage, and went on to have at least seven children with Ben. Peace had been restored at last.

But too late for Clem. His childhood ended when his mother passed away. Now, fed up with all that had gone on at home and anxious to be out in the world earning money, he left school and started work. He was just twelve years old.

CHAPTER FIVE

Work and War
(1913-1919)

In 1913, when Clem started work at twelve years of age, he could not claim to be skilled at anything, of course, but he knew enough about many trades to make himself useful as a "boy". A lot of the jobs possibly open to him, and other young country-lads at that time, would be recognised today; dairyman, cowman, shepherd, blacksmith and thatcher for example. The description of the job is obvious from the title and the basic duties have remained much the same through the centuries, even though many of the tasks would now be mechanised.

A dairyman/maid in the early part of the twentieth century would still have had to milk the cows, but by hand then, not machine. The "De Laval Milker", for example, would not go on sale until 1918, and the unpasteurized milk would go in large churns and not in a huge tanker. The churns would be loaded onto a wagon, pulled by working horses, and taken to the nearest train station to be transported, via the railway system, to a growing urban population.

In the early 1900's, every village would have had a blacksmith who would spend most of his day shoeing horses that would either be ridden or driven to him. Nowadays, we have very many fewer blacksmiths and those we have take their forge to the stables, rather than the other way round. And because there are probably not enough horses to shoe full-time, they have specialised in other ironwork, such as staircases, fancy weathervanes and the like.

A thatcher's job is much the same as it has always been, even down to making the hazel spars that secure the reed to the roof. In the old days, however, spar-makers shared the hazel copses with hurdle-makers, who spent a solitary existence out in the woods weaving hurdles (fences) from strips of split hazel. (The hurdles were used to pen sheep.)

Like spar-makers and hurdle-makers, other jobs have gone forever, for example a hedger and ditcher. Where a hedgerow of various bushes, shrubs and trees was carefully cut, and skilfully woven together, to form an attractive barrier and become a haven for wild-life, now a giant machine noisily tears and rips and cuts the twigs, boughs and branches into submission, leaving in its wake an ugly scar along the country lane, instead of, what some would have no hesitation in calling, a work of art.

Ploughman or carters were once a common sight in Sussex fields but they too have disappeared. Of course fields are still ploughed, but by machine. The days of hitching a couple of shire-horses to a plough, and trudging about eleven miles a day behind them as they plodded slowly up and down the furrows, are long gone. Of course the working-horses were used for harvesting too, for a shire-horse could pull five times its own weight. Gone with the horses, are the beautiful horse-brasses and the skill of "tracing". (This was plaiting the tail and mane and interweaving them with coloured ribbons.) In those days an average-sized farm would employ about twenty-four people; just three or four would be employed today.

And it is not just the land that has lost the old trades; Sussex flint-knappers have also disappeared. Flintstones, gathered from the fields and the sea-shore, usually by women paid a few pence for a basket-load, were used by the "knappers" to build the distinctive flint walls that are so much part of picturesque old Sussex in the western part of the county. The walls and buildings vary in appearance, depending on which stones were used, the irregular field stones, or the smoother, more rounded, sea-shore ones. Sometimes they were kept whole and other times they were cut in half, or "knapped", giving a shiny appearance.

Wheelwrights did not only make wheels, they made the whole wagon or cart, and they slowly fell by the wayside when lorries took over. Coopers made wooden barrels; now they are mass produced and used mostly as garden ornaments, because beer is delivered and dispensed from stainless steel barrels.

Brick-makers were another occupation common in the early part of the century. Each brick was made by hand and dried in the sun, although the clay was ground by horse-power. Nowadays the vast majority of bricks are mass-produced but a few are still made by hand in the old-fashioned way (without the assistance of the horse!) for specialised building and renovation projects.

So it appears that there was quite a lot of choice of employment for a young lad in the early 1900's and, if they did not fancy any of the above, and they did not want to join the Armed Services, or go into domestic service, many young men in 1913 might have decided to leave the countryside, and the trades it offered, and try a job in a city or town, taking advantage of the opportunities the new industrialization had created; a job on the railways perhaps, or in a factory, or on a building site. The steam train had made places accessible to the working man that had previously been a distant dream, but in reality most boys did what they had always done; they followed their father into their father's trade. Clem was no exception.

By this time, the family were living in Bedingham, near Lewes, where his father was employed as a carter on a local farm, and Clem was taken on as a carter-boy, working under his father. His wages were just 2/6d a week for six days work, though it was soon raised to 3/0d. This provided a very useful extra income for the family finances as all but 6d was handed over to his step-mother.

After a few months he was offered a better position as a cowman on a neighbouring farm at Firle. Here he had to start work at 4am, and leave home at 3am, in order to walk the four miles to work. He worked six and a half days a week, and often walked home after dark, but the wages were 7/0d a week, more than twice what he was earning at Bedingham. One of the duties of a cowman would have been to wean the calves off the mother's milk and this reminds me of an incident in my own childhood. I was about eight years old and our father took my sister and me to Guildford Market. It was a proper market in those days, with animals for sale and an auctioneer, and we went to view some calves that were to be sold. There he showed us how he used to wean the calves off their mother's milk by putting his fingers in the calves' mouths and directing their heads down to a bucket of milk instead of to a teat. I can also recall being thoroughly disgusted by his saliva-ridden fingers and declining to follow suit!

There were no televisions or radios in 1914, but there were newspapers, and around this time they were full of the problems in the Balkans. Conflict between the different ethnic groups was escalating as they tried to divide up the spoils from the collapse of the Ottoman Empire in 1912. The Balkan Wars were to give Europe a foretaste of what would become known as "ethnic cleansing" and the human cost of this war cannot be understated, although it paled in comparison with what was to come.

Bosnia and its neighbour, Herzegovina, had been taken into the Austro-Hungarian Empire from the Ottoman Empire, modern Turkey, and they and their independent neighbour of Serbia objected. Archduke Franz Ferdinand of Austria, and his morganatic wife, went to inspect the troops in Sarajevo, the capital of Bosnia, and were assassinated. Austria accused Serbia of complicity in the murders and declared war on all the Balkan states on 28th July 1914. (Of course, the reasons were more complicated than this but I have tried to simplify it!) Russia was pledged to assist Serbia, and Kaiser Wilhelm of Germany promised to support Austria. Thus, before anyone really knew what was happening, we have Germany and Austria against the Balkans and Russia. Then Russia called on France to honour an old treaty agreement and suddenly France is dragged in. Germany formally declared war on Russia on 1st August and on France on 3rd August 1914.

Then Britain said if Germany attacked French ports, the British Navy would be forced to intervene, and furthermore if they dared to attack Belgium, Britain would be obliged to go to her aid under the terms of the 1839 Treaty of London. This must have been like red rag to a bull because Germany responded by pouring troops into Belgium! The rest, as they say, is history and Britain declared war on Germany on 4th August 1914.   Italy and Rumania joined the fray in 1915 and 1916 respectively so now there were these countries plus the Balkans, Russia, France, Belgium, Britain and its Empire, pitted against the mighty Germany and Austria.

Suddenly the whole country must have seemed to be on the move as men voluntarily left farms, mines, shipyards and factories to join-up and "fight the Hun".   In the beginning, no-one expected the war to last long but as it dragged on month after month, the propaganda to persuade yet more men to enlist was huge.   *"The War to End All Wars"*, they proclaimed. *"Peace in Our Time"*, they promised.   And the poster of the moustachioed Lord Kitchener with his penetrating stare and his index finger pointing out at them, beseeched and beguiled men in their thousands to respond to the plea *"Your Country Needs YOU!"*

Clem was too young to join up at the beginning, but how he envied these brave young men going off to foreign shores to fight for their country. At age thirteen, in 1914, it all sounded so exciting, so exotic, so heroic, but he had to settle for something a lot more prosaic. He would move away from home and not just around the corner; he decided to go right across the county of Sussex and return to the area where he was born, to Sidlesham near Chichester. It meant he had to walk from the family home in Bedingham to Lewes, take the train to Chichester, and then walk the four miles to his new place of employment. To add to the excitement, this was the first time he had journeyed on a train alone and he well remembered the thrill of travelling across the whole county, with the engine belching out clouds of black smoke and the fireman sounding the warning klaxon, as it raced across the country lanes and disappeared into tunnels. (No electric or diesel trains in 1914!) The job he was going to involved looking after, and working, three Suffolk Punch working horses and was a big responsibility for a thirteen year old boy. In fact, he said he preferred Suffolk Punches to Shires or Clydesdales. They were slightly smaller but he thought they had a better temperament.

At Sidlesham he lodged with a lady called Mrs Grant, paying her 2/6d every fortnight for a room he shared with another farm worker. He was responsible for buying his own food, however, which Mrs Grant cooked for him. He was already a heavy smoker and would indeed remain so more or less until he died. Also he had started to drink beer and he and the other workmen would go to the local public house at lunch-times for a hunk of bread, a chunk of cheese and pickled onions. (The fore-runner of what we now call a "ploughman's lunch", only then it really was!) The lunch would be washed down with a pint of the local brew and the land-lord turned a blind eye to any licensing laws they may have had then by making the comment that if he was old enough to do a man's job, then

26

as far as he was concerned, he was old enough to drink a man's drink!

He stayed in the west of Sussex for his next job, moving approximately twenty miles north-east to a village called Fittleworth, only a stone's throw from where he was born. This was to work as a carter again but the fields he had to plough were so full of flints that, on more then one occasion, the plough jumped into the air and almost hit him in the face!

Meanwhile the war in Europe raged on. At this stage, there was still no conscription, so all the volunteers, who may never have been out of their village, let alone been abroad: may never have even seen a car, nor handled a gun: perhaps had never kissed a girl, found themselves on the battlefields of the Somme, or Ypres, or Loos. They had unknowingly, unwittingly and unwillingly stepped into the jaws of Hell. Later analysis of the war would note that poor leadership at the General Officer level and a callous disregard for the lives of the common soldier, that would be called criminal today, combined with the invention of the machine gun, all contributed to a huge loss of life. Tens of thousands would not return, but still Lord Kitchener pointed his finger, and still young men left these shores in their millions. And not only these shores; men came from all over the Empire: from Canada, Australia, India and Africa. They all answered the call for help from the "Mother Country".

All too soon, the battle of Marne had been fought and, in 1915, the merchant ship "Lusitania", carrying many American passengers, was sunk by a German U-boat. Also this was the year that the Germans started using poison gas as a weapon, and the year that the second battle of Ypres took place.

In the closing months of 1915, the British Government realised that they could no longer find enough volunteers, so, from January 1916, conscription was introduced. All men between the ages of 18 and 41 were liable to be called up, unless they were married, widowed with children, or served in certain reserved occupations.

In 1916, the battle-grounds of Somme and Verdun flowed with the blood of thousands. In 1917 Mata Hari, born Margaretha Geertruida Zelle but also known as "Lady MacLeod", Dutch-born and married to a Dutch army officer, was executed by the French for being a spy for the Germans.

It was in 1916 that Clem changed jobs again (he was his father's son, after all!) travelling all the way to Addington in Surrey, to take up work as a cowman. This was the first time he had been out of his native county. Here he was supposed to be one of a team of six men, but three had joined up, leaving the remaining three to do the work of six. It was here that he had an incident with some cows that caused him to chuckle even many years after the event, though at the time I am sure he did not find it so funny. He was told to take a herd of cows to market and this involved getting them all to go over a bridge. They all got across when one of the new-fangled motor-cars came up behind them and hooted for him to get out of the way. The cows promptly took to their hooves and scattered in all directions. It took him the rest of the day to round them all up again! Needless to say, he missed the market.

In 1917 he decided to return to his original job at Bedingham but this time as a fully-fledged carter in his own right. Still the Lord Kitchener posters were reminding young men that *"Your Country Needs YOU!"* and so, in November 1917, at just sixteen years of age, he travelled to Brighton, lied about his age and enlisted in the Royal Artillery. He was posted to Chichester but when he arrived he discovered to his disgust that he was not in the RA at all but the infantry. The thought that he had swopped one lot of walking for another, filled him with dismay but he had "taken the King's shilling" and the dye was cast. Nevertheless, he comforted himself with the thought that now he was with the 7th Battalion of the Middlesex Regiment, he would soon be sent abroad to fight the "beastly Hun". Instead he found himself in Tunbridge Wells testing gas-masks! What a letdown! He was so disappointed!

It was to be the effect on the merchant shipping of Britain's allies, suffering at the hands of the German U-boats, which decided the United States of America, on 6th April 1917, to declare war on Germany.

As America joined the conflict, Russia left it. It conceded defeat to Germany for it had serious problems on its own doorstep. It had begun on 22nd January 1905, with "Bloody Sunday" and the death of hundreds of unarmed demonstrators in St Petersburg. This incident is regarded as the start of the "Russian Revolution". Although the Tsar had brutally put down this uprising, the people felt more empowered than ever before and in their "February Revolution" of 1917, they had forced the abdication of Tsar Nicholas II. A Provisional Government had taken control but in October 1917 a bloodless coup put Vladimir Ilich Lenin and the Bolsheviks into power. However one month later they lost an election and a civil war ensued between the Bolsheviks (now called Communists) and the "Whites" (White Guard Volunteer Army). In 1918 the Bolshevik-Communists murdered Czar (Tsar) Nicholas and his entire family. After their own hostilities with the Germans ceased, Great Britain, France and the United States supported the "Whites" but they finally withdrew their troops in 1920. The "Russian Revolution" was over and the Communist regime of the Soviet Union, under Vladimir Ilich Lenin, then began.

Meanwhile the *First World War* ended with Germany's surrender at 11am on the 11th November 1918, bringing to a close the worst conflict the world had ever seen and it would become known as *"The Great War"*. It is impossible to estimate the exact numbers of people killed but it could not have been less than ten million. Six million men had served in the British Forces and nearly one million of them had died, including two hundred thousand from the Empire. The country also had one and a half million seriously injured, many suffering the permanent effects of gas, loss of limbs, blindness. In France, the losses were even more severe with 1.3million dead and one third of the young male population dead or mutilated. Over the whole of Europe, a generation of young men had been wiped out and there was hardly a family in any land who was not affected in one way or another.

How to summarize in a few short sentences a war that lasted for over four years, killed so many, maimed so many more, devastated France and families throughout Europe, and wrecked the economies of that continent for over a decade. It was a war the like of which had never been fought before. For the first time U-boats (submarines) patrolled the seas; Zeppelins (airships) and bi-planes bombed and reconnoitred from the sky, and on land, tanks, machine-guns and heavy artillery made their deadly debut. The Germans invented one gun, nicknamed "Big Bertha", that could fire a shell over seventy miles, laying waste to towns many miles away and inflicting huge casualties, for the first time, on civilian populations, way behind the battle lines.

The European armies had traditionally worn brightly coloured uniforms, stood up in full sight of the enemy "like a man", fixed bayonets and charged. With the newly-invented machine-gun, this was now literally suicide, so tactics and uniforms had to change and eventually battles were fought from the protection of muddy trenches, the British forces in muted khaki and the French in pale blue. The trenches became "home" for months on end and one, 750kms long, was dug by the allied forces from the North Sea to the Swiss frontier, in an attempt to keep the Germans out of France. This was known as "The Western Front" and thus many of the worst battles were fought along its border; names that now go down in history: Somme, Ypres, Loos, Verdun, Marne, to name but a few.

Britain and its allies lost men from its workforce but France gave men and animals. Thus, when the heavy horses went to the Front, there were only old women left to yoke a plough to their shoulders and attempt to do the work, not only of their men folk, but of their horses too. Not only that, but much of the livestock was killed and eaten by various armies, and so many battles were fought over the arable land that no crops could be planted, let alone harvested. Not surprisingly France was soon short of food. The endurance and stoicism of Europe in general, but France in particular, cannot be underestimated. Basically all because one man, Kaiser Wilhelm of Germany, had wanted to expand his empire.

At the end of the carnage, "Kaiser Bill" was allowed to abdicate and lived a luxurious and peaceful life in Holland, while Germany had to pay huge sums in reparations. Frontiers were re-drawn, with the Austro-

Hungarian Empire dismembered and a South Slav Kingdom of Serbs, Croats and Slovenes brought into existence as Yugoslavia. An independent Poland was established and Czechs and Slovaks joined forces to become the new Republic of Czechoslovakia. In Europe a League of Nations was established in Geneva, with the aim of avoiding future wars by submitting disputes to international arbitration. Parliaments and people were united in the hope that the "Great War" would truly be the war to end all wars.

King Edward VII had died in 1910 and his son, George V, was now on the British throne. The new King was advised to change his surname as it sounded too German, bringing to an end the Royal House of Saxe-Coburg-Gotha. The Royal House of Windsor began, and with it came a greater affection from his people than any sovereign had enjoyed since the Hanoverians had come to power in 1714.

By the time the war ended, the car was becoming a more frequent sight on the roads, and was no longer a source of curiosity and wonder, but horses still outnumbered cars and, as the motor-car was noisy and unreliable, accidents frequently occurred with the nervous, unpredictable animals. Although actual car production had been severely curtailed during the war years, the pressure to manufacture machinery for war encouraged the development of mass-production techniques in all industries, including the motor industry, and soon it would not be uncommon to see jeep-like cars and even small box-like lorries taking the place of horse-drawn wagons and carts. The 1914-18 war had also witnessed the birth of the first aeroplane, or a flimsy-looking bi-plane to be precise, and if a car had been a source of amazement, imagine what it would have been like to see your first aeroplane.

Despite not having seen active service, I am proud to say my Dad lied about his age in order to fight for his country in the First World War. The fact he did not fire a gun in anger is neither here nor there; he had been prepared to do his duty and die for his country if necessary. Clem had signed-on with the army for nine years so, with the war over, he was posted to a camp in Gillingham and, in 1919, he passed his riding test at Woolwich Barracks. After a short spell in Brighton, he was drafted to India and there he would remain for the next seven years.

CHAPTER SIX

India
(1919-1926)

The East India Trading Company (latterly known as the British East India Company) was set up in 1600, initially to pursue trade with the East Indies, but it ended up trading mainly with the Indian subcontinent and China, in goods such as cotton, silk, indigo dye, saltpetre, tea and opium. In 1757, after the battle of Plessey, the Company came to rule large swathes of India, exercising military power and assuming administrative functions, to the gradual exclusion of its commercial pursuits. However, the Company was largely incompetent, arrogant and ignorant of local customs and culture, and, in 1857, the Indian Army mutinied against the British authorities in the so-called "Great Rebellion". The ensuing bloodshed sent shock-waves throughout colonial Britain and forces had to be despatched to restore the imperial authority. The administrative powers of the country were then taken over by the British Crown and the Company's troops were transferred to the British Army. Therefore, from 1858, the Crown, supported by the Army, became an occupying force, attempting to keep the peace between the various States and the two main religious groups, Hindus and Muslims.

But the new regime also brought with it a change of attitude. Instead of trying to force English culture, religion and taxes on a largely disenchanted and resentful population, and replacing old rulers with more sympathetic pro-British ones, the new Royal Government of India promised that it had no intention of imposing *"our convictions on any of our subjects"*. It distanced itself from the Christian missionaries and made huge investments into the country's infrastructure with railways and irrigation canals. The Suez Canal, which opened in 1869, linked Indian farmers with world markets, and universities, colleges and schools proliferated in towns and cities, most of them opened by Indian initiative. Hindu and Islamic culture flourished alongside British influence and, by the end of the 19th century, a modern India was emerging that fulfilled the aspirations of Indians rather than becoming a colonial idea of what a modern India ought to be. Thus, by the time Clem arrived in 1919, the British Army had maintained a relatively peaceful presence, in a slowly modernising India, for over sixty years.

What an exciting adventure the voyage to India must have been for a young man of eighteen years, who had only seen three counties of south-east England in his whole life! Of course, some of his fellow shipmates might never even have seen another village, except their own, let alone another country! I should think Clem must have set foot in

31

Africa en route, at least, but he never talked about the journey, so I only know that he docked in Karachi in 1919 and was immediately posted to the Army Headquarters at Lahore.

Here he found there was little soldiering to do except "show the flag" occasionally and in many ways, therefore, I think this must have been the least physically taxing of all his jobs. The main task of the officers seemed to be to keep the men occupied, and thus the mornings were devoted to "spit and polish", marching, firing practice, caring for and exercising the horses and general soldiering, and the afternoons to playing cricket and football, attending voluntary classes and suchlike. Sadly, I know very little about Dad's time in the country from the peace-keeping angle because he never once mentioned firing a gun at a rioting crowd, or dealing with insurgents, for example. The impression he gave was of stifling heat and trying to keep boredom at bay and thus this is what will be reflected here.

Every so often a shipmont of wild horses would arrive from Australia and Clem spent many a happy hour breaking them in. He became so adept at riding that he and the other men used to perform what can only be described as circus tricks. They would run alongside the horse, holding the saddle, and then spring onto its back. They would stand on the saddle and canter around, ride backwards, bareback, double and triple-up and leapfrog onto the horse from a standing start.

Whenever a new batch of horses arrived, the colonel and the officers would come to inspect them and one day the colonel decided he would have a beautiful black stallion as his personal mount. Before the horses could be broken-in, they had to be branded. Clem had the job of throwing the horses to the ground so the branding could be done. He had done this a thousand times; it was not difficult, there was just a knack to it. So he duly threw the colonel's horse, and promptly broke its neck! I do not think the colonel was too pleased!

He had many happy memories of all the sport, especially cricket and football, which he had played in India, especially when they travelled to Simla where the air was cooler. In later years, he maintained that his bad knees were due to all the games of football he had undertaken there.

He was immensely proud of the fact that he studied *English, Imperial History, Mathematics* and *Map Reading* while abroad and that he obtained certificates to say he had passed the Army's examinations. He kept the certificates all his life and they have now passed to me. He was never much of a letter writer but he used to leave me notes if he knew I was going to pop in and neither he nor Mum would be at home. They would always be written in pencil; he never seemed to take to ballpoint pens unless he had to! In these notes, I never knew him to make a spelling mistake or a grammatical error; he had his "their" and "there" sorted out and all the apostrophes in the right place. And when I went to grammar school, he did his best to help me with my mathematics homework, a subject in which I struggled. For someone who left school at aged twelve, I thought it was pretty good! Although whether it was the education he received as a child that could take the credit, or the later Army courses, I do not know.

He also learned to drive in India; cars and lorries with gear-boxes that required the driver to double de-clutch. I believe he carried on with this technique for the rest of his driving years, despite the later improvements in modern engines.

I think it must have been in India also that he trained to be an "Army Signaller", becoming proficient in sending and receiving orders via semaphore flags and Morse code. Many years later, he and I would stand on opposite sides of our lawn, waving our arms about sending messages to one another; he was helping me practise for my *Girl Guide Signallers Badge*!

On the whole, he enjoyed his time in India, although he had less than happy memories of the jaundice and malaria he contracted out there. I can remember him suffering bouts of malaria even when I was a child, some thirty years later. But at least they had quinine in the 1920's.

However, he hated the dirt, the flies, the dust, the heat and the poverty of India. And curry! He had so much curry out there that when he returned to England, he vowed never to eat it again.

In 1924 he was posted to Meerut and in November 1926 he sailed home on the troopship *Derbyshire*. On his return to England he left the Army but remained on the "Reserves", and thus, in later years, he would boast that the Army had been paying him since 1917!

All through his Army service in India, Clem had kept in touch with his family, especially his brothers, Ted and young Jack, and his sister, Blanche. Most of the soldiers usually sent just a post-card home, with the minimum of news on the back, and a local scene, or a photograph of the sender in full-dress uniform, on the front. Clem was no exception; the few postcards that have survived from this era have the back left blank, so we have to assume his news was non-existent!

When the *Derbyshire* docked in 1926, he found an England much changed since he had left in 1919, but his father was living now at Grove Farm at Yapton, near Arundel, and, with most of his family living in the vicinity, he came back to West Sussex where he obtained a job with a firm of landscape gardeners, nurserymen and fruit growers at Barnham, not far from Littlehampton..........

CHAPTER SEVEN

Sussex by the Sea
(History of Littlehampton to 1905)

When Clem returned to England, he could not have known (or cared!) that he was now living and working near the town where a certain Annie Martin had been born in 1905. However, Littlehampton was about as different from Duncton, where he had been born, as it could be. Duncton was small, insular, inland and hilly, and predominately engaged in farming. Where Duncton might be described as a sleepy little village, hardly changed for centuries, in 1905 Littlehampton was go-ahead, thriving and forward-thinking. It was also on a flat, coastal plain, with a wide variety of industry, and was a rapidly expanding community of some six thousand souls.

Littlehampton is on the Sussex coast, approximately mid-way between the cities of Portsmouth and Brighton and is situated at the mouth of one of Sussex's major rivers, the Arun. In the old days, it was possible to travel inland, on small boats, a considerable distance from the mouth of the river and thus it was always a useful arrival and departure point for trade and warring armies.

Sufficient evidence has been unearthed to conclude that a community of sorts has been here since Roman times, and probably before that. Domesday records refer to the place as "Hantone" and that, at the end of the Saxon era, the manor was held by a Countess Goda, an association which lives on in the name of a Littlehampton street, Goda Road. The reason Countess Goda, or Princess Goda, held the manor was that she was the daughter of *King Ethelred the Unready.* She was also mother to *Ralph the Timid*! The Saxons made up these quaint pseudonyms because surnames were not used in the British Isles until the Normans conquered England in 1066. (At the Battle of Hastings!) Under the Normans, surnames were usually patronymic (son of), after a place of residence or birth, a trade name or a nickname. The surname "Martin" is said to be of Norman origin.

The Normans regularly used the area as an entry-point to their conquered domains and, in 1097, William Rufus, the elder son of William the Conqueror, landed in Hantone from Normandy when he arrived to take over the throne of England on his father's death. In 1139, Queen Matilda (known as Empress Maud) also disembarked here when she came from France to try and seize the throne from her cousin, Stephen. "Hantone" eventually became "Hampton", then Little Hampton until it evolved into one word sometime in the 1800´s when, perhaps, it could no longer be called "Little".

However, the estuary was several miles wide and subject to flooding, leaving the land very marshy. Also it was not deep enough to allow larger vessels, with a bigger draught, to sail far inland and, furthermore, the river mouth was constantly moving eastwards, due to a continual build-up of sand from the west, creating sand spits. These things combined to make the area largely uninhabitable and not suitable for use as a port, although King Henry V111's royal dockyard was located here in the 1500's.

In 1723, permission was granted to stabilize the river mouth by building an embankment along both sides of the river, ending in two substantial piers, one on the east bank and one on the west bank, both running out into the sea, and thus channelling the water through one permanent outlet. The work was completed in 1735 and, almost immediately, the river became a safe harbour for sailing ships of all sizes; wharves were built on the eastern bank and shipyards on the west. Then, in 1787, the Arun Navigation Canal came into being, making the Arun River fully navigable from the coast to Newbridge Wharf, near Billingshurst, and, in 1816, a second canal, the Wey and Arun Junction Canal, was completed making a fully navigable route up as far as London. Additionally the Arun connects to the River Rother near Pulborough so it was also possible to travel west as far as Petworth and Petersfield. Littlehampton was on the map and in the one hundred years between 1801 and 1901, the population increased tenfold from 500 people to over five thousand. Sadly the popularity of the port was not to last. No-one could have foreseen that in one hundred and fifty years, sail would start to be replaced by steam and that the sand-bar at the river mouth would mean many of the larger steamships would require too much water under their keels to get in and out of the harbour, except at high tide. This might not have mattered so much if Littlehampton had been able to offer a round-the-clock direct rail link to the capital but sadly, though promised, it never materialized and, therefore, over the years, much of the cargo trade was lost to the port of Newhaven, which did not have these problems and could give the shipowners a quicker turnaround. Sadly the canals also lost their battle against the railways and the roads, and eventually fell into disuse with the waterway system becoming known as *"London's lost route to the sea"*.

But in 1905, when Annie was born, the harbour still positively throbbed with sailing ships, large and small, unloading cargoes such as lime, timber, coal and gravel and taking on things like potatoes, strawberries, cherries, packs of butter, eggs and even, on at least one recorded occasion, live sheep. (This was in fact in 1877 and was on the maiden voyage of a barque, called "Trossachs" built and owned by a local shipbuilder. She carried Scottish shepherds, with sheep kept in pens on the deck, that were destined to form the nucleus of the sheep rearing industry of the Falkland Islands.) In 1905, the shipyards, too, were still busy turning out sailing ships, but these were now mostly smaller ships for coastal traffic, latterly ketch-rigged barges. The days of building the eighteen-gun sloops for Admiral Nelson's navy and the beautiful, wooden, ocean-going sailing vessels of 500-600 tons or more, were already gone. But the ship-building industry had spawned rope-making and sail-making, an iron foundry (to make anchors and other iron-work for ships) and the harbour trade gave birth to ships' chandlers shops, a large timber-yard and gravel and coal depots, all on the river's eastern bank.

One of the common sights on the river at that time was the harbour work-horse, "Jumna", a paddle tug that towed the sailing vessels in and out of the harbour. From about 1910, however, a lot of the sailing ships were fitted with auxiliary engines and in 1921 she left the harbour for good. By that time, what little towing needed to be done was undertaken by motor launches.

A vessel that caused great excitement whenever it was launched was the Littlehampton lifeboat. In 1904 the town celebrated the arrival of a new oared and sail-assisted boat called the "Brothers Freeman" and on Lifeboat Day each year it was paraded through the streets with all the crew on board and onlookers could throw pennies into it. By the 1920's however, the Royal National Lifeboat Institution (RNLI) was replacing these boats by power-assisted vessels and less boats were needed. So Littlehampton lost its lifeboat and for over forty years was covered for sea rescues by the lifeboats at Selsey and Shoreham. By a cruel irony, however, the boatyards of *Osborne* and of *Hillyard* established a reputation for building lifeboats for the RNLI. But in 1967, thanks to the popular children's television programme, *Blue Peter*, and contributions from viewers, Littlehampton was the first place to receive one of their inflatable rescue boats. Used mainly for inshore and river rescues, it has saved hundreds of people and also saved the main lifeboats being called out so often.

It was the eastern side of the river that had been developed as the town and, by 1905, there was a High Street with an ironmongery and builders materials, a chemist, a brewery, a greengrocers, a poulterers and game suppliers, a butchers, a cartwright, a corn merchant, a cabinet maker, the gas company and at least two public houses. The adjacent Surrey Street had a grocery store, a tailor's shop, an orchard, a bakery and another two public houses, but was best known for hosting the annual fair which was held on May 26th every year. In other parts of the town were at least three churches, two Anglican and one Roman Catholic, plus a Congregationalist church and a Methodist chapel. There was a school built in Sussex flint, two farms, a dairy and an old coaching inn from which, prior to the arrival of the railway, a coach had run daily to

36

Fetter Lane in London, taking seven hours. They had their own weekly newspaper, and their own Urban District Council, complete with offices. There were gas-lamps in the main streets, a sewerage system (albeit going into the sea!) and most of the houses, shops and churches had gas and water piped to their premises.

Also on the eastern side of the river was the original pier with a pepper-pot lighthouse, and near to it the Arun Mill (the site is now known as the Windmill Theatre) and an old oyster pond. Sadly, around 1860, the oyster industry had been destroyed by over-fishing, (by the French!) but the pond had been kept as a recreational feature and small children still sail their boats on it. For many years after the First World War, an annual children's regatta was held here with the toy ships racing against one another, and their owners partaking in swimming competitions, all in aid of the local hospital.

Just north of the pier, the local fishermen moored their boats and sold some of their catch on the quayside. This would include mullet and mackerel, bream and sea-bass, plaice and whiting, mussels, crabs, winkles and shrimps. At low-tide, it was possible to see "Winkle Island" about two hundred yards off-shore, and this was a favourite place to collect your own winkles, if you were so inclined.

Between the first line of buildings and the sea, many years ago, someone had had the foresight to leave a grassy strip of common land running from the east pier and the adjacent oyster pond, all the way to the next village, Rustington. This has created a peaceful backdrop to the stony east beach, for sand only appears when the tide goes out. Even in 1905, there was an illuminated promenade between the grass and the beach, with shelters and seats installed at periodic intervals. However, this attracted the hooligan element and the problem of lamps and glass being smashed by vandals had to be faced! Despite this, it was (and is) one of the nicest beach areas on the south coast and attracted many visitors, including the five year old Rudyard Kipling, who delighted in making sandcastles, enjoying donkey rides, watching the acrobats and taking boat-trips up the river to Arundel, with its impressive castle and park, seat of the Duke of Norfolk, Earl Marshal of England. By 1905 the increase in leisure-time and rail transport had made a seaside holiday an annual event for many better-off families.

The beach on the western side of the river is even better, although much of the pier disintegrated many years ago. This area is still almost completely undeveloped, although in 1905 there was a mill here with an adjoining house and a newly constructed golf-course. The beach this side is stone free, just miles of sand, backed by sand dunes and topped with marram grass. For centuries, there was only a rowing boat, grandly called a ferry service, linking the two sides of the river mouth. It was adequate for foot passengers but all horses, carriages and carts would have to travel all the way to Arundel before they found a bridge on which they could cross to the other side of the river. This would add at least ten miles to the journey. So, eventually, in 1825, a wooden chain ferry, or floating bridge, came into being. It was said at the time that it was big enough for a "*carriage and four...and there is nothing in its use to alarm the most spirited horse or the most timid lady.*" It was built by one of the local shipbuilders, who had his yards only a stone's throw from the point where the ferry was to cross, and it required two men to pull it across the stretch of water. It lasted for about seventy years until it was replaced by a steel pontoon, but in 1905 thoughts were (again) turning to the thoughts of a bridge. As they did not want it to impede the river traffic, it was decided to build a swing-bridge and the foundation stone would be laid by the Duke of Norfolk on August 7th 1907.

For centuries Sussex had had the reputation of having notoriously atrocious roads, where any existed at all, so the arrival of the main-line of the railway system in 1846 must have been a godsend to passenger and freight alike. This was just north of Littlehampton, at Lyminster, although this was not a proper station, just a halt. Then, in 1863, a branch-line opened in Littlehampton, linking it to the main-line at Ford Railway Station. Labourers were required to build these lines; the labourers needed houses and thus a building boom ensued, which as the town expanded, seemed by 1905 to be ongoing.

Farming had been undertaken in the area from earliest times but since the river had been brought under control, as it were, and more people were living in the area, that too expanded, so by the turn of this century, Littlehampton enjoyed construction, shipbuilding, railway, fishing and farming industries, a brewery and various shops, services and merchants. In addition a library and hospital were planned, as well as the new swing-bridge. The town was booming and perhaps that was what had attracted a certain Thomas Martin to come to Littlehampton in the late 1890's and look for work.......

CHAPTER EIGHT

The Martin Clan
(Up to 1905)

Annie's father, Thomas Martin, was born in 1870, in Burgess Hill in Sussex, and not much is known about him except that he was a bricklayer by trade and that he had several brothers, all bricklayers, so I guess this must have been his father's trade as well. Annie could only remember going with her father once to visit his family in Burgess Hill, when she was about nine years old, and it snowed very heavily. Many years later she could only recall that her paternal grandmother struck her as being tiny; she remarked that her mother's mother was quite small but her father's mother was smaller still! However, she did keep in touch with a cousin in Burgess Hill, Peggy (Margaret?) Boyd, more or less until she died.

Her father was another strict Victorian, rather taciturn and extremely careful with money! My Aunt Ethel (married to Mum's youngest brother, Dick) was of the opinion that all the Martin men were rather more than just "careful" with money but Mum did not agree, so let us be kind and say "careful" rather than call him a tightwad! He was about 5-feet 6-inches tall, stocky and with dark bushy eye-brows, so typical of all the "Martins". All the photographs we have always show him sporting a very bushy moustache (to match the eye-brows, perhaps!). He smoked a pipe, as was very common in those days, was an enthusiastic gardener and loved reading, mostly cowboy books and adventure stories. He was a staunch Labour Party supporter and Trade Union Member and encouraged his sons to follow his example. Many years later, when I had just started work, I can remember his son, my Uncle Les, encouraging me to join my trade union. I did as he suggested and remained a member all my working life. Indeed, although I am now retired, I still have honorary membership.

The very first "Independent Socialist" Member of Parliament had been Keir Hardie in 1892. In the general election of 1906, they were calling themselves "The Labour Representation Committee" and Grand-dad Martin must have been delighted when twenty-nine out of their fifty candidates were elected. It would not become known as the "Parliamentary Labour Party" until 1911, by which time they had forty-two Members of Parliament after the general election of 1910. It was in 1911 that Parliament voted to pay MP's a salary, and those who benefited the most were the members of the new "Parliamentary Labour Party". Eventually Littlehampton had its own "Trades and Labour Social Club" and Grand-dad was a keen supporter of this too, popping down at least

39

once a week, invariably with Mary, for a pint of beer and a game of darts or cards.

He met his wife soon after he came to Littlehampton to work and it was love at first sight. Mum said he adored Mary right to the end and she could never remember hearing them have a cross word. Her maiden name was Love and she was a local girl born and bred. She was small and dark, of a rather anxious, nervous disposition and just eighteen years of age when they married in 1898. Tom was ten years older, dependable, reliable, a hard worker and besotted, so it is not hard to imagine the mutual attraction and the reason for a quick marriage. She loved reading as well, mainly romances, women's magazines and the like. And she must have loved a chat because it is from her that Mum learned about her family. Information that was passed to me eventually.

Soon after their marriage they went to live in London and while there Mary Martin suffered two miscarriages and a still-birth. She could not seem to pick up from this and a doctor advised Tom to bring her back to the south coast and the cleaner air, for London was highly industrialised at this time and infamous for its "smogs" (a mixture of fog and smoke). They went to live in number 15, Stanhope Road and it was there that their first son was born in 1901 and named Thomas after his father. The air must have agreed with her because two years later another son was born, Leslie, and two years after that, Annie Elizabeth Ellen arrived, but not at number 15. They had moved a couple of doors down by this time so Mum was born at number 11.

She was blessed (she would say cursed!) with all these Christian names after her mother's three sisters but she grew to hate the name "Annie". She said it was a typical servant's name and it reminded her of her years "in service" when her employers ordered her to "Annie do this" or "Annie do that". So as soon as she reached her late teens, she started to call herself "Anne". Most people called her Anne, except perhaps her parents, certainly her employers, and her brother, Dick. Some years after she had died, I mentioned to him, just in passing conversation, that she had hated to be called "Annie" and he was mortified to think he had unwittingly offended her, all her adult life basically. I rushed to try and put things right.
"Not YOU!", I said. "She never minded YOU calling her Annie because that was part of her childhood."
It was true but I do not think he was convinced and it was my turn to be mortified. I had not meant to hurt his feelings. Of course, when she married Clem Oakley, she became the original "Annie Oakley" of "Get your gun" fame and had to suffer the inevitable jokes .... and that was from people who did not know she really was Annie Oakley. Anyway, in accordance with her wishes, I will stop referring to her as Annie. From

here on in, she is Anne!

Stanhope Road is about a mile from the town centre, a cul de sac leading off the main thoroughfare of East Street. Not far up from the Stanhope Road turning, East Street ends in a T-junction, in the centre of which was a huge elm-tree, with a raised grassy verge all around it and a kerb to sit on. The right hand fork is St Flora's Road and leads to the sea about a mile distant; the left hand fork is Horsham Road and takes you north, past the cemetery, to one of the main west-east roads out of Littlehampton. In those days Horsham Road was bordered mostly with farmland, market gardening, orchards and the like and if you walked past the cemetery and crossed the main road onto yet more farmland, you could walk along various footpaths to Lyminster, Poling, Crossbush, Burpham and Arundel. If you did so, you would have to cross a stream called "Black Ditch". This was all that was left of the old estuary of the River Arun before it was "tamed" and was a magnet to all the children through the decades as a place to collect frogspawn and tadpoles. My mother and her brothers used to go there and many years later so did we, coming home with the poor creatures in a jam-jar. The internationally famous (to the scientific world at least!) Glasshouse Crops Research Institute was the first to build on this land, followed, some years later, by the factory and headquarters of the also internationally famous, *Body Shop* empire. The founder, Anita Roddick, was a local girl. Recently a huge housing estate has been developed here as well, so what remains now of Black Ditch, and its tadpoles, is anybody's guess.

Back in 1905, the northern side of East Street had the most development, including shops, a public-house, cottages, a farm, a large private house (later to become a convent and now a nursing home run by the order of St. Francis), more private houses, more farmland and a large private school for boys, *Dorset House*, founded in 1784. On the southern side was the flintstone school, private houses and a large private house on the corner of Goda Road called Winterton Lodge. (This would later become part of the *Rosemead School for Girls* campus which was founded in 1919, on farmland right next door to the *Dorset House School*.) An embankment right up to the junction of St Flora's Road completed this side of East Street with farmland behind it. It had trees and shrubbery on the top and a muddy track running through the greenery, made by countless feet of children and, once again, including Mum and her brothers and, later on, my sister and me!

The houses in Stanhope Road were reasonably modern in 1905; each one a set of three, so number eleven was actually semi-detached with a narrow alley-way running between it and the next set of three. There were four rooms upstairs, one quite small which would invariably become the bathroom in later years, and two rooms downstairs plus a scullery. (This room would become what we would call a "kitchen" in later years.) The back room had a kitchener, fuelled by coke or coal, and the scullery had running water with a sink and tap. Soon after they arrived, gas was installed, although Grand-mother Martin was too nervous about this new-fangled invention to use the gas-lights, preferring to stick to the paraffin lamps. She did however have a gas ring in the scullery which she used regularly as it saved lighting up the kitchener. Just outside the back-door were two outhouses side by side. One housed the copper and the other was a water closet, a toilet with a flush! The garden was long and narrow for growing vegetables. Definitely no pig!

So not only was the town very different to Duncton but the life-style was so much more sophisticated. Some things, however, were the same. Still no bathroom, so baths were taken in a galvanised tub in the back room in water heated by the copper or the kitchener. Births were still at home, and carts, carriages and wagons were still pulled by horses on stone or dirt roads, although some streets in towns and cities might be paved or cobbled. But cars were becoming more common, albeit only for the chosen few.

Although cars were still few and far between on the roads, motor vehicle manufacture was taking off around the world. In 1903 Henry Ford had opened his first factory in Detroit, although it would be 1911 before he expanded into Europe. The *Ford Motor Company* is now the largest family-controlled business in the world, and has been in continuous family control for over 100 years. However, although *Ford* was destined to become among the most prolific of car producers, Henry Ford was not the first car-maker. Germany and France can be credited with developing the first motorised vehicles in the late nineteenth century and, using their experience, other countries followed in their tyre-treads, so to speak.

The *Daimler Motor Company,* which was founded in Coventry in 1896 by Harry J. Lawson, made the first serial production car in the UK, followed by the *Humber Motor Company* in 1898. However, production in the UK of these new "beasts" were hindered by the so-called "Red Flag Act". This severely restricted the use of motor-propelled vehicles on the public highway, so, in 1896, Lawson and his fellow enthusiasts, successfully campaigned for a new law to be introduced, which allowed a higher speed limit (14 mph instead of 2 mph!) and would no longer require a minimum crew of three people per motor-car, one of whom had to walk in front of the vehicle waving a red flag!

To celebrate the new freedoms, Lawson organised the "Emancipation Run", to take place on 14th November 1896. (Since 1927, this has been commemorated by the annual "London-Brighton Veteran Car Run" and nowadays vintage as well as veteran cars are permitted to take part.

Bryan and I, and Mac and Sheila and their sons, have many happy memories of standing for hours watching these much-loved and beautifully-preserved old crocks putter by. Many of them are so valuable, and so fragile, that this is their once-a-year outing.)

So, with the change in the law, during the early years of this new century, a veritable plethora of motor companies sprung up: *Sunbeam* in 1901, *Vauxhall* and *Standard* in 1903, *Rover* in 1904, *Singer* and *Austin* in 1905, *Morris* in 1910 and *Riley* in 1913, just to name the most well-known companies. By 1913 there were about 100 companies in the UK, producing approximately 16,000 vehicles. (And by 1922 there were 183 companies. But an "economic slump" was just around the corner and, by 1929, only 58 companies remained.)

With the rise of motor vehicles, and other oil burning engines, came the rise of oil exploration and extraction, particularly in Persia for Britain and Texas in America. Companies such as *Shell, British Petroleum, Castrol* and *Texaco* can trace their roots back to these years.

But not only oil companies benefited from motor vehicle manufacture; tyre companies also sprang up to meet the new demand for tyres. The pneumatic, or air-filled tyre, had been invented in 1845 but it was not until John Boyd Dunlop re-invented the pneumatic tyre in 1888, for use on his son's bicycle, that the idea truly caught on. Then, in 1895, Andre and Edouard Michelin used the pneumatic tyre (instead of solid rubber tyres) on one of the new-fangled automobiles, and the rest, as they say, is history!

But the automobiles brought new problems. In 1903 the speed limit was increased to 20mph, but many vehicles were already capable of travelling at least twice that speed. They were also heavier than a carriage, and they needed better roads. A Scottish engineer, John Loudon McAdam, had designed the first modern roads in the early nineteenth century. These were made with three layers of hand-broken stones, with the smaller stones on the surface and each layer compacted by heavy rollers. He had insisted on the surface being higher than the surrounding terrain so water would drain away. Road builders improved his initial design by filling in the gaps on the surface with sand and clay but the finished product was still not impervious to water and storm damage and, without constant maintenance, they soon became rutted and full of potholes. Something was needed to bind the top surface together and make it waterproof.

In 1901, on a road near the *Denby Ironworks* in Derbyshire, a barrel of tar had fallen from a dray and burst open. To avoid a nuisance, someone from the ironworks had spread the tar and thrown waste slag from the furnace over the sticky black mess. The world's first tarmacadam (tar-McAdam) surface was born by accident.

In 1902, a British patent was obtained for mixing tar with the slag and

43

the product was called "Tarmac". In 1903, the *Tarmacadam Syndicate* was formed and although later re-named the *Tarmac Group,* it remains the UK's largest leading supplier of road building materials, and has given its name to aircraft parking areas throughout the world.

But the biggest problem for the car driver was the availability of fuel. In the early days of motoring, petroleum spirit had to be collected from general stores, blacksmiths and chemists in two-gallon cans, with bulk deliveries in barrels being made by rail and horse and cart! But cans were awkward and dangerous. Suppliers and motorists wanted an easy and safe method for re-filling vehicles and the world's first purpose-built gas station was constructed in St Louis, Missouri, in 1905. (Although the first place to sell gasoline/petrol had been a pharmacy in Wiesloch, Germany, in 1888. Bertha Benz refilled the tank of the first automobile here on its maiden trip from Mannheim to Pforzheim and back.)

But motoring in the UK got off to a much slower start than in America or the rest of Europe. Britain did not have its first filling station until the *AA* (Automobile Association) began a service to its members in 1919 It was then that motoring for the masses began to arrive and with it filling stations started to proliferate. In 1921, *British Petroleum* had 69 filling stations in the UK, but all the early petrol pumps would be unrecognisable today, coming in all shapes, sizes, materials and colours. It would be the 1950's before pumps became standardized.

As the number of cars increased, another problem was how to make traffic flow more smoothly at road junctions. Initially called "traffic circles", the first one-way rotary system was "Columbus Circle" in New York City, installed for the very purpose in 1904. Across the Atlantic, a similar idea was being implemented around the *Arc de Triomphe* in Paris. But the early "traffic circles" encountered serious safety problems, especially when the volume of traffic increased, and they gradually fell out of favour to be replaced by the later development of traffic lights (1914).

But motorised vehicles, tarmacadam roads, petrol pumps and traffic circles were not the only innovations of these early years. By 1905 Kodak had introduced its first *Brownie* camera; the first Nobel Prizes had been awarded; the first trans-Atlantic radio signal had been received; the teddy bear had been produced. The first silent movie had been watched, the first sod broken on the Panama Canal. A regular motor 'bus service was inaugurated in London, the New York City subway had opened and the Wright Brothers had got their powered aeroplane off the ground. The twentieth century was truly off to a flying start.

CHAPTER NINE

The Carefree Years
(1906-1912)

At opposite ends of the journalistic spectrum, two items of news came out of the United States of America in 1906. While San Francisco was still trying to recover from the catastrophic earthquake of this year, in which 2,500 people died and 250,0000 lost their homes, *Kellogg's* started selling cornflakes. Originally *Kellogg's* was formed by Dr John Harvey Kellogg and his younger brother Will Keith Kellogg and known as the *"Battle Creek Toasted Cornflake Company"*. Dr John ran the "Battle Creek Sanitarium" (sic), a health and wellness spa, emphasising "nutrition, enemas and exercise" and he was an enthusiastic advocate of vegetarianism. Although best-known for the invention of the world's first breakfast cereal, the brothers Kellogg also patented a process for making peanut butter and the first "granola" biscuit-bar. They changed the breakfast habits, not only of a nation, but of the world, and cornflakes would be only the first of many products.

In 1907, in southern Africa, the Boer Republics of the Orange Free State and the Transvaal gained their independence from Britain, bringing to an end an ignominious chapter in British imperialism. Between 1899 and 1902, the country had been involved in the latest war with Dutch (Boer) settlement farmers who had been fighting for independence, on and off, since 1880. The British had "won" this latest war, after making heroic stands in the beleaguered garrisons of Ladysmith, Kimberley and Mafeking, and a peace treaty had been signed in 1902. But this *Boer War* is now best remembered with shame, for it was during these hostilities that Britain introduced the world to "concentration camps".

For the first time in modern warfare, the heavily-outnumbered Boers were making commando raids on the troops, and being very successful at it. The British never knew when or where they would be hit, so the commander of the British troops, Lord Kitchener, decided to burn all the farms, destroy the crops and the livestock, and herd the people into so-called concentration camps, with inadequate sanitation, facilities, food and water. Over 100,000 men, women and children were thus imprisoned and over 30,000 died. There was such a public outcry of disgust when the British public learned what had happened, that the British Government paid £3-million in compensation to the Boers so they could restock and repair their farms. (In their *"Act of South Africa of 1909"*, the British brought the colonies and republics of the Orange Free State, the Transvaal, Cape Colony and Natal together as the "Union of

South Africa". The Union remained British territory but allowed home rule for the Boers of Dutch descent, known as Afrikaners. This put it on a par with the three other British dominions of Canada, Australia and New Zealand.)

On 1st August 1907, Lord Robert Baden-Powell, of Makeking and Boer War fame, held a camp on Brownsea Island, in Poole Harbour, for teenage boys from varying backgrounds. The camp is considered to be the start of the worldwide Scouting movement and thus it celebrated its centenary in 2007, still going strong.

1908 saw the car industry in the news again when what was to become *"Rolls Royce"*, and the elite of vehicle manufacture, opened its first factory in Derby, England. Also the *"Ford Motor Company"* in America introduced their *Model-T*. A mix of motor and horse would soon become a regular sight in town and city streets.

And motor and horse could now use the new swing-bridge at Littlehampton, the official opening date having been May 1908, with some of the brickwork contributed by a certain Thomas Martin.
The toll charges were:-
Foot passengers 1d
Bicycles 2d single and 3d return
Motor cars 1s
Carriages drawn by one horse 1s, by a pair of horses 1s 6d
(NB The abbreviation "d" stands for "penny" or "pence" and "s" for "shilling(s)")

In 1909, another son arrived for Tom and Mary Martin, William (Bill). The birth was a special joy because I think it must have been in 1907 that Mary was delivered of another healthy daughter who sadly lived only a few days. As was the custom then, the newborn was placed in bed with its mother. Tragically Mary accidentally rolled over onto her in her sleep, smothering the baby who did not recover. Sadly this was not an uncommon occurrence and Mum said Mary mourned the loss of this little girl all her days, as indeed did Mum mourn the loss of a sister. And, as Bill saw the light of day, his parents saw their four year old daughter, Anne, off to school for the first time.

1909 was the year Louis Blèriot made the first crossing of the English Channel by aeroplane and Robert Peary became the first man to reach the North Pole. Also Halley's Comet made an appearance.

1910 saw one of the most famous murder trials in British history, still remembered today for creating a series of "firsts". The American physician, Dr Hawley Harvey Crippen, was accused of the murder of his wife, Cora Turner. She had been poisoned and dismembered. Her bones and limbs had been burned on the kitchen stove, her organs dissolved in acid in the bathtub, and her head placed in a bag and thrown overboard on a day-trip to France. What little remained of her torso was buried under the brick floor of the cellar of Crippen's house.

Suspicion was aroused among Cora's friends because, although Crippin had said she had returned to America, his lover, Ethel Le Neve, had moved in with him and was wearing Cora's clothes and jewellery. The friends alerted the police but by the time they found Cora's remains in the cellar, Crippen and Le Neve had fled to Antwep. From there they had taken the Canadian Pacific liner *SS Montrose* to Canada, with Ethel masquerading as a boy. However, the Captain recognised them and sent a wireless telegram to the authorities in London, alerting them to his suspicious passengers. This was the first time this system of communication was used to apprehend a criminal. This is the best-remembered "first" of the infamous case but it is not the only "first".

Chief Inspector Walter Dew raced across the Atlantic in a faster boat, the White Star liner *SS Laurentic,* and with the help of the Royal Canadian Mounted Police, arrested Crippen and Le Neve before they even disembarked. They returned to England to face trial.

It would be the first murder trial for Scotland Yard's first full-time forensic pathologist, Bernard Spilsbury. He was only able to identify the remains in the cellar by a scar on the abdomen, which matched a hysterectomy scar Cora had. The toxicologist, William Henry Wilcox, found poison in the tissues and made crystals of it. The jury was able to look at the scar and the crystals under a microscope; the first time such an instrument had been used to clarify evidence in a murder trial.

Crippen was found guilty after just twenty-seven minutes deliberation by the jury and was subsequently executed at Pentonville Prison on 23rd November 1910. At a separate trial, Ethel Le Neve was acquitted of murder. She died in 1967 from natural causes.

In 1911 the final member of the Martin clan was born, Richard (Dick), the same year that David Lloyd George, as Chancellor of the Exchequer in the Liberal Government of Harold Asquith, introduced possibly the most far-reaching piece of social legislation ever to come onto the UK statute books. It was called the "1911 National Insurance Act" and gave birth to the beginning of the contributory system of insurance against illness, unemployment and old age, that we still have today. Every worker between 16 and 70 years had to pay 4d per week, the employer 3d and the State 2d and these contributions were to be used to fund free medical attention and medicines, provide 7s 0d a week for fifteen weeks when unemployed, and pay a small old age pension when aged over 70 years. When unemployed, the recipient would be obliged to register at a local Labour Exchange where the money would be paid in cash and information on jobs available in the area could be obtained. It would run alongside a non-contributory scheme Lloyd George had introduced in

1908. This was the "Non-Contributory Old Age Pension Act" which paid 5s 0d a week to every person over the age of 70, if they had an annual income of less than £31.10s 0d. This was one of the first national pension schemes to be adopted anywhere in the world. In 1909, 647,494 people qualified, two-thirds of them women, and over the years the amount paid would be increased until, in 1932, it was 10s 0d a week.

These two pieces of very modest legislation, wonderful though they were at the time, were no help to the thousands of destitute, uninsured persons who were under the age of 70, including those who were permanently disabled or widowed. They would still have to rely on the old Poor Law, parish relief and workhouses, but at least these statutes of 1908 and 1911 were the beginning of the comprehensive welfare system we have today.

It was in 1911 that King George V was crowned Emperor of India, at a magnificent public ceremony (called a *Durbar*) in Delhi, which was then proclaimed the capital of India in place of Calcutta

An event that would change the course of Chinese history happened at the beginning of 1912, although it had begun in earnest some years before. For centuries, China had been ruled by successive tyrannical dynasties, which made the rich get richer and the poor remain poor, and then (to add insult to injury) over the last decades, China had been the victim of imperialist expansion involving European opium traders, political invasion (by Japan, Russia, the United States and most of the European countries), economic manipulation and Christian evangelism. The peasants had suffered enough.

Beginning in 1898, groups of them banded together into a secret society called the *"Righteous Fists of Harmony"*, later dubbed the *"Boxers"* by the Western press. At first they wanted to overthrow the Ching Dynasty, which was of Manchurian extraction and had ruled the country for nearly 350 years. But when the Dowager Empress, surprisingly perhaps, backed the *"Boxers"*, they decided to kill all foreigners instead. Thus on 2nd November 1899, the *"Boxer Rebellion"* began. The worst single event of this bloody upheaval was in July 1900 with the "Taiyuan Massacre", when more than 18,000 Christian missionaries and converts were killed, and not with a merciful bullet to the head, but hacked to death with big, old, rusty knives and swords. Foreigners and Christians were also under siege in the Legation Quarter of Beijing, so an eight-nation alliance brought 20,000 troops to the country to defeat the *"Boxers"* and the rebellion ended on 7th September 1901.

The Ching Dynasty was greatly weakened by this event but went ahead with the enthronement of a new emperor, Pu Yi, in 1908, when he was just two years old. However, the majority Han Chinese still resented being dominated by an ethnic minority of Manchurian descent. Also they were incensed at the corruption of the government and frustrated with its inability to restrain the interventions of foreign powers.

On 10th October 1911, the anger, frustration and resentment came to a head with an uprising in Wuchang and this began the "Xinhai Revolution". In less than four months the "Chinese Revolutionary Alliance" ousted the hated Ching government and deposed the now-six-year-old emperor, Pu Yi.

They elected Sun Yat-sen as provisional leader of the new republic and set 1st January 1912 as the first official day of the "Republic of China". They agreed to treat the emperor and his family as foreign royalty and gave them an extremely generous allowance, so, on 12th February, the Dowager Empress, on behalf of the boy-emperor, agreed to abdicate. On 5th April, the United States became the first foreign country to officially recognize the new republic. In the summer of 1912, Sun Yat-sen's party absorbed another four revolutionary parties to form a new party, the *Kuomintang* or *Nationalist Party*. Sun Sat-yen resigned and handed over the presidency to Yüan Shih-Kai.

(However, this was not the end of China's internal conflict, as we shall see in later chapters; the nation would have to endure a Second Revolution, a Warlord Era and a Chinese Civil War before the communists took control in 1949 but, to this day, China, and Chinese people living abroad, celebrate the anniversary of the "Xinhai Revolution", as the first attempt to establish a republic in China and revere Sun Yat-sen as the "Father of the Republic".)

Also in 1912 was Captain Robert Falcon Scott's ill-fated expedition to the South Pole. When his party reached their goal in January, they discovered a Norwegian, Roald Amundsen, had got there just one month before them. All of Scott's team perished from starvation and cold on the return journey.

Something that would save thousands of lives in the years to come saw the light of day in 1912; the parachute was invented, but this was not the only innovation of a remarkable year.

Alexander Graham Bell, a Scot living in Boston, USA, is credited with inventing the first experimental telephone in 1875, although this is disputed in some quarters! The first telephone he installed in the UK is said to have been for Queen Victoria, on 14th January 1878, linking her retreat of Osborne House on the Isle of Wight, with Buckingham Palace in London. Thus this line could be said to be the first carrying "overseas" calls. Soon afterwards another *"point-to-point"* line was installed between the House of Commons and the press in Fleet Street.

As more telephones were provided, it was obviously necessary to allow interconnection to all the other lines in the system and thus telephone exchanges came into being, the first being in London in 1883. A network of lines between these exchanges in the larger cities grew and the junctions were called "trunks", hence the expression "making a trunk call".

By 1912, a lot of private telephone companies had sprung up to operate all these lines, and this was the year the General Post Office (GPO) took them over and made it easier for people not only to acquire a 'phone but to make a telephone connection.

But telephones were still only available in selected cities. By 1914, companies in London, and its affluent residents, could be connected with Brighton, Canterbury, Guildford, and Stratford, and north to Birmingham, Liverpool, Leeds, Sheffield and Hull. It would be 1938 before the system could be said to be available nationwide.

But as important as family, local and international news items were, the big story in 1912 must have been the sinking of the "unsinkable" *Titanic*. Britain's splendid new liner was on her maiden voyage to New York when she struck an ice-berg and sank. Just 703 lives were saved out of a total of 2206, and that was only thanks to the newly-introduced wireless telegraphy system.

1912 was the year Littlehampton Cottage Hospital opened, brickwork for this also contributed by Thomas Martin. In fact Tom left his mark all around the town and surrounding area, wielding his trowel on Littlehampton Library, the large convalescent home on the seafront for the "Worshipful Company of Carpenters", and many places in Angmering and East Preston. He never owned a car, (or a horse!), nor even a bicycle, and walked to work, even when it was miles away. When he was unemployed (as you always are at some time if you are in the building trade) he would trudge miles and miles looking for work.

In 1912 Tom Junior was eleven, Les aged nine, Anne aged seven, Bill aged three and Dick just one year old. It must have been about this time that her mother suggested that Anne wheel Dick out in the pram. It had a shallow top part and great big wheels and she dutifully pushed it down to the bottom of the road where it promptly turned over and Dick fell out! She ran back the (fortunately) short distance home, crying and saying "I tipped Dick out of the pram and he's on the road!" Of course her mother rushed to the scene, luckily to find Dick unharmed but just screaming his head off. With supreme irony, Mum remarked to me, "I can't remember taking him out much after that!"

The only childhood illness that Anne could remember any of them having was mumps and that only affected Tom and Les. Many years later she still chuckled as she recalled their big, fat faces! The only malady she could recall that she had was ringworm, which makes me wonder if they had a pet cat? Alas, I do not know if they had any pets but it would not surprise me to learn they had a cat as Mum loved animals, especially felines. The ringworm took a long time to go and she

50

had the scars on her forehead for months.

In photographs of the early 1900's, both men and boys appear to wear flat cloth caps that resembled pancakes, and the boys wore short trousers down to their knees or knickerbockers, with jackets or sweaters. The men always seemed to wear a jacket and tie. For ladies long skirts or dresses, down to the ankle, were still in vogue, long sleeves on blouses and dresses, and always, always wearing a hat, usually with a wide brim. Girls were allowed to wear their skirts a little shorter and over the dress they invariably had a white cotton pinafore, with frills on the shoulders, and they too wore hats, usually a straw boater. Anne still remembered with affection one Sunday-best dress of her childhood; it was a plaid pattern and she was so proud of it! Both sexes wore leather boots, the men's had laces and the ladies and girls wore "button-boots", called this because they had small bead-like buttons that fastened up the side with the aid of something called a button-hook.

Anne's mother always made her daughter's pinafores and her underclothes. She wore a white cotton chemise next to her skin and long cotton drawers, or pantaloons, that came down below the knee and had a frill around the edge. On top of this was a cotton petticoat and in winter she wore a liberty bodice. This was like a thick, white, flannelette waist-coat with white cloth buttons down the front. She has no memory at all of ever wearing a cardigan or sweater in her youth, so for warmth she must have worn a shawl.

As her childhood progressed, Anne had to come to terms with the fact she was sandwiched between two sets of brothers and neither really wanted to include her in anything, "Coz you're only a girl!" How she longed for a sister but, despite this *crie de coeur,* she must have found some playmates because she could remember coming home from school in the summer months and playing outside until it was dark. They played games such as hopscotch, skipping-jenny, whip-the-top, beat-the-hoop and "tearing about generally". The boys played soldiers, hide-and-seek, and the like, and disappeared into the fields at the top of the cul de sac to climb the elm trees and hunt for birds´ nests.

Milk was dispensed from churns, towed around on a hand-cart, and the housewives bought it daily by the can or jugful. Coal, however, was delivered by a horse and cart and it came up the road several times a week. This created another fine game for the boys because when it turned around at the top of the cul de sac, the horse knew it was going home and it got a move on. This was the signal for the boys to jump on the back of the wagon as it hurtled down the road. Those who had not managed to hitch a ride, shouted to the driver, "Whip behind, mister! Whip behind!" The driver then cracked his whip round the back of the cart, forcing one lot of boys to jump off so the next lot could jump on!

Another game Tom junior and Les indulged in was throwing Anne's doll to and fro while she tried to retrieve it. It had a beautiful, china face and a soft, cloth body and, of course, the inevitable happened and it fell to the ground, its lovely face smashed beyond repair. She said she never wanted another one after that. One thing the horrors did not destroy, however, was her doll's house. This was nothing fancy, just a home-made, open-fronted box divided into four "rooms". Her father made little bits of furniture and her mother sewed a miniature family for it. She did get hours of pleasure from that and for years and years it stood on a little table just inside the front room. It was still there long after she had outgrown it, surviving the onslaught of four brothers because they knew their lives would not be worth living if they dared even to breathe on it!

Each of them always had a Christmas stocking, even if there was not much in it. There was always an orange (a rare treat) stuffed into the toe, chalks with a little slate blackboard perhaps, pencils, crayons, possibly a book, and Anne might have a few handkerchiefs, a skipping-rope or a whipping-top and the boys a pen-knife or a set of skittles. There might be a few sweets like a sugar mouse. There was no decorated tree; the only Christmas tree she could remember seeing was at Sunday School.

Her parents were not regular church-goers but all the children had to attend Sunday School at the nearby parish church of St Mary. The older ones were in charge of the younger members of the family and Tom and Les (again!) took this "power" to the extreme by delegating to Anne the responsibility of carrying all the prayer-books home. She dutifully did so for weeks, then decided to make a protest and told them they could carry their own books in future, and promptly placed theirs on the ground and walked off home. The boys ran off and when they got home they told their father, "Annie wouldn't carry our books. She's left them by a tree!" Her father told her to go straight back and get them, adding, "..... and if they aren't there, you'll be in trouble, my girl!"

So back she went and, of course, they were gone. She had to go home and report the loss and got "an awful walloping" for her wilfulness. To her dying day, she thought this most unjust, convinced she had taken the blame for the laziness of her brothers who went unpunished. However, as she got older, it was more a source of amusement than anger.

Many years later, I asked Uncles Tom and Les if they could remember the doll and prayer-books incidents and they could not. They were both horrified to think they could have been so awful! But these were isolated incidents in an otherwise easy-going, happy family. In fact, in his old age, Uncle Les´ wife, my Auntie Dorie, asked him if they had had many family squabbles when he was young and he said he could not remember any at all. She did not believe him, so she asked Mum the same question. Mum thought for a bit and then gave the same answer. Dorie replied, "That's what Les said and I didn't believe him but if you say the same, it must be true!"

Every Saturday, after their father had eaten his mid-day meal, the children queued up for their pocket money, ½d each, and they did not dare ask for it before every bit of his dinner was finished. Then they scampered off to *Palmers*, the sweet shop on the corner of the road, and there big decisions had to be made as to what to buy: sherbet drops, mint humbugs, liquorice sticks, nougat, gobstoppers, lollipops, or their favourite *Callard Bunkers* toffee slabs. This came in a big square, wrapped in greaseproof paper, and they would ask for ½d worth, and could they have the toffee paper please! This was because there were tiny flakes of toffee sticking to the paper so they got a little bit extra!

Saturday nights were also bath-nights and, after their weekly dip, they had to swallow a dose of a foul-tasting liquorice powder. It was "to keep our tummies working properly", as my mother so delicately put it! Victorians were obsessed with daily bowel movements but even after all those years, Mum still screwed up her face remembering the horrible flavour.

Of course, they all had chores to do, that was very much part of the Victorian work ethic, and Anne felt very hard done by to be the only girl, and therefore her mother's only dogsbody. She said she was always in trouble from her father for continually having her head stuck in a book and not helping her mother enough! It would have been unheard of for a boy to wash-up or help his mother change the sheets, for example, so all this fell to her while the boys completed their duties in record time (because there were more of them) and then rushed off out to play and enjoy themselves. Anne vowed if she ever had any daughters they would not have to help with any housework. And we didn't!

There was one chore, however, that all the children had to undertake at some time, and they hated it, but before I can tell you about that, I need to introduce their maternal grand-mother, Jemima Love.

CHAPTER TEN

Love by Name and Love by Nature
(Jemima Love)

What an evocative name it is, Jemima Love! And Mum said she was one of the loveliest people you could wish to meet: kind, gentle and caring. Her favourite saying was, "*If you can't find something nice to say about someone, then it's best to say nothing at all!*" and she lived by this maxim. In all the years Mum knew her, she never heard her utter an unkind thought or comment about anyone. She was truly, Love by name, and love by nature, but it would seem to us today that she had little to love about her life, for it appears to have been one of sheer drudgery for little reward.

Jemima could read, and this is not as obvious as it may sound, for she was born in Byworth near Petworth, in 1852, and this was a long time before free education was introduced in 1891. In her day, she would probably have attended a so-called "penny school" and although 1d sounds ridiculously cheap now, it was money a lot of people could not afford, so by 1900 there were many adults who might be able to write their name, but they would not be able to read a newspaper.

By the time Anne was born, in 1905, Jemima had been a widow for just over ten years and very little is known about her husband, except he was a seaman on one of the many sailing ships that berthed in Littlehampton Harbour, and that he was a local lad, born in Lyminster, in 1834. Anne did not even know his name, nor when, nor how, he died but a search of the records has revealed that his Christian name was James and he died in 1896 in East Preston, not far from Littlehampton. Anne did remember one story that her grand-mother told, however. It was on Jemima's wedding day and her new husband got so drunk that he fell asleep in the chair. Jemima was so fed up that she went out for a stroll, and then got in into awful trouble when he woke up and found his new wife (his bride!) had gone off for a walk ..... with the best-man! But the marriage must have survived this early hiccup because they went on to have seven children; three boys, James (known as Jim), Richard (known as Dick) and Arthur William (known as Bill), and four girls, Elizabeth (known as Liz), Ellen (known as Nell), Annie (known as Nance) and Mary, of course.

When her husband died, their eldest child, Jim, was 23 and married; Liz was 20 and Mary 17, both would probably have been in domestic service. Nell was 15 and although was probably able to do some daily work, she was most likely to still have been living at home. That left Dick, aged 13, Nance, aged 9, and baby Bill, aged only 2 years, all of whom would still be relying on their mother. They were all born in East Preston, so we can only assume that after her husband's death, Jemima, as the widow of a sea-farer, must have been offered rent-free (or very low rent) accommodation in Littlehampton, because Mum only ever knew her to live in a tiny waterman's cottage in Pier Road. By the time Anne was born, all the children, except Bill and Nell, were married or in service. Eventually Bill joined the Army and became a career soldier but Nell, who was constantly ailing, continued to live with her mother.

Pier Road runs alongside the river and thus afforded grandstand glimpses of the river traffic as there was only a road, wharves and warehouses between the single row of terraced cottages and the water. It is the link between the town centre and the old Oyster Pond, the East Pier, and, in those days, the Arun Mill and the lighthouse. The first gas-works were built to the north of the cottages and St John's Church, known as the Fisherman's Church, was constructed, mainly of wood, between Pier Road and Fisherman's Hard. Jemima's house was right next door to *John Eede Butt's Timber Yard* and Anne remembered it as a funny little place where she went straight into the sitting room from the front door and from there into the kitchen. Then four *"horrible, dangerous, little steps"* took her down to the scullery where there was a tap and a sink, just down on the right. When she went to the tap, she said it felt as though she was still standing on the steps. In fact, although Anne did not know this, these houses were quite historic and a real part of old Littlehampton, for they were known as Mussel Row and were built in 1829, perched on top of the far edge of the original embankment, which, as we know from a previous chapter, was constructed in 1735 to cut off the old delta of the river when they wanted to make a permanent outlet for the Arun. Thus all the cottages were deeper at the back than the front, hence the *"horrible, dangerous, little steps"* inside.

There were no widows' pensions in the early 1900's, even for widows with dependent children. Indeed it would be 1925 before state widows' pensions were introduced, and then it was only payable to widows of insured men with children aged under 14 at the time of the husband's death. Widows without children would not be entitled to any kind of state benefit for widowhood until 1929 when the above entitlement was extended to all widows of insured men, from age 55. If their husbands were not insured, they would have to wait until they were aged 70 and the Non-Contributory Old Age Pension (introduced in 1908) would be paid, or until the means- tested "National Assistance Act" came onto the statute book in 1948. Thus the only way Jemima could have money was to earn it, and the only way she could do this was to take in other people's washing. This was where her grand-children came into the picture, for they had the job of collecting the dirty washing from the homes and then delivering it back again when it was clean and asking for the money. At first it was Tom and Les who did this, but as Anne came of age, Tom dropped out and she did it first with Les and then with Bill. I suppose when Mum left school, and started work, Bill undertook the duty with Dick.

The first electric washing machine had actually gone on the market in 1907 but it would be many years before the appliances became standard in people's homes and I doubt if Jemima even saw one in her lifetime, let alone owned one. The first thing she would have to do on wash-days, was to heat up the water in the copper by making a fire underneath it, with bits of wood collected from the timber yard, by kind permission of the owner. This was another job for the children and each week they had to scavenge in the saw-dust searching for bits of wood that were big enough to burn. My mother absolutely HATED this chore above all others!

The next job for Jemima (or the children) was to grate a large bar of hard soap into flakes so it would dissolve in the water and then each article was washed by hand, scrubbing every seam with a small brush. Everything that could be boiled was then placed into the copper and boiled up, taking off the wooden lid from time to time and agitating the contents with a large wooden stick or something called a "dolly-stool". This looked like a small three-legged stool with a long handle on the top and it was submerged into the water and swirled around.

Then, when the washing had been boiled, it had to be hauled out of the copper and rinsed several times in cold water. A "blue-bag" would be added to the final rinse so the whites looked whiter and then it was starched if necessary.

The next process was to put the whole lot through an old-fashioned wringer or mangle. Granny-Love kept her mangle outside, so, summer and winter, the wringing would have to be done in the elements. And these were the years when there was always frost and snow for weeks on end in the winter months. The machine was a wrought iron contraption with two large rollers, one on top of the other, made of wood and adjustable. The rollers could be made to revolve by a wheel at the side and, as the operator held the article between the rollers, and turned the handle on the wheel, the wet washing was dragged between them, thus squeezing out the excess water. Because of this wringing exercise, a lot of clothes at this time had rubber or cloth buttons which would not break as they passed between the rollers. No spin dryers in the early 1900's!

Then it all had to be dried on lines, preferably outside but hanging down from lines strung across the ceiling indoors if the weather was bad. No tumble dryers in the early 1900's!

The final process was to iron it all, with flat-irons heated by the fire, or on the kitchener, summer and winter. No electric irons in the early 1900's! Anne said her grand-mother put so much effort into her laundry. Tablecloths, for example, were huge and they had a fringe all the way round which had to be combed so it was not matted together. Anne said she put in hours and hours of work for so little reward; 2d for a sheet perhaps and a whole big basketful would only fetch about 2/6d.

In spite of this hard work, Jemima often could not make ends meet and the children would have to take a note from her to the vicar of St John's Church, asking for a "ticket" so she could get 2/6d worth of free groceries. With this she could buy some tea, a little sugar, and margarine, a bit of cheese perhaps and a few bacon bits so she could make a bacon pudding.

The children also went to the dairy for her and, armed with her own can, they would buy ¾d worth of skimmed milk. Then they would trudge down to the Beach Hotel on the sea front and beg a few crusts, or leftover bread, on her behalf, so Gran could make a bread and butter (i.e. margarine!) pudding.

After the death of her husband in 1896, times must have been desperately hard for Jemima and if it had not been for the kindness of the local vicar of the "Fisherman's Church", the charitable efforts of the seaman's mission, the support of her family and her own hard work and determination, she, and her children, would probably have ended up in the dreaded work-house.

CHAPTER ELEVEN

On the Brink of Change
(1913-1918)

The 12th December 1913 saw the world's first-ever crossword puzzle. It was first developed in the shape of a diamond, by newspaperman Arthur Wynne for his *"New York World"* newspaper. It was an instant success, although it would take until the 1920's for it to become a popular international pastime and it would be 1942 before the *"New York Times"* deigned to publish its first crossword puzzle.

By this time, a Frenchman, Albert Kahn, was well into compiling his "Archive of the Planet", with the assistance of his project director, Jean Brunhes. Kahn was a millionaire banker, businessman and philanthropist who had the foresight to realise that the world was on the brink of change and that certain crafts, traditions and customs would soon be lost forever.

So, from 1908 until the war began in 1914, he sent teams of people to over fifty countries all over the world in order to photograph the ways of life that were quickly disappearing. In fact, as we know from a previous chapter, cameras producing black and white, or sepia, pictures had been around since the 1850´s but, like many of the new advances, such as cars, telephones, washing machines and the like, although invented and available, they were well beyond the pocket of the "man in the street" and not particularly user-friendly.

Kahn's records were often the very first images of ordinary people, doing everyday tasks, that had ever been taken. His photographers employed the most up-to-date equipment that money could buy, including the new hand-cranked cinematography technique of moving pictures and the latest "autochrome" plates that produced still pictures in colour, although it was difficult to get some of the subjects to stay motionless long enough for the eight to ten seconds needed to record the image.

Albert Kahn and his team found dignity and nobility in the most humble of scenes, and in the most surprising places, and recorded 72,000 still photographs and 183,000 metres of moving pictures, documenting the last chapters of the Edwardian era before war, upheaval and loss took its toll.

With the outbreak of the "Great War" in 1914, Albert Kahn and his team did not stop taking photographs but, with restrictions on travel, they were limited to recording images of the French Army, and its allies, in battle and at rest, highlighting the endurance and the stoicism of the average soldier and providing a powerful, intimate and humane portrait of the French at war. For a pacifist like Kahn, it must have been a heart-breaking comment on the futility of conflict.

Meanwhile films of a very different genre were being made across the Atlantic for it was in 1914 that the American public were introduced to Charlie Chaplin's unique brand of slapstick comedy in *"The Little Tramp"*. This was also the year in which the Panama Canal was officially opened and the year the *"American Traffic Signal Company"* installed its first set of traffic lights, in Cleveland Ohio, on 5th August.

In 1916 the newspapers reported that a strange new retail outlet had opened for business in the United States. It was the first self-service grocery store, the forerunner of the modern supermarket. Mary Martin was convinced such an alien concept would never catch on in Britain!

1916 began a period of "Warlordism" in China. It had already suffered a period of dictatorship under a power-hungry president, Yüan Shih-kai, who had shown that all he really wanted to be was a new emperor. By 1914, he had expelled the Kuomintang as a political party and its leader, Sun Yat-sen, had fled to Japan in fear of his life. Provinces started to secede from his rule and China fragmented into a series of independent states, under the control of military leaders or warlords. When Yüan died in June 1916, they were free to pursue aggressive policies against neighbouring provinces for the most trivial and illogical of reasons. China was in a state of chaos.

The 1914-18 "Great War" had little direct effect on the Martin family for Thomas was already married with children, and thus exempt from conscription, and the boys were too young. However two of Anne's uncles were involved; her mother's brother, Bill, was a regular soldier with the Horse Artillery and he was the first to leave for France. Then Fred Joyce, the husband of her mother's sister, Nance, decided to join up and while he was away, Anne went up to Wick, just north of Littlehampton, to sleep with her aunt as she was nervous of being alone in her house at night.

All of Jemima Love's daughters were inclined to be "nervy" but none more so than Nell. Mum said she was really strange; hearing voices no-one else could hear, seeing things other people could not see, laughing uproariously one minute and sobbing the next, all interspersed with periods when she seemed "normal". Poor Nell. It sounds as if she was more psychotic than neurotic and without treatment was destined only to deteriorate but there were no suitable drugs for mental illness in the early decades of the twentieth century. And poor Jemima, but she never complained, only trying to cope as best she could.

Although Anne spent her nights with her Aunt Nance, she spent the days at her own home or at school. One day at school, they heard a strange noise gradually becoming louder and louder and they were all rushed out of their classes to stand in the playground and look skywards. After a few minutes, a biplane flew over, the first time they had ever seen such a thing, and Mum remembered the wonder of it all her life.

During the war years, Anne and her younger brothers, Bill and Dick, amused themselves collecting shells from the beach and then bringing them back to the elm tree that grew in the middle of the T-junction at the end of East Street. There they used to sit on the edge of the kerb-stones and make grottoes out of the shells, decorate them with flowers and put a candle in the middle. Passers-by would admire their efforts and, if they were lucky, the better-off ones would reward them with a penny.

She remarked that after 1917, when the United States had entered the war, they often spotted American soldiers in Littlehampton because a battalion of them was stationed in Rustington, a village just to the east of the town. She recalled that one of them regularly used to sit on the kerb chatting to them. He used to carve things out of wood and one day he made them a star, like a Star of David, to hang in their grotto.

When she told me this in later years, she made the comment that her parents never seemed to worry about them talking to strangers, as parents would today, and the front door was always left unlocked when her mother was home alone. She did lock it when she went shopping but the windows might still be left open. Anne could not remember hearing about any incident of robbery or molestation in her youth.

In 1918 workmen laid down their tools, housewives ceased their chores and schoolchildren were taken out into their playgrounds, all so they could stare in wonder at an eclipse of the sun. Mum remembered being given bits of coloured glass to look through for the event! Definitely NOT recommended today and it is fortunate no child's eyesight was ruined.

In 1918, as the war came to its bloody conclusion, an indiscriminate, silent killer swept across the world: an influenza epidemic, the like of which had never been seen before and, thanks now to vaccination, hopefully will never be seen again. It had started in the spring of 1918 when large numbers of soldiers in the trenches complained of a sore throat, headaches and a loss of appetite. Although it was highly infectious, recovery was rapid and doctors called it the "three day fever". In the summer, the symptoms became much more severe and about a fifth of the victims developed pneumonia or blood poisoning. A large percentage of them died. The virus soon spread worldwide and was exceptionally aggressive, striking young adults rather than the elderly, which was (and is) unusual with this type of virus. By the time the pandemic had affected populations around the globe, some estimates put the total number of people killed at 70 million. The highest mortality rate was in India with 16 million dead from the disease within one year.

In the United Kingdom 228,000 people died, 400,000 in Germany and 675,000 in the United States. The high mortality rate lowered the average life expectancy in the USA by ten years and ten times more Americans were killed by this 'flu virus than died in the war. Indeed of the US soldiers who died in Europe, half of them died of 'flu and not by enemy action. 43,000 British servicemen, mobilized for the war, died of the virus and not from battle wounds.

It was unfairly known as "Spanish 'flu", probably because that was one of the earliest countries affected and it allegedly killed an unbelievable eight million people there by May 1918. However it is now thought that it most likely originated in China from a rare genetic mutation of the influenza virus.

When Fred Joyce returned to Littlehampton after fighting for his country, he was to find that his wife, Anne's Aunt Nance, had lost her personal fight for life; she had contracted 'flu and died, so they never saw one another again. Bill Love returned safely too, left the army and married a Littlehampton girl. Their daughter, Joan, eventually went to live in Australia. His brother, Jim Love, was already married to a local lass (from Wick, just north of the town) and they too had a daughter. (She married a man from Bermuda and their son was later to become a friend of my husband. Small world!) Alas, I do not know what happened to the third of Jemima's sons, Dick. Of her remaining daughters, Anne's Aunt Liz was in service in London. She had always suffered badly with asthma and soon after the war she had a bad attack and she also died. So, of Jemima's daughters, that left just Mary and Nell. Nell, of course, suffered with her "nerves" and Mary had developed dreadful varicose veins which would plague her for the rest of her life.

Women had done their bit for the war effort too. Although they were not allowed to fight, they had joined up as nurses, clerks, and messengers, and six million of them had worked in essential services, in industry and in munitions factories. Many young woman and girls had lost their marriage partners, before they had even had the chance to meet them, and they would be destined to be forever "on the shelf". In 1918, in recognition of the huge contribution women had made to the war effort, (not to mention sacrificing sons, fathers, husbands, brothers, future husbands, future children) women over the age of thirty were at last given the right to vote. It would be another ten years, however, before they were enfranchised on an equal footing with men.

This brought to an end the decades of struggle that women had undertaken in order to obtain this right, culminating in the formation of the suffragette movement in 1903 under the leadership of Mrs Emmeline Pankhurst. From then until the outbreak of the war in 1914, they had conducted a series of nuisance tactics such as breaking windows and chaining themselves to railings. When this did not work, they bombed the houses of politicians, burned down churches and vandalized golf-courses. They had been imprisoned, force-fed when they went on hunger-strike, and one, Emily Davidson, had even thrown herself under the King's horse in the 1913 Derby and died of her injuries. Now the war had achieved what they had failed to secure in peace, the right of women to vote.

So 1918 saw an eclipse of the sun, the end of the bloodiest war in history (at that time), a pandemic of influenza killing millions, the murder of the entire Russian royal family, and the enfranchisement of women. It also heralded the end of Anne's childhood. Soon she would be fourteen years of age and the time had come to leave school and start work.

CHAPTER TWELVE

Out in the World
(1919-1923)

By the time Anne started work in 1919, her eldest brother, Tom, had already left school and, in 1916, after a year working as an errand boy for *Colethorpe's The Bakers*, he had started his apprenticeship as a bricklayer with his father. Les, too, had left school, in 1917, and, like his brother, worked as an errand boy before he too began his apprenticeship with his father. In reality, children leaving school had very little choice of occupation in those days and boys tended to follow in their fathers' footsteps but, at least, unlike their father, Tom and Les rode bicycles to work!

I would guess that more than 90% of girls who left school at that period went into domestic service, as parlour maids, kitchen maids, scullery maids and the like, or daily work, which was more of the same but living out. Of the lucky 10% who escaped this life, two out of one hundred possibly became shop assistants, another two perhaps obtained clerical jobs, one might get work in a factory (if there was one near enough), a couple might work on a farm, one might be kept at home to care for an ailing relative, and the remainder would probably work for parents, looking after younger children, running errands, possibly learning their mothers' trade of seamstress, for example. I would not imagine that more than one in a thousand would go on to become a nurse, governess or teacher. A lot would depend on who, and what, your parents were, what connections they had, how affluent they were, and where you lived. Anne was in the 90% category and she knew domestic service was to be her lot in life. For her there was no other option.

Her first job was as a daily for an elderly lady, called Mrs Wray, who lived in East Street. Mum remembered it particularly for an incident that occurred soon after she began to work there. Apparently Mrs Wray's daughter, a Mrs Pennicott, came to stay bringing her precocious nine year old daughter with her. The youngster thought it would be a great lark to make "Annie the Servant" dress up in a mop-cap and apron and then send her to post a letter. Anne felt totally humiliated and a little way along the road, she took off the hated cap and apron and rolled them up in a ball. When she got back to the house, she said that she had bumped into her mother in the street and her mother had expressed the opinion that she was too big to be dressed up in things like that and had told her to take it off! All the years later, Mum still hated the thought she had told a deliberate lie but I replied by saying I thought it was a very clever ploy! Despite this humiliation, she stayed with Mrs Wray for about a year.

While Anne was with Mrs Wray, in 1919, John Alcock and Arthur Whitton Brown made the first direct flight across the Atlantic Ocean in a Vickers Vimy aeroplane, taking sixteen hours and twenty-seven minutes. In the same year, a British airship made the double crossing and Ross Smith flew from London to Australia in one hundred and thirty-five hours. The days of international air travel for all were just beginning.

Towards the end of 1920, Anne obtained another daily job, this time for Mr Reeves, the local riding master, and his wife. They lived in a big house in Selborne Road, near the beach, and every summer they let their house and moved into a flat above the stables. As well as her domestic duties, Mr Reeves used to yell up the stairs for her and she would have to go down and hold the bridle of the horse "so the kiddies could mount". There was one old, white pony in particular that he used for them and Mr Reeves said as soon as this old equine heard her coming through the doors that led to the stable-yard, he used to whinny for her and that would set all the other horses off.

She was with Mr and Mrs Reeves on the 24th September 1921 when Littlehampton's War Memorial to "the fallen" was unveiled near the Council Offices, on the crossroads of Beach Road, New Road, St Catherine's Road and Maltravers Road. Eventually every town and city in the country would have a similar monument and on it would be inscribed the names of the local members of the Armed Services who had given their lives for their country. As the century progressed, and more wars were fought and more lives lost, more names would be added.

Services are still held at War Memorials throughout the land on "Remembrance Sunday", the nearest Sunday to the 11th November, "Remembrance Day", and the anniversary of the signing of the armistice ending the "Great War". In Littlehampton, in common with many other towns without formal troops stationed nearby, uniformed members of the local youth movements march through the streets, led by the *Sea Cadet* band. At the memorial, wreaths of poppies, in memory of the dead from all the wars, are laid by various civic dignitaries, and a bugler will usually play "The Last Post", while all the flags are lowered in their honour. Normally someone will intone the immortal words of Laurence Binyon, from his *"Ode For the Fallen",* written in the early months of the First World War when thousands and thousands of names were being recorded in obituary columns of national newspapers, day after bloody day.

They shall not grow old, as we that are left grow old:
Age shall not weary them, nor the years condemn.

64

At the going down of the sun and in the morning
We will remember them.

In the week before these ceremonies take place, red poppies are sold in aid of the charity, the "Royal British Legion", which aims to help ex-service people and their families. The poppy was chosen as the symbol because it was the only thing which grew on the battlefields of Flanders in the aftermath of the devastation; a sea of red making a powerful image of the bloodshed of trench warfare. Members of the "Disabled Society of the Legion" still make the poppies at the Poppy Factory, founded in Richmond in 1922. The original poppy was designed so that workers with a disability could easily assemble it and this principle remains today.

In 1920 and 1921, newspapers were again carrying articles about the seemingly-never-ending "Irish Problem". It is almost impossible to simplify the difficulties of this dilemma but it all started centuries ago when various conquerors under the British flag, such as Oliver Cromwell and William of Orange, cruelly confiscated vast tracks of land from native Irish Catholics and handed it over to an English, or Anglo-Irish, mainly Protestant, aristocracy. These often-absentee landlords cared only for profit and used local Protestant agents to manage the estates on their behalf, while they lived lavishly in London or Europe, off the rents paid by Catholics for land their ancestors had once owned. The landlords and the agents treated the tenants with a cruel and callous disregard for their living conditions, their families and indeed their lives.

The peasants found themselves paying higher and higher rents for smaller and smaller plots, as the agents kept sub-dividing the land in order to get yet more rent, and, by 1835, the people were among the poorest in the Western World, often reduced to living with their animals in a single-roomed, windowless mud cabin that did not even have a chimney. The peasants could just about exist if they grew potatoes, for it is possible to stay healthy on a diet of these alone, so rich are they in protein, carbohydrates, minerals and vitamins. But this meant "all their eggs were in one basket", so to speak, and thus when the potato blight hit their crops in 1845 and subsequent years, they were truly in a desperate situation. Without doubt, not only had the landlords and their agents been criminally negligent over the welfare of the people on its offshore island, but so too had all the English parliaments ..... and never more so when the potato famine struck.

Thus it was hardly surprising that the Irish wanted to govern themselves and in 1870 formed a "Home Rule Association" with the aim of dissolving the union between Great Britain and Ireland. The Protestant (surprisingly!) Member of Parliament, Charles Stewart Parnell, became its leader in 1877 and, under his leadership, the Association stepped up its campaign by disrupting the business of the House and adopting terror tactics on its opponents in the Irish countryside. This resulted in the Crimes Act of 1886 authorising trial without jury. Evictions of recalcitrant tenants increased to unprecedented levels and when the Home Rule Bills of 1886 and 1893 were both defeated, Ireland was a tinder-box waiting to explode.

On Easter Sunday 1916, the extremist wing of the Home Rule Association, calling itself "Sinn Fein", seized Dublin Post Office and declared a republic. This is known as the "Easter Uprising" but it lasted only until the Friday of that week when the rebels surrendered. Fourteen of the leaders were executed for high treason and Eamonn de Valera was only spared because he was born in the USA. He was sentenced to life imprisonment instead.

The problem dragged on until, in 1920, the English government proposed that the "vexed question of the Irish problem" could be solved by the three (largely Catholic) counties in the south of Ireland having a measure of independence if they agreed to accept dominion status as the "Irish Free State". Meanwhile, the six (largely Protestant) counties in the north would remain, as the majority of residents wished, in the United Kingdom. The rebels refused to accept this compromise because this "home rule" only gave them very limited power and in any case they still wanted a united Ireland (even if the north wanted to stay in the United Kingdom) so they intensified their terror campaign. The English Government responded by sending in the hated "Black and Tan Regiment" who answered violence with violence.

In 1921, the "Provisional Irish Government" capitulated and agreed to accept dominion status for the three counties in the south and it became the Irish Free State, renamed Eire in 1936. Full independence as a republic was to come in 1949 but Northern Ireland remained part of the United Kingdom and future years would see that the "Irish problem" was far from solved.

In 1921 the Nobel Prize for Physics was awarded to Albert Einstein *"for his services to Theoretical Physics and especially for his discovery of the law of photoelectric effect"*. This is just one of his many contributions to science, and he is regarded as the father of modern physics and one of the best known scientists and intellectuals of all time. He was born in Germany in 1879, but during the rise of Nazi-ism in the 1930's, he emigrated to America and became a US citizen in 1940. He published more than 300 scientific and over 150 non-scientific books. His great intelligence and originality has made the name of "Einstein" synonymous with genius and he is, without doubt, the most amazing intellectual of the 20th century. He died on 18th April 1955, aged 76 years, at Princeton, New Jersey.

One of the great medical breakthroughs of the 20th century was discovered in 1922 with insulin becoming available to combat diabetes. Alas, it was too expensive for most people but, at least, it was the beginning of hope for thousands of diabetics.

Another discovery of a different kind also occurred this same year, on 4th November 1922, in Egypt. While clearing away some debris near the base of the tomb of Rameses VI, workmen unearthed a hidden step. The archaeologist, Howard Carter, found it led to the tomb of the boy Pharoah Tutenkhamun, and the priceless treasures therein had lain undiscovered for over 3000 years.

In the same year, Littlehampton's new combined post office and telephone exchange was opened, a sure sign that 'phones were becoming more common.

At about this time Anne changed jobs again. This time she went to work for a widowed lady in Beach Road who had just returned home from Jamaica. Her mother soon came to live with her and Anne basically kept house for them. Unfortunately, after she had been there for about eighteen months, Mary Martin had a nervous breakdown and Anne had to give up her job in order to look after her and the family. No-one really knows what caused Mary to become quite so ill but Anne felt it was the worry over her sister, Nell, worry over her mother who was finding it increasingly difficult to cope, and worry over her own health as her varicose veins now tended to ulcerate and, in these pre-antibiotic days, there was little anyone could do except bed-rest and wrap the affected part in a bandage spread with honey. But the remedy did seem to work. After all, honey is a natural antibiotic, and its use for medicinal purposes has been well-documented for centuries.

In 1923 Anne's third brother, Bill, left school. Bill must have been the brightest of the children because he was selected by the junior school to go onto a grammar school, rather than the ordinary secondary school which was what most children attended. However his parents could not afford to pay for the uniform, so the offer was turned down, and thus Bill travelled the same work route as his male siblings, errand boy for a year and then apprentice bricklayer with his father.

CHAPTER THIRTEEN

The Roaring Twenties
(1924-1929)

In 1924 the leader of the 1917 Russian Revolution, Vladimir Lenin, died and Joseph Stalin took over. This was also the year Adolf Hitler published his book, "Mein Kampf". Neither event would bode well for the coming decades.

As for Anne, in 1924 she was just nineteen years of age and, with her mother fully recovered, she had to look for employment again. Her old job, with the widow and her mother, had been taken by a certain Blanche Oakley, but her ex-employer recommended that she work for her sister who lived next door. Thus she started work for Mrs Sims and family; for the first time she was living-in and could therefore be regarded as truly being in domestic service. Little did she realise then that this was to be the start of a lifelong association, and in more ways than one!

When Anne started in domestic service for Mrs Sims, she had accepted the conditions of service that was the norm´ for this employment: The pay was £2.10s 0d per month, living-in-all-found, and one half-day off per week and a whole day once a month. I think all of the local girls must have contrived to have the same half-day, or at least the same clique had the same half-day, because there did not seem to be any problem in meeting friends even with this very limited "social window".

Anne also adopted the fashions of the other girls, shorter skirts and shorter hair, stylish shoes with a small heel and a strap across the front, buttoned at the side or fastened with a thin lace, tied in a bow in the middle; a cloche-style, felt hat, summer and winter, and a tailored coat. It was in this up-to-the-minute apparel that she and the other young women would parade along the High Street on their half-days off. Up and down, up and down, they went, chatting to the girls they knew and surreptitiously eyeing up the young men who had contrived to have this as their half-day off as well.

One day she saw an old school-friend who was in service in Goda Road and she introduced her to two sisters, who were in service in the house next door to hers. Their names were Edith and Carrie Starte and Anne took to them straight away. Edith was a little older, and was the cook, and Carrie a little younger, and was the parlourmaid. They went off for a walk together and this was the beginning of a life-long friendship. How she envied them having each other; she had always wanted a sister of her own! But the three became like sisters, sharing

68

confidences and dreams, going for walks, to the cinema and to socials (dances) together. They walked for miles, across the fields to Lyminster and Burpham, along the beach to Angmering-on-Sea, up the river-bank to Arundel, and often they ended up having afternoon tea with one another's parents and Anne became very fond of their mother. She maintained it was Mrs Starte who encouraged her to save a little bit of money each week from her meagre earnings and on her 21st birthday, some two years after the first meeting, the "Startes" gave her a string of pearls which she treasured until the day she died.

It was also soon after she had started work for Mrs Sims, that Anne had her first boyfriend, a young man by the name of Fred Warner, who lived in Essex Road in Bognor Regis, a town about eight miles to the west of Littlehampton. He was working in Littlehampton and had a brother who had married a girl called Kitty. They lived in Lewes and one weekend, early in November, Anne and Fred went up there by train to see the town's communal bonfire and fireworks.

Of course bonfires have been lit for centuries as a mark of celebration, even as far back as Celtic times, but the origins of having a communal late-Autumn bonfire are many and varied. Suffice to say that all the reasons coalesced in 1605 because it was on November 5th of that year, that a Papist, called Guy Fawkes, attempted to blow up the Houses of Parliament and return Protestant England to the Roman Catholic faith. He was caught, just as he was about to light the fuse, and he and his fellow conspirators were tried, convicted as traitors, and sentenced to be hung, drawn and quartered.

Ever since, in memory of this act of treason, a ritual search of the cellars of the Houses of Parliament is carried out every year before the "State Opening of Parliament" but no-one really knows why Sussex has maintained its communal commemoration of this event, when the rest of the nation celebrate Guy Fawkes´ Night with a family bonfire in the garden and a few fireworks, if they bother to remember it at all. Be that as it may, Lewes, as the county town of old Sussex, (before it was divided into East and West) is the centre of these annual festivities to this day, and the various Bonfire Societies organise a stunning, costumed procession to parade through the streets, illuminated by flaming torches held high above their heads, and accompanied by banners and bands. The procession winds its way to a large, open space where a huge bonfire is lit, with an effigy on top, called a "guy" and a spectacular firework display ends the evening's entertainment. Strange to say, in Sussex it is not called "Guy Fawkes´ Night" but "Bonfire Night".

Eventually the romance between Anne and Fred just fizzled out but

Anne stayed friendly with Kitty for many years and treasured a china biscuit barrel that the couple gave her on her marriage a few years later.

Then she had another boyfriend who lived just across the river-mouth, in the village of Clymping, but she discovered that he was two-timing her so, "That was the end of that!" she declared, many years later, adding, "He's dead now anyway!" His name was not revealed but I doubt this was a deliberate omission. She may have imagined he was not worth a mention!

In 1925 Dick, the youngest of the Martin children, left school, once again to follow the now well-rehearsed pattern of his older brothers, which was errand boy, followed by apprenticeship. By now both Tom and Les had finished their apprenticeships and were fully-fledged tradesmen. Although Tom was fully qualified, however, he actually preferred, at this stage, to work as a labourer with less responsibility. He was always the less confident of the brothers. Les had already acquired the nickname of "Swallow" (as in swallow-martin) and many years later my husband would work in an elderly bricklayer's home who could remember working with "Swallow". (Small world again!) Les was a very good brick-layer, confirmed by the fact he later worked as a "corner-man", the highest paid "brickie" on the site, because they all take their lines from his work; if the corners are not accurate, nothing will be right. But Les said Bill was the most-skilled of the brothers and had a natural fluidity of movement that just could not be taught. Les thought it might have been because Bill was the tallest of them and slimmer than himself and Tom. Also Bill would be recognised as the fastest of the brothers, laying up to 1200 bricks a day. Dick (also taller and slimmer than his two eldest brothers) could be regarded as the most ambitious as he eventually became a site foreman for the big building firm of Lovells. However, he never regarded himself as good a tradesman as his brothers were.

(By a strange co-incidence, I would marry a brick-layer! Years later my husband would chat with my uncles for hours, whenever he had the chance, about the jobs they had worked on, the people they had worked with, and how techniques had changed over the years, for better or worse! My Uncle Tom even gave Bryan his tools! But Mum said the co-incidence did not end there and often commented that Bryan reminded her very much of her father. Not so much in appearance, although both were dark, but in temperament. Both were "worriers" and inclined to be highly-strung, as were her brothers, especially Tom and Les. All of them were rather reserved, not particularly sociable and not easy to get to know. They were all hard-working, immensely loyal, conscientious, trustworthy and inclined to be "careful" with money! They all had a very dry sense of humour, not ambitious, not materialistic, gentle, proud but not arrogant. My mother thought of Bryan as a "Martin-clone" and would come to regard him as the son she never had.

But one trait not shared by them all was a love of gardening! Grand-dad Martin and Uncles Tom, Bill and Dick were very keen gardeners, but Les' daughter (Peggy) feels her father only gardened because he had to! (Like Bryan!) Mum never gardened at all, except to pick the sweet-peas that Dad grew for her, and perhaps to harvest some peas for lunch. She did not share all the "boys'" traits either for she was more sociable than they were.

All the older "Martin" children were now courting but Anne's second eldest brother, Les, was the first to be married, to Dorothy Minnie Pelling in May 1926. Dorie (as she was known) was from Angmering, a village about four miles away, but was in service in Littlehampton for the "Richmond" family when they met. She was born in the same year as Anne and they were destined to become good friends as well as sisters-in-law.

But things were not so good for the country in general. After the war, the Liberal Coalition Government of Lloyd George had promised the populace "A Land Fit for Heroes" but, in the event, thousands of demobbed soldiers could not find work. In 1922 this Government collapsed and was followed for a short period by Conservative rule. Then, for the first time, the Labour Party ran a minority government headed by Ramsey MacDonald. He called for "a vote of confidence" in the general election of 1924, but lost due to what we would now call a dirty tricks campaign. The Conservative Party won the election and Stanley Baldwin became Prime Minister instead.

With little action from any of the ruling parties, the total number of unemployed in 1926 had soared to over 2million. Disillusioned and demoralised, with rising profits for the owners but falling wage rates, miners, dockers, builders, printers, transport workers and those in heavy industry decided to strike. Known as the General Strike of 1926, the miners held out for three months but the main body of it collapsed after just nine days. When eventually the miners went back to work, it was on the mine owners' terms; more hours for less money. Stanley Baldwin, known for his love of the quiet life, had backed the mine-owners. The workers had been defeated and the next year the Trades Dispute Act made general strikes illegal and this remained on the statute book until 1946.

So, in 1926, Clem had returned to an England gay in parts and grey in others, officially at peace but far from peaceful. But with the worst of the unemployment in the north, he had had little trouble in securing the job as a landscape gardener for *Barnham Nurseries*. With his first week's pay, he decided a celebration was in order and jumped on the back of his brother Ted's motorbike and off they roared to toast the new job, and a new life, at a country public house. They were exceedingly "happy" when they came out .....and promptly got arrested for being drunk and disorderly! A five shilling fine, if my memory serves me right, and Dad forever after disparagingly referring to the offending hostelry as "The Ruptured Duck", when its proper name was the more salubrious, "The White Swan"!

Alas, I do not know what work Ted was doing at this time but he was living and working in the area and he and Clem used to go out together looking for girls to chat up! (Some things don't change!)   Jack had learned how to thatch hayricks from his father and now, aged sixteen, he was working with a master thatcher called George Dilliston, thatching roofs of cottages. He would eventually become a master thatcher in his own right and go into partnership with George.

All of Clem's sisters would be "in service" by now but only Blanche, as we know, was in service in Littlehampton and she was a useful source of possible "dates", and even blind-date material, for her brothers from the young women she knew. Sometimes she set up Clem, sometimes Ted, and sometimes both of them together. Dad said he would arrange to meet the blind-date at a bus-stop and then if he did not like the look of the (poor) girl, he stayed on the 'bus! So there must have been 'buses in the area in 1926!

Clem enjoyed his time at *Barnham Nurseries* but the only garden of significance that he could remember building and planting-out, was for Gladys Cooper, the well known star of stage and film, who lived nearby at Amberley.

So many people were buying wireless parts and building "cat's whisker" DIY radios, in order to listen to any message that might be floating out there somewhere, that manufacturers decided to transmit proper programmes and set up a British Broadcasting Company. They appointed a Mr John Reith as its manager and in 1926 the Government agreed to allow them to finance the venture by imposing licence fees from all the owners of the receivers. The Company was duly reborn, in 1927, as the British Broadcasting Corporation, the BBC, and John Reith (later Sir John Reith, then Lord Reith) became its first director-general. The "wireless" had arrived.

Other technical advances now opened up the possibilities of making and breaking air and land speed records and names like Henry Seagrove and Malcolm Campbell came to the fore. In 1924 Imperial Airways operated long distance flights across land masses, while British Airways ran services to and from the continent. In 1926 Alan Cobham tested the possibilities of long distance air routes between England and South Africa and England and Australia. On 20th May 1927 the U.S. pilot Charles Lindbergh became the first man to fly across the Atlantic, from

New York to Paris, in the *Spirit of St Louis,* winning $25,000 prize money put up by a Frenchman, Raymond Orteig. He had travelled 3600 miles in 33.5 hours, flying solo and fighting fatigue, fog, ice and cold, every lonely mile. Four million people lined the streets of New York to welcome him home with the largest ticker-tape celebration the world has ever seen. A new aviation hero was born, and international air travel for all, if not actually taking off just yet, now, at least, was ticking over on the tarmac.

In 1927 Edwin Hubble discovered that galaxies recede from one another and that the universe is expanding in all directions. In 1925 he had already discovered the first galaxy outside the *Milky Way,* 2million years away from earth.

By now the so-called, unbelievably perhaps, "Roaring Twenties" were well under way with jazz music, the Charleston dance, flapper dresses and bobbed hair styles all the rage. Portable, wind-up gramophones (and their 78rpm records) had been invented and the improving quality of recording established the new sounds as the trend-setters of the twenties. It was the dance music of the "gay young things" and a "must-have" at any youthful social gathering. But the most popular entertainment, for all ages, was the new medium of the cinema, complete with live music provided by any keyboard, from a mighty Wurlitzer organ to a modest upright piano. Although talking movies had been invented in 1923, it would be 1927 before the first talking picture, "The Jazz Singer", made its debut and soon there was a picture-house in every town, and sometimes more than one. Eventually Littlehampton boasted no less than three cinemas; the *Regent* came first, followed by the *Odeon* a few years later and finally the *Palladium.* Each one had the "cheap" seats downstairs, 6d in Mum's time and the dearer 9d seats upstairs. The *Regent Cinema* became known, rather unfairly, as the *Regent de Flea* in my husband's youth, in the 1950's, and still had the original fittings including the old gas-lights, which the lads delighted in blowing out and nearly asphyxiating the patrons! I do not know if this went on in my parents' day but, at that time, Douglas Fairbanks and Rudolph Valentino were the heart-throbs, while Joan Crawford and Greta Garbo provided the glamour. Slapstick comedy routines by the likes of Charlie Chaplin and "Laurel and Hardy" (Stan Laurel and Oliver Hardy) supplied the laughs and in 1928 the first "Mickey Mouse" cartoon made its appearance. The genre of "star" had begun in all fields of cinema entertainment and Littlehampton could make its own claim to fame with Ronald Colman, a middle-class son of an import merchant who was educated locally at "Hadley School", and who survived the transition from silent movie actor to "talkie" roles.

Clem and Ted came to Littlehampton quite frequently and often would meet Blanche for a walk and a chat. One day in the spring of 1928, the three of them were walking along the road and four young women came towards them. Blanche set about introducing them to her brothers: Edith and Carrie Starte, Blanche Warren and Anne Martin. They stood talking for a while. Anne had taken an immediate liking to Ted but, unfortunately for her, Ted fancied Blanche Warren and offered to walk her home. Clem gallantly asked Anne if he could do the same for her. She thought for a moment. It was either this or walk back on her own, so she rather reluctantly accepted his offer. But she always had a soft spot for Ted!

A few months later, Anne and Clem were still seeing one another but the romance between Ted and Blanche was becoming quite serious and Blanche asked him to go up on his motorbike to visit her parents near Horsham.

That same Saturday evening, Clem met Anne on a date but she felt "out of sorts"; fidgety and unsettled, but she could not say why. Clem asked what she wanted to do. Go to the cinema? Go for a walk? Anne could not decide.

"Well what DO you want to do?" he asked in exasperation.

"I don't know!" she wailed. "I feel sort of jittery. I can't explain it!"

The next day, they learned that Ted had been killed on his motorbike, a few miles from his destination, at about the same time that Anne felt "jittery". The 'bike had skidded on a bend in the road and he had died instantly. Although major roads were now tarmac'ed, there were no crash helmets in 1928. Indeed crash helmets would not even be conceived as a possibility, or necessity, until 1935 when a neurosurgeon, Hugh Cairns, was involved in the treatment of T.E. Lawrence (better known as *Lawrence of Arabia*) for severe head injuries, sustained after a motorcycle accident near his home in Dorset. Lawrence died six days later (on 19th May 1935) and this began Cairns' long study into what he saw as unnecessary deaths of motorcycle riders and what could be done to avoid them. Eventually his research would lead to the use of crash helmets by both military and civilian motorcyclists but helmets would not be compulsory in the UK until 1st June 1972.

Meanwhile, Clem had not only lost his brother but his best friend. Luckily, Blanche was not a pillion passenger on this fateful day, but I doubt whether she had ever even sat on Ted's motorbike. With the fashionable straight skirts, to a mid-calf length, it would not have been "seemly" for a lady to sit astride a motorbike! And trousers did not become acceptable for every day wear for women until the mid-60's, although they would be worn extensively during the war years (1939-1945) for factory and farm work.

At some time during China's period of "Warlordism" that had begun in

1916, Sun Yat-sen had returned from his exile in Japan and re-organised his Kuomintang troops. He managed to seize Canton in 1921 and established a republican government in that province. He declared this government to be the national government of China, in direct opposition to the warlord government of the capital, Beijung, but he was unable to unite the country, and died in 1924, believing his dream of creating a Chinese republic to have been a failure. But, hiding in the wings of history, was a young general named Chiang Kai-shek who was fanatically devoted to Sun's vision. He continued Sun's efforts to crush the warlord governments and, in 1928, with his Western-supported Kuomintang army, he brought about the unification of which Sun had dreamed.

But it was a unification not agreeable to all its people. The Chinese Communist Party had been formed in 1921, supported by Russia. During the purge on the warlords, there was an ideological difference between the two parties that could not be reconciled and, in 1927, civil war commenced between the Kuomintang and the Communists.

1928 also saw what was to be one of the most important medical breakthroughs of all time; Dr Alexander Fleming made the accidental discovery of penicillin but with insufficient support from the medical community, his research had to stop. However, in the late 1930´s other scientists found a way to mass-produce the drug and British and American pharmaceutical companies began to manufacture it in large quantities, in time to cure many infections from thousands of wounds in the war that was to begin in 1939. Since then Dr Alexander Fleming´s 1928 discovery has saved literally millions of lives and in 1945 he was presented with the Nobel Prize for Medicine. 1928 also brought forth two more ground-breaking inventions; sliced bread and chewing gum!

By now Anne´s eldest brother, Tom, had married Myrtle Peace Lettis (on 26th December 1927). Myrtle's parents lived in Amberley and on Sunday afternoons, weather permitting, they would walk along the river-bank in order to visit her family. It was a journey Myrtle had made many times when she had worked in Littlehampton, in domestic service, of course. However, because the river winds along the Arun Valley, the journey was actually twice as long than if they had travelled by road. It was much more pleasant, however, for the sailing barges were still using the river at this time and they would have walked passed the new swing-bridge, and the watercress beds at Arundel; seen Arundel Castle and the Norman church at Clymping; picked primroses and wild flowers from the river-bank; watched lambs gambolling, and cattle and deer grazing in the meadows, and swans nesting on the bank. Depending on the tide, the Arun can look very benign as it meanders along but in fact it is one of the fastest flowing rivers in England, second only to the Severn at Bristol, so appearances can be deceptive and the currents and eddies can be extremely dangerous. In inclement weather, they would return by train, for Amberley was only two stops up the line from Littlehampton.

Tom and Myrtle's first son was a honeymoon baby they named Geoffrey Thomas, born on 27th September 1928. He was not the first grandchild for Tom and Mary Martin; their second son, Les; and his wife Dorie had had a daughter, Jean, in June of that year. By this time they lived on a new housing development in Streatham Vale, in London, where they stayed until their retirement. Uncle "Swallow" worked on some very prestigious projects in the capital and their home would act later as the launch-pad for brothers Bill and Dick, who also tried their luck in the metropolis in future years. But Tom stayed put. He and Myrtle, and baby Geoff, were happy enough in Littlehampton and they were thrilled when eventually they were offered one of the first council houses in the town, not far from Tom's parents' house in Stanhope Road.

1929, and Jemima's little waterman's cottage, with its "horrible little steps", and the whole of the historic Mussel Row in Pier Road, was about to be demolished and replaced by a new row of terraced houses. Mary and Tom Martin's children were flying the nest, so they asked Mary's mother, Jemima Love, to go and live with them. The health of Anne's Aunt Nell had deteriorated and she had been admitted to the East Preston Infirmary on an indefinite basis, although later she would be transferred to the Graylingwell Psychiatric Hospital at Chichester.

At this time brother Bill was courting Violet Ellen Poole and even seventeen-year-old Dick was walking out with fifteen-year-old Ethel. Love was definitely in the air and perhaps it seemed like some kind of lucky omen for Anne and Clem when they learned that Anne's grandmother, Jemima Love, had been born in Byworth, the adjacent village to Duncton where Clem had been born. What a strange co-incidence! Possibly it helped to forge one of those indefinable links that turn courtship into romance, and then into love, for in September 1929 Anne and Clem became engaged.

Clem had met Anne's parents very early on in the courtship and from day one, Mary thought he was a "good sort"; a steady, dependable man who was obviously besotted with her daughter and who would make her a good husband. Indeed she would often take his side against Anne and would tell her off "for nagging him" and "talking nasty"! If you knew my mother you would find this very hard to believe! She never nagged and she tried (successfully) to live by Jemima's maxim of "*If you can't find something nice to say…etcetera, etcetera*" so I asked Mum what kind of things her mother had in mind. She could not remember! Anyway Dad could not have been very bothered by the "nagging and the nasty words"; he remained her adoring slave until the end.

76

Of course, they also had to tell Ben and Ada Oakley the glad tidings of the engagement. Ben informed his future daughter-in-law of the family tradition where the Christian names of the first-born son (of the first-born son), were reversed and thus their son should be called after him, Benjamin Clement. Anne retorted, "Well this is where the tradition stops!" These words would come back to haunt her in the years ahead.

About this time Anne went to Brighton with Edith and Carrie Starte and, for a lark, they visited the fortune teller at the end of the pier. When it was Anne's turn, the gypsy-lady peered deeply into her crystal ball and looked perplexed. "The picture is unclear", she mumbled. Then, after pausing for thought, she continued, "I see you with two children........but I'm not sure if they are yours......Yes! They are yours....... but you have waited such a long time........"
What a load of old rubbish, thought Anne as she exited the tent. And immediately dismissed the revelation.

On Thursday 24th October 1929, the largest stock market in the world, the New York Stock Exchange, began to crash. Monday 28th and Tuesday 29th saw more catastrophic losses and stocks continued to fall in value at an unprecedented rate for the next month. It was the most devastating stock market crash in the history of the US and anyone who was unfortunate enough to invest mid-1929, would see his, or her, whole adult life pass by before recouping the loss.

The so-called "Wall Street Crash" caused an American economic collapse that reverberated around the globe and officially began the years that were to become known as the "Great Depression", or the "Great Slump". Not an auspicious start to a new decade.

CHAPTER FOURTEEN

On the Move!
(1930-1933)

I believe three of the enduring figures of 20th century history will prove to be Mahatma Gandhi, Adolf Hitler and Mao Zedong and, strange to say, they all came to prominence in the 1930´s, although Gandhi was the first to make international headlines.

Early in the decade, the Indian National Congress made a *"Declaration of Independence"* from British rule and appointed Mahatma Gandhi to organise the campaign to achieve this. Gandhi believed in the principle of non-violent protest and thus, on 12th March 1930, he set off for Dondi, some 200 miles away, in order to mine salt. The British, via the Raj, controlled and taxed salt production and therefore this was an act of civil disobedience. Thousands of people joined him along the route and at the conclusion of "Gandhi's Salt March", on 6th April 1930, hundreds of non-violent protestors were violently beaten but they would not be deterred and large-scale acts of disobedience against the "Salt Laws" began. On 5th May Gandhi was arrested and imprisoned. Despite their mentor being in jail, protests against the "Salt Laws" continued and, as a result, over 80,000 Indians were jailed within the year. Extensive newspaper and newsreel coverage drew attention to Gandhi's plight, the people's struggle for independence, and the activities and suffering of the protestors, but failed to convince the British Government of the need for change.

Time Magazine declared Gandhi "Man of the Year" and likened his march to the sea to defy the salt tax, to that of the so-called "Boston Tea Party", the protest of the American New Englanders in 1773 when they sank the vessels in Boston Harbour over the British tax on tea. This is said to have been the flashpoint for the American War of Independence.

Mahatma Gandhi was released after a year in prison but he remained the figurehead for Indian independence. Also he became the icon for the "Untouchables" of his own country, and for struggling peoples worldwide, including, it is claimed, the American Civil Rights leader, Martin Luther King, who drew inspiration from the non-violent teachings of Gandhi in his own fight for civil rights for black Americans in the 1960´s.

Still in 1930, Anne and Clem were married on 27th September in St James´ Church, Littlehampton. Mum would have preferred it to have been the parish church of St Mary, where she had gone to Sunday School, but the church was being rebuilt and in fact would not be in use again until 1934. She had four bridesmaids, Edith and Carrie Starte, Blanche Oakley and her future sister-in-law, Violet Poole, by now betrothed to her brother Bill, and the newlyweds spent their honeymoon with her brother Les and his wife, Dorie, at their home in Streatham, London. Dad's best man was his brother, Jack, and the only hitch on a perfect day was his father not arriving at the church on time. Clem and Jack had to race around trying to find him but luckily they knew where to look. The nearest public house...... where he was slightly the worse for wear! The bride was not impressed! Photographs were not taken on the day, although this was becoming more fashionable in the cities. The only recorded image of the event was the happy couple in their wedding finery, taken in a studio a few days after the ceremony and the honeymoon. But one face was missing from the celebrations; sadly Jemima Love had been taken ill with pneumonia a few months before the wedding, and had passed away in East Preston Infirmary, so she had just missed seeing her grand-daughter married. She was 79 years old.

Of course there was no way that a married woman could be in resident domestic service, unless her husband was in service with the same employer, so Anne reverted to being a "daily" with Mrs Sims. In fact Mrs Sims had tried to find them a cottage to rent by writing on their behalf to a Mrs Willets who owned Winterton Lodge at the end of Goda Road, but by the time she replied they had found something to rent by themselves; two rooms and a shared bathroom on a small estate of terraced bungalows that had been built very recently near Stanhope Road, on the land where the boys used to climb the elm trees and hunt for birds´ nests. It was not far from her parents' house and all was right with their world, but sadly not for the world in general.

When the American stock market crashed in October 1929, Europe had still not recovered from the economic fallout of "The Great War" that ended in 1918. Although Britain had not borrowed money to fund the war, it found its trading position in world markets had been permanently eroded by disruptions in production and shipping losses that had occurred throughout the war years. This was because overseas customers of traditional exports, such as textiles, steel and coal, had been forced to find new suppliers and, when they did, they found them more modern, more efficient and cheaper than the traditional British exporters. Thus, even with the war over, they declined to "buy British".

The North of England and South Wales, where these "traditional" industries were sited, and the shipbuilding industries of Central Scotland and the north-east of England, were the worst hit. Shipbuilding production alone declined by 90% and this had a knock-on effect on the coal and steel industries. Millions of unemployed people and their families in these areas were left destitute, relying on soup kitchens to survive and scrabbling about in slag-heaps for hours on end, searching for tiny chips of coal in order to provide a little heat for their homes. The Government implemented special programmes to help the unemployed, such as road building, but the programmes were too few, and the unemployed too many, to make any real difference.

By the end of 1930, 20% of the insured workforce, 2.5million people, was unemployed and exports had fallen by 50%. Measures taken by a coalition government in 1931 only made matters worse and soon unemployment soared to 3million.

It was not until the exchange rate of the pound sterling fell 25%, from $4.86 to $3.40, and interest rates were cut from 6% to 2%, making production costs cheaper and exports more competitive, that the economy gradually began to recover. From 1933 onwards, the numbers of unemployed began to fall but the North of England remained severely depressed for most of the decade.

London, the South-east of England and the Midlands were cushioned from the worst of the "Slump" because these areas became the centres of the new emerging industries created by the advances in technology. Factories were now able to mass-produce items such as electric cookers, washing machines, radios and the like. Nearly half of all the new factories that opened between 1932 and 1937, were in the London area, although the motor industry found its way to the Midlands. Motor manufacture boomed in the 1930's with the number of cars on the road doubling within the decade. Agriculture also flourished and the cut in interest rates fuelled a building boom in London and the South-east, but Britain was a divided nation; poverty in the North and relative prosperity in the South.

So when Anne and Clem started their married life in 1930, it was destined to be a decade of a north-south divide and they must have felt extremely fortunate to be in the latter half of that division. But they were both born with an easy-going temperament that always saw the best in people, the bright side of life and made the best of what they had. To have jobs, to have found their two rooms, to be young and healthy....they would have felt truly blessed.

In 1931 "EMI" opened the largest recording studio in the world at Abbey Road in London. Perhaps it was the ongoing effects of the "Great Depression" that this era not only heralded the explosion of recorded music, but gave birth to live "swing". People in Europe and America seemed to have the need to listen to upbeat music and to dance their cares away. Americans such as Louis Armstrong, Count Basie, Duke Ellington, Glenn Miller, Benny Goodman, Buddy Rich and Arty Shaw became the popular exponents of jazz and "swing" and formed large dance bands in both continents.

In Britain, the frenetic *Charleston* dance had given way to more romantic close dances, the modern waltz, the quickstep and the foxtrot, and thus it became the era of the big dance bands on that side of the Atlantic too, with British band leaders such as Ted Heath, Ambrose, Geraldo, Henry Hall, Jack Hylton, Joe Loss, Jack Parnell, Ronnie Scott and Victor Sylvester all forming "big bands" or even orchestras. Large ballrooms and dance halls sprung up everywhere to accommodate the musicians and their lively "swingers".

Some of the musicians were also vocalists, the most well known must be Louis Armstrong, of course. But solo singers were used as well and the likes of Anne Shelton, Lita Roza, Dennis Lotis and Dickie Valentine, all became household names along with their "big band" accompaniment. Many others had their start with a "big band" and went on to become solo artistes in their own right: Ella Fitzgerald, Bessie Smith, Patti Page, Lena Horne, Billie Holiday, Rosemary Clooney, Doris Day and Connie Francis, just to name a few.

The bands grew in popularity throughout the 1930's, 1940's and were even going strong in the 1950's. Every town would have their own dance band, and often several. Littlehampton was no exception and my husband (born in 1939) well remembers his teenage years in the local *"Top Hat"* ballroom listening to "Ronnie Smith and his Orchestra", although he was never much of a dancer! Even the smaller Arundel had a band called the *"Melodaires"*. The "Regent Ballroom" in Brighton also had its own resident orchestra as did the "Assembly Rooms" in Worthing. These were golden decades indeed for live music!

"Swinging" back to 1931, this was also the year South Africa and Canada became independent, followed by Iraq in 1932, under the rule of King Faisal. However, if the black South Africans had thought independence from British rule would be to their advantage, they were sadly mistaken for, in 1934, the whites introduced apartheid.

Meanwhile, in the Oakley household, life settled into a routine with Anne taking her weekly laundry to her mother's house every Monday, because she had no facilities to do it in her two rooms, and there they did the washing together. Anne also had no access to a kitchener so she did all her cooking on an open fire, with her mother making her oven facilities available for the baking of Anne's pies and cakes.

She and her mother started to go to the cinema every Wednesday afternoon and they were as fascinated by the *Pathe Newsreels* as they were by some of the films. The happiness, and horrors, of world news seemed more real somehow when they watched it in moving pictures. Perhaps, in 1931, they saw that a Rio de Janeiro hilltop now boasted a spectacular Christ Monument and viewed the newly-built, but equally spectacular, Empire State Building in the United States. The United States also gained a "monument" of another kind in this year; its national anthem became official and I am sure *Pathe News* would have broadcast this in all its glory.

Apart from the news, there were always two films, one main release, preceded by a so-called "B movie", which might be a comedy by the *Marx Brothers*, for example, or one of the new cartoons. Anne and Clem also went to the pictures most Saturday nights; if they felt extra well-off that week they would go in the nine-penny seats upstairs but they always purchased a bag of sweets from *Woolworth's* before they went in.

In the early 1930′s, despite the soup kitchens and the "dole" queues, it was claimed that a new "*Woolies*" was being opened every eighteen days. Perhaps the popularity of this American import lay in the fact that larger necessities, like a saucepan, could be bought in parts; 6d (sixpence) for the lid and 6d for the pan. Spectacles were sold in a similar fashion, 6d for the frames and 6d each for the lenses. The shop prided itself on selling almost everything under the sun and soon an *F.W.Woolworths* store was on every High Street.

Once a week Anne and Clem walked to Stanhope Road for supper and there they played cards, or listened to Mary's pride and joy, a new gramophone, or just sat and chatted. Every month or so, Anne and her mother would undertake another outing which was not so welcome; they went to visit Anne′s Aunt Nell in Graylingwell Hospital. Mary had accompanied Jemima until Jemima was too ill to go and now Anne took her place. They both hated it. Although Nell was well looked after, and they always saw her in a day-room and not on the ward, they found the experience thoroughly depressing. Also it was not the easiest place to get to as it involved a train journey to Chichester and then a long walk from the railway station to the hospital.

Back in their rented rooms, their landlord made them one of the new DIY radios and they would sit together in the evenings listening to the programmes on the BBC, or perhaps Anne would read and Clem would make a rag-rug for the bedroom. Mum was never much of a knitter or sewer, but she loved her books, especially romance novels!

After they had been married for about eighteen months, Anne was making her way to her mother's house with her weekly wash, when a neighbour called out a greeting and then added, "I'm glad I've seen you! I wanted to ask if you would be interested in renting this place? Only my husband and I want to move in with my sister for a time and we need to find tenants for the bungalow before we go?" Anne replied that she was sure they would be interested but she would have to ask Clem when he came home from work. At this precise moment, the neighbour's brother came riding up on his push-bike and asked his sister if she had found a tenant yet because he knew a couple who were definitely interested. Without a moment's hesitation, Anne chimed in, "We'll take it!"

So Anne and Clem moved just a few doors away from their rented rooms, on Friday 13th May 1932, and while 1932 brought a big change for Anne and Clem, Littlehampton experienced its own transformation. In 1930, a certain entrepreneur, by the name of Billy Butlin, had purchased the land between the pier and the Oyster Pond, on which stood one of the town's most prominent landmarks, the Tower Windmill, although it had ceased its working life in 1913. In 1932 Billy Butlin had the site flattened, the mill demolished and in its stead the whole place was covered with a funfair. It is still there today, although no longer a "Butlin" amusement centre. Billy Butlin, later Sir Billy, went on to build his famous holiday camps, dotted all over the country, including one just along the road at Bognor Regis. In their day, before package holidays to the continent became readily available, they were hugely popular holiday destinations for their working class patrons as they gave accommodation, food and plenty of "free" entertainment, for all ages, all on one site, at a very reasonable price.

1932 also saw Littlehampton lose another piece of its history; the village pump was removed. A sure sign that the motor-car was becoming more important than the horse.

And yet another change took place in 1932, for on 8th October, (Clem's birthday!) Bill Martin married Violet Poole at the Church of St Gertrude, South Croydon. All of Anne's brothers were now married for Dick and Ethel had also tied the knot by now and had a son, Keith.

On 15th August 1931, Tom and Myrtle had been blessed with another son, Derek Arthur. Thus the news in 1932 of the kidnapping and murder of the baby of the American aviator, Colonel Charles Lindbergh, which made headlines around the world, must have seemed even more poignant to the rapidly expanding "Martin Clan". The subsequent trial of Bruno Hauptmann received as much publicity as did the crime. He was found guilty and executed, though he maintained his innocence right to the end. The crime was responsible for the "Lindbergh Law" which made kidnapping a federal offence. It is said also to have inspired Agatha Cristie to write her novel "On the Orient Express".

In 1933 Adolf Hitler became Chancellor of Germany and the first Nazi concentration camp was established at Dachau. At first only their known political opponents (Communists, Social Democrats) were incarcerated but gradually Jews, Jehovah Witnesses, gypsies, dissenting clergy, homosexuals and anyone voicing criticism of the regime were among those imprisoned. Unfortunately this was just the beginning.

By 1933, much of China was in chaos and corruption was endemic.

Ever since Emperor Pu Yi had been deposed in 1912, miscellaneous war-lords, mandarins and generals had fought for supremacy of this vast country. Many foreign nations too had tried to exploit the country's huge natural resources, and none more so than Japan. History would reveal that as early as 1931, Japan's Emperor Hirohito, and a small coterie of his most trusted advisors, had drawn up a secret document with the stated intent of conquering China and using this country as a launch-pad to conquer all of Asia, Russia and then the rest of the world. By 1933, they were already well-entrenched in the Manchurian region of northern China, more by stealth, treachery and brutality than by fighting, and were able to export much of Manchuria's ore, minerals and food to a power-hungry Japan. Vast numbers of Japanese had immigrated to Manchuria and thousands of its indigenous people had "disappeared", most of them in horrific circumstances. They had even re-named the province Manchukuo and had installed China's deposed emperor, Pu YI, as its Head of State, albeit a puppet one. Then, in 1935, they made him "Emperor of Manchukuo". Another meaningless title that Pu Yi came to despise. The province was now set to become the powerhouse for Japan's industries, and a major supplier of its food.

Meanwhile, in the rest of China, civil war still raged between, on the one hand, the Western-supported Nationalist Party, or Kuomintang, and its allied warlords, under the command of Chiang Kai-shek, pitted against the Soviet-supported Communist Party of China (the Red Army), under the eventual leadership of Mao Zedong and Zhou Enlai. In the autumn of 1933, Chiang Kai-shek had launched a huge attack against the Communist base in south-east China. Within twelve months, the Communists had lost 50% of the territory they had controlled and 60,000 of their soldiers had been killed. The Red Army decided to retreat, and regroup with another communist enclave in the north-west of the country. Thus began, what has come to be known as, "The Long March".

86,000 men left Jiangxi in October 1934 with the intention of travelling some 12,500 kms (8,000 miles) over some of the most difficult terrain in the whole of China, including the Snowy Mountains, which boast some of the highest peaks in the world, and the Chinese Grassland, which is an area of deep marshes. Not only was the terrain treacherous in the extreme, but part of the area was under the control of Chinese warlords, so, if they were spotted, they had to fight their way through, but because Mao had split them up into smaller groups, they were more difficult to find. The retreating soldiers took 370 days to reach their target and less than 10,000 men, of the original 86,000, survived the journey. But at Yanan they combined with other communist troops to make a fighting force of 80,000. The journey sealed the personal prestige of Mao and his supporters as the new leaders of the Communist Party in the following decades.

On a much, much lighter note, the Loch Ness Monster was first spotted in 1933 and prohibition ended in the United States. Also, in our family, at least, it is around this time that black and white snap-shots begin to proliferate and to replace the formal studio portraits, so popular in the 1920's. I can only assume that personal cameras, and the cost of developing the film, had come down so much in price that they were another item now well within a working man's budget. But not for Anne and Clem. It would be another two decades before anyone in our family owned a camera and another three decades before colour film became popular.

1933 was also the year Anne finally gave up domestic work for the Sims family because Mr Sims had been appointed headmaster of *Dorset House School for Boys* in East Street and the family would live in an apartment there. A short while after moving in, Mr Sims visited them and offered Clem a position as a head gardener cum handyman at the school. Clem talked it over with Anne and decided to take the job. The wages were on a par with what he was earning at Barnham Nurseries but the big advantage was that the new job was only a five minute ˊcycle ride from home.

After about eighteen months as tenants, the landlord wrote to them and said they had decided not to return to Littlehampton and asked if they would be interested in taking over the mortgage from them, £2.14s.3d a month. They readily agreed and repaid the £60 deposit he had paid. From tenants, they were now home-owners.

The bungalows are built in threes, like the houses in Stanhope Road, and theirs was in the middle. For some reason I have never been able to determine, the properties were a mixture of privately-owned and council-rented and theirs was sandwiched between two of the latter. They are very modest dwellings, a bit box-like in appearance, with a tiny strip of garden between the building and the pavement. There was a square, built-in porch in the middle leading to the front door, which opened onto a long narrow hall. To the left was "the front room" (it was never called anything else, for example sitting-room, parlour, best room, lounge, or the like) and on the right was the main bedroom. Further down the hall on the left was "the back room", complete with a kitchener, (which became a dining/sitting room but was never called this!) and on the right was another bedroom. Between these two rooms was an INDOOR bathroom. A real "mod con" in 1930, it came with water closet, basin and bath! When Anne and Clem moved in it only had these five rooms and a long narrow garden at the back, which was accessed via an alleyway between neighbours' houses.

Clem set about building a fence at the front to separate the plot from the pavement, installed a gate and planted a hedge along the fence. He may have regretted the gate in later years, as my sister and I delighted in swinging on it, and despite being constantly told off, carried on until it fell off its hinges! He also planted a hedge around the back garden and laid a concrete path right down the middle. They decided the top third of the garden would be for leisure and pleasure, laid with a lawn and flowerbeds, and the bottom two-thirds would be used for growing vegetables. To separate the two sections, he installed a trellis and cultivated climbing roses to cascade over it and, in the flowerbeds underneath, he planted daffodils, polyanthus and lobelia so Anne could look out of the window and see a vista of flowers instead of beans and sprouts!

He went to the farm in East Street and arranged for a wagon-load of manure to be delivered and dug and fertilized every bit of his domain, planting potatoes as a first crop to break up the soil. Later he grew every vegetable he could think of, plus a row of sweet peas and a patch of chrysanthemums, so Anne would have cut flowers throughout the year.

They persuaded Anne's father, Tom, to build a large scullery onto the back room, complete with walk-in larder. He also built two coal bunkers, discreetly placed near the back-door. They acquired a cat, Blackie.... or perhaps Blackie acquired them in the way that felines do. With their own little house, an indoor bathroom, a kitchener, gas lights, garden and cat, there was only one thing missing from their perfect world....no babies.

CHAPTER FIFTEEN

On the Brink
(1934-1936)

By the early 1930's, the town was growing so fast that the building the Littlehampton Urban District Council occupied in Beach Road was much too small, so in 1934 the Council opened their new offices at Manor House, Church Street, the old home of the Drummond-Murray's. Mrs Drummond-Murray had been well-respected for all the charity work she undertook for the town's less privileged citizens and one hopes she would have been pleased to see her old home put to good use. The site came with quite a large piece of ground, allowing for additions to be built at later dates, and was right next door to the newly re-built St Mary's Church which was consecrated in the same year.

Quite a creative year, 1934, apart from council offices and churches, as both the cheeseburger and the game of *Monopoly* went on sale for the first time. Also Violet and Bill had their first child, a daughter they called Barbara.

As Anne had no job now, and over one week's wages went every month on the mortgage and the rates (the tax paid to the Local Authority), from about Easter 1934, they decided to do "bed and breakfast" for holiday makers, and family and friends were pleased to pay a few shillings to come to the sea-side for a week. As well as providing "B & B", as it came to be known, it was the custom then that if the visitor supplied the meat, the land-lady would prepare an evening meal, so Anne offered this service as well. Sea-side holidays in guest-houses (or private houses) were becoming very popular for working families, travelling to their holiday destinations by train. One of Anne's first visitors was Clem's cousin Evelyn Dodson, née Standage, the eldest daughter of Rosina and Edwin Standage who had taken in toddler Jack and baby Elsie when their mother died. Evelyn had married Bert who was born profoundly deaf and although she had taught him to speak, it was always difficult to understand him. He said his hearing had been even more damaged than it might have been, when a schoolteacher boxed him around his ears for not paying attention in class. Be that as it may, he was one of eight children, four of whom had severe hearing difficulties but one thing the "Victorians/Edwardians" did do right, they made sure handicapped people could earn their living and Bert had been trained as a boot and shoe repairer, a cobbler. They had a daughter, Joan, fortunately not born deaf, and often if Bert did not come with them on holiday, Evelyn was accompanied by his (also deaf) sister, Ellen, known as Nellie. Eventually all the "Standage" cousins, their spouses and their children would be regular visitors but the payment fell by the way-side as the visits were reciprocated. Anne and Clem were very sociable and they loved having visitors, especially children.

At some stage, Clem must have renewed contact with his mother's family in London because there is just one photograph of two of his maiden aunts, Bertha and Mabel Pilkington, holidaying in Littlehampton. It is safe to assume they were also regular visitors.

It was also around this date that Clem's brother, Jack, met Daisy who was in service at Dorset House School. It is not known if Clem introduced them, or whether it was a chance encounter when Jack visited Clem at work, but domestic service certainly brought girls from the surrounding villages to a larger town and, if nothing else, was a useful way of meeting prospective husbands! Daisy was from Lavant, near Chichester, Myrtle had been from Amberley, Dorie from Angmering and Ethel from Rustington and that is just one family. (Violet was the local exception. She was from Croydon and Bill met her when he was working in London.)

It was in 1934 that Anne and Clem had the gas lights taken out of the bungalow and electric lights installed. Anne had inherited her dislike of gas from her mother and had never been really happy using it. In fact they would not have gas there again until they had central heating installed many years later. When the workmen had finished the wiring and installed the meter and the sockets, Anne said she was like a child, constantly going around the house switching all the lights on and off. She thought it was a wonderful invention and it was months before the novelty wore off.

By now Anne was already showing signs that she would be afflicted with the "Martin disease"; varicose veins. She dreaded the thought that her legs would become as bad as her mother's but the doctor assured her that there was an operation now that should help. He suggested leaving well alone for a few more years until the operation was really necessary. Anne was greatly reassured by this as she had nursed her mother through several episodes where Mary's legs had ulcerated, requiring complete bed rest, so she knew the pain, discomfort and sheer frustration that this disability caused. Of all the things Mary Martin had suffered, problems with her legs would be top of her list.

On 7th June 1935, a second daughter, Margaret (known to the family as Peggy), was born to Dorie and Les Martin.

Penguin Library Paperbacks were the brainchild of one man, publisher Allen Lane. The first title appeared in 1935, at a price of just 6d, and his idea revolutionised not only an industry, but the reading habits of the general public, forever. It meant, for the first time, ordinary people could buy good, well-produced books at affordable prices. Anne and her parents must have been thrilled to bits!

1935 must have been the year for simple but "brainy" inventions for this was also when Percy Shaw of Boothtown, in Halifax in West Yorkshire, thought of the "Cat's Eye". He got the idea when he realised he used a strip of polished steel to navigate. He called his invention "Cat's Eye" from the eyeshine of a cat in the dark when a light falls on it. In its original form it consisted of two pairs of reflective glass spheres set in a white rubber dome, mounted on a cast-iron casing, but these days they come in many colours and are used around the world.

"Cat's Eyes" were not the only new innovation to be seen on the streets of Britain in 1935 for this was the year the distinctive, red telephone kiosks made their appearance nationally. Public telephone kiosks had been introduced in 1924, but they were made of concrete, and a better design was sought by holding a competition. It was won by Sir Giles Scott, but his design was expensive and only used in London. A cheaper version, based on Scott's idea, was manufactured in 1935 and used extensively throughout the country until 1985, when a newly-privatised "BT" decided they needed kiosks that were cheaper to maintain, easier to clean and more vandal-proof. Along with red pillar-boxes and red London 'buses, the telephone kiosks had been an instantly recognizable symbol of the UK. Some 2000 boxes were given listed status, and several thousand others were left on low-revenue, mostly rural, sites, but many more were just sold off, most of them relegated to people's gardens, where they could only be used as a decorative feature.

One of the world's greatest engineering projects, the Hoover Dam, was completed in 1935. Situated in the Black Canyon of the Colorado River, on the borders of the two American States of Arizona and Nevada, it immediately made two claims to fame as it was both the world's largest electric power producing facility and the world's largest concrete structure. The Hoover Dam came at a high price, however, as there were officially 112 deaths associated with its construction but many more workers also died from carbon monoxide poisoning in the tunnels from the use of generators. Most of these deaths go unrecorded as the company maintained it was from natural causes, pneumonia. Just ten short years later, the Hoover Dam lost both its "largest" titles when the Grand Coulee Dam, on the Colombia River in Washington State, was constructed.

1935 also saw *Alcoholics Anonymous* open its doors for the first time, and Social Security was enacted in the United States. However, things were going from bad to worse in Germany with their Chancellor, Adolf Hitler, introducing the Anti-Jewish Nuremberg Laws which excluded German Jews from Reich citizenship, took away their right to vote, deprived them of most political rights and prohibited them from marrying or having sexual relations with persons of "German or related blood." For a brief period after this became law, the Nazi regime actually moderated its anti-Jewish attacks and rhetoric but this was only because they were hosting the 1936 Olympics in Berlin and Hitler did not want to risk incurring criticism of his government which might result in the Games being transferred to another country.

Berlin had been chosen as the venue long before the Nazi regime came to power but now it was the perfect vehicle for Hitler to demonstrate to the rest of the world the supremacy of "The Master Race". Unfortunately for him, the "racially inferior" black American athlete, Jesse Owens, won four gold medals, broke eleven Olympic records and defeated the German Lutz Lang, a brilliant long-jumper who easily fitted the blond, blue-eyed Aryan stereotypical image that Hitler was trying so hard to promote. There were ten African-American athletes at the Games and between them they won seven gold medals, three silvers and three bronze, more than any national team won in track and field events at the Games, except America itself, of course. Hitler refused to place the gold medal around Owen's neck and was reputed to have remarked privately, "*The Americans should be ashamed of themselves, letting Negroes win their medals for them. I shall not shake hands with this Negro....do you really think I will allow myself to be photographed shaking hands with a Negro?*"

In July 1936, in Spain, parts of the army led by General Francisco Franco, attempted a *coup d´etat* on the democratically-elected, socialist government. The rebels were backed by the Church, the monarchists and the ruling classes because the government was threatening to implement what were considered to be communistic ideas of re-assigning land, owned by the church and the aristocracy, to the people. A civil war ensued and the government appealed to other democracies, like Britain and America, for help. However, their pleas fell on deaf ears, for the idea of breaking up vast estates for the masses filled them with horror too! The Soviet Union and Mexico did give help, however, and 32,000 socialists, communists and sympathisers from fifty-three other countries, including 9,000 from France, 3,000 from Germany, 3,000 from Poland, 2,800 from America and 2,000 from Britain, joined so-called International Brigades. This side, the Government, Socialists, Communists, Russians, Mexicans and the International Brigades, was broadly called the "Republicans" and the opposing side, consisting of the Army, the Church, and the Monarchists, under the command of General Franco, broadly called (in English!) the "Nationalists". They were backed by Italy, Germany and Portugal.

Known officially as the Second Spanish Civil War, hostilities began on 17th July 1936 and continued until 1st April 1939 and pitted brother against brother and father against son. The advent of the mass media gave unprecedented coverage to the atrocities committed by both sides and Germany is said to have used the conflict to test out its theories on saturation bombing, with the town of Guernica as its guinea-pig. Pablo Picasso's masterpiece of the devastation of Guernica remains a poignant and permanent reminder of the horrors of war in general, and civil war in particular.

The war ended with a victory by the Nationalists and thus began Spain's decades of dictatorship led by General Francisco Franco. He ruled with an iron fist; secret police were introduced, no elections held and all opposition ruthlessly dealt with, but, despite this, Britain, France and America recognised Franco as the legitimate leader of Spain with almost indecent haste, for he was considered a bulwark against the dreaded spread of communism.

The reverberations of the "Depression" were still continuing and on 5th October 1936, 207 men, from a small town called Jarrow in the north-east of England, began a protest march to the Houses of Parliament in London. They wanted to hand in a petition drawing attention to the dire consequences of mass unemployment in their area, caused by the collapse of their ship-building industry. Perhaps they were inspired by Gandhi's Salt March, or Mao's Long March but, be that as it may, the men had no resources other than their own determination and their desperation. Donations from the general public supplied every man with a decent pair of boots, and sympathisers along the route provided food and shelter. When they arrived at their destination, nearly a month later, the Prime Minister, Stanley Baldwin, claimed he was too busy even to meet them.

(However, by 1938/39, a ship-breaking yard, engineering works and a steel-works had been established in Jarrow and, as the nation's need for re-armament increased, so did the fortunes of one of the most depressed areas in the whole country. By this time, however, it had already earned its place in the history of the nation's Labour Movement with its "Jarrow Crusade".)

Ironically, also in 1936, John Maynard Keynes published his book "The General Theory of Employment, Interest and Money" which claimed that government spending was required to end economic recession; this became known as the "Keynesian Theory".

After the Stock Market Crash in 1929, Albert Kahn, the banker, philanthropist and photographer, lost all he owned and was declared bankrupt. In 1936, the last of his possessions were sold and his mansion in Paris and his "Archive of the Planet" passed to the French Government. His beautiful garden was turned into a public park but, perhaps because of the powerful and influential connections he had made over the years, he was allowed to stay in his house as its tenant.

His photographs, mostly on glass plates, were considered too fragile to move, so they stayed too. (As a French Jew, he was spared the worst horrors of the Nazi occupation of Paris by dying, at home, in his sleep, aged eighty years, on 14th November 1940. The "Archive of the Planet" must have been considered to have little monetary value for the Germans left it untouched and intact, and thus it stayed, largely forgotten, until the 1970´s and a new administration realised its historic importance and set about cataloguing the collection. Eventually Albert Kahn´s mansion was re-opened as a museum, where selections from his "Archive of the Planet" are regularly exhibited, as he wished, a lasting memorial to a disappeared world.)

1936 also saw the transatlantic liner *Queen Mary*, the pride of the Cunard fleet, travel from Southampton to New York in just four days. On 4th July, Jack Oakley married Daisy.

A newsworthy year indeed, and it would end with the biggest constitutional crisis Britain has ever seen. It had begun at the beginning of the year, on 20th January, when King George V had died and his eldest son, Edward VIII, ascended the throne. Only months into his reign, he proposed marriage to the twice-divorced American, Wallis Simpson. The Prime Minister, Stanley Baldwin, and his government argued that the people would never accept her as Queen, and as the King was supposed to be "Defender of the Faith", the Church of England could not accept her either. In December 1936, Edward chose to abdicate rather than give up "the woman I love" and thus became the only monarch of Britain ever to have voluntarily relinquished the throne.

Edward VIII was succeeded by his brother, Albert, who took the title King George VI. He was already married to Elizabeth Bowes-Lyon and they had two children, the Princesses Elizabeth and Margaret. Edward VIII, the King who was never crowned, took the title the Duke of Windsor and married Wallis in June 1937.

(What was not known at the time, and indeed would not come to light for over sixty years, was an allegation that Wallis and Edward had had an illegitimate child in June 1934 who they named Elizabeth. The scandal would have been so great that she was taken from them. It is claimed that Elizabeth subsequently married, and had children and grandchildren, but she did not learn the true identity of her biological parents until 1995. The "Windsors" remained childless.)

August 1937 saw the rise of a young Welshman who some would say was the century's best UK heavyweight boxer, Tommy Farr. He became one of only three boxers who went the full distance of fifteen rounds with the legendary "Brown Bomber", Joe Louis. The fight was a "first" in that it was broadcast on the wireless to millions of listeners, and I can imagine how excited Clem became as he listened to the commentary. Dad loved all sport but his favourites, to listen to, or later to view, were boxing and football. To watch him, watching or listening to a match, was an entertainment in itself because he would sit right on the edge of his armchair, his head and upper body moving from side to side as he witnessed every move, puffing heartily on his rolled-up cigarette, making comments and waving his arms around. And woe betides us if we dared to interrupt the action!

After Anne and Clem had been married for a few years, there was still no sign that Anne was going to become pregnant, so she took herself off to the doctor who arranged for her to go into hospital for a small operation and an examination under anaesthetic, just to make sure there were no obvious problems with conception. There were not. Dr Waddington suggested her husband visit the surgery. It was a simple task to test his ability to father children, he explained. Clem would not go. No amount of cajoling, nagging or begging could persuade him.
"What will be, will be," he declared and eventually Anne had to be satisfied with that. How she wished she could take back the words she had pronounced to his father before their marriage, "And this is where it stops!" Had she tempted fate? The doctor told her that there was still hope; they were both healthy and sometimes these things just took their time. So she lived in hopes. Month after disappointing month. Sometimes there would be a false alarm and she would allow herself to dream. She would make up names for the baby and find herself looking at knitting patterns. Then the hopes and dreams were dashed, yet again. It even got to the stage where she could not bear to hear that someone she knew was to have a baby, when she could not conceive one. But she knew they were blessed with many other godsends and Clem was right, what will be, will be. So they just kept hoping that their prayers would be answered eventually and she tried to be genuinely delighted when family and friends were pregnant and to enjoy being an aunt to an ever-increasing number of nephews and nieces.

CHAPTER SIXTEEN

Preparing for War
(1937-1939)

As 1937 dawned, the world must have seemed in turmoil. Civil war was raging in Spain and China, Gandhi was orchestrating civil unrest in India and in Germany the Nazi government stepped up the persecution of German Jews by requiring them to register their properties and forcing them to sell their businesses to non-Jews for knock-down prices, fixed by the Nazis. Jewish doctors were forbidden to treat non-Jews and Jewish lawyers not permitted to practise law. It was hard to believe that things in Germany could get any worse but this was just the beginning, and not solely for German Jews. Gypsies, communists, "social misfits" (as defined by the Nazi dogma), dissidents, disabled and mentally handicapped people, and many others who did not conform to Hitler's vision of an Aryan race, also were forced into concentration camps.

With the benefit of hindsight, it seems incredible that Europe and its Allies allowed Hitler not only to persecute his own citizens, but to violate so blatantly the Versailles Treaty that Germany had signed at the end of the 1914-1918 war. From his election in 1933, he was re-arming his country: building massive fortifications in the industrial heartland of Germany: speeding up re-militarization: introducing conscription: all with the declared aim of bringing more of Eastern Europe under his control. But there were two big considerations that worked in his favour; the British people were terrified of another conflict engulfing Europe and he was seen by conservative governments, both sides of the Atlantic, as a bulwark against Communism, along with General Francisco Franco of Spain. France knew it could not tackle Germany alone; Britain hoped it would all turn out right in the end and America turned a blind eye and a deaf ear to what they regarded as Europe's problem. So Hitler carried on regardless and even signed treaties with Italy and Japan; these became known as the "Axis Powers". Spain was invited to join but declined.

Not all was going well for Germany, however. The *Hindenburg* was a German zeppelin, one of the two largest rigid aircraft it had ever built but, on 6th May 1937 during its second year of service, it burst into flames at Lakehurst Naval Air Station in New Jersey. Thirty-six people died in the accident and the event was widely reported by film, photographs, newspapers, newsreels and radio, much to the Fuehrer's embarrassment.

Later this month, on 27th May, the *Golden Gate Bridge* opened, linking the city of San Francisco with Marin County in California. At the time it was the longest suspension bridge in the world and carried six lanes of traffic, plus pedestrians and bicycles. Since its inception, however, it has earned a less desirable reputation by becoming one of the most popular locations for committing suicide. So far more than 1200 people have jumped off the bridge into the icy waters of San Francisco Bay, some 67metres below. Very few people have survived the fall but debate still continues on the feasibility of a suicide barrier.

However the news of the opening of the bridge was overshadowed by the mystery of Amelia Earhart. In 1932 she had become the first woman to fly the Atlantic solo, overcoming near fatal weather conditions and equipment failure, and she came to symbolize women's invasion of the male world with her feats of endurance and adventure. On 21st May 1937, she set out with her navigator, Frederick Noonan, to circumnavigate the globe, and at first all went well. But about seven hours after leaving Lae in New Guinea, they went missing and this spawned one of the most famous missing persons' stories of the 20th Century.

Supposition, suspicion and speculation abound over the incident, with blame at first being attached to Noonan, who was known to be an alcoholic, and then to Earhart because some professional pilots thought her flying skills left a lot to be desired, despite her reputation. Some theories have her ditching into the sea, others that she landed on an island. Some claim they tried to make radio contact and others that they were captured by the Japanese, but nothing conclusive could be proved. Only one thing is certain; the mystery remains but the legend lives on.

News of war, unrest, civil disturbances and the like would not be out of the headlines for long in these turbulent times. By now, Japan fully-occupied the northern province of Manchuria/Manchukuo and, in July 1937, they decided the time was right to expand their Chinese empire and began by invading another part of China, on a flimsy excuse about being fired on by Chinese troops at the Marco Polo Bridge in Beijing. At last, hostilities between the Chinese Nationalists and the Communists came to a halt, but only to combine to fight a common enemy, Japan. The Sino-Japanese war had begun.

Initially the Japanese troops came up against little organised resistance, so much so that by the end of the year, all of the major cities in China were under Japanese control. But China is a vast country so the Japanese concentrated their resources fighting the enemy they could see, the Kuomintang, or Nationalists, under Chiang Kai-shek. However, they also had to fight an enemy they could not see, communist guerrillas trained by Mao Zedong. These tactics would serve Mao well when the common enemy was eventually defeated and the Communists and the Nationalists could go back to fighting each other for supremacy of China.

By now Saturday morning pictures were becoming popular with

children. For a few pence they could join their local cinema club and every Saturday watch a slapstick comedy, or a cartoon, and a cowboy film such as *Hopalong Cassidy* with his trusty steed, *Topper.* Soon *Hopalong* and *Topper* would be in competition with the likes of *Roy Rodgers* and his horse, *Trigger,* or *The Lone Ranger,* or *Whip Wilson* and generations of children learned to play "Cowboys and Indians" as well as the tried and tested games of soldiers and adventurers.

Imaginations were also fired by the many children's comics and story papers coming onto the market, for the period 1938-1943 was to become known as the "Golden Age of Comics". The likes of *Magnet* and *Gem,* with their *Billy Bunter* and *Sexton Blake* characters and their stories of "the fat owl of the remove", the "super sleuth" and all the goings-on at "St James College in Sussex" had been around since the early 1900's. They were soon joined by the characters from *Wizard* and *Hotspur.* Then the comic *Dandy,* launched in 1937, was followed by *The Beano* in 1938 and *Desperate Dan, Lord Snooty,* and *Korky the Cat* became familiar names to children of all ages for successive generations.

Meanwhile children were also able to enjoy another kind of treat. Out in the streets of Britain, some 7500 *Walls* ice-cream salesmen were now riding tricycles displaying the slogan "*Stop Me and Buy One*". The idea had begun in London in 1923; by 1927 *Walls* ice-cream tricycles could be seen throughout the country and sales had expanded to nearly £½m per annum - a huge amount of money in 1927. They were selling 2d choc ices, briquettes, and small tubs of ice-cream served with a little wooden spoon, and children watched wide-eyed as these delicious treats emerged from the chilly depths of the square, box-like refrigerator fitted to the front of the vehicle.

After the disappointment of the operation, and still no babies in sight, in the spring of 1938 Anne and Clem decided to try and adopt a child. Anne wrote to an adoption society (name unknown) and to *Dr. Barnardo´s,* the charity synonymous with orphans and orphanages. Dublin-born Dr. Barnardo had opened his first "Home for Boys" in Stepney in 1870 and later a "Village Home" for 1500 girls in Barkingside. By the time he died in 1905, the charity he founded ran 96 Homes caring for 8500 children. Over the years the policies of the charity changed; for instance, after the First World War, some *Barnardo´s* children were sent to Australia, as it was thought they would have a better life, but this was discontinued in 1946. Gradually the charity, and society in general, came to believe that the best way to care for children was in foster homes, and not large Children's Homes, and the last *Barnardo's Children's Home* closed in 1970. (I believe it was St Margaret's House in Aldwick, Bognor Regis, not far from where I then lived.)

I do not know if the charity ever had an adoption scheme, but when

Anne received the reply from them in 1938 regarding her adoption enquiry, she maintained that they told her that when a child came into their care, their policy was for that child to remain with them, until he or she could go to work. She was dismayed, believing this policy to be short-sighted and not in the best interests of the child, and vowed not to donate money to *Barnardo's* ever again.

The other adoption society she wrote to did send an application form back for them to complete but subsequently informed them that in their opinion, *"The wages of the head of the household are insufficient to support a child."* I expect this letter, along with the one from *Barnardo's*, was torn up in disgust and thrown in the bin. So with their dreams of conception fading, and their hope of adoption shattered, they resigned themselves to a married life without children.

Perhaps they were comforted by the thought that it might be better not to bring a child into such a chaotic world. Or perhaps they were reassured in this regard, like millions of others, at the Prime Minister's efforts to find a peaceful solution to Hitler's stated intent to create a new and enlarged Germany. These conciliatory attempts culminated in September 1938 with a conference in Munich between Britain, Germany, France and Italy when the Fuehrer stated, *"We are determined to continue our efforts to remove possible sources of differences and thus to contribute to assure the peace of Europe."*

Neville Chamberlain was euphoric and returned to Britain waving the agreement to jubilant crowds declaring, *"We have peace for our time."* But many people were more sceptical and accused him of "appeasement" to German aggression in Europe.

Just one month later, on 30th October, the day before Halloween, Orson Welles caused mass panic in America when he broadcast his fictional story *"The War of the Worlds"* about a Martian invasion of earth. In order to heighten the dramatic effect, he made it sound like a news report with "up-to-the-minute news bulletins" interspersed in the script. With the talk of a possible war in Europe so prominent, perhaps it is hardly surprising that millions of Americans believed the story to be true and thus mass panic (and massive publicity) ensued. This may have been the first time it was realised that it was possible to confuse, or manipulate, a population en masse, with misinformation.

Just ten days later, on 9th November 1938, violence against the Jewish community broke out across Germany. In just two short days, over one thousand synagogues were burned and seven thousand Jewish businesses trashed and looted. Jewish cemeteries, hospitals, schools and homes were robbed or destroyed, and all this carried out while police and fire brigades looked on. Dozens of Jewish people were killed and the night of destruction became known as "Kristallnacht", the

"Night of Broken Glass", from all the shattered windows that littered the streets. The next morning 30,000 Jewish men were arrested for the "crime" of being Jewish and sent to concentration camps. Life for a Jew in Germany was ever more difficult and most families tried desperately to leave, not often successfully.

Some however did manage to get away, for in January of 1939, the *Kinder Transport Scheme* was launched. This arranged for Jewish children, trapped in Europe, to escape the Nazis and to be brought to Britain, there to live in safety …… but without their parents.

By this time, Europe had to accept the inevitable; it was only a matter of time before war broke out with Hitler's Germany. Preparations were begun and, in February, one of the first measures in Britain was to deliver *Anderson Shelters* to London homes. These were small, cheap, outdoor shelters designed to protect families from bomb blasts. Although they would not withstand a direct hit, they would still save many lives.

The worst fears were realised in March when Germany invaded and occupied Czechoslovakia and, if there had been any doubt before, now France and Britain knew for certain that Hitler's promise to *".... assure the peace of Europe"* could not be trusted. Appeasement had failed and they had to act. They realised the next obvious target for him was Poland, so they gave immediate guarantees to that country that they would go to their aid if it was attacked by Germany.

Meanwhile, on 16th March, *Pan American Airlines* made the first commercial flight across the ocean, from Baltimore in Maryland, USA, to Foynes in Ireland, with a scheduled flight time of twenty-nine hours.

With the situation in Germany and Europe deteriorating daily, Britain could delay no longer one urgent need to prepare for war. From April, all British men aged 20 and 21, who were fit and able, were now required to undertake six month's military training.

Wall's Ice Cream realised that, in the very near future, fewer men would be available to sell their products, so now women could be seen pedalling their tricycles with the *"Stop Me and Buy One"* slogans. Sadly their foresight was short-lived, for the rationing of sugar and milk would severely curtail the manufacture of ice-cream during the war years, and the familiar and much-loved vehicles would be requisitioned for use at military installations. Tricycles selling the refreshing treats would not be seen back on the nation's streets until 1947.

It was also in April that Britain installed a top secret radar station on the east coast, designed by the Scottish physicist, Sir Robert Alexander Watson-Watt, who invented the system of radar (Radio Detection and Ranging) in 1935. In a short while, radar stations were built all around the south and east coasts in order to give early warning of an imminent attack by air.

In the same month, the WRENS (Women's Royal Naval Service) was re-formed. It had been disbanded after the 1914-1918 war but was needed again for women to undertake shore-based, mainly clerical, duties for the Royal Navy, thus releasing men for active service. The WAAF (Women's Auxiliary Air Force) was formed in June for the same reason; women could carry out ground duties, freeing men for combat. And in July the Women's Land Army was re-formed to train women for farm work, because so many men who worked on the land would have to be called up.

In June 1939, a ship called the *St Louis,* and carrying one thousand Jewish refugees fleeing the persecution in Germany, was turned away from Cuba and then from Florida, USA. To the world's eternal shame, no country would accept the refugees, so the ship was forced to return to Germany where the passengers disembarked into the hands of the Nazis. Most of them died in concentration camps.

In July, the Government issued advice on air raid warnings; a continuous warbling siren would warn of a raid; a constant wail would sound the all-clear.

In August, lights in London were switched off in a blackout trial and the Government announced plans to evacuate children from major cities to safer areas as a "precaution".

Still in August, a top secret team of code-breakers, posing as "Captain Ridley's shooting party", arrived at Bletchley Park (known as "Station X") in Buckinghamshire. Included in their number was Alan Turing; a brilliant and inspirational mathematician. They would eventually be responsible for deciphering the codes transmitted by German High Command and for breaking the famous *Enigma Code.* A research team, led by Tommy Flowers, an engineer from the war-time Post Office Research Station at Dollis Hill, designed and built the world's first production programmable electronic computer, called *Colossus,* for the codes had to be cracked by carrying out complex statistical analysis that could take weeks with a human brain. *Colossus* could read paper tape at 5000 characters per second and thus could perform the same task in a matter of hours. A total of ten *Colossus* machines were built and used at Bletchley but these, along with technical drawings and diagrams, were destroyed after the war in order to keep their existence a secret.

Late in August 1939, Germany and Russia signed a non-aggression pact which, it was soon to be learned, included secret clauses for the division of Poland.

On the 31st August, the last of the *Kinder Transport* brought Jewish children from Austria, Germany and Czechoslovakia to live in Britain. Most would never see their parents again.

On 1st September, Adolf Hitler invaded Poland, deriding the

agreement he had made with Neville Chamberlain the year before by calling it, *"Just a scrap of paper"*. On 3rd September 1939, Britain and France declared war on Germany. The Second World War was officially about to begin.

Almost immediately, conscription was extended to make all able men between the ages of 18 and 21 liable for call-up into the armed services, although it was decided to call-up single men before married men, and they took the youngest first. By October men aged 20-23 were being called up but it would be June 1941 before 40year olds had to register. By the end of 1939, more than 1.5million men had been conscripted to join the British Armed Services: 1.1million into the Army, and the rest split between the Royal Navy and the RAF. Conscientious Objectors could ask to be excluded from the war effort, or to be considered for non-combat war work. 60,000 men applied and although the system for judging their claim was reasonably fair and just, some of those who were rejected still spent time in prison rather than enlist or work in the occupation they had been given. No posters this time around, pleading for volunteers to respond to the call, *"Your Country Needs YOU!"* The next war would be fought with regular soldiers and conscripts.

At the outbreak of war, Anne's brother Bill was 30 years of age and Dick was 28 years. Clem's brother, Jack, was also 28 years and all of them would eventually be called up. Dick and Jack would serve in Europe but Bill would be sent out to Burma and would earn the *"Burma Star"* medal, which his son, Peter, now has. Tom and Les would be declared exempt from active service and would instead be put to work in the construction industry. Tom was sent all over southern England to undertake war damage repairs, especially in the Portsmouth area. Les was put to work all over the south and east of the country, building new aerodromes. Regrettably, in true male Martin-Oakley tradition, none of them ever talked much about their war-time experiences, any more than they had about their childhood ones!

As an ex-regular soldier on the "Reserve List", Clem was one of the first to be recalled into military service. His job at Dorset House School would be kept open for him, in accordance with Government regulations. He did not know when, or where, he would be posted but on one thing he was certain; he would not be testing gas-masks in Tonbridge!

All non-essential hospital operations were cancelled as beds had to be kept free for possible war casualties. Thus Anne's operation on her varicose veins was suspended until hostilities ceased. By the time it was all over, her legs were beyond surgical help and she would be plagued by "her veins" for the rest of her life.

But Anne had more to worry about than her varicose veins. Her mother, Mary Martin, was fighting her own battle, against stomach cancer, although in those days the "big C" was not mentioned. It was called a growth. Her mother had been ill, on and off, for months with this "tummy trouble" but she had always rallied and Anne thought this latest bout of illness would gradually disappear. At least with Clem away, Anne was able to devote her days, and nights, to nursing her mother and caring for her father. As it happened, their own home was not unoccupied because Anne had given refuge to a couple from London who had thought it prudent to escape the expected air attacks. They had taken over the front two rooms of the bungalow, using one as a sitting room and the other as a bedroom and sharing the bathroom and cooking facilities. Anne had been asked to take in child evacuees but, rather surprisingly perhaps, she had declined but offered to take adults instead. She explained to me many years afterwards, that she felt she could not bear to become fond of a child, only to see it return home at a later date, or when hostilities ceased.

While Europe spent 1939 preparing for war, on the other side of the Atlantic, Americans enjoyed the spectacle of their Civil War in celluloid; the legendary film *"Gone with the Wind"*, starring Vivien Leigh and Clark Gable, played to huge audiences. It was one of the first films to use the new technology of colour which transformed film-making into an art form. Now historical and biblical epics, comedies, musical extravaganzas with, for example, Fred Astaire and Ginger Rogers, and the full-length, colour fantasy of Walt Disney's *Snow White*, raised the standard of cinema entertainment to new heights, although Britain had to wait until 1940 for their first showing of *"Gone with the Wind"*.

Music also became very upbeat, for American swing was becoming the latest rage with Glenn Miller leading the way with his "In The Mood", recorded in August 1939, and Latin American dances, the rumba in particular, became popular in dance halls.

But little did anyone realise just how important music, film and dance would become in raising morale in the difficult, dangerous, and often dreary, years ahead.

CHAPTER SEVENTEEN

The "Phoney War"
(1939-May 1940)

One of the first things the British Government did after war was declared on Germany was to send a "British Expeditionary Force" (BEF) to France, although for about seven months little happened as they sheltered behind the massive fortifications of the French defence barrier, the *Maginot Line*. Clem was part of this BEF and sent regular "field cards" and post-cards back to his wife while he and the rest of the British and French armies watched and waited, with growing impatience and impotence, as the defeated Poland was divided between Germany and Russia. Then Finland was attacked by the Soviet war machine and at one point Britain seemed on the point of taking on Russia as well as Germany but decided against it. And still Hitler made no move on France. It seemed he did not relish a war of attrition, such as he himself had experienced in the trenches of the 1914-1918 war. Perhaps he hoped the Allies would compromise as they had done so many times before. Meanwhile Britain and France were equally reluctant to start shooting and the RAF contented themselves with dropping propaganda leaflets on the enemy instead of bombs.

The armies were billeted in whatever shelter they could find, ancient rat-infested barns mostly, with the officers taking over the farm-houses. The men were kept busy digging endless latrines, deep anti-tank traps and defensive positions (i.e. trenches!) in the mud and clay, for it was a particularly cold and wet winter. Most of the troops had received parcels of knitted socks and balaclavas from their womenfolk back home, and these had been most welcome. There were endless fatigues and training sessions, for example in compass and map reading, and, in what spare time they had, they sought out local farmers who were prepared to sell them eggs and potatoes and the occasional chicken, to supplement the boring Army rations.

Sometimes they would be ordered to go out on patrol and then they would cross over the *Maginot Line* to see what the German soldiers were up to on their defence barrier. Theirs was called the *Siegfrede Line,* hence the song *"We'll hang out the washing on the Siegfrede Line"* which became a war-time favourite with British soldiers in France and civilians at home.

Nothing much seemed to be happening on the war-front back in Britain either. People living in cities, or near ports, airfields or other strategic targets, had been warned to expect imminent attack by air and had dutifully allowed their children to be evacuated to safer parts of the country and the whole nation co-operated in a blackout where no lights were allowed to shine at night. As soon as it became dark, windows were covered with blackout material and also the windows had been permanently taped to stop glass flying about in the event of a bomb blast. Barrage balloons, tethered onto strong steel cables, were installed over all major cities to deter low flights by enemy aircraft and a "Dig for Victory" campaign was launched, urging the populace to use every spare piece of land, gardens, parks, golf courses, tennis courts and the like, to grow vegetables.

In December the "*Graf Spee*", a German pocket battleship, attacked supply ships sailing to Britain but was forced into dock by the Royal Navy where it was scuttled by its captain. This was the first major naval battle of the war and came to be called "*The Battle of the River Plate*". By this time the first Canadian troops had disembarked in Britain, and the first members of the Royal Australian Air Force had flown in, both to offer their support in the fight against Germany. But despite the naval engagement and the arrival of Commonwealth troops, by December people were calling it a "Phoney War" and some evacuees returned home and people stopped carrying their gas-masks.

1939 ended with the singer, Vera Lynn, being voted "The Forces Sweetheart" by the BEF. In 1940, she started her own BBC radio show, "*Sincerely Yours*", during which she read out messages from men fighting abroad to their wives, families and sweethearts. Her songs, especially "*The White Cliffs of Dover*" and "*We'll Meet Again*", became war-time classics. She also travelled abroad to entertain the troops, to such far-flung, inhospitable venues as Burma. After the war she continued to do charitable work for organisations like the "*Burma Star Association*" and in 1975, in recognition of all that she had done in and for the entertainment industry, Vera Lyn was made a *Dame of the British Empire*. Her name has become synonymous with the morale boosting efforts of war-time artistes.

Of course, Vera Lynn was not alone in providing war-time entertainment both at home and abroad. The singer Gracie Fields also evoked nostalgic memories and comedians like Max Miller and Tommy Trinder kept up the spirits of the public when times became difficult.

One not-to-be-missed radio programme began during this period of "The Phoney War". It was called *ITMA*, which stood for "It's That Man Again" and starred the comedian Tommy Handley. These were the years of endless form-filling and government directives, with German spies suspected to be lurking around every corner, and the programme lampooned all these fears and frustrations with the "*Ministry of Twerps*", featuring such characters as *Colonel Chinstrap, Fusspot, Funf, Mrs Mopp, Claude and Cecil,* and *Ali-Oop.* They became household names and introduced catch-phrases spoken throughout the nation such as

"Can I do you now, sir!": Good Morning! Nice day!": "I go - I come back!" :
"TTFN": "Funf speaking!" and "I don't mind if I do!"

As the likes of Vera Lynn and Gracie Fields united the nation in song, Tommy Handley's *ITMA* and Arthur Askey's *Bandbox* united it in comedy. Indeed it is said that in some places of war-torn, Nazi-occupied Europe, people tuned in to the forbidden programmes, at the risk of death if discovered and even though they could not understand the dialogue, just to hear people laughing.

Of course, morale boosting efforts were not limited to radio, nor to Britain, nor to names I have mentioned here, and it seems invidious not to mention two of the greatest entertainers the 20th century produced, co-incidentally born within days of one another in May 1903, and both of whom did a huge amount for the morale of US personnel serving abroad. They are Bing Crosby and Bob Hope and one of their best-known, war time efforts was a joint enterprise, beginning with *"The Road to Singapore"*, premiered in 1940, and ably assisted by Dorothy Lamour. Altogether they did seven *"Road to ....."* movies, not all of them during the war years. The films had a minimal plot as a back-drop to light-hearted adventure, comedy, romance and music, and were an ideal vehicle for the Crosby-and-Hope type of gags and ad-libs, for which the couple would become famous.

Bing Crosby had a unique bass-baritone voice that made him the best-selling recording artist well into the 1960's and he is credited with being the inspiration for most of the well-known male singers that were to follow in the coming decade: Perry Como, Frank Sinatra and Dean Martin. He is probably best known for his recording of *"I'm Dreaming of a White Christmas"* , by Irving Berlin, first broadcast on Christmas Day in 1941 and still aired during the festive season to this day. It is the best-selling single of all time, with over 50-million copies sold world-wide. He is also known as an actor and won an *"Oscar"* for his performance in *"Going My Way"* in 1944. *"Yank"* magazine would come to recognise him as the person who had done the most for American GI's during WW2. He died in 1977, aged 74 years.

Bob Hope was an actor and comedian who would also come to be noted for his work with the American armed services, in every theatre of war during the whole of the century. During a long career, spanning nearly eight decades, he would appear in, or host, 199 known "United Service Organisation" (USO) tours, ending every one with his signature tune, *"Thanks for the Memory"*. In 1996 he was made the *"First and only honorary veteran of United States Armed Forces"* by the US Congress. He died in 2003, at 100 years of age. Probably the greatest ad-libber we have ever seen, it is said that on his death-bed his wife asked him where he would like to be buried. "Surprise me!" he replied.

1940 started as the Government meant to go on; food rationing was introduced. Adults were to be allowed just 4ozs of butter, 4ozs of bacon or uncooked ham and 12ozs of sugar per week. Anne knew Clem had a sweet tooth so she resolved to stop taking sugar in her tea. This would save some of her sugar ration so that when (she never allowed herself to think "if"!) Clem came home, he could still enjoy his "cuppa" with his usual two teaspoonfuls of sugar.

Also in January 1940, a campaign was launched to recycle waste. The first item on the list was waste paper; this could easily be recycled and thus save on imports. Also the Government maintained scrap metal was needed in order to build more tanks, guns and ships, so they confiscated all the railings surrounding parks, gardens and cemeteries, and those in front of houses, mansions, government offices and buildings. People donated their old saucepans, bicycles and the like, in the belief they were helping the war effort. (Many years later it was disclosed that most of the donated metal was useless as it was not suitable to make a tank, or gun, or ship, but it was nevertheless a clever propaganda ploy to make the "man in the street" feel he was doing his bit! After the war, many of the railings in front of government buildings and mansions mysteriously found their way back to their original owners but that was not so for all the "ordinary" dwellings that had also had their railings forcibly taken.)

On 14th January, Violet Martin (wife of brother Bill) gave birth to their third daughter, Diane, a sister for Barbara born in 1934. Sadly their middle daughter, Valerie, had died in infancy. Many, many years later, when Valerie would have been middle-aged, Auntie Vi told me hardly a day went by when she did not still think of her beloved baby who had died.

It was also around this time that Mary Martin passed away. She was just 60 years of age. The family doctor had called earlier in the day at home in Stanhope Road, examined her and remarked sadly to Anne, who was sitting with her at the time, that he was sorry but there was nothing more he could do except give her morphine for the pain. Anne was horrified. Mary had had these problems before but she had always got better. Anne had believed that this episode was no different to all the others.

She continued to sit beside her, stroking her hair and holding her hand. Her mother opened her eyes and whispered, " Promise me that you'll look after the boys, Annie."

"Of course I will, Mum," she replied as Mary Martin drifted off into a deep sleep.

Anne carried on sitting beside her, quietly reading, when her mother made a funny noise and then was still. Anne carried on reading. Some while later, her brother Tom's wife, Myrtle, came up the stairs. She had been making a cup of tea for her father-in-law and she had brought up a cup for Anne.

"How is she?" she asked.

"She's very quiet now," replied Anne with gross understatement. "She made a funny noise a little while ago but she's OK now."

Myrtle went over to Mary and murmured, "Oh dear! I think she's gone, Anne."

Poor Anne was in total shock. She had just not been expecting her mother to die, or at least not so quickly. And she always maintained her father, Thomas Martin, never recovered from the loss of his beloved wife. He could not bear to carry on living in the house that he and his wife had shared so he moved in with Anne. When Anne told her evacuees that her father would be coming to live with her, and that she would need the use of one of their rooms as a bedroom for him, she expected them to say they would find alternative accommodation but instead they asked if they could stay and they turned the front room into a bed-sitting room. It worked very well and the four of them lived harmoniously together, even enjoying occasional card games in the evenings.

Clem, of course, was unable to come back from France for the funeral and he would have regretted not being able to pay his last respects to the woman who had become a second mother to him, for she had always treated him as another son and they were very fond of one another.

So Thomas, now aged 70 years and retired, busied himself with Clem's garden and grew the vegetables to supplement the rations and put himself in charge of the blackout curtains that had to be put up every evening. Eventually, if Anne went out on a Saturday evening, he would take himself off to the *Trades and Labour Club* and thus their life settled into a routine without their much-loved wife and mother.

While this was going on, Britain, of course, still had a war to run and in February the Government made fresh plans to evacuate 400,000 children to rural "safe" areas and introduced campaigns with the slogans *"Careless Talk Costs Lives"* and *"Keep Mum! Don't Say a Word!"* to discourage people from gossiping and thus inadvertently allowing useful information to fall into the hands of the enemy. Britain also announced that its merchant ships would be armed, which drew the response from Germany that, in view of this, they would be classed as ships of war in future.

February 1940 drew to a close with the discovery of part of an *Enigma* code machine on a wrecked German U-boat. It was immediately despatched to the top-secret "Station X" (Bletchley Park), much to the excited delight of the scientists there. In April the scientists cracked the *Enigma* code used by the Germans in Norway. The Germans had made de-coding as difficult as possible by changing the code at least once a day.

In March meat rationing was introduced; each person was allowed meat worth one shilling and sixpence (1s 6d) per week with children under six years of age allowed half of that.

On 18th April some lucky Londoners were able to escape the problems of war for a few hours by going to see the premiere of the blockbuster classic, *"Gone With the Wind."*

Neville Chamberlain's half-hearted prosecution of the war was drawing contempt from all quarters and it was obvious national unity could only be achieved by a coalition government. Thus on the 13th May a new Prime Minister, Winston Churchill, rose in the Commons and pledged, *"I have nothing to offer but blood, toil, tears and sweat."* He appointed Ernest Bevin, a Labour Member of Parliament, as Minister of Labour and, with his working class background, he was able to cajole, bully and organise "fellow workers" into ever-increasing productivity throughout the war. Lord Beaverbrook was appointed Minister of Aircraft Production and he was successful in increasing the output of fighter 'planes.

None of these efforts came a moment too soon, for across the Channel plucky little Finland had finally been beaten into submission by the might of Russia and had been subjected to harsh surrender terms. Just one month later, in April, German troops had invaded Denmark and Norway. A British expedition to Narvik had fought gallantly on their behalf and had succeeded in re-capturing the town but, on 3rd May 1940, all British and French forces were withdrawn because the Germans had attacked the Benelux countries. On 10th May Germany launched its *"Blitzkrieg"* on Holland and Belgium, bombing airfields, ports and cities almost to extinction. Then, at last, in May 1940, Hitler invaded northern France. The "Phoney War" was at an end.

CHAPTER EIGHTEEN

Dunkirk
(May/June 1940)

When the Germans invaded France in May 1940, and brought an end to the so-called "Phoney War", the British Expeditionary Force (BEF), under their Commander-in-Chief, General John Gort, finally advanced and attempted to engage the enemy in order to stop further German incursions onto French soil. However, by 14th May 1940, the Germans had already crossed the Meuse and opened up a fifty mile gap in the Allied Front. Just six days later the Germans were at the Channel and there were only twenty miles of beaches around the town of Dunkirk still under Allied control. Surrounded by the elite Nazi Panzer Divisions of tanks, the BEF and the French and Belgian armies were trapped, with just a narrow corridor between them and the sea. The BEF and its Allies had been out-manoeuvred with hardly a shot fired, and the elaborate defences that the BEF had so laboriously dug during that long, cold winter were never used.

When he heard the news that his army was trapped in France, Churchill ordered the immediate implementation of *"Operation Dynamo"*, a plan to evacuate the troops and equipment from the beaches of Dunkirk, and this swung into action on 27th May. Boatyards along the River Thames and beyond were searched by Admiralty Officers and more than forty serviceable motor-boats or launches were commandeered and assembled at Sheerness. At the same time lifeboats from liners in the London docks, tugs, private yachts, fishing craft, lighters, barges, paddle steamers and pleasure boats, indeed anything that could be of use along the beaches, was called into service. Fishing boats from as far afield as Scotland answered the call for help.

Between 27th May and 4th June 1940, a total of 693 ships, including 39 destroyers, 36 minesweepers, 77 trawlers, 26 yachts and a variety of small craft, left the relative safety of the English Channel ports and set sail for France. Some made the trip no less than seven times, with little or no sleep between each voyage. The thought of all those thousands of men waiting in the hell of Dunkirk, praying for their sea-going comrades to rescue them, kept them going. Each time they made the crossing, all the vessels, large and small, had to run the gauntlet of mines, submarines, shore batteries and the *Stuka* dive bombers. Some would not make it.

The RAF did their best to patrol the sea and protect the shipping and flew up and down the coast near Dunkirk looking for enemy aircraft to attack. They commented that during the days of the evacuation, the

Channel between the French port and Dover was solid with shipping. Indeed from the air it looked as if you could step from one ship to another without getting your feet wet. Many aircraft were themselves shot down.

But the BEF and the French army still had to get to the Dunkirk beaches. For up to two weeks they motored and marched across France and Belgium, leaving burning tanks and equipment in their wake and scrounging what little food and water they could from embittered citizens who knew they were being left to face the Nazis alone. Not all the locals intended to stay put, for the roads were also choked with the milling masses of tens of thousands of refugees and their many different modes of transport. They were mostly women, children, the elderly and the infirm, for able-bodied men were in the services. Often the women were carrying their children and pushing a pram loaded with a few pathetic possessions. Some of the elderly and infirm were on carts being hauled along by loving relatives. However they were hindering the evacuation of the British and French armies and their military convoys, so Military Police went ahead and just pushed all the refugees and their miscellaneous assortment of transport, off the road, turning a deaf ear to all the pleas and the curses that were thrown at them.

Clem remembered the retreat all his days. The unending sound of gun-fire in the distance day and night and, at night, the sky illuminated by the artillery flashes. During the day the sky was dominated by German aircraft flying in formation and machine-gunning the congested roads. Eventually they had to abandon the lorries and proceed on foot. The lorries were destroyed and what equipment they could not carry was trashed and thrown into the ditches at the side of the road. Then the horror of leaving an exhausted comrade who could walk no further; the hunger and thirst that never left you; the effort of just putting one foot in front of the other; the shame and humiliation of defeat; the faces of the local people left to their fate under Nazi domination; the smell of burning; and all the while one thought kept him going. *"Anne. I must get home to Anne."*

When eventually he arrived at Dunkirk, it was like Dante's inferno. The buildings along the promenade, and the oil tanks just inside the harbour, were ablaze, with flames shooting into the sky, accompanied by a huge pall of black smoke mushrooming upwards. The conflagration could be seen from as far away as the Thames estuary and it was all choreographed to the sound of incessant bombing.

The dead, the dying and the injured were laid out on the promenade where a café had been turned into a makeshift field-hospital. The beach was a seething mass of khaki. Some soldiers had dug slit trenches in the sand to give some protection from the bombers, others took their chances in the open and just dived flat when a bomb hit, still more hid as best they could in the sand-dunes; a rag-tag mob, some separated from regiment and friend; unwashed, dishevelled, demoralised, hungry and thirsty and all desperate to get home. Some would not make it and an occasional flash of white would be spotted; a navy nurse or doctor from one of the destroyers trying to tend to the injured. Stretcher bearers and Army medics were moving amongst the khaki mass and armed naval personnel were trying to sort out who would be next onto a boat. And the boats. What a glorious sight they were. The larger ships, such as destroyers and minesweepers, were anchored about a mile out, but between them and the shore were smaller vessels, fishing boats, barges, yachts and the like, scurrying back and forth, back and forth, ferrying men from the beach to the bigger ships or taking as many men as they could on board and heading for home. Thousands of men lined the shore-line, knee-deep, waist-deep, shoulder-deep, in the cold sea waiting to board a boat. And all under attack from the German Luftwaffe. Rescuers and rescued alike were at risk from bombs and strafing from the sky.

At night the embarkation had to stop and they were all under orders not to light fires or to smoke, despite the conflagration raging all around them, but many broke the smoking rule and the beach became a mass of orange glow-worms ....until 'planes were heard overhead and the glow-worms were quickly extinguished!

Clem had managed to stay with some of his comrades, cajoling and encouraging the younger ones to keep going, but now he could collapse into the relative safety of the sand dunes and he fell into an exhausted sleep until it was his turn to board a boat. Daylight revealed again the sheer scale of the operation that had been launched to pluck them from the beaches.

Eventually it was time for Clem's small group to move from the sand-dunes. He turned to the man sleeping next to him.

"C'mon, mate," he encouraged, "Time to go!"

The young soldier could not be roused, so Clem shook him harder. Still no response. He had died in his sleep. Clem could not believe it. The man had walked all those miles only to die of exhaustion within sight of rescue. Of all the things that he saw at Dunkirk, this incident haunted him all his life.

His group debated whether to join the queue of thousands waiting to board a destroyer from the east *môle* of Dunkirk Harbour (a massive stone jetty encircling the port) where men were being lifted directly onto the deck of the ship but as they walked towards it, a bomb hit the destroyer and seemed to lift her right out of the water for a few seconds. Suddenly soldiers and sailors were scrambling to get off the ship as she listed dangerously against the jetty. They were unlucky. It is said that two-thirds of the men who were evacuated from the beaches at Dunkirk, were lifted directly from the "*môle*" onto Royal Navy destroyers. This decided Clem and his group to take their chances with one of the small ferry-boats so they waded into the sea.

Clem could not swim so he was at the mercy of a boat coming near enough to enable him to struggle on board but he helped his weaker mates to get away first. The incident on the beach had made him realise that he was tougher than many of the younger ones! Nevertheless he was in the water all day. Just as he was beginning to think he would have to spend the night on Dunkirk Beach in wet clothes, hands gripped his battledress and he was hauled unceremoniously aboard a life-boat and they were motored out to a waiting destroyer.

There they were taken below decks and their clothes were taken off them to dry off as best they could in the engine room. Some of the rescued in some of the destroyers were given tea and toast but Dad never made any mention of this. What he did say was that when they eventually arrived in port, someone had taken his trousers and he was given a pair several sizes too big. He often chuckled at the thought of a larger man struggling to get into his smaller pair!

The WRVS (Women's Royal Voluntary Service) and the Red Cross were lined up on the quayside dispensing cups of tea and eggs and bacon. For some reason he was chivvied into the food queue, when all he wanted was a "cuppa", and he remembered that the well-intentioned eggs and bacon, (a rare treat in war-time Britain) going down on empty stomachs, "*Damn near killed us!*"

He was one of 120,927 men rescued between the 30th and 31st May 1940 in *Operation Dynamo*. Altogether 338,226 men, including 139,997 French and Belgian troops, with a smattering of Dutch soldiers, were brought back from the beaches of Dunkirk between 27th May and 4th June. It had been anticipated that a maximum of 45,000 would be able to be rescued, so to snatch nearly ten times that number helped, in no small measure, to turn an ignominious defeat into a glorious retreat. One of the greatest, if not THE greatest, evacuation by sea the world has ever seen.

At a cost, of course. 30,000 British troops died, including some from the 51st Highland Division and the 2nd Battalion of the Royal Norfolk Regiment who were left behind, with many French and Belgium troops, to cover the Allied retreat. At least another 10,252 allied soldiers were killed; 42,000 men wounded; 8,467 missing; and a colossal 1,212,000 Dutch, Belgian, French and British prisoners taken, including many of the medics who had remained on the beaches tending to the wounded and dying, even as the last boat sailed away.

Of the 39 destroyers involved in the evacuation, only 13 were fit for immediate service and many of the smaller boats were so riddled with machine gun bullets they were not worth repairing.

The Allies left behind 2,000 guns, 60,000 trucks, 76,000 tons of ammunition and 600,000 tons of fuel supplies. The Germans gained 1,200 field guns, 1,250 anti-aircraft guns, 11,000 machine guns and 25,000 vehicles.

The question remains "How on earth did the British get away?" With the Allies surrounded by the elite Panzer divisions, the Germans had the BEF at their mercy and, at the time of the evacuation, all but five kilometres of coastline at Dunkirk was under German control.

Theories abound, as they always do. One reason might have been that Hitler did not want to risk advancing his tanks any further over the flooded areas between them and the Allies. Another is that the Luftwaffe's Commander-in-Chief, Field Marshall Goering, is believed to have insisted that the annihilation of the BEF should be left to the squadrons under his command. Still another, that Hitler personally intervened to allow the British to escape as he "did not want to destroy the British Army and force them to fight to the bitter end." Perhaps he still had hopes that the two countries could become allies in his vision of creating an "Aryan race".

A simple thing like the weather also played its part, for an unusual meteorological pattern occurred in late May of 1940. First it rained much more than usual at this time of year, threatening to bog down the German tanks. Then the weather remained cloudy for prolonged periods, grounding the Luftwaffe for extended periods over the crucial days. Finally there was very little wind, making the sea less choppy and enabling the smaller vessels to cross the Channel.

Whatever the reason, or reasons, the fact remains that a total of five nations participated in the remarkable evacuation of Dunkirk: Britain, France, Belgium, the Netherlands and Poland. After the war, a marble memorial was erected at the French port. Translated it reads:-

"To the glorious memory of the pilots,
mariners and soldiers of the French and
Allied armies who sacrificed themselves in
the Battle of Dunkerque May June 1940."

CHAPTER NINETEEN

The Threat of Invasion Looms
(June -October 1940)

On the quaysides all along the south coast, after being fed, watered and dried off, and clean, dry clothes and boots supplied where necessary, the soldiers were despatched to a central point where they would be given instructions on where, and how, to re-join their regiments. Clem was ordered to proceed to barracks in Warwick and from there, on Friday 1st June 1940, he sent the following telegram to Mrs Sims at Dorset House School, Littlehampton.

TELL ANNE AM SAFELY HOME*CLEM*

Then he sat down and wrote a letter, in pencil of course, which Anne kept all her life and which I will reproduce here in full. It is just as he wrote it, warts and all, but it is straight from the heart.

My Dearest Anne
Friday
Hello Darling here I am with a few lines, which I know will be a change, for I'm sure you have not had a letter from me for some time, according to what I have heard happened to them, but still that is over now and I am safe and sound in England again. I do hope you are still keeping well, also Dad. I'm still very well in spite of everything. Well darling I got here last night but it was too late to get news to you, so I had to wait until this morning, and so as not to give you a shock, I sent a telegram to Mrs Sims to tell you. I think that left here about 11, I couldn't get it through before, so I hope it wasn't too long in coming. Well I've been saying I'm here but I haven't told you where. I'm at Warwick, quite a long way from home but still it's nice to be here all the same. I don't know what is happening yet, if we are staying for a few days or what, but what might happen is, they will fix us up with a new rig out, and then send us home on leave, which I hope is right, but we shall not be sent out again for a while until we are reorganised and I'm sure that will take quite a while, anyway I hope so. I will not tell you anything now of what happened for I can do that better when I get home, if I did it would be like reading a book, and I want to get this off as soon as I can, so as you get it first thing in the morning , but if you get the news of that telegram, I know your mind will be at rest. I am sure you have been very worried,

113

darling, for I am sure you guessed where I was and as you were not getting my field cards, as I know now you didn't, I know quite how you felt, but I was always thinking of you, duck, and hoping for the best and all my hopes have come off, so we are alright now and no need to worry. I am looking forward now very much to seeing you again and hope it will not be too long. After reading this duck, you will be able to go to the pictures or somewhere tonight, which will be Saturday and enjoy it. Well my Darling I will not stop to say any more now, but I will let you know what is going to happen as soon as I can get to hear, so I will close with all my love and kisses.
So Cheerio Dear, Yours Always,
Xxxxxxxxxxx Clem
Xxxxxxxxxxxxxx

Dad's favourite way of greeting members of the opposite sex, whom he knew well, was, "'ello, Duck!", hence the fowl reference in the above missive! I think it is a Sussex expression, as "Chuck", "Lovey", "Dearie" and the like, would be in other parts of the country.   And the Sussex dialect always drops the "h's", (as it does with a lot of the "t's") so to an untrained ear, it could sound a little like "yellow duck"! A family in-joke and that is why a yellow duck is swimming in the Channel on the front cover of this book.

Although Clem did not know it when he wrote this letter, in fact his fighting days with the army were over. Indeed I do not know if they ever began for Churchill is said to have been scathing about the performance of the BEF and to have complained privately to General Gort that he did not order his troops to put up more of a fight adding the comment, *"Of course if one side fights and the other does not, the war is apt to become somewhat unequal."*

Be that as it may, Clem did return home on leave for a few days and subsequently volunteered to go abroad again but he was informed he was now considered too old for a fighting unit and was posted instead to Cumbria.   (Army records showed him older than he actually was because he had lied about his age in order to join up for the First War in 1917.) He was promoted to Sergeant and there he spent the remainder of the war training new recruits to drive army vehicles, double de-clutching up and down all the mountains of that area, some learning to drive more successfully than others!   He called them "the goons"!   I think he had quite a happy, if frustrating, war but he was always very aware of the fact he fared a lot better than most of the population. Stuck in the wilds of Cumbria, while cities were being bombed, was not his idea of what a trained soldier should be doing when a nation was at war. But a soldier does what a soldier is ordered to do, and so he counted his blessings, as he always did, and counted the days until he could be with Anne again.

For the country, of course, "active service" was far from over and the withdrawal of the BEF from France, and the defeat of the French army, had had serious consequences. Parliament passed a Bill giving the Government complete control of all persons and all property in the country. It was unprecedented, for now banking, munitions, businesses and profits, wages, hours and conditions of service, were all brought under Government control.

The loss of so much weaponry, left behind or destroyed in France, meant that Britain was in no state to defend herself, so munitions and aircraft factories, shipyards and coal-mines worked around the clock in shifts, seven days a week, in order to re-supply the armed services. Everyone had to do their "bit", for the people knew there was only a strip of water between them and the might of the German Army. The air positively bristled with the threat of invasion and on 4th June, as the last of the troops arrived back from Dunkirk, Churchill's famous "We shall fight them on the beaches...." speech was broadcast to the nation via the BBC. (Many years later it was revealed that an actor's voice had been used as Churchill was too busy to go to the studio.)

On the 10th June, Italy joined Germany and declared war on the Allies. The month also saw the opening of the Nazis' biggest concentration camp, at Auschwitz in Poland.

Also in June 1940, Germany bombed the Channel Islands and thus, by the 1st July, they added Guernsey and Jersey to their list of occupied territories.

By July 1940, a million men had responded to a plea the War Secretary, Anthony Eden, had made in May, calling for volunteers to join the "Local Defence Volunteers", later known officially as the "Home Guard" (and unofficially as "Dad's Army"!) With the invasion a very real threat, they busied themselves in their spare time building concrete pillboxes (fortified huts) and anti-tank obstacles. They also removed all the signposts, supposedly to make it difficult for invaders to find their way around. (Would they not have had maps and compasses?) Hindsight is a wonderful thing but actually all this achieved was confusion and frustration for the indigenous!

July also saw the launch of the "Special Operations Executive", the SOE, which was brought into being to help French people, and fluent French speakers, currently living in Britain and who wanted to join in the fight against Germany. They would be trained and then dropped into France by air for sabotage activities. Many of them linked up with the French Underground Resistance Movement.

Also in July, the Government banned church-bells from ringing; they would only ring again if an invasion was imminent. And tea and margarine were added to the list of rationed foods.

Back across the Channel, the evacuation of the BEF and its allies had given   the Germans the opportunity of an almost unopposed advance through the rest of northern France, so that by early June they occupied Paris.   Two thirds of the country was now under Nazi rule.   The remaining one-third, in the south, became known as "Free France" and the French soldiers, who had escaped to Britain from the beaches of Dunkirk, went there to from the nucleus of a Free French Army under a little known General, Charles de Gaulle.

After the evacuation of Dunkirk, it took several weeks for the Luftwaffe to take over, repair and re-stock the abandoned airfields in its newly acquired territories of France, Belgium and Holland.   Meanwhile the German Army prepared for "Operation Sealion", their code name for the invasion of Britain.   They moored thousands of barges in the ports, canals, and rivers of northern France and Belgium in readiness for the vessels to carry them, and their fearsome weaponry, across the Channel.

But before this fleet could set sail with any hope of arriving in safety, the Luftwaffe had to destroy Britain's air and naval power.   Goering told Hitler that this could be done in a few massive air strikes and he proposed to begin on 13th August 1940, "Eagle Day".

Thus began the famous "Battle of Britain" between the Luftwaffe and the RAF.   Perhaps if Goering had concentrated on bombing airfields, harbours and naval bases, as he first intended, he might have succeeded in making Britain impotent in the face of an invasion.   But on 7th September he changed tactics and subjected London to massive daylight raids.   It became known as "The Blitz".   Bombs were also dropped on major ports and cities such as Liverpool, Southampton, Manchester, Bristol and Cardiff.   Apparently Goering believed that British resistance would crumble and the RAF would be forced to bring its reserve squadrons into the fray for a final showdown.   In fact it gave the RAF chance to make its airfields in Kent operational again and from there they launched massive counter-attacks.   German losses mounted.   The Luftwaffe was not invincible and, on 17th September, Hitler postponed "Operation Sealion" until further notice.

On 30th August 1940, Churchill made another of his famous speeches in the House of Commons.   He praised the RAF and said, "Never in the field of human conflict was so much owed by so many to so few."

When France fell, he was also reputed to have said, "Britain stands alone" but this can be forgiven as a bit of Churchillian rhetoric, for Britain was not alone.   Soldiers, sailors and airmen from throughout the British Empire had arrived to defend the "mother country" and now they were joined by substantial numbers of allied soldiers from the evacuation of

Dunkirk. Free French, Poles and Czechs, who had made their way to England after the fall of their own countries, also joined the fray; many of these were formed into their own units and fought with valour and distinction throughout the war. There were even Americans who had joined the RAF as volunteer fighter pilots and had distinguished themselves flying "Spitfires" and "Hurricanes" in the "Battle of Britain". Some became famous flying aces but many lost their lives. Some of the survivors stayed in the RAF throughout the war; others eventually transferred to the USAAF, but all contributed in no small measure to the Allied cause throughout the war.

CHAPTER TWENTY

The War Continues
(November 1940-February 1942)

The "Battle of Britain" is generally considered to have ended on 31st October 1940 but of course this did not mean an end to the bombing, nor to the war. Just two weeks later the mediaeval city of Coventry was destroyed and in December more than 22,000 fire bombs were dropped on London. Attacks continued on the capital and other cities the length and breadth of Britain, from Southampton to Liverpool, Bristol to Newcastle. In March 1941 the Luftwaffe started night-time raids and, in April, London was bombed by land-mines which fluttered down on parachutes. Several hospitals were hit, as was the famous St Paul's Cathedral. In May the House of Commons was hit by conventional bombing, and so it went on.

On 22nd June 1941, when everyone had been expecting Hitler to invade Britain, he invaded Russia instead. He thought Russia would collapse quickly under a mighty *Blitzkrieg,* and thus provide living-space for his "*Master Race*", with the populace fit only for slave labour. In this he grossly underestimated the Russians' tenacity, perseverance and capacity for suffering .... and Russia's bitter winters. Immediately Britain offered an alliance, and the USA offered arms to the beleaguered nation, and thus Russia became one of the Allied countries. After a long and bitter struggle, in which men literally froze to death and the elite Panzer tanks were frozen solid, history would show Hitler had bitten off more than he could chew on his eastern borders.

On 7th December 1941 the Japanese launched a huge air attack on US ships in Pearl Harbour, Hawaii. It caught the Americans completely by surprise and the very next day the USA, Britain and allied nations declared war on Japan. Three days later, in accordance with the "Tripartite Pact", Germany and Italy declared war on the United States. So, as 1941 ended, another European war had escalated into a world conflict.

After Pearl Harbour, Japanese troops stormed through the Far East, invading Thailand, Malaya, the Philippines, Burma, British Borneo, Wake Island and Hong Kong. On 15th February 1942 Singapore surrendered to the Japanese army, leaving hundreds of thousands of military and civilian prisoners (men, women and children) at the mercy of the invaders.

Now the hostilities encircled the globe and would be fought on many fronts, on the land, on the high seas and in the air. As well as central Europe it would be fought on the frozen steppes of Russia, in the deserts of North Africa, in the steamy jungles of Burma: in the Mediterranean and Baltic Seas: in the Atlantic and Pacific Oceans: in the Middle East and the Far East: in Italy and in Greece: on the islands of the Pacific and the Mediterranean.

But it was fought too by the civilian populations; a battle against sleeplessness from constant bombing; the problems of rationing and shortages, and joining endless queues to purchase food; the never-ending worry of family and friends fighting, or imprisoned, in far-off shores; the worry of just getting from one place to another without encountering an air raid attack. It was a war fought at home as much as abroad.

In April 1942 the Luftwaffe ordered the so-called *Baedeker* raids, named after the German travel-guidebooks. They bombed historic cities such as York and Bath in the hope of demoralising the British people. In August 1943 Portsmouth suffered its worst attack by air and in June 1944 the Germans launched the first of the deadly V1 flying bombs, called *Doodlebugs*. The new long-range V2 rockets came as late in the war as September 1945 and, just two months later (in November) a V2 rocket hit a Woolworth's store in London, killing sixty and injuring two-hundred; all that was left was a huge crater.

Of course the RAF and its allies attempted to give as good as they got and the German city of Nuremberg was attacked in October 1941. May 1942 saw parts of Cologne destroyed, including its cathedral and chemical plants; Berlin and Hamburg were hit in 1943 on round-the-clock raids, and so on. It was the first time a war had been directed so intensely, and deliberately, on civilian targets, by both sides.

Protection against air attack was provided in Britain, though nothing would be of use against a direct hit. Evacuation was by far the best of the measures and hundreds of thousands left their homes in the cities for safer rural areas. In the beginning children were evacuated; often the parents did not know where they were going or to whom. For some it was like a holiday and it is said children from the slums in the East End of London were mesmerized by the sight of cows for the first time, for example. For others it was one long nightmare as they were used as child slaves (or worse) on farms, in businesses and private houses. For the majority, the homesickness was awful and many wrote heart-rending letters back to their parents begging to be brought home. Many did return, for parents felt they would rather all die together, than go through the heart-break of separation.

For those not evacuated, outdoor *Anderson* shelters were supplied but these were cold and damp in winter with the floor awash with water after a rainstorm. Many families tried to build bunk-beds inside but they were still so inhospitable that eventually a lot of people stayed put indoors, sheltering under the stairs perhaps, and took their chances there with the Luftwaffe's aim. Indoor *Morrison* shelters were provided for folk without gardens, or for those considered at less risk from bombing. These were large, heavy-duty, steel tables under which people could shelter in the event of an air-raid.

Underground tube stations were eventually officially permitted to be used as refuges from bombing and some time later the Government even got around to providing bunk-beds and washing facilities. Public shelters were also constructed with the same amenities.

As the war went on, conscription rules were changed; as early as November 1940 the Government were releasing builders from active service so they could re-build and repair houses damaged or destroyed in air raids. This was followed by the release of fire and rescue personnel in March 1941. In October 1942 men as young as 18 could be called-up to serve in the armed services and in September 1943, boys and girls aged 16 and 17 had to work in munitions factories. For some reason miners were not exempt from the conscription regulations. Instead, in December 1943, the Minister of Labour, Ernest Bevin, announced that young men under 25 years of age would be called-up to serve in the mines. They became known as "Bevin Boys".

In December 1941 unmarried women aged 20-30 were called up to serve in the armed services, police force or fire service and by May 1943 all women aged 18-45 could be forced to do "war-work", unless they had children under the age of 14 years.

Rationing became a way of life. By the end of the war, tea, margarine, jam, cheese, meat, eggs, rice, dried fruit, sweets, chocolate, biscuits, milk, oat flakes, breakfast cereals, tinned tomatoes, tinned peas and condensed milk were all rationed ... but available if you had the money to pay for it on the thriving black market. Some things simply disappeared from the shelves because they were just not available; bananas, for example, were no longer imported after November 1940. Once again people living in rural areas fared better than those in the cities because they had the growing-space to be more self-sufficient and could sell-on their excess produce to local customers only too pleased to obtain something "under the counter" and above the allotted ration.

Clothes were also rationed through the issuing of coupons, although good quality "utility clothing", without any trimmings, was introduced in September 1941. Coal was rationed and driving on non-essential journeys banned to save petrol.

Various campaigns were launched throughout the war years. After *"Dig for Victory"*, *"Keep Mum! Don't Say a Word"* and *"Careless Talk Costs Lives"* came *"Make Do and Mend"* and the BBC introduced *"V for Victory"* in July 1941. (People in Britain and occupied Europe were encouraged to display the letter "V" and to beat out the "V" sound in Morse code, three dots and a dash.) In September 1941 Lord Woolton, the Minister of Food, introduced the nation to a character called "*Potato Pete*", aimed at encouraging the populace to fill up on potatoes, which was one of the few items still readily available. For the same reason "*Dr Carrot*" soon followed in "*Potato Pete's*" footsteps.

In March 1942 the white loaf disappeared and a "National Wheatmeal Loaf" took its place. It was supposed to be making the most of wheat grains but it did not have the nutty brown colour that we associate today with wholemeal bread; it was an unappetising dirty grey! The *Savoy Hotel* did its bit for the war effort by inventing a dish called "*Woolton Pie*"; stewed root vegetables in an oatmeal base.

Books and magazines were full of cooking tips and war-time recipes and hints on how to save, conserve or preserve food, clothes and fuel. Gardening suggestions were also popular, as was advice on how to rear livestock, for many people had started to keep rabbits and chickens in their gardens to supplement the rations.

Airfields proliferated around the south and east coasts and British and foreign troops were stationed everywhere, especially Canadian soldiers and American GI's. There were 1.5million of the latter alone and they were very popular in some quarters for their ready access to nylon stockings, tinned fruit, chocolate and chewing gum, but others said they were nothing but trouble being "overpaid, over-sexed and over here!" (They earned seven times the wage of the average British soldier.)

Nylon stockings had come onto the American market in 1940 but, due to the war, were unseen in Britain until they arrived with the GI's. They were like gold-dust. Most young women still had to make-do with staining their bare, shaved legs with cold tea and asking a friend to draw a line with an eye-brow pencil up the back of the calf to simulate a seam. Seamless stockings and tights, of course, had not been invented.

The foreign troops brought a certain *joie de vie* to the country and a "*Live today, for tomorrow we may die*" philosophy. Social barriers and British etiquette, even morals, were breached and, with "swing" music all the rage, dances (or "socials" as they were known) were a very popular way of introducing foreign man to local girl.

Most towns had troops stationed nearby. Littlehampton had Ford Aerodrome on its doorstep, full of the Fleet Air Arm troops practising deck landings on make-believe aircraft-carriers. And, in nearby Arundel, Canadian soldiers were stationed.

Anne loved to dance. Not the ultra-modern American dances like the jitterbug and the jive but the waltz, foxtrot and quickstep and often she would go with her friend, Carrie, to one of the local "socials", normally the one held every Saturday night at the Beach Hotel. A lot of the young men based at Ford had been stationed previously at Shoreham and they used this venue as the meeting place for the girl-friends they had made there. Anne became very friendly with some of the couples and after the dance the young women would stay overnight with Anne before returning to Shoreham on the Sunday.

At the dance, one Saturday in August 1942, rumours were circulating that the men would soon be sent on a mission to France. They were. On 19th August, 5000 Canadian soldiers and 1000 British troops, mainly commandoes, attacked the French port of Dieppe. It came to be called the "Dieppe Raid" and it was a disaster. Two-thirds of the troops involved were killed, wounded or taken prisoner. The RAF and the RCAF waged their most intense battle of the war and on this single day they lost 106 aircraft. The young men stationed at Ford and Arundel had been part of that mission and most did not return.

Just one month later, Anne returned home from the dance and was surprised to find the front door unlocked. The black-out curtains had been put up, so that meant her father had returned home after his pint at the *Trades and Labour Club* but it was unlike him not to re-lock the door. She called out to him but there was no reply. There was no sign of him in the house but eventually she found him, collapsed in the garden. He had suffered a massive stroke and had died immediately, aged 72 years. Although the death certificate said differently, Anne always maintained he died of a broken heart. At the funeral service in St Mary's Church, they played the hymn *"Abide With Me"*. It had been his wife's favourite and had been sung at her funeral too. It seemed appropriate that Tom and Mary Martin should depart this life on the same note. Tom was laid to rest with his beloved Mary in Littlehampton Cemetery and, after their names, the headstone bears the single word, "Reunited".

At least this time Clem was able to obtain a 48 hour pass to come home for the funeral but Anne would be destined to spend the rest of the war on her own for her evacuees had already left. They had moved to the West Country when Littlehampton itself became a target for the Luftwaffe, although I believe only one bomb was actually dropped there during the whole of the war, near the gatehouse of Rosemead School in East Street. A bit too close for comfort!

About the same time that they left, Anne had been made a "fire-watcher". This involved going out with a neighbour a couple of times a week, at night, and being ready to sound an alarm if a fire was spotted in the vicinity. This was not however her only contribution to the war effort. In 1943 she had to register for "war-work" and was sent to assist a Naval Commander's wife with her housework! (There was no munitions factory nearby so I suppose this was the best the authorities could come up with!) Captain Seymour, and his wife and family, lived in Blackheath but had packed up their London home when the bombing became too severe and Mrs Seymour and the children had evacuated to Rustington. In the event Anne became very fond of Kitty Seymour and soon became more of a friend than an employee. As I said, war was breaking down normal social barriers.

As early as February 1942, it was realised that the threat of an invasion of Britain by Germany had passed but it was June 1943 before the Home Guard started to replace all the road signs they had so laboriously taken down. They also removed the barbed wire and dismantled the anti-tank traps but the Home Guard itself was not disbanded until December 1944.

So no invasion was imminent but the hostilities, and shortages, continued unabated.

CHAPTER TWENTY-ONE

The War Ends
(March 1942-1945)
(+ Attlee's Government 1945-Oct 1951)

Throughout the war Hitler was still obsessed with his idea of creating his "Master Race" and his inhumanity to Jews, dissidents and "social misfits" continued. In July/August 1941 he decided the final solution was to gas all Jews and in December of that year the first extermination camp, at Chelmo, was opened. The second, at Belzec, opened in March '42 and by December all the camps had become extermination camps. Hitler had added gypsies to his list of undesirables and ordered that they too should be sent to Auschwitz for extermination.

Meanwhile the war was still raging and in November 1942 the Germans occupied "Free France", or "Vichy France" as it was also known. However, not everything was going Hitler's way for, just six months later, on 17th May 1943, nineteen Lancaster bombers, from the elite *617 Squadron,* dropped a new, unique type of weapon, called bouncing bombs, (designed by Dr Barnes Wallis) on three dams in the industrial heartland of Ruhr in Germany. The pilots became known as *"The Dambusters"* and were later immortalised on celluloid by the Hollywood film industry. The leader of the *Dambusters* was Wing Commander Guy Gibson, who was awarded a Victoria Cross for his heroism on that day; sadly he was killed in action on 20th September 1944. Three months after the death of Guy Gibson, the "King of American Swing", Glenn Miller, also was killed. The aircraft in which he was travelling disappeared as it crossed the English Channel, from Britain to France, on 16th December. Neither his 'plane, nor his body, was ever found.

Early in 1944 yet more bombs rained down on London and one scored a direct hit on the house belonging to Dorie and Les Martin in Streatham. Uncle Les was at work, and their daughters were at school, but Auntie Dorie was at home when the bomb struck. Unfortunately, after the air-raid warning, she had left it a second too late before she vacated the house to make her way to the air-raid shelter at the bottom of the garden. She was almost there when the force of the explosion actually blew her into the shelter. She was lucky. Her arm was broken in three places and she had severe concussion, but she was alive. She was taken to hospital where her arm was set and a few days later she was evacuated to a nursing home in Edinburgh. She stayed there for six months, recovering from her injuries.

124

Their younger daughter, Peggy, was eight years old and was collected from school by a neighbour, who took her to her home for the night. Jean, aged fifteen, was met at her school-gates by another neighbour and she in turn met their father at the railway station as he came home from work. They went home to find their house reduced to a pile of rubble. Not a stick of furniture, nor an item of clothing, remained but they scratched away in the rubble with bare hands and a bit of debris and eventually managed to unearth a tin-box with some cash in it and a few salvageable personal items. This was all that remained of their family home but they were all alive and they were grateful for that.

Of course this was happening hundreds, maybe thousands, of times a day, all over the country, so relatives and neighbours, and the rescue and support services, were well geared to offer assistance. That night Uncle Les and Jean were offered the refuge of a neighbour's air-raid shelter and then the Red Cross stepped in and found them temporary accommodation. Within the week, the Council had re-housed them until their own home could be rebuilt.

Jean was on the threshold of leaving school and starting work, so she stayed in London with her father. Peggy, being younger, was sent to her mother's sister, her Auntie Alice, in Angmering, until her mother came out of hospital.

Personal buildings insurance did not cover war damage on property so the Government undertook to pay for all the repairs. However, in their case, it was four years before their house was rebuilt and they could all move back in.

By April 1944, the war was at last turning in the Allies' favour. All foreign travel was banned, for an invasion of northern France was planned. Lessons had been learned from the disastrous Dieppe Raid in 1942, so in May '44 northern France was bombed first, to prepare for the troops to land. On 6th June the allied forces invaded France in "Operation Overlord". The Normandy Landings, or D-Day, as the invasion came to be known, took place on five French beaches code-named Utah, Juno, Sword, Gold and Omaha. And this time there would be no retreat. On 15th August allied troops invaded the South of France enabling Paris to be liberated on 25th August. Just five days later the capital was handed over to the Free French, amidst much rejoicing by the French people, and within days German troops surrendered in the French ports of Boulonge and Calais. Also in September, the allied troops were successful in liberating Brussels, the capital of Belgium, and the port of Antwerp. Allied troops entered Germany but the Allies suffered a massive defeat at Arnhem, in Holland, after defending the bridge for nine days. The war was not yet over.

The Russians liberated Majdanek Concentration Camp in July 1944 and by November of that year it had already been turned into a museum. In October 1944 the gas chambers at Auschwitz were shut down and the Germans began destroying the evidence of the murders of two million Jews, gypsies, "asocials" and prisoners that had taken place there. Auschwitz, however, would not be liberated, also by the Soviets, until January 1945. As each camp came to be discovered, and the true horror of what had happened there emerged, even battle-hardened troops, and their generals, openly cried. The surviving prisoners were little more than walking skeletons and the tales they told of their suffering almost defied belief.

By February 1945 the war in Europe was all but over but Allied leaders still made the controversial decision to bomb Dresden. It left 50,000 citizens dead, with many British people and politicians wondering if this was not an unnecessary slaughter of a civilian population. The last German bomb fired against Britain was on 29th March; it was a V1, a "doodlebug", and was shot down in Kent without causing any casualties.

Italy had surrendered in September 1943, after sustained attack by air and on the ground, but the Germans fought back on their behalf and German forces did not surrender in Italy until April 1945.

April was also the month that the last of the concentration camps was liberated. Hitler finally accepted defeat and, on 30th April 1945, he committed suicide. He had succeeded in ending his life where others had failed, for there had been no less than forty-two known attempts on his life during the war. One of the first was as early as November 1939 when a bomb intended for him exploded in a beer hall, but he had already left. Of the more well-known endeavours was another in March 1943 when a bomb, planted in his 'plane, failed to explode. Then, in July 1944, he survived two more bomb attacks; one when he left a conference early and another when his briefcase (complete with hidden bomb) was moved during a strategy meeting with his advisors. One of his top generals, Rommel (who had won many victories in the deserts of North Africa with his *Afrika Corps)* was implicated in the last attacks and in October 1944 he committed suicide on Hitler's orders. The Germans told the world that he had died of war wounds.

Germany surrendered unconditionally to allied forces on 7th May 1945. The war in Europe was over. Churchill declared that the 8th May should be celebrated as VE Day, (Victory in Europe) and church bells rang out throughout the land and people waved flags and sang and danced in the streets. Impromptu street parties were held with residents sharing their carefully hoarded rations and children played games like the three-legged race and the sack race, without the fear of an air-raid siren interrupting the festivities. Music blared out from gramophones and wirelesses, and all seemed right with the world, at last. Similar celebrations took place in America, France and the USSR. They were euphoric. But the war was not over. Japan had not surrendered.

The Second World War is generally thought to have started on 3rd September 1939 but in truth it could be said to have begun in July 1937 when Japan invaded China. When Japan aligned itself with Germany, allied troops and American arms were despatched to China to help her in her fight against Japan but in 1942, when Japan over-ran much of the Far East, China seemed to be offering only limitless manpower against a far superior enemy. The Japanese were ruthless, ruthless and barbaric. It is said they carried out a reign of terror against China and its people, (men, women and children) that is unsurpassed in its bestiality and savagery in modern times. I do not propose to detail their atrocities here, as I would like my readers to sleep tonight, but taking young girls as "comfort women" and burying prisoners alive, for example, is the least of it. The captured allied troops and civilians fared little better. Any soldier who surrendered, rather than die fighting, was treated with contempt. They were herded into camps with no better facilities, or food, than the Nazi concentration camps.

In June 1942 the Japanese decided to put their allied prisoners of war (POW's) to work building a railway line through the jungle from Thailand to Burma. The conditions were appalling; it was stiflingly hot and humid, very little water to drink and just a handful of rice to eat. Dysentery, typhus, beriberi, cholera and tropical diseases were rife. The Japanese wanted the men to die; there were plenty more prisoners and their deaths would mean less mouths to feed, if you can call a handful of rice, "food". Any minor infringement, or none, was severely punished, often resulting in the death of the prisoner.

At the fall of Singapore it was estimated that there were between 500,000 and 600,000 allied prisoners of the Japanese, not including Chinese prisoners. Estimates vary as to how many of them survived but 116,000 men alone expired building "Death Railway", as it came to be known. Probably only about one quarter of those taken prisoner in Singapore, between 125,000 and 150,000 people, lived to the end of the hostilities, including 37,583 UK and 14,473 US troops. But to put even this dreadful statistic into perspective, only 56 Chinese POW's were released after the surrender of Japan. It is unknown how many Chinese POW's were killed by the Japanese but some estimates put the figure at 10 million, plus another 4-10 million from Java. These horrific figures make the carnage worse than the numbers of deaths in the Nazi concentration camps, but the horror and savagery has received much less coverage in the international press over the years.

At first it was the US Navy who started to win against the Japanese but in March 1943 the USAF (United States Air Force) destroyed a Japanese convoy of ships in the Battle of the Bismarck Sea, and slowly the tide was turning. In November 1943 the Gilbert Islands were taken by American Forces, followed by the Marshall Islands in January of the following year. Just a few months later, in July 1944, US troops invaded Saipan and saw Japanese civilians and soldiers throw themselves off the cliffs rather than surrender. On 26th October 1944 the Japanese Navy was destroyed by the US Navy in a three day battle.

In March 1945 the USAF firebombed Tokyo killing 83,000 and making 1million people homeless. In June 1945, with the war in Europe already won, the last island held by the Japanese, Okinawa, was taken by American troops. Most Japanese fought to the death, and many threw themselves off the cliffs, but a few were captured. The taking of Okinawa meant the Americans now had the ability to bomb mainland Japan into submission. But still the Emperor of Japan would not surrender.

So, on 6th August 1945, an entirely new weapon, the atomic bomb, was dropped on Hiroshima, killing 100,000 immediately. Thousands more would die from burns and radiation sickness in the coming months and years. But still no surrender.

On 9th August another atomic bomb was dropped, this time on Nagasaki and on 14th August the Emperor, on behalf of the Japanese people, surrendered, at last. I would like to record that at least he had the grace to "fall on his sword", in true *Samurai* tradition, but he did not.

On 15th August 1945 the people in Britain and America celebrated VJ Day, Victory in Japan. The Second World War was really over at last.

It had been the deadliest conflict in history with a total of over 60million people dead, mostly civilians. Of the Allied nations 14million active combatants had been killed and 36million civilians, mostly Soviet and Chinese citizens. The defeated Axis powers lost 8million military dead and 4million civilians. There were over 12million people who had died in the Nazi extermination camps, of whom 6million were Jews.

It had involved over 100million military personnel worldwide, making it the most widespread war in history and it was the most costly war ever in terms of capital expenditure as well as lives. (Estimates put the cost not less than one trillion US dollars at 1944 values)

The effects of the war had far-reaching implications worldwide. Even before the official surrender of Germany, at the "Yalta Conference", the victorious nations re-drew the borders of many countries, making the Soviet Union the main beneficiary. Large populations of Germany, Finland, Poland, Romania, Estonia, Latvia and Lithuania suddenly found themselves in hostile territory, although Poland was compensated for its losses to the Soviet Union by receiving most of Germany east of the Oder-Neisse line, including the industrial region of Silesia. In the "Yalta Treaty", Stalin had promised to hold free elections in his newly acquired territories. They never happened. Churchill's fears were therefore proved correct for, before the ink was hardly dry, he had commented to

President Roosevelt that he feared they had signed a false treaty.

Germany was partitioned into four zones of occupation with American, British and French zones grouped as West Germany and the Soviet sector as East Germany. Its capital, Berlin, was also divided into two parts; West Berlin under allied control; East Berlin in the charge of the Soviets. Austria was again annexed from Germany and divided into four zones of occupation but eventually it re-united and became the Republic of Austria. Korea was divided along the 38th parallel into two sections; North Korea, controlled by the Chinese, and South Korea occupied by the Americans. Partitions were initially informal but as relations between the victors deteriorated, the "Cold War" began creating two military blocs, NATO and the Warsaw Pact.

Now that China was free of Japanese troops, it could renew its civil war between the Kuomintang, under the leadership of Chiang Kai-Shek, and the Communists, under the command of Mao Zedong. By August 1945, the Communists already controlled more of China than they had before 1937, mainly because their soldiers had tried to help the peasant population during the war, thus spreading the word of communism, while the Kuomintang had taken the brunt of fighting the Japanese "head-on" in the cities. The ensuing hostilities were to be to the death, for neither could tolerate the existence of the other.

The victors also demanded payment of war reparations; Russia received many millions of dollars plus dismantled manufacturing plants and 3million former German POW's who were forced to work in Russia. Some did not return to their homeland until well into the 1950's. Free coal and machinery, dismantled factories and 700,000 former German and Italian POW's, as forced labour, went to France. 100,000 POW's were also sent as forced labour to Britain. The USA and the UK settled for appropriating German patents and blueprints (worth about $10billion then) and the US took all the German Company assets and all the German scientists and technicians (mainly to deny their expertise to Russia). The Japanese were required to make similar reparations to China and America.

Originally the plans against Germany were very harsh. Franklin Delano Roosevelt was the American President who had led the United States through the war years but he had died on 12th April 1945, having been ill for some time. Harry S. Truman had replaced him and, in July 1947, the Truman administration realised that the economic recovery in Europe could not go forward without the reconstruction of the German industrial base and the "Marshall Plan" was implemented. The West German people could begin to rebuild their country at last.

However, this was not to the liking of Joseph Stalin, the leader of the Soviet Union. His armies and territories surrounded West Berlin so in 1948 he decided to try and starve the people there, so that he could take charge of that part of the city as well. Thus he blocked all the rail lines, canals and roads to prevent food getting in. So, in order to keep the people alive, the British, American and French Air Forces flew in supplies; day after day, month after month. This became known as ·"The Berlin Airlift" and, at its height, one 'plane was landing every minute. Some of the American pilots "bombed" the city with chocolate bars for the children and they became known as "the candy bombers". After eleven months Stalin gave up and re-opened the access routes.

The economic recovery of individual nations varied hugely. The defeated countries of Germany and Japan soared ahead and within two decades had strong economies with a solid industrial base. France and Italy's recoveries were a little slower but the poor old UK struggled for decades. Some would argue (in the country's defence!) that the war had saddled the economy with a huge National Debt, which, with interest payments added, did not make for a level, economic, playing field. Others would say it was just poor management by successive governments. The US economy had suffered very little in the war, however, and was already set to become a formidable manufacturing power. Despite the losses of its military personnel and civilian casualties, the USSR was in a better economic and strategic state than any other continental European power. Thus the stage was set for the emergence of the "Super Powers" and with it the "Cold War" which lasted for 45 years. Indeed, as early as August 1945, Winston Churchill talked about the Soviet Union's increasing power and made a speech in the House of Commons saying an "iron curtain" was descending across Europe. Sadly he was to be proved right.

The war gave birth to the "United Nations", in place of the "League of Nations", in the hopes of preventing another conflict. Also the war would be instrumental in creating the new nation of Israel, a Jewish homeland at last, but only brought about by the displacement of hundreds of thousands of "Palestinians" who had lived in that area for thousands of years. It was founded in 1948 but alas not even the United Nations would be able to prevent the decades of conflict this single decision would bring to the Middle East. The war also accelerated de-colonization in Africa and Asia, while Europe moved towards integration.

Many high-ranking German and Japanese leaders were prosecuted for war crimes, mostly for the mass murder of holocaust victims, civilians and POW's. Some were executed by hanging; most received long prison sentences. Although the deliberate targeting of civilians was already defined as a war-crime, it had been used so extensively by both sides that no-one was ever tried for this specific offence.

On 15th October 1945, Pierre Laval, the Head of Government in German-occupied France was executed by firing squad for collaborating with the enemy.

The most well-known broadcaster on the British airwaves during the war was William Joyce, nicknamed "Lord Haw-Haw". He had been born in America, of Irish immigrant parents, but eventually settled in England where he became involved in the British Fascist Movement. At the outbreak of the war, he fled to Germany and immediately offered his services as a propaganda radio broadcaster. He did his best to undermine British morale throughout the war and, when the hostilities were over, he was tried for treason. He was found guilty and executed by hanging at Wandsworth Prison on 3rd January 1946.

In military terms the war marked the coming of age of air supremacy over huge battleships and fixed coastal artillery. The major powers would come to rely upon small highly-trained and well-equipped armed forces, rather than huge conscript armies. As well as the SOE, the SAS came into being during the war. A British officer, David Stirling, formed the "Special Air Services" in July 1941. It was a highly-trained force, which we still have today, specialising in going behind enemy lines on sabotage missions.

In technological terms the war gave a kick-start to the possibility of nuclear power and saw the beginning of electronic computer technology and the birth of the jet engine, initially for military aircraft. The first jet to fly in the UK was the *Gloster E28/39* on 15th May 1941, although as early as 1939, a German 'plane can claim to be the first ever jet aircraft to take to the skies. The mass-production of penicillin was accelerated by the huge number of casualties in the conflict.

Hundreds of thousands of pre-fabricated homes (pre-fab's) were built across the land in the months and years after the war, initially to house people whose dwellings had been bombed during the hostilities. Pre-fab's had gone on display at an exhibition in London in April 1944 and demonstrations had shown that they could be erected in three days. Although they were only supposed to be temporary, some stayed occupied for decades. They went some way to easing a huge housing shortage, for many demobbed men, who had remained single during the war, were now anxious to settle down and this added to the housing crisis. The price of rented accommodation soared and the Government encouraged Local Authorities to build permanent council-houses for their residents. (Houses that were owned and maintained by the Authorities and rented to tenants at a reasonable rate.)

Women's attitudes to working practices changed because of the war. They had become accustomed to working in a factory, or the armed services, or on the land. Thus the idea of working outside the home, and also working alongside men on an equal footing, was beginning to take hold. However, because so many de-mobbed men were looking for work, these aspirations were not encouraged ... but it gave women the confidence, in later years, to try jobs traditionally reserved for men.

As demobbed soldiers returned home, a so-called "baby boom" ensued. By the late 1940's the number of births in the UK peaked at almost 900,000 per annum, one-third more than the usual annual birth-rate. The baby boom in America was even greater and the effects reverberate to this day as all these "baby-boomers" reach pensionable age.

The Allied troops stationed in the UK had also left their mark. In the early months of 1946, forty thousand women who had fallen in love with American GI's would set sail to a new life in America. Some had already married in the UK and the rest would marry in their new country. Thousands more would be left broken-hearted as they watched their boy-friends sail back home without them. Many would be left literally "holding the baby". Not just Americans, of course. Canadian, Australian and British soldiers stationed far from home, married or not, had succumbed to feminine comfort. And not just with single women. More than a few married ladies had some explaining to do when husbands arrived home to find an unexpected child they could not possibly have fathered. The war had breached normal social boundaries in more ways than one and, as well as the birth-rate, the divorce-rate soared.

Everything must have seemed to be on the increase, except the availability of food. Europe was in ruins and was extremely short of all edibles, so what little Britain had, or could now import, had to be shared with the rest of the continent. Germany, especially, was suffering a desperate food shortage; some of their main agricultural areas were now in Russian hands and Russia refused to part with any produce, saying it was needed for its own people. So if British citizens had expected rationing to cease with the end of the war, they were sadly mistaken; rationing was increased.

The end of the war would mean Winston Churchill's coalition government had to cease. He had steered the country through the difficult war years magnificently and felt confident that he would win another term in office, so when his Labour Party ministers insisted on a general election, even before the war in Japan was won, Churchill was not concerned and called an election for early July 1945. But there were tens of thousands of servicemen still stationed abroad, and everyone over the age of 21 years was entitled to a vote. So the results were delayed a few weeks until all the votes could be counted. When the result came in, the election would produce one of the biggest shocks of British political history. Churchill lost!

Although Churchill had steered Britain through its darkest days, the people remembered only too well how a Conservative government had promised *"A Land Fit for Heroes"* after the last war, and delivered unemployment, soup kitchens and a depression. They hoped a Labour (Socialist) administration would give them a better deal. The voters had shown they wanted change. They wanted an end to wartime austerity and no return to economic depression. They wanted the implementation of the Liberal economist William Beveridge's suggested reforms, which promised *"cradle to grave"* protection, and they felt the socialist Labour Party was the political group to deliver it.

The Labour Party had secured a staggering 393 seats in the House of Commons, the Conservatives 210 and the Liberals just 12 seats, changing the face of British politics, possibly forever. The two main parties would now be Labour and Conservative, with the Liberals (at least in my lifetime) relegated to a minority party.

The new Prime Minister, Clement Attlee, was an unprepossessing man. It was lucky that a television set was not sitting in every home, because he lacked any charisma for the small screen, coming across as painfully shy, and reserved to the point of coldness. Yet he was a man of integrity, with a steely resolve and deeply devoted to social justice for all. A small man who would prove to be a giant among men and who headed one of the greatest social reformist administrations of the 20th century.

With this huge majority, Labour could push through almost any legislation it proposed and thus it was in 1946 that a new "National Insurance Act" established the welfare state as envisaged by the *"Beveridge Report"* of 1942. It introduced compulsory contributions to cover unemployment, sickness, maternity, widows, old age benefits and funeral grants. Despite much resistance from the medical profession, in 1948 the "National Health Service Act" was passed, providing a free and fully comprehensive health service to all citizens. Also in 1948, the "National Assistance Act" came into being. This abolished the "Poor Law" (with its hated system of work-houses), which had been on the statute books since 1598, and created "National Assistance Boards" to provide help to people whose resources were insufficient to meet minimum needs. (This became the "Supplementary Benefits Commission" in 1966 and "Income Support" in 1983.) But not only were health and social security issues dealt with, the Acts also covered housing, education, and the welfare of children, the disabled, the sick and the aged. All these Acts came into force on 7th June 1948, with the Health Service implemented on 5th July 1948. ("Family Allowance" had already been introduced in 1945. This provided a regular sum of money for second and subsequent children, paid to the mother.)

It was a huge amount of legislation to get through Parliament and it did not stop there. In 1949, the "National Parks and Access to the Countryside Act" was introduced, creating the first national parks in England and Wales. Our national parks are quite different to those of other countries as they include substantial human settlements and vast tracts of land, largely in private ownership, but giving protected status to *"conserve and enhance the natural beauty, wildlife and cultural heritage of the area."*

The Labour Party manifesto had also promised nationalization of the Bank of England, fuel, power, iron and steel industries and inland transport. One by one the key industries of post-war Britain were taken into the public sector, and none was more popular than the nationalizing of the coal mines. Many of the pits had dire and dangerous working conditions and the new "National Coal Board" was seen as an humanitarian improvement as much as an economic one.

But eventually the nationalized industries would become bureaucratic and not cost-effective, and the dreams of full employment, secure jobs with fair wages, decent homes for all, and financial protection for all disadvantaged citizens, would prove to be a never-ending millstone around the neck of an increasingly reluctant tax-payer. Cracks in a would-be socialist Utopia would begin.

CHAPTER TWENTY-TWO

A New Arrival
(November 1945-June 1948)

When the war ended, it would take many months for all the troops to be brought home, and many thousands would still have to remain as an occupying force, but mass de-mobilization for British servicemen began as early as 18th June 1945, despite the war in Japan still raging. Each was given a "demob suit" so that they would have something to wear other than their uniform. Clem was not de-mobbed until November 1945 but he must have felt so lucky to have a wife, a home and a job to return to, when so many people had lost so much. When he returned home to Anne, he found a new face in the Oakley household; at some time during the war Blackie, the cat, had died and he had been replaced by another black feline called Mister Tibbles, or Tibbles, or even Tibbs, for short.

However, his pride and joy, his garden, was sadly neglected. After her father died, Anne had tried to carry on growing a few vegetables for herself, and to keep the grass cut and the flower-beds weed-free, but most of the vegetable plot, and the surrounding hedge, were badly overgrown so, in his spare moments at the weekends, Clem concentrated on bringing some order back to his domain. He cut the hedge, and enlarged the small plot Anne had kept going, and planted some onions, late broad beans and potatoes. The rest would have to wait until the spring, with the longer evenings and the better weather, when he would soon bring it under control. The main thing was just to enjoy being home, to make the most of their first Christmas together for many a long year, and to look forward to the New Year and whatever 1946 might have in store.

It would seem a strange festive season, for other Christmases had been spent with Anne's parents, and now they were both gone. Gone too was Anne's Aunt Nell, her mother's sister who had been admitted to Graylingwell Psychiatric Hospital many years before. After her mother died, Anne had carried on visiting her aunt every month, on her own, and hated it! Then one day a letter arrived from the hospital (most "ordinary" people would still not have a telephone at this time) informing her that her aunt had passed away. Anne was sorry that her aunt had had such a sad life but guiltily relieved that she would no longer have to visit her. Strange to say, as ill as she was, Nell was the last of the "Love" sisters to die.

With Clem returning to his job at Dorset House School, perhaps it was not surprising how quickly he and Anne settled into a routine again, counting their blessings as they always did, for they had resigned themselves to the disappointment of not having children and had decided to make the best of it.

Then, on Monday 11th February 1946, a letter arrived as they were eating breakfast. (It was written in pen and ink, not pencil! Ballpoint pens (biros) had been invented in 1944, but it would be twenty years before they were readily available, cheap, and acceptable socially, and in business, as an alternative to the fountain pen.) It was postmarked "Guildford" and was from Evelyn Dodson, Clem's cousin; the lady who had married Bert, the deaf man, and who had often come to stay with them before the war.

"It's from Evelyn," Anne commented, as she started to read the letter. "I expect they want to come and stay this summer." A few moments passed and she looked up at Clem, sitting there munching his toast and drinking his tea.

"I don't believe it! I just don't believe it!"

"What?" replied Clem, his voice full of concern and his mouth full of crumbs. "What's the matter, duck? What don't you believe?"

"I think you had better read it for yourself!" was her reply as she thrust it into his hands.

So here is the letter, reproduced in full. Clem duly read it with Anne sitting there, shell-shocked, watching his face.

Sunday , 10th February '46

Dear Anne and Clem

We hope you are both well and settling down again to a life without the threat of bombs or invasion, as we are.

This letter will come as a bit of a shock but I am writing to you on behalf of Bert's sister , Nellie. I am sure you remember Nellie. She accompanied me several times when Joan and I came to stay with you before the war. The thing is she has had a baby, a healthy little girl born on Friday (8th February). The father is a Canadian soldier who promised to marry Nellie after the war but it turns out he is already married and has a wife and family in Canada. I don't know if you ever met him? He often visited us with Nellie during the war and you might have seen him here? Anyway he has let her down badly and she is heartbroken. To make matters worse, she cannot keep the baby as her sister will not allow her to take the child home. Nellie would like her to be adopted but she does not trust the agencies to find a loving home for her. She was wondering if you were still interested in adopting a child? I realise it is a huge commitment and that you will want some time to think about it. At the moment the baby is being looked after by foster-parents in Aldershot. (She was born in the Military Hospital there.) We hope they can keep her for a few

136

months if necessary and then if we can't find a home for her, she will have to go to Barnardo's.

Please do not feel guilty if you are not able to help. We will all understand.

With much love to you both,

Evelyn

"Well I'm blowed!" Clem gasped. "A baby! Just what we've always wanted, duck. I can't believe it either!" And tears started to fill his eyes and roll slowly down his cheeks.

"Don't start crying, Clem! You'll set me off!" Anne responded. Then, bringing a note of caution into the conversation, "You do realise that she could be deaf?"

"Then she'll need us all the more, won't she, duck?" he replied. "I'm glad it's a girl! I see too many little boys all day at the school!"

"I'm glad it's a girl too. I've always wanted a sister but a daughter will be even better!"

There was no dissension, discussion or hesitation. It was an answer to a prayer; what they had always wanted to make their lives complete and, just when they had got used to the idea their destiny was to be without children, suddenly the chance of a baby popped into their lives. It did not occur to them to turn down the offer, even though they were no longer young, aged 44 and 40 years. They were both in total agreement. So Anne penned their reply straight away as Clem peddled off to work, late, in a euphoric haze.

Monday 11th February '46

Dear Evelyn,

What a lovely surprise your letter was. We would love to adopt Nellie's baby. Poor Nellie. I know how heartbroken she must feel. Please tell her thank you from the bottom of our hearts and we promise to love and care for her baby as we would our own.

Please send details of the foster-parents and we will visit on Sunday, if that is all right with them. Do NOT let her go to Barnardo's. They hang onto a child forever and she will not have the chance of going to a family.

I am committed to helping Kitty Seymour pack up her home in Rustington for the next month but that will give us chance to sort out the paper-work and also give us some time to gather some things together for the baby. Will the foster-parents be able to look after her for another month?

We look forward to hearing from you. Meanwhile thank you, and Nellie, so much for thinking of us. Perhaps you, Bert and Joan will be able to visit us in the summer?

With much love to you all,

Anne and Clem.

And so the dye was cast. Anne and Clem travelled to Aldershot by train the following Sunday and saw their daughter (me!) for the first time. Many years later, I asked Mum what her first impressions of me had been, thinking/hoping she would say something like, "Oh! You were beautiful! I fell in love with you at first sight!" Instead she pronounced, "Oh! You were such a funny little thing! So tiny! I had never seen a baby so tiny! Oh you were such a funny little thing!"

But I think for Dad it was love at first sight. His giant hands encircled this helpless bundle and it frowned a greeting. From then on, I do not think he cared if I grew two heads. I still do not understand how they left me in Aldershot that day, but they did. Two weeks later the foster-parents decided to have a day at the sea-side and they brought me to Littlehampton, where Mum and Dad played *Mummy and Daddy* for a few hours, while my foster-parents walked along the promenade and their daughters explored the fun-fair at the end of the pier. Still Mum and Dad allowed me to return to Aldershot, for Mum was still helping Kitty pack up her house. Meanwhile they were steadily accumulating the paraphernalia of baby accoutrements and friends and relatives rallied round with a second-hand cot and a pram and Kitty Seymour donated some beautiful, expensive baby clothes that her children would no longer wear. The four weeks flew by until, with Kitty and family back in Blackheath, I finally arrived, permanently, at the bungalow.

The adoption process in those days was much easier than it is now. For one thing private adoptions, as I was, were allowed. Back then a parent, usually the mother, was permitted to find a couple who wanted her child and just hand him, or her, over. Of course there were checks, but if a home could be provided, character references supplied, and the adopting parents seemed respectable and solvent, the adoption would go ahead. Three months after the adoption, the prospective parents had to produce the child in a Family Court, before a judge, so he could see for himself that everything seemed all right. Then the adoption was more or less "rubber-stamped". It had to be easy because there were so many of us at that time! Anne and Clem's referees were the family doctor, Dr Waddington, and Dad's employer, Mr Sims.

My arrival changed all their plans. Dad now thought it would be a good idea to turn part of his precious vegetable plot into a chicken run. The chickens would enjoy scratching in the weeds for snails and worms and the extra eggs (and occasional chicken) would be good for the baby. It would mean sacrificing their egg ration but they would be entitled to chicken-meal instead. Also he suggested to Mum that it would be a good idea to keep rabbits too, for the extra meat would be useful for them and the baby. Once he had got the chicken run built and the garden dug, he could build some rabbit hutches at the bottom of the garden. Did Anne agree? Of course she did.

Meanwhile there was little he could do until the days lengthened and the weather improved so he concentrated on digging over the bit that would still be used for growing vegetables, ready for a spring planting. Many years later I found a great contentment in watching my father quietly digging because he made the whole process look so easy. Just a steady rhythm with the spade; in-out-turn, in-out-turn. It was poetry in motion.

As he would have less growing space, he decided to put his name down for one of the new allotments that the local Council had organised. On behalf of the residents, they had purchased a piece of farmland, just up the road from our home, and divided it into small plots. For a nominal rent, families could use the plot to grow vegetables and fruit. Eventually Dad ended up with two plots, side-by-side; the Council allotted him one and the man who had the next door plot offered him his. I am not sure if this was done with official approval, or even knowledge, but, as far as I know, no-one complained and he carried on with two plots until the farmland was sold and turned into a housing estate. I remember the day he was informed that he would lose his allotments very well; it was one of the few times he was almost incandescent with rage!

The chickens, their "house", and surrounding fence arrived that summer, from where I have no idea, but by the autumn Clem was all-set in his modest efforts at self-sufficiency. He must have worked so hard during these months but Mum was to say, many years later of course, that our arrival gave them a new lease of life.

I was a small baby, 5lbs 4ozs, and I cried a lot. Mum thought this was because I had been spoiled at the foster-home, for they had three teenage daughters who all rushed to be the first to pick me up as soon as I opened my mouth!

I had come to live with them about the middle of March 1946 and Mum wanted me to be christened on Easter Sunday, 21st April, but as the adoption had not been formalised by then, special dispensation had to be sought from the Bishop before it could go ahead on that date. They decided to call me "Maureen", because they liked the name. It must have been a popular choice at the time as I was destined to come across many "Maureens" of the same age in later years. Apparently it can mean "*Long waited for*", which seems entirely appropriate. My second name is Anne, after Mum.

One of my God-parents was an Army pal of Dad's, Bill Roberts, and he and his wife and two teenage sons travelled all the way from Aylesbury in Buckinghamshire, in their new, second-hand, *Ford Popular* car, for the christening. Obviously they stayed with us for a few days and he thought it a great joke as he listened to his old buddy trying to pacify me, especially as their own "baby-days" were long gone.

After I had been with them for a few weeks, Mum was feeding me one day and we looked into one another's eyes, as babies do, and she whispered, "I can't believe you're not really mine." Had I been able to reply I would have added, "I am yours. Nature made a mistake but God put it right."

That summer we were bombarded with visitors, including Evelyn and Bert and, later on, Mum's brother, Bill, and his wife Violet and their two daughters and baby son, Peter, born in 1945. Auntie Vi told me, many years later, that while they stayed with us that summer, they lay in bed in the front room in the wee small hours, listening to Dad walk up and down, up and down, trying to get me to sleep. She went on to say that she had never known a man to have so much patience with a crying baby as Dad had with me. And he never complained. Not once. And when she told him how impressed she was, he just chuckled.

Another example of my father's infinite patience was with feeding. I was a fussy eater, so to get me to eat, he would play "eating" games with me, often while his own meal was getting cold. One was the ever-popular, tried-and-tested "trains" where the spoon, loaded with food was the train and my mouth was the tunnel. "Open wide, here comes the choo-choo-train! Chuff-chuff. Chuff-chuff!" he would say, mouthful after mouthful until the "train" went into the "sidings" to await the next course.

Another game he devised was to invent a family of starving rabbits. They lived at the school and I would have to eat a mouthful for *Mummy Rabbit, Daddy Rabbit,* all the baby rabbits by name, aunts, cousins, *Uncle Tom Cobley-Rabbit* and all, until the meal was in my tummy and not on the plate. Later on my sister and I would get Dad to play this game even when we were feeding ourselves. "What rabbits are at the school today, Daddy? I'll eat a mouthful for them!"

When I was middle-aged, I made a quiet, and I hope not too obvious, point of thanking all my aunts and uncles (individually!) for welcoming us so open-heartedly into their family, for not one of them ever treated us as anything other than "the real thing".

Auntie Vi replied, "Why wouldn't we? We were all so pleased that Anne and Clem had the babies they had waited so long for."

Another of Mum's brothers, she was sure it was the youngest one, Dick, although he could not remember it, brought me a teddy-bear back from Belgium, just before he was de-mobbed. I loved that bear! Indeed I still love this bear! He looks a bit moth-eaten and well-worn now but once upon a time he was a fluffy pink on his tummy and a fluffy brown on his back. He used to sit in my cot with me and one day one of our young visitors decided to "borrow" him. As small as I was, I grabbed his head as his body disappeared through the bars and a tug-of-war ensued. I screamed and Mum came to the rescue but Teddy was mortally wounded; I had his head and the little boy had his body. I was inconsolable but luckily Mum was able to perform emergency surgery and he was soon restored to a whole being again. Some years later I gave him the name "Mister Tumpkins", or "Tumpy" for short, (after my namesake in a story-book who had a bear of that name, so it was not very original) and now he lives wherever I live, with new paws in brown corduroy.

The first soft toy my parents bought for me was a fluffy white dog, with black button eyes, I later called "Snowy". Alas he is no longer fluffy, and no longer "snowy", but I still have him as well, now bald, blind and a dirty grey but another much-loved memento from my early days.

As soon as I could sit up and take notice, Mum took me to our family doctor, Dr Waddington, and asked him if he thought I was deaf. He told her to keep me on her lap facing forward, while he made different noises behind her back. Rather a primitive test but as I seemed to be aware of all the different sounds he made, I was declared to be "a perfectly healthy baby". Mum then asked him if my children were likely to be born deaf. He made a rather extraordinary statement that I am not convinced is correct but nevertheless it put Mum's mind at rest at the time. He claimed that a disability of this nature usually occurred only in every seventh generation, so it was highly unlikely to happen to my children. If this was the case, why were four of Nellie's family deaf, and four not? Anyway she was sent on her way rejoicing, with the words, "Stop worrying, Mrs Oakley. Just enjoy your lovely daughter."

One day during that summer, Mum wheeled me out in the pram, dressed in the finery that Kitty Seymour had given her. A neighbour stopped to peer in and remarked, "Oh she's beautiful, Mrs Oakley. Just like a little princess!" It was not the baby she was admiring as much as the lovely dress and expensive matinee jacket!

By this time, Anne's friend, Edith, had her own little boy, Peter, and often Mum would meet them down at the beach and Peter and I would play in the sand together, while the two old friends chatted and compared baby-notes. Carrie was also destined to have two sons, who were born soon afterwards, and then we would all meet on the beach.

Meanwhile there was still a world outside the Oakley enclave and, co-incidentally in 1946, "The Common Book of Baby and Child Care" by Dr Spock was published, although I am sure Anne did not feel the need to rush out and buy a copy.

Also in 1946, on 5th March, at Fulton, Missouri, USA, Winston Churchill made his by-now-famous "Iron Curtain" speech once again.

The snowiest UK winter of the 20th century occurred in 1947, although no-one suspected that this would be the case for, after two cold snaps, the weather had initially turned unseasonably mild. Then snow started to fall on 22nd January and fell every day, somewhere in the UK, until 17th

March 1947. February became the coldest February on record but while the Midlands and southern England hardly saw the sun that month, parts of north-west Scotland were unusually sunny and western Scotland set itself a precedent by having no precipitation at all in February, wet or white!

There were several snowfalls of more than 60cm and even a record 150cm in Upper Teeside and the Denbighshire Hills. Most of the snow was powdery and all over the UK strong winds soon whipped it up into deep drifts. Some drifts were 5m deep and blocked roads and railways. Whole villages were cut off for days and supplies were dropped to isolated farmhouses by helicopter. Despite this, farmers were unable to reach their livestock and thousands of sheep, ponies and cattle starved to death.

February was bad enough but March was to be even worse beginning with yet more gales and heavy snowstorms. Then on 10th March mild air edged into the south-west bringing rain. The ensuing thaw was rapid and soon vast areas of southern England were under water, for, after weeks of frost, the ground was frozen solid and the rain had nowhere to go. Then melt water from the Welsh mountains poured into the valley of the Severn and Wye. The rivers of the Midlands burst their banks and the dykes of East Anglia gave way. The town of Selby in Yorkshire was almost completely under water and hundreds of homes were flooded in Nottingham.

The cold and snowy weather had ended at last but the misery of the floods continued for months, aggravated by the fuel and food shortages that were still ongoing after the war.

The snowy conditions were an ideal opportunity to take photographs of the landscape, for taking black and white photographs on personal cameras was widespread amongst the general population by now. However, very few people would have been able to afford the "Polaroid Camera" which was invented in 1947. These clever little machines developed the picture inside the camera but without producing a negative.

In Spain, General Franco was still Head of State and, in July 1947, he orchestrated a law which ensured he had this appointment for life. Regrettably, most people would say, Franco enjoyed a long presence in this world and it would be 1975 before Franco died and the country could become a democracy again under a restored Bourbon constitutional monarchy.

Also in July, Auntie Vi gave birth to their final child, another daughter named Andrea. Clem's side of the family had not been as productive as the Martin clan but by now his brother, Jack, and his wife Daisy, had a daughter, Brenda, and three sons, Brian, Christopher and Dennis. Added to his sister Nellie's two boys, this made a grand total of six cousins for me on his side but nine on Mum's.

History was made on 14th October 1947 when the American WW2 flying-ace Chuck (Charles) Yeager broke the sound barrier for the first time in a rocket-powered *Bell X-1* bullet-shaped aircraft. He had named it *"Glamorous Glennis"* after his wife. A few years later, in 1952, he went on to break the air speed record, flying at twice the speed of sound. He is unquestionably the most famous test pilot of all time, and perhaps the most decorated. He is one of a very few enlisted men to have gone on and achieved the rank of general. In 1979, his biography, called *"The Right Stuff"* and written by Tom Wolfe, was published and became an instant bestseller. In 1983, Yeager was immortalised on celluloid when a movie based on the book was premiered. Glennis died in 1990 but Chuck re-married in 2003 and currently lives in California.

But perhaps the single, most important, international event of 1947 happened on 15th August with the independence of India. Since his famous "Salt March" in 1930, Gandhi had travelled around his vast country, seeing for himself how people of all castes lived, including the "Untouchables", and advocating the power of non-violence wherever he went. However, the Muslims in northern India wanted their own State, Pakistan, so when Independence arrived, India and Pakistan went their separate ways. The end of British rule brought to a close the custom of referring to the British monarch as "Emperor (or Empress) of India" but the British left behind eight times more irrigated land, marked improvements in public health and life expectancy, a massive rail transportation system, Common Law, cricket and the English language. Hundreds of millions of people celebrated India's Independence on August 15th and paid tribute to Gandhi's wise and fearless leadership. Less than six months later, on 30th January 1948, Gandhi would be assassinated but India continues to be the world's largest democracy and a member of the British Commonwealth of Nations.

Also independence came for Ceylon and Burma in 1948. That same year the Federation of Malaysia was created under British rule, although it would not become independent until 1957.

On 22nd June 1948, the *MV Empire Windrush* docked at Tilbury in London. On board were 492 West Indian migrants, mostly Jamaican men who were responding to job advertisements, placed by the UK government in their own countries. Britain was desperate for unskilled labour in a burgeoning economy and the *Empire Windrush* migrants were to be just the beginning of a mass exodus of people from the former colonies of the British Empire, for all that anyone needed in order to have the right to settle in the UK, at that time, was to hold a British passport. Many of the immigrants who arrived in the coming decade had fought for the "mother country" and their sense of patriotism and the invitation to work here, combined with the lack of jobs at home, made the

UK seem an attractive, and welcoming, place to live and work.

Alas, not all their hopes and dreams were to be fulfilled, for their arrival brought about a massive change in British society, introducing many different customs, religions, cultures and skin-tones. The indigenous, white population began to feel overwhelmed by the new, black communities springing up in their midst and, as mass immigration gathered momentum, so did racial prejudice, intolerance and violence. Eventually race riots would break out in many cities and legislation would be introduced to make it harder for non-white British passport holders to settle in Britain.

The *Empire Windrush* sank in the Mediterranean Sea in March 1954 but she remains a potent symbol of the birth of multiracialism and multiculturism in Britain. In 1998 an area of open space in Brixton, London, was re-named Windrush Square to commemorate the fiftieth anniversary of the arrival of the first West Indian migrants to Britain's shores.

Now that I was on the scene, Anne and Clem's evenings out together were a thing of the past. Dad joined the local *United Services Club* and would disappear down there on Saturday nights for a pint of beer and a game of snooker. Mum did not object for she was quite happy to sit at home and read a book instead. Indeed she was never much enamoured with "Dad's Club"; she thought it noisy, smoky and she had little in common with the other wives. She was not one for gossip and she could not drink alcohol because it made her varicose veins itch like fury. On the other hand, for his one night a week, it was home from home for Dad; I think it brought back memories of the camaraderie of the Sergeants' Mess.

Naturally Anne could not bear to think that I, like her, would grow up without a sister, so after a couple of years they approached the Local Council to see if they could adopt a baby through them. Due to the baby-boom of post-war years, there were many more children and babies needing homes, so this time they were not turned down, but put on a waiting list for a baby girl. And thus it was, in July 1948, they were told another baby was waiting for them.

CHAPTER TWENTY-THREE

Double Trouble!
(July 1948-September 1951)

Sheila was born in Zachary Merton Hospital, Rustington, on 1st July 1948. She was two weeks old when she came to live with us and going to collect her is my earliest memory. I remember waiting in a garden with a lady wearing a "funny hat" and a long apron and being taken to see some big, white birds. I remember looking through a window and seeing my Mummy and Daddy standing beside a cot in a room full of cots.

I later learned that the "funny hat" was a nurse's cap and the "big, white birds" were geese. I was not allowed into the hospital so a nurse looked after me while Mum and Dad went to the nursery to collect their new daughter. The nurse entertained me by showing me some geese that lived in the grounds and then she guided me to a window where I could look through and see where my Mummy and Daddy where. I expect I was anxious at being separated from them, for I always hated for them to be out of my sight.

A few years later, when I was able to verbalise the memory, Mum was surprised that I could recall the geese for she had forgotten all about them. It seems an odd thing for a hospital to keep in its grounds but I can only think, in these post-war, food-rationed days, that someone was fattening them up for Christmas!

As Sheila was an official adoption, my parents knew very little about her birth-mother except that she had given her the Christian name of "Mary", which was an odd co-incidence as they had already decided to have that as her second name, after Mum's mother, of course, Mary Martin. This was only the first of many co-incidences about her birth that Sheila would discover in later years.

At a young age, we looked reasonably alike for we both had blonde hair, blue eyes, rosy cheeks and chubby bodies but Mum said two differences were immediately apparent. Having got used to "tiny" me, Sheila seemed huge, although her birth-weight was about average at 7lbs. The other obvious difference was that she hardly ever cried; she was a really happy baby, which must have come as a great relief after me.

Although Mum must have been thoroughly absorbed with her new baby (and toddler) she did not miss the news that spread like wild-fire throughout the local community in the middle of August 1948. Nor did she, or anyone of her generation living locally, ever forget it, for a young

145

woman's body was found in an isolated area of Arundel Park. It was that of Joan Woodhouse, a 27 year old librarian from Blackheath in London. She had been sexually assaulted and strangled some ten days before, on 31st July, a bank holiday weekend.

Despite months of investigation, it could never be determined why she had come to Arundel that weekend, for she had told her room-mate that she was going to visit her father in Barnsley.

The man who found the body was a local housepainter who lived in Arundel and knew the Park well. He was known to be a little "odd" and had the habit of following young girls. Although he was strongly suspected of the crime, nothing could be found, in these pre-DNA days, to link him with the murder.

Two years later, Joan's aunts employed private detectives to investigate the case and, in the light of their findings, her father applied for a private warrant against the housepainter. However, after a four day hearing, the magistrate decided that there was not enough evidence to justify a trial. Had it gone ahead, it would have been the first private prosecution for murder for one hundred years. As it was, the case remained officially unsolved, but never forgotten.

When Sheila was about six weeks old, she contracted whooping-cough. Vaccination for this disease was not introduced until 1957 and, in these pre-vaccination days, there were about 100,000 cases each year in the UK, so it was quite a common childhood ailment that is potentially life-threatening. Whether she caught it from me, or one of our many small visitors, I have no idea but one evening she "whooped" and could not get her breath. I do not know what took Mum to her cot at that precise moment; a funny noise she had made or a premonition, but Sheila had stopped breathing and her lips were turning blue. Mum was transfixed to the spot in panic and screamed, "CLEM! CLEM! The baby's stopped breathing!" Dad rushed in and, without a moment's hesitation, he grabbed her by the ankles with one large, loving hand and with the other, slapped her on her upside-down back. She sucked in her breath and began to cry. Never was there a sweeter sound. The crisis was over. Already my baby sister owed our Dad her life. Incidentally after vaccination in 1957, the number of cases per annum dropped to about 2000.

Some months later, I contracted measles so I was isolated in the back bedroom, on my own, while Mum took Sheila into the front bedroom with them. I had the cold-like symptoms for a few days but once the rash appeared, I improved rapidly. However, by this time, Dad had caught the disease so he was isolated with me, in the double bed which was still *in situ* in the back bedroom for visitors. Poor Dad felt very ill, for so-called childhood illnesses often affect adults much worse than

146

children. I was well on the way to recovery, however, and was full of energy. My second childhood memory is being told off by "my hero" for using the bed as a trampoline and rocking him about like a boat on a storm-tossed sea.

He growled," If you don't stop jumping about, you'll have to go in the other room on your own!"

I was very good after that; fed-up but well-behaved! Sheila managed not to get measles this time around as it rarely affects babies under eight months old. Mum also stayed germ-free. A vaccination for measles was not introduced until 1968 but it was not compulsory and there were still 100,000 cases every year until the combined MMR (Mumps, Measles, Rubella) vaccine came in twenty years later.

One day Mum realised it had gone eerily quiet in the garden and put her head out of the back-door to see what I was up to. I was toddling back up the path with a handful of Dad's prize chrysanthemums, just their heads, no stems. "Flowers for you, Mummy," I purred.

"Did you tell her off?" Dad enquired when he came home at lunch-time.

"How could I?" she replied. "She thought she was giving me a present."

"Well there hardly seems any point in growing them if she pulls off all their heads!" he grumbled. He grew cabbages there instead.

As the elder sibling, I feel inclined to take responsibility for the next tale but in truth we do not know who the offender was and, in her old age, Mum was quite unable to remember which of us was at fault. Be that as it may, apparently one of us took to biting the other on her arm. The first time it happened Mum very firmly told the culprit off. Then it happened again, so Mum administered a smack on the hand of the offender with a warning that if she did it again, Mum would bite her back. She did it again, so Mum steeled herself to bite the offender. This would probably constitute child abuse today but it worked! Once the wrongdoer knew how much it hurt, the biting ceased. Recalling the incident, Mum might not have been able to remember which of us was to blame but she did remember that it was one of the hardest things she had ever had to do. I can well believe it because corporal punishment was a form of discipline that was just not used in our family....well not often, but that story comes later.

On 18th June 1949, our cousin Geoffrey Martin (eldest son of Mum's eldest brother, Tom and his wife Myrtle) married Pamela George at *All Saints Church* in Weston-super-Mare, Somerset. A big day for them and a big day for me too because I was invited to be a bridesmaid, via Mum of course! I wore a short pink "party-dress", with a garland of artificial flowers in my hair and carried a posy. I can only guess how proud Mum and Dad felt that day.

Geoff had met Pam when he was stationed at RAF Locking, near Weston, while doing his *National Service*. This had been introduced after the war to replace conscription and was formalized as a peacetime measure from 1st January 1949. All young men between 17 and 21 years of age were then required to serve in the Armed Forces for 18 months and to remain on the reserve list for four years, although the service could be postponed if they were serving a Government-approved apprenticeship. It was compulsory until 31st December 1960, when *National Service* was brought to an end. Some people would argue that "youth" has been going downhill ever since!

The "Martin contingent", plus a few Lettis's and Oakley's, travelled down to Bristol by train on the Friday before the wedding and were accommodated overnight by members of Pam's family. Then, as Pam and Geoff set off on their honeymoon to Jersey, via another train and a boat from Southampton, Geoff's family returned to Littlehampton. Quite an undertaking with a baby, a small child and wedding finery but cars were still something of a luxury for the average working-man.

Dad must have wished heartily that they owned their own transport, however, when the Oakley family very nearly missed catching the train taking them to Bristol. They had left home in a rush as usual, for the Oakleys were seldom on time! Mum was pushing Sheila in the push-chair, me trotting along at the side and Dad carrying a case, when Mum suddenly remembered I was not wearing any knickers! She had left them off in case I had "an accident" at the last minute and had then forgotten all about them. Poor Dad was duly despatched back home to retrieve the missing item and then had to run, still carrying the case, all the way to the railway station; no mean feat as it was about 1½ miles away.

Pam and Geoff settled in the Littlehampton area and celebrated their Diamond Wedding Anniversary in 2009.

The wedding was probably the last time my parents made a long journey by train, because Sheila and I think it was about this time that Dad must have bought his first car, a second-hand *Austin Seven*. Perhaps the incident of rushing for the train to Bristol had finally persuaded him life would be an awful lot easier if he was to join the ranks of car-owners. Be that as it may, obviously he was keen to show off his new purchase and took us all out for a drive that Sunday. This was the beginning of a family tradition to go out for a "run" in the car every Sunday afternoon. Sometimes we would go bluebell-picking in Barlavington Woods, or pick primroses in Slindon Forest, or walk to the top of *The Trundle*, set high on the South Downs, just above Goodwood Racecourse. The trips were very varied and when we were a little older we would often end up in a country pub' where we would all sit in the garden, Dad drinking his "pint", Mum sipping her fruit-juice and us slurping our orange squash and munching our crisps. No breathalyser tests back then and it was still not illegal to pick wild flowers!

This first Sunday Mum had cause to remember very well and often repeated the story. We went in a big circle through Amberley and Pulborough, returning to Arundel, and then Littlehampton, via Bury Hill. Bury Hill is probably one of the steepest hills in West Sussex, and one of the longest. In those days it was narrow and winding, as well as being steep, and for some unaccountable reason, Dad stalled the engine on the hill. What a good job his "goons" could not see him! Anyone who can drive, knows there is no real danger in this, especially in those days when there was much less traffic on the roads, but Mum could not drive and she was already nervous of their new acquisition. Unfortunately, Dad rolled back a bit before he brought the car under control and thus she was terrified. From then on, whenever we came up Bury Hill, which was frequently, she would lean forward in her seat, grip the dashboard and literally urge the car forward. I can hear Dad now, grumbling under his breath to her, "Will you stop that, Anne!" I think if she could have got out and walked up the hill, she would have done so! It did not matter how many decades passed, or how many cars he had, she remained the same whenever Dad drove up that hill.

We were probably one of the first working-class families in our street, possibly in the town, to own a car and this makes us sound very affluent. We were not. Dad earned only a modest wage at the school but he did manage to provide us with most of our vegetables, eggs from the chickens and meat from the rabbits. It was around this time that he took his "self-sufficiency" to even new heights by buying an incubator in order to rear his own hens. He had to shine a light through every egg to see if it was fertilized, and then placed it in this metal box-like structure, which was connected to the electricity supply in our front room. I can remember peering through the glass-door of the incubator when the chicks were pecking their way out of their shells, and watching with fascination as these featherless, wet creatures emerged. As they dried off in the gentle heat, they moved about and fell an inch or two into the bottom of the incubator. It was amazing to see these "aliens" gradually transform into fluffy, yellow chicks. As they got bigger, they were transferred into one of our coal-bunkers which had been turned into a nursery. However, I do not think the enterprise can have been all that successful because, after a few years, Dad sold the incubator and went back to buying-in laying hens.

Mum also did her bit to stretch the family finances. She was a good money-manager and an excellent cook; I never knew her to buy a shop-made-cake and she made all our pies, puddings, pickles and jam, even salad cream. She also made our ginger-beer which was delicious. Apart from their mortgage, they never bought anything on hire-purchase; everything they had, including the cars, they saved up for and paid cash. They did not have a bank account; in fact they never had a bank account, and put their modest savings into the Post Office, as most working people did back then.

Another economy measure most housewives carried out in those days, my mother included, was to "sides-to-middle" single sheets. Single sheets wear out in the middle, thus, when they become thin, she would cut down the centre and then sew it back together again, sides-to-middle, and neaten the newly-cut, raw edges. She would make pillow-cases out of the double sheets. For all these domestic sewing tasks, she would use the sewing-machine Dad had bought her as a wedding present in 1930. It was a hand-wheel *Frister Rossman* model. Sheila owns it now and it is still in use to this day. Not that Sheila uses it very often. Like our mother, my sister has never been much of a needlewoman! However Mum did make our curtains back then and even claimed to have made a few dresses for us when we were little.

Another thing Sheila has in common with Mum is a love/hate relationship with another kind of needle: the knitting needle. When we were aged about 3 and 5 years Mum decided to make us matching cardigans in a blue, tweedy-kind of wool with coloured flecks. She started off in a burst of enthusiasm but one "back" and half of one "front" later, she gave up and stuffed the unfinished project in a cupboard. A few years on, she came across the wool, unpicked what she had done and started to re-knit one larger cardigan. That too ended up, unfinished, in the cupboard. Twenty years later, when Sheila had her boys, out came the wool again, to make a sweater for one of them. Needless to say it was never completed and by this time the wool and her knitting was a family joke. After she died, I found the would-be sweater, still with knitting needles attached and all the wool. If Vicky (Sheila's grand-daughter) had been born at that time, I would have finished it; instead it was donated to a charity shop, just as it was, with very fond memories, a wry chuckle or two, and a few tears.

Incidentally the only knitted article I can recall my sister actually completing was a sweater, about four inches long, for a teddy-bear! This was not so many years ago and the project was undertaken while I was staying with her on holiday. For some reason I can no longer remember, she wanted to clothe this nude bear so I undertook to knit a pair of trousers while she did the top. Even then I had to sew it up!

In May 1950, Mao and communism emerged victorious from the civil war in mainland China and re-named the country the *People's Republic of China*. All that was left for the opposing forces was Taiwan, Penghu, Kinmen, Matsu and several outlying Fujianese islands. They were to come under the jurisdiction of the separate *Republic of China*. To this day no armistice or peace treaty has been signed but the two sides have close economic ties.

"Emperor" Pu Yi of Manchuria had been deposed (once again) in 1945, when the Japanese were defeated. He was captured by the Soviets and detained in Russia as a "war criminal", albeit in relative comfort. When Mao won the civil war, he was returned to China and would undergo nine years of "rehabilitation", under Chairman Mao's administration, until he was declared to be a "remoulded man". With Party approval, he spent the last few years of his life working in the archives of the *"China People's Political and Consultative Committee"* and talking to survivors of his days in the "Forbidden City". With co-writer Li Wenda, his book *"From Emperor to Citizen"* was published in 1964. He died in 1967, aged 61 years, from cancer, declaring his proudest moment to have been in 1962 when he became a full citizen with voter's rights. In 1987, his extraordinary life was made into a film called, appropriately enough, *"The Last Emperor"*, parts of which were actually filmed in the "Forbidden City".

On 25th June 1950 another war broke out, the Korean War. It started as a civil war in a dispute over the border the victors of the Second World War had created along the 38th parallel, to divide North and South Korea. However the "Super Powers" became involved and the whole thing escalated, with the Soviet Union and China supporting North Korea, and America and its allies sending troops to South Korea. The hostilities lasted until a ceasefire agreement was reached on 27th July 1953 and, despite a tremendous loss of life on both sides, it ended with nothing resolved and a border stalemate.

1950 also saw the birth of the infamous "McCarthyism" in America, named after the US Senator, Joseph McCarthy, who is credited, or discredited, with starting the whole thing. It was paranoia against communism, and alleged communist sympathisers, carried to extraordinary lengths and resulted in the loss of employment, destruction of careers and even imprisonment for many American citizens. Although the phenomenon bears McCarthy's name, the crusade was taken up with unwarranted fanaticism by the Director of the Federal Bureau of Investigation, J. Edgar Hoover. At the time he was one of the nation's most fervent anti-communists and one of its most powerful citizens. The appalling witch-hunt did not cease until the late 1950's.

The year also saw two more famous "births"; the first modern credit card was introduced and the "Peanuts" cartoon strip saw the light of day.

Travelling by road in our new family car in 1950 did not prevent another knickerless journey, although on this occasion it was Sheila's turn to go out inadequately dressed. We were on our way to Guildford but this time Dad refused point-blank to turn back. Instead he stopped at Arundel and Mum popped into *Herrington's the Drapers* in "The Square" to buy a new pair. Thus, with modesty restored, Mum permitted us to continue on our way.

On our return trips from Guildford, Mum would often get us ready for bed before we left. So washed, teeth brushed and dressed in our pyjamas, we would curl up on the back seat of the car, traversing the miles fast asleep. No seat belts in the early fifties! Indeed it would be 1983 before legislation was introduced making compulsory the wearing of front seat belts and 1989 before they had to be worn by children in the back seats. The pyjamas ensured that Dad could carry us into bed when we got home, without us even having to wake up. As we became older, and larger, the back seat did not accommodate us so readily and I well remember the squabbles we had as we fought to share the limited space! We also got too big for Dad to carry us and I hated having to wake up and walk indoors half asleep!

The acquisition of the car, and the easy access it afforded to friends and relatives, meant that friendships with Dad's cousins, the "Standage's" had been cemented. Most of them lived in the Guildford area. Edwin Standage (Uncle Ted to us, although strictly speaking he was a second-cousin and not an "uncle") had even asked Dad to go into partnership with him in his carpentry/building business. Mum was very keen for him to do it but Dad was a steady plodder, not one to take chances, not very ambitious, nor was he materialistic, so after a lot of thought he decided he would rather stay in his safe, secure, little world at the school. In no way is this meant as a criticism of him; he might never have set the world on fire …. but he would have been the first there to put out the flames.

"Uncle" Ted had married "Auntie" Phyllis and they had three children; the eldest, Terry, was a little older than us, about twelve years old in 1950. Ivan was next, aged six, and Gwendoline about three years old, to our ages four and two years. As well as day trips to Guildford, we often stayed with Uncle Ted and Auntie Phyllis and they in turn often stayed with us.

Evelyn Dodson, the lady who had written to Mum and Dad about me, was Uncle Ted's eldest sister and, as we know, had a daughter, Joan, who was considerably older than we were. Neither of us can remember "Auntie" Evelyn, for she died in 1950 at a fairly early age. His sister, Gladys, must also have died because we never knew her at all. His next sister, Margaret, had never married but his sisters, Dora and Irene, had "tied the knot" and both of them had produced two children. Irene's family did not live in Guildford but Dora's two boys, Clive and Rodney, were about our age and lived locally, so it was with them and the younger members of Uncle Ted's "brood" that we forged special friendships that last to this day.

Tragedy was to strike however. Auntie Phyllis became ill with cancer and, over a number of months, became increasingly frail. I can remember going to see her shortly before she died and Mum warning me to be very quiet *"because Auntie Phyllis is not very well"* as we climbed the stairs. I can even remember seeing her lying in bed, very pale and with her hair fanned out on the pillow. According to Mum, she was a lovely lady; always so gracious and appreciative of our visits, even though she must have felt dreadful. Mum was particularly upset, therefore, at her passing, for she was extremely fond of her. After every holiday with one another, they would exchange gifts and Mum treasured a blue vase and a painting of a bluebell wood that Phyllis had given her. The painting was especially poignant because it reminded her of a walk they used to take together, not far from their Guildford home.

When she died in December 1950, their eldest son, Terry, was old enough to remain with his father but, until Uncle Ted could make permanent arrangements for their care, the younger two, Ivan and Gwendoline, went to stay with his sister Dora, husband Reg, and their two boys, Clive and Rodney. Then, when the summer holidays came, they came to stay with us for a few months. Thus it was that the "favour was returned in kind", for Uncle Ted's parents, Rosina and Edwin Standage, had taken in Dad's little brother, Jack, and his baby sister, Elsie, when their mother died in 1911.

So from having no children at the beginning of 1946, in the summer of 1951 Mum and Dad suddenly found they had care of four youngsters under the age of seven years. I think they were in their element! We were all blue-eyed blondes in those days and when Mum went out she put Sheila and Gwendoline at each end of the pram and Ivan and I would hold onto the handles at either side of her. One day an elderly lady walked by, shook her head in disbelief and commented, "You poor, poor woman!" Mum chuckled over this incident all her days.

I think Uncle Ted and Terry must have come down every weekend to see the younger two children but, in September, school beckoned. Uncle Ted found a neighbour to look after the children when they came home from school and so Ivan and Gwendoline returned home. But there was always a special link between the two families and we were destined to spend many happy holidays together. After a year or so, Uncle Ted re-married and thus the children had a step-mother and we had a new aunt, Kathleen, but neither Mum nor Dad was ever as fond of Kathleen as they were of Phyllis. She was just a very special lady.

CHAPTER TWENTY-FOUR

Challenges and Change
(October 1951-1953)

On 8th October 1951 Dad celebrated his 50th birthday. What changes he had already witnessed in his lifetime! To name but a few, cars were now commonplace on tarmacadam roads, although a few deliveries were still made by horse and cart in some areas and in our locality the "rag and bone man" made his collections using this form of transport; aeroplanes were regularly seen in the sky; connections to mains water and electricity were now possible to all houses, except those in very remote areas and some of the smaller islands, and gas and mains drainage were available to most of the population. Advances in technology, engineering, science and medicine were unprecedented and still ongoing. The National Health Service (NHS) had been introduced and, with a little luck and good management, the working man could afford to buy his own property and his own transport. He could look forward to being protected by the recent birth of the Welfare State with its system of sickness, unemployment and retirement benefits, now among the best in the world. Clem was not a man for looking back; he lived very much in the present and the future but I wonder if he did find a few moments to pause and ponder the amazing half century (including two world wars) through which he had lived.

Less than three weeks after Dad's birthday, on 25th October 1951, Winston Churchill defeated Clement Attlee, to become Prime Minister of Britain again. However, his narrow success in the general election was totally eclipsed by the hugely successful "Festival of Britain", instigated by Attlee's Labour Government. It had been conceived *"to demonstrate to the world the recovery of the United Kingdom from the effects of war in the moral, cultural, spiritual and material fields."* It also celebrated the centenary of the Great Exhibition of 1851. It was held on the south bank of the River Thames, near Waterloo, and through it Britain discovered it could still produce young designers in all fields of human endeavour. It was a tremendous boost for the nation after the austerity of the war years, and the 8.5 million people who visited the festival before it closed in September were exhilarated by the achievements of which the country showed itself still capable. With much of London still in ruins from the bombing, and therefore in urgent need of redevelopment, the layout was intended as a permanent showcase of new principles of urban design, such as multiple levels of buildings, elevated walkways and avoidance of a street grid. However all the buildings and exhibits, except the Royal

Festival Hall, were destroyed by the incoming Churchillian Conservative Government who thought them "too socialist" for their taste. Battersea Park Funfair and a public housing estate at Poplar were also built as part of the festival but they were allowed to stay and are still in existence to this day.

The Churchill Government must have been in "demolishing mode" for one of the first things they did was to repeal the "National Registration Act", thus abolishing the need to carry identity cards. The Act had been introduced as a war-time measure but had become increasingly unpopular in peace-time.

At some stage in 1951 the first colour television set was invented but, as with all these new devices, it would be some years before it became standard in people's homes. Indeed black and white TV's were still relatively rare at this time.

Also in 1951, zebras started to proliferate on the streets of Britain. Not the animal kind, but black and white striped pedestrian crossings. As well as the distinctive road markings, black and white striped poles with a flashing amber globe on top are placed near the crossings. These are called Belisha beacons, after the Minister of Transport, Leslie Hore-Belisha, who had first introduced them to the UK in 1934. Initially these beacons, and a row of studs, were all that marked a pedestrian crossing, but blue and yellow stripes were added for visibility in 1949, becoming black and white in 1951. Nowadays the UK can also rejoice in tiger, pelican, puffin, toucan and Pegasus crossings, but they all began with the dear old zebra in 1951.

1951 was a big year for me, for I was five years old and it was time for me to go to school. However, I always hated to be parted from my mother. When we went to *Woolworth's*, for example, and I wanted to look at the toys, I would not go to that counter unless she came with me. But inevitably my big day had to come.

A new infant and secondary school had been built not far from our house, so we did not have far to walk. I cried and cried when Mum left me so, when break-time came, I walked straight through the gate and ran back home! This does not say a lot for play-ground security! Of course Mum had to take me back. Every day that first week she took me to school and every day I found a way to "escape". Then the Headmistress, Miss Judney, a wise and intuitive lady, thought up a ploy to make me stay. I was offered "the most important job in the school"; she claimed that she needed someone to greet all the visitors and then escort them to her office. But to do the "job" properly, I had to promise to stay put. It worked. I think I can say, from that day, I never looked back!

Part of the new school complex included a children's health clinic. Mum had taken us there as babies, for as well as regular check-ups by a nurse, this was where she obtained the free orange juice and "cod liver oil and malt" that was offered to all children under school age. In fact we had the cod liver oil and malt for most of our childhood but Mum may well have paid for it once the "freebies" ended because we LOVED it! It came in large brown jars and was the consistency of treacle. It was delicious and we really looked forward to our dessertspoonful every day.

The clinic also organised the regular check-ups we had once we started school. Every year the little girls would be lined up in their vest and knickers and examined by a school-nurse. Our height and weight would be recorded, I suppose they took note of any skin problems or unusual bruising, and finally our hair would be examined for nit infestation. The boys would have their own examination separately.

A free school dentist was attached to the clinic too. Mum took me to see him soon after I started school but I took fright as soon as I walked into the surgery. I did not want to sit in the funny chair, or open my mouth for this strange man in a long white coat. Of course I started to cry; this seems to be the one thing I was very good at in my early years!
"I think it would be a good idea if you waited outside, Mrs Oakley," the dentist suggested. In these days a working-class housewife would be in the habit of obeying a diktat from a professional with a posh voice, so she reluctantly left the room.

Of course, as soon as she left, the whimpering became a heart-rending sob. He smacked me. My sobs became a wail and Mum rushed back into the room, full of concern.
"He hit me, Mummy!" I howled.
"She was hysterical!" the dentist retorted. It took a lot for my mother to show anger, for she was the very epitome of patience, but this time she was like a lioness protecting her cub.
"How dare you hit my daughter!" she raged. "You've no business being a school dentist if this is the way you treat frightened children! I would sooner pay than bring either of my children to see you again!" And we stormed out of the surgery.
"When I grow up, Mummy, I'm going to become a policewoman and come back and arrest that horrible man!" I declared, not realising then that I would never achieve the height requirement!

Thus both my sister and I attended Mr Horsfield's practice and had nothing to do with the school dental service. I don't know if it was free treatment back then but it certainly came under the NHS banner eventually, which was just as well as I needed a lot of dental work in my teens and twenties. Mr Horsfield was the complete opposite of the "horrible" school dentist. He was geared for frightened children (and adults!) for on the little "table" in front of the chair, were things to distract the nervous patient, like a nodding turtle for example and a little Bunsen-burner contraption with a tiny frying-pan on top. Well it looked like a frying-pan to my five-year old eyes! He went to a great deal of trouble to restore my confidence and I shall be forever grateful for his kindness and understanding.

One day Mum picked me up from school, with Sheila in the push-chair, and as we walked along I asked, "Mummy, what does "adopted" mean?" I can imagine her brain racing at a thousand knots as she thought, "This is it! The moment of truth!"

"Why do you want to know that?" she replied, playing for time and also probably wondering if some small child had "*let the cat out of the bag*", so to speak.

"It was in a story our teacher was reading to us. This little boy had been adopted."

"Well", she began, no doubt breathing a sigh of relief, "It means he was very special because his mummy and his daddy had chosen him to be their little boy. You and Sheila are very special too because Daddy and I chose both of you, out of all the little babies in the whole wide world."

"REALLY? Really and truly? We're special because we are adopted too? I can't wait to tell all my friends tomorrow that I'm special like the boy in the story!"

And thus it was that we learned that we were adopted. In adult years I realised that I had chosen my moment to be told but I felt Sheila had been denied that privilege and I often wondered if it had increased her insecurities.

Mum passed her love of reading on to us from an early age, by reading us a story every night, but I could not wait to be able to read for myself. I would like to report that I had been weaned on Beatrix Potter's "*Peter Rabbit*", or A.A. Milne's "*Winnie the Pooh*" and the characters of "*100 Acre Wood*" but in truth I fell in love with Enid Blyton's "*Noddy*" and all his chums in "*Toyland*". "*Noddy*" was first published in 1949 and I spent all my Christmas and birthday money on his books. After "*Noddy*" I followed the adventures of "*The Famous Five*" and then "*The Secret Seven*" but my hero, or heroine, was Susan Coolidge's *Katy* from "*What Katy Did*" and "*What Katy Did Next*". How I wanted to emulate Katy's patience and stoicism....but not to the extent of falling off a swing and breaking my back!

By the early 1950's, something of a tradition had already been established in the family. Every year, on one Sunday in August, the various "Guildford families" and the "Oakley's", with assorted friends and sundry relatives, would meet at Goodwood for what became known as "The Family Picnic".

The place where we gathered was a large, grassy car-park, like a big field. It was completely flat, despite being on top of the South Downs, and surrounded by woodland. In those early days, apart from us, it was relatively vehicle and family free. We parked our cars around the edge of the big open space, in the shelter of the trees. As the years went by, the picnic paraphernalia became more sophisticated but back then it was just a blanket to sit on, sandwiches and a fruit cake to eat, and a paraffin stove to boil water for the necessary "cuppa".

After our picnic lunch, while the mums sat and chatted and caught up on family news, the men organised themselves into two teams for a friendly, but competitive, cricket match. Uncle Ted headed one team and Dad the other and they took turns to select their team members, carefully choosing the hardest hitters first. All the children were included and from an early age I showed my complete lack of sporting talent. Year after year, I was always the last to be chosen and I never really forgave my Dad for leaving me on the sidelines while my sister and my peers disappeared into teams.

Still one year Dad was "punished" for ignoring me! He was fielding (at silly mid-off, no doubt) and ran backwards to catch a wayward ball.
"I've got it! I've got it!" he screamed in delight as the ball fell into his outstretched hands and he fell straight into a rubbish-bin. He was left with his head, legs and upper body in the air and his *derriere* firmly wedged in with the trash! Amid much laughter, the other men had to haul him free but he still had hold of the ball!

After the match we would all be rewarded with a frozen delicacy from the ice-cream van that visited during the afternoon. The losing captain had to pay for the treats and my memory seems to recall that this was always Dad! One day we were queuing up with all the other children, while we made our choice as to what to have, and the man in the van commented, "Treating all your grand-children then, guv'nor?" Dad just chuckled in his usual fashion but until that moment I had not appreciated that our parents were considerably older than most other mums and dads.

There was always time for the children to play hide-and-seek in the woods or climb the trees. For some reason my cousin Ivan was my special pal and one year he encouraged me to climb higher and higher.
"It's all right," he said, "I'll get you down again!" And I am sure he would have done so but I had completely lost my nerve.
"No! No!" I quivered, "Please go and get Dad". So poor old Dad had to leave his chums, and tales of work and football or whatever it is that men talk about, and come to my rescue. He always wore a suit to these "do's", never being one for slacks or casual clothes, so climbing a tree in his dress trousers and best shoes cannot have been easy. Perhaps this was why he was grumbling away as he made his journey through the branches, "Why did you climb so high if you couldn't get down again?" Then as we reached the safety of the woodland floor he threatened, "If you do it again, you'll have to stay up there!" My lack of sporting talent obviously included heights and climbing.

Of course, not every year was sunny but without universal 'phones it was difficult to make last-minute adjustments to the plans, so the stalwarts turned up, rain or shine, and hoped for the best. But one year the weather was so bad that the whole picnic de-camped to our house. The children's lower limbs were so muddy that each of us had to sit on the draining-board and have our feet washed off in the kitchen sink.

The picnic days ended with the families setting off from Goodwood in a convoy, wending its way to a nearby hostelry where we would all have "one for the road", of various brew, before we dispersed back to our respective homes. The tradition of a "Family Picnic" was carried on for decades, even though the venue had to be changed eventually as Goodwood became more accessible to the increased number of car-owners, and thus too popular with other families, for the obligatory family cricket match to take place in safety.

Another tradition well established by this time was our annual birthday parties. Because mine took place in February, in later years Dad hired the top floor of "his" (United Services) Club. There was plenty of room for my chums to run around and many spare chairs to set up games such as *"Pass the Parcel"* or *"Musical Chairs"*.

Sheila's birthday was in the summer so we always had her party in the garden. I do not remember it ever raining! The jellies, blancmange and ice-cream, along with sundry sandwiches and, of course, the cake complete with the requisite number of candles, were set up on trestle tables borrowed from Dorset House School and we all sat around the feast on benches, also borrowed from the school. Although the venue for my party seemed more upmarket, I always envied Sheila her *al fresco* celebrations.

Often my birthday present would be combined with my Christmas gift; a new bicycle, for example, would be too expensive for one celebration but I could have it as a joint gift. Hence I had a new bike but Sheila preferred to have separate presents and opted for a second-hand one. As always, our parents attempted to treat us fairly.

When we were younger, Dad would often make our gifts. One Christmas he made us identical little cots for our dolls and Mum sewed little sheets, pillows, blankets and bedspreads. He painted the cots in a duck-egg blue colour and stuck transfers of ducks and teddy bears on the ends. Another time he made a blackboard and easel so we could play *"Schools"* , with me being the teacher, naturally! Sheila can remember being given a dolls' house one year. It was made out of match-boxes by a friend of our Uncle Jack (Dad's brother).

As we became older, Sheila favoured tom-boy toys like a cowboy outfit and a train set. I stuck with the more "girly" gifts like a dolls' pram but neither of us was greatly enamoured with dolls. I always preferred soft toys and at one time I lined up fifteen of them between my pillow and

159

the sheet to sleep with me. It was a wonder I was not forced to sleep on the floor!

In 1952 Britain exploded its first atomic bomb. Other countries had already achieved this but, at this time, Britain did at least lead the world in harnessing atomic energy for peaceful purposes by beginning to build the first nuclear power stations.

Britain also led the world in aircraft development in 1952. Since the end of the war, passengers now regularly flew in piston-engined aeroplanes across the Atlantic Ocean and to other previously distant countries like Africa and Australia. But, on 2nd May 1952, the world's first jetliner took off from London to Johannesburg. The British *de Havilland Comet* was an immediate success. It flew at 35000 feet where the air was less turbulent, so it was a much smoother and faster journey. New York was now only twelve hours away, where the trip took eighteen hours on a conventional aircraft. Airlines were soon beating a path to the *de Havilland* factory door to order a *Comet*.

The British lead in jet aircraft design seemed insurmountable but, after only a year of commercial service, *Comets* started to fall out of the sky. Extensive investigation over many months revealed a devastating design flaw - metal fatigue. The jet was redesigned and re-entered service in 1958 but its reputation was forever damaged. Airlines opted instead for the new American-built *Boeing* and *Douglas DC-8* jets. Even though the *Comet* had become the first jet airliner to fly non-stop between London and New York, Britain's lead in commercial aviation was lost, never again to be regained. But jet travel, as a normal mode of transport financially accessible to all, was now not only on the tarmac but cleared for take-off.

In February of 1952, King George VI had died. The coronation of the heir to the throne, his daughter, Queen Elizabeth II, took place on 2nd June 1953 in Westminster Abbey. For this auspicious occasion Mum and Dad decided to buy a television set. Not a newly-invented colour one but a very modest black and white version. Once again we must have been among the first of the families in our street to own a television because I can remember our front room being full of neighbours and friends who wanted to witness the ceremony. It seemed to go on for hours and for my sister and me it was incredibly tedious! We kept running in and out of the room, disturbing the ambience, and I can remember Mum encouraging me to sit down and "watch history in the making". Alas I was not impressed.

The new television did give us access to Children's TV however and we were much more enthralled by the antics of *Andy Pandy,* followed by *Bill and Ben the Flowerpot Men* and their sidekick, *Little Weed!*

(Pronounced *Weeeeeed!*)   But television ownership did not mean forsaking the radio, for it was on for most of the day, and my sister and I have many happy memories of listening to programmes such as *"Sing Something Simple"*, *"Music While you Work"*, *"Workers' Playtime"*, and *"Friday Night is Music Night"*.   Mum was not much enamoured with the (later) comedy programmes, like *"Hancock's Half Hour"*, *"The Navy Lark"*, and *"The Clitheroe Kid"*, thinking them to be rather silly, but in this she was out of step with the rest of the country as most of the population loved them!

Our prime-time listening , however, was on Sunday lunch-times as we tucked into our roast lamb with all the trimmings, followed by apple pie and custard!   First we would tune into *"Two Way Family Favourites"*, which played record requests to link families in the UK with loved ones in the British forces stationed overseas, particularly West Germany.   Then it would be *"Billy Cotton's Band Show"*, with his distinctive *"Wakey! Wakey!"* greeting, followed by *"Educating Archie"*, by which time Mum was probably doing the washing-up so she did not have to suffer the full force of the "silly" humour!

All meals in our house were taken seated around a dining-table, which was properly laid with a cloth, cutlery and condiments.   This was the only chore we were ever asked to do, to lay the table!   No balancing a plate on our laps for us!   And we had to maintain proper table manners and ask permission to leave the table.   But this was not unusual; I think most families then had this discipline, even if they were fairly easy-going in other respects.

However, one thing was perhaps a little unusual for a working-class family.   At tea-times we never had milk-bottles placed on the table!   The milk was always decanted into a jug before it was put on display, for bottles on tables were anathema to our mother!   This was probably a habit she had retained from her days in domestic service.

Strange apparitions appeared on the streets of Britain in the early 1950's.   They had first been spotted in London but rapidly spread throughout the land.   In 1953 a newspaper headline gave a name to these strange phenomena and a new word entered the language:- *Teddy Boy.*

Young people's disposable income had increased in the boom of the post-war years and some of them wanted to spend their spare cash on looking different from their parents.   They took to wearing clothes inspired from the Edwardian era (hence *Teddy)*: long drape jackets with velvet collars and lapels: high-waisted "drainpipe" trousers, often showing brightly-coloured socks above their large, crepe-soled, suede shoes (known as "brothel creepers"): a narrow "Slim Jim" tie on a white shirt with a high-necked collar and a brocade waistcoat.   They sported long side-burns and their hairstyles too were distinctive with a strongly-moulded, greased-up quiff at the front and cut into a "duck's ass" at the back.

The *Teddy Boys* were the first youth group in England to identify themselves as "teenagers", thus helping to create a whole new market aimed solely at this age-group. *Teddy Boys* made it acceptable for young people to dress purely for show, instead of having clothes only for work, or school, or Sunday best. They were the peacocks of the post-war years but, like all fashion items, they would not last.

Also in 1953, arguably the biggest discovery of the 20th century was unveiled, although it probably meant little at the time to anyone not in the scientific field; Francis Crick and James Watson discovered the double helix of DNA. This was to be just the beginning of unravelling the remarkable mysteries of genes in general and the human species in particular.

This was also the year New Zealand's Edmund Hilary and Nepal's Tenzing Norgay conquered Mount Everest. They were the first men ever to reach the summit.

Russia's leader, Joseph Stalin, died in 1953. After a brief power struggle, Nikita Khrushchev succeeded him and just three years later Khrushchev would denounce the "cult of personality" that had surrounded Stalin. He also accused the former leader of committing crimes against the populace during the so-called "Great Purges". The process of "De-Stalinization" had begun.

I was seven years old in 1953 and going to school, once I had been persuaded to stay, had worked wonders for my confidence. I was no longer frightened to let my mother out of my sight and I was anxious to spread my wings a little. I had a brief flirtation with ballet lessons but it was soon obvious I had as little talent for dance as I had for sport. I decided I would like to become a "Brownie" instead. However Mum was not sure I would last any longer with the Girl Guide Movement than I had with the ballet school and, having spent her hard-earned money on a tutu, a leotard and ballet shoes, she refused to buy the Brownie uniform until I was sure I wanted to stay. She need not have worried. I loved Brownies. I had found my niche.

1953 was also the year I moved onto "primary education" at Mum's old school, the flint-stone building in East Street, and Sheila started her formal education at "Elm Grove Infants"; at least she did not try to run away even if she did wet her knickers on the first day! At the same time as Sheila went to school, Mum began working there. Auntie Myrtle (her brother Tom's wife) was already employed there in the school kitchens and, when a vacancy occurred, she recommended Mum for the position. It was hard work in those days, as there were relatively few labour saving devices, but the extra money was useful and the hours fitted in nicely with school-hours. It meant, of course, that we had to have "school meals" but Mum cooked in the evening for Dad so we ended up with two dinners!

In those days all the schools provided a two-course, cooked lunch at very modest, subsidised rates. Free school milk was also standard. It came in small one-third-of-a-pint bottles which invariably froze solid in winter and forced the silver top off the bottle. We used to try and thaw them on top of the radiators. No cast iron wood-burning stoves for us! All public buildings now had central heating but it would be several decades before most home-owners would contemplate installing this luxury.

After Mum had finished her stint in the kitchens, she would wait and pick us up from the school-gates and one day Mum noticed Sheila was dragging her leg.

"What's wrong with your leg?" she asked.

"Nothing!" came the reply.

Despite this reassurance, Mum thought it wise to check with Dr Waddington. To her horror she learned that Sheila had contracted polio. Luckily relatively mildly, and only in her right leg, but it would always be thinner, weaker and slightly shorter than the other one. Over the years it has not given her any real trouble but as she goes into old age, the spectre of PPS (Post-Polio Syndrome) hangs over her.

95% of polio' victims have only mild 'flu-like symptoms and it is thought that exposure to this virus in early life gives life-long immunity. If, however, the poliovirus invades the central nervous system, it can destroy or damage the nerve cells and cause anything from mild paralysis to death. Young children are more vulnerable to the virus although adults can also be affected.

Poliomyelitis is an infectious disease which is believed to have been around for thousands of years but for some reason epidemics of it only started to occur in the late 19th century. The largest epidemic in the UK was in 1950, affecting 8000 people, but epidemics continued to bubble up throughout the 1950's and early 1960's until the oral vaccine was introduced.

The first polio vaccine had been created in 1952 but it used a live virus and could thus actually cause the illness it was trying to cure. It would be 1962 before a vaccine was developed using an inactivated form of the virus and then this was offered to all children on a sugar lump.

Sheila was dreadfully unlucky to have succumbed to the disease but, of course, she was not the only child to suffer. One of the other mothers, waiting at the school gates to collect her child, confirmed her son had also been a victim.

Over the following months, the two mothers compared notes and both said they had noticed a change in their child's behaviour. They had been happy, easy to manage children; now they seemed fractious, difficult and demanding. I do not know if the virus had somehow affected the brain, or whether the parents over-compensated out of misplaced guilt, or even if it was just a co-incidence, but Mum always felt the virus was the catalyst. From then on our sweet-tempered five-year old became a miniature *Jekyll and Hyde*. She was a charming *Jekyll* all the time she was getting her own way but a little monster when she was not. The *Hyde* side of her character was only on view to the immediate family however; she was always absolutely delightful to strangers and visitors and therefore most people had no idea how difficult and disruptive she could be. Our parents had never experienced such a wilful temperament and I do not think they knew what to do. So they adopted the path of least resistance; they gave in to her and just hoped her sunny disposition would return as suddenly as it had disappeared.

CHAPTER TWENTY-FIVE

Family and Friendships
(1953-1955)

By the time Sheila started school in 1953, many family traditions had already been established, apart from birthday parties and the family picnics, and, of course, a lot of these traditions were related to Christmas. There were very few artificial decorations then so we always had a real tree, with roots, which was adorned with huge "fairy" lights in the shape of stars, glass baubles, lots of tinsel and a fairy on the topmost bough. It was placed in all its splendour in the front sitting-room and Mum tied tree presents, chocolate figures (wrapped in gaily-coloured silver paper) and chocolate money to the branches. (The latter must have been when sweet rationing ended!) We were not allowed to open the tree presents, or any of the chocolate, until Boxing Day.

The living-rooms were decorated with boughs of holly, balanced on top of pictures, paintings and wall mirrors, and paper chains were strung from corner to corner. In the early years, we sat night after night making the paper chains from strips of coloured paper that were formed into a circle with a dab of glue and then other strips were added, until you literally made a chain. (I believe newspaper, cut into strips, was used in the war years but this was before my time!)

We coloured fir-cones with glue and sprinkled silver and gold glitter over them and then turned our efforts into table decorations, with the addition of a red candle and a bit of holly.

On Christmas Eve we always left stockings at the end of our beds and by the chimney we placed a mince-pie and a glass of sherry for Santa and a carrot for his chief reindeer, Rudolph. On Christmas Day we would awake at the crack of dawn to find that Santa had not only left our presents but our Christmas stockings had been filled with goodies. There was always an orange in the toe, pink and white sugar mice, a colouring book and a card-game like *Snap* or *Happy Families*. Santa seemed to know I preferred a box of *Turkish Delight* while Sheila would find *Peppermint Creams*. There would be an orgy of opening and then we would clamber into the marital bed to show Mum and Dad what Santa had left us. Dad would get up and clear the ashes from the grate of the coal-fire and re-lay and re-light it and then make us all a cup of tea. (As he did every morning! Served with two biscuits!)

Mum would be up early too to put the turkey in the oven but of course she had been busy for weeks making Christmas puddings, Christmas cake (with home-made marzipan and royal icing), mince-pies (with home-made mincemeat) and sausage rolls. She had pickled the shallots and boiled a bacon joint; literally shopped and cooked until she dropped (well almost!).

Dad's contribution was to grow and harvest our Christmas vegetables: potatoes, carrots, parsnips, and sprouts. He also purchased the turkey at a wholesale auction (in Petworth, I believe) so it came complete with feathers and innards and he would have the job of plucking and drawing it. It would be hung in the cool of the shed until the time came for Mum to stuff it with sausage meat and sage and onion stuffing mix. In those days we always had cold winters!

The children's Christmas drinking treat was something we called "raisin wine". It was dark red, thick and syrupy and absolutely delicious, to a child's palate at least. Of course it was not alcoholic but we liked to pretend it was! And then there were the Christmas crackers with the silly jokes and mottoes, the useless little gift and the paper hat. Happy, happy memories!

Of course, to a greater or lesser degree, most of the above took place in most homes throughout the land but we had one tradition that was a little unusual. Dad made Christmas wreaths. Some weeks before the festive season, he would cover the front-room carpet with a dust-sheet. Then shrubbery he had nurtured and harvested from the school, wire cutters and frames would litter the floor. He would make dozens of wreaths, in all shapes and sizes, weaving laurel, fir and holly around the frames and securing each piece with wire. They were very popular, for this was before artificial wreaths became available. Some were made for the local florist but most went to regular customers for them to place on their family grave or to decorate their front door. One wreath always found its way to the "Martin" grave in Littlehampton Cemetery.

A summer tradition was always to have two weeks holiday away from home, even if it was only visiting relatives. Throughout the 1950's we forged links with aunts, uncles and cousins with these protracted excursions and, of course, they holidayed with us in return. Those we did not stay with, or who did not stay with us, we visited, and thus our parents ensured we were very much part of a large, extended family.

One year when we were still quite young, Dad and Uncle Ted decided to take the respective families on a joint camping holiday to Swallow Falls in North Wales. They purchased some Army surplus tents and miscellaneous equipment at a very reasonable rate and off we set.

As soon as we arrived, Dad and Uncle Ted busied themselves with digging latrines. I think it was at this point that Mum began to have grave doubts about the wisdom of this kind of vacation! Then it rained. And rained. And rained. Trying to cook on primus stoves in a downpour, plus straddling a latrine, was not my mother's idea of an enjoyable holiday! Then one of the children fell in the mire of the trench, I cannot recall whom it was but it was not Sheila or me, we would certainly have remembered that! It is amazing that the wives did not stage a revolt and insist we head for home but we did manage to last the two weeks. However, it was the one and only time the Oakley's had a family camping holiday in the United Kingdom. Uncle Ted and his family were made of sterner stuff and they did try camping again and then caravanning at a later date.

For the next couple of years we tried house-swapping; this was many years before this kind of holiday became popular. The first place we went to was a house in Tenterden in Kent which smelled of mildew and the next was a pre-fab' in Cheltenham. Mum was not enamoured with the mildew and Dad was disappointed with Gloucestershire as he felt there was very little to do, so after these excursions into the unknown and untried, Mum decided the safest bet was to go to relatives where at least we knew what we were getting!

Mum's brother, Bill, and his wife Violet and family, by now had moved to the wilds of Romney Marsh in Kent and we stayed with them a few times. At that time they owned a village store that sold everything under the sun. It was a fascinating treasure trove for children and sometimes Auntie Vi would let us "serve" one of her customers which was a real treat, like playing shops but for real!

One of Dad's sisters, Elsie, had married and moved to London and also owned a shop, a pet shop. As children it was great to go downstairs and see the kittens and puppies for sale. We did spend Christmas with them once, and the occasional weekend, but they did not have the room to accommodate us all for long periods.

Dad's brother, Jack, and his family lived near us in Fontwell, near Arundel, so we often popped in to see them on our Sunday afternoon drives and we normally spent Boxing Day with them; one year we went to them and the next they came to us. Dad's sister, Blanche, always joined the two families on Boxing Day. Also Dad always made sure we kept in touch with his father and his step-mother, Ada, who by now lived in Slindon, also near Arundel.

So by the early 1950's we had been well and truly introduced to the Martin and Oakley clans. Included in the Guildford family get-togethers were meetings with Uncle Ted's sister, our "Auntie" Margaret. As we know from an earlier chapter, their sister, Evelyn had died and some time after that Margaret had gone to live with, and care for, Evelyn's deaf husband, Bert. Auntie Margaret was herself profoundly deaf, although her disability must have come later in life because her speech was not too badly affected and she did wear a hearing aid. It therefore made sense for her and Bert to set up home together; they were company for one another, their living costs were cheaper and each could look after the other. Because they lived together, any invitation to Auntie Margaret naturally included "Uncle" Bert. He was "uncle" to all the other cousins only by marriage to Evelyn, but to me he was indeed my biological uncle, although I had no idea of this at the time. He never appeared to favour me over the other cousins but for some strange reason I was drawn to him and from quite a young age I would make a special effort to try and talk to him, if only for a few minutes. Even then I could see how his deafness isolated him from the other adults, from their conversations and from their activities. I might have made even more of an effort to communicate with him if I had realised how close I came to inheriting the same disability.

Many friends of our parents also came to stay, including Dad's old army pal, my god-father, Bill Roberts, and his wife and sons. Sheila can remember going to the beach with them on one occasion when a little boy got caught in the tidal currents at the river-mouth and drowned. The only real memory I have of one of their visits is being given 2/0d (two shillings) at the end of their stay. Sheila was given 2/6d (two shillings and sixpence) and I was really hurt! Probably because our parents made a point of always treating us equally. They never showed any favouritism and extended this principle to our play-mates too. We were not allowed to eat sweets, for example, unless we shared what we had with our little friends. We would never sit down and eat a meal, or a sandwich, without a guest being offered the same. And as soon as a visitor came through the front door, they were always offered refreshment of some kind.

One of our young chums spent a huge amount of time with us, sharing our holidays on occasion and even our bathtub as Mum often got her ready for bed if her widowed mother was working late. Her name was Ellita and they had moved to a house opposite us. Age-wise Ellita was right in the middle of Sheila and me. She had been born in Canada of an English mother and a Canadian father who had been stationed in Arundel during the war. They had subsequently married and moved to Canada but, when he died, Ellita's mother came back to Littlehampton to be near her own mother who lived at the top of our road.

One day the three of us peered through the hedge at the bottom of our garden and saw three young brothers playing in the garden backing onto ours. Greetings were exchanged and they explained they had just moved in. The two mothers were summoned and conferred through the leaves that it was alright for us to play together. There was a small hole in the bottom of the hedge so through we crawled, for their garden appeared much more interesting than ours. Ours was full of boring vegetables and livestock while they had a large lawn with a roundabout, a swing and a slide and plenty of room to run around or play ball. Eventually the boys would move away and Ellita's mother would remarry and immigrate to Canada again but until all this transpired, the six of us spent a lot of time in one another's company.

I was eight years old when I decided to run away from home! It was a constant bone of contention between my parents and me that I did not clean the cage in which my two pet mice lived, at least without being nagged to do so. I was always going to do it "in a minute" and the minute seldom arrived! Consequently, unnoticed by me, the poor creatures chewed their way to freedom and Dad found them that morning, floating in the gold-fish bowl. Poor mice! Poor fish! Of course, I got told off and, as Mum would say, I got into a " right old paddy"! I was so upset I decided to leave home. *That would show them,* I thought. So I stomped off, through the front door, up the road and out of sight. No-one followed so I carried on walking. *No-one cares how I feel,* I thought. *I didn't mean my mice to drown. It wasn't really my fault, was it?* (Well, yes! Actually it was but I did not want to face this fact!)

Eventually I arrived at the swing-bridge that crossed the river, about two miles from home. I stood at the bridge and pondered my options. *If I cross,* I decided, *I'll never be able to go home.* (Childish logic but it seemed the point of no return.) I was still feeling hard done by but I had no money, and I was getting hungry, so I turned back and the return journey seemed ten times as long as it had been to get there.

When I arrived home, it did not seem that I had even been missed. How humiliating!

"I ran away!" I announced proudly to Mum.

"Did you? Well you're back now."

"But I didn't mean my mice to die."

"No, I know you didn't. But actions have consequences and if you want a pet you have to look after it and that means cleaning up after it regularly. If you'd cleaned the cage last week, you'd have seen the hole they were making. But it's done now and we'll say no more about it."

"I'm sorry my mice died ..... but I might run away again if you tell me off!"

"Yes, well. Have your dinner before you go. I'm about to dish-up."

It amazes me now that an eight-year-old could walk all the way to town and back and that her parents would not be frantic to know their child had done so! How times have changed!

On 30th June 1954, there was an eclipse of the sun and by a strange co-incidence I was at the East Street School when this took place, just as my mother had been thirty-six years previously. We too were taken out into the playground to view this strange phenomenon and I wonder if I stood in the very same spot where Mum had watched all those years before? I cannot remember being given coloured glass to look through, however, but nor can I remember being given any warnings about not looking directly at the sun.

Soon after the eclipse, Mum developed a thrombosis in her legs. The family doctor, Dr Waddington, visited her at home and wrapped both limbs in a very tight sticky bandage. Round and round and round it went from ankle to groin. Then he recommended complete bed rest for at least one month.

Luckily we were both at school at the beginning of her illness and I can only think Dad finished work early in order to give us our tea and put us to bed. Also fortunate was the fact that Mum had purchased her first washing machine with the money she earned at the school, so doing the laundry was not too onerous for my father, but I know he was struggling to iron our little dresses when someone Mum worked with, Mrs Reeves, popped in to visit her. She spotted his inadequate attempts with the iron and immediately offered to take all the ironing home and return it the next day. Mrs Reeves did the ironing for him the whole time Mum was laid up and Mum never forgot her kindness.

After Mum had been on her enforced bed-rest for about two weeks, we broke up from school for the summer holidays and, with at least another two weeks of idleness for Mum to endure, Uncle Ted and Auntie Kathleen offered to look after us, even though by this time there had been another addition to Uncle Ted's "brood" for Auntie Kathleen had given birth to a daughter, Yvonne, early in 1953. It was the first time we had been anywhere to stay without our parents but we had stayed with them many times before as a family, so it did not seem too strange.

Very near to their house in Guildford was a common and we all spent many happy hours there building "houses" out of tree branches, playing hide-and-seek or collecting odd-shaped stones or wild flowers. In those days no-one seemed to have heard of child molestation or abduction. Ten year old Ivan was in charge and sometimes he would take us all to Guildford's *Lido*. This was a huge outdoor swimming pool, surrounded by landscaped lawns with man-made hillocks and miscellaneous shrubbery. It was a great place to relax in the sun after our dip in the pool. All in all, we had a great time.

One of the meals Auntie Kathleen used to prepare for us all was a large shepherds' pie and she would mix *Armour's Baked Beans* in with the minced meat. As we all sat down to eat we would chant "*Armour's beans are so, so tasty!*" just like they did in one of the new television commercials that was popular at the time. I still cannot eat baked beans without thinking they are "so, so tasty!"

The two weeks flew by and then Ivan and Gwendoline came to spend a few weeks with us. This was not the first time they had come without their parents. Ever since their mother had died, they had spent part of the summer holidays with us and, many years later, Ivan told me that this was the highlight of their year; going to the beach and the funfair, riding on the ferry across the river and just being with Auntie Anne and Uncle Clem. Auntie Kathleen did tend to be a bit of a nag and our easy-going, non-critical, non-confrontational parents were a welcome relief from their step-mother's constant fault-finding.

In later years, Mum told me that having the bandages taken off, when the thrombosis had dispersed, was one of the worst experiences of her life. Dr Waddington cut his way through the sticky layers and then ripped them off in one fast movement. The pain as they came off, hairs and all, was something Mum never forgot and Dr Waddington actually hugged her when he had finished, saying, "I'm so sorry. It's the only way to do it but I know how painful it is."

From that time Mum had to wear special prescription stockings. They were very thick, white elastic but with flesh-coloured stockings on top, they actually improved the look of her legs, apart from giving her the necessary support. Neither my sister nor I have ever seen varicose veins as bad as my mother had; her legs were a complete mass of discoloured mounds. It is the only thing about her that we can honestly say we are glad we cannot inherit.

Mum and mice were not the only members of the family to suffer in 1954. Mr Tibbles, the cat, got into a fight and sustained a nasty wound to his head. Dad decided to take him to the vet' in a cardboard-box, balanced on the cross-bar of his bicycle. Not surprisingly, the cat jumped out and ran and hid in some nearby shrubbery. Dad hunted high and low but could not find him so he came back home and recruited Sheila and me to help him catch poor old Tibbs. We did locate him eventually and Dad made the decision to take him in the car instead. Sadly Tibbs was an old cat and the vet' felt the wound was too severe to heal, so he was put to sleep.

Hardly was poor Tibbs in his grave, than I started to pester my parents to buy me a dog. As much as I loved cats and Tibbles, I also loved dogs. Indeed I loved dogs so much that I would walk up to any canine and pat it, regardless of size or ferocity. Sheila was the complete opposite; dogs scared her to death. So my parents thought having a dog was not such a bad idea; I needed to learn a bit of respect for the animal and Sheila needed to learn not to be so frightened of them. So they acquiesced. I could have a dog as a joint present for Christmas of 1954 and my ninth birthday in the following February. I was allowed to choose whether I wanted a corgi or a Sealyham. Corgis seemed a common dog; even the Queen had corgis, so I decided to go for the more exotic-sounding: a Sealyham.

Sealyhams are medium-sized dogs, belonging to the terrier breed. They were bred in the late nineteenth century, from a mixture of the bassett hound, the bull terrier and the West Highland White terrier, by a Captain Edwardes in the Welsh town of Sealyham. He wanted a dog that could flush badgers out of their setts and therefore they are fearless and strong, but very friendly, especially with children. More by luck than judgement, I made a good choice!

We went to view the litter and I was supposed to be allowed to have my pick. I chose a tiny little runt of a pup, cowering in fright at the back of the cage. It was adorable with a black patch over one eye but Dad would not let me have it because it was a bitch.

"Have this one instead!" he urged and pressed a fluffy ball of white fur into my arms. I could just see a little black nose and black eyes peering at me through the fur. I cast one last, forlorn look at the tiny pup we had to reject and carried my new pet back to the car. My very own dog! We called him "Laddie", although his pedigree name was the more imposing "Tiny Tim of Basingham". Of course, I had promised to walk him and groom him every day ...... and, despite my supposed "lesson" with my mice, kept it up for less than a week, to my eternal shame. I did walk him occasionally but poor old Dad got lumbered with the chore on a regular basis, twice a day, and I cannot remember ever grooming him. Mum and a professional dog-groomer did the necessary in that direction. But I did love him and he features in many of my childhood memories. Even Sheila grew to love Laddie. Indeed he was such a character, it would be hard for anyone not to be fond of him. He was a great favourite at our family picnics and just loved chasing the ball during the cricket match. Had his antics interfered solely to the detriment of Uncle Ted's score, Dad might have turned a blind eye but as Laddie was completely impartial, Dad used to shout across the field, "Anne! Will you keep that dog under control!" Poor Laddie would then have to be tied up on a long rope for the duration of the match.

As he grew older, one of his favourite tricks was to walk slowly down the garden path until he got to the chicken-run and then break into a gallop, barking all the way past the birds, making them fly into the air in fright. At the end of their fence, he would turn around with a silly smirk on his face, and then saunter back up again. Anyone who says a dog cannot smile, or that it has no sense of humour, has never owned a dog. Dad would growl at him, "Will you stop that! You'll stop the hens laying!" but Laddie carried on regardless and the stupid chickens never got used to his antics.

Another of his tricks took place after his bath, which he hated. It was a mammoth undertaking requiring the joint efforts of both my parents. After they had washed him, and dried him and he was all nice and clean and a fluffy white again, he would run straight into the coal-bunker. He would scrabble about in there for a while and then re-appear with a black face and the silly grin.

The first summer holiday we took after we had him, Dad decided to return him to the kennels where he was born, thinking he would be well looked after while we were away and that this was better than taking him to a strange place. When Dad went to collect him, he was horrified to see Laddie had sores all over his back and around his neck. They had nicked him badly while clipping the fur on his back and the neck wounds looked as if he had been tied up for the whole fortnight and had tried to get away. Dad was incandescent with rage and refused to pay the bill. He also threatened to report the kennels to the RSPCA (Royal Society for the Prevention of Cruelty to Animals). Laddie was beside himself with joy to be home with his human family again but Mum was heartbroken when she saw his wounds. My parents resolved that he would never be parted from us again and subsequently Laddie spent many happy holidays with us and adapted to every place in which we stayed.

He used to know when it was Sunday and that we would all go out in the car for a drive and then take him for a walk in the woods. If we ended up in a country pub', he would be treated to an arrowroot biscuit. He was very much part of our family and his favourite spot to sit and watch television with us, was on Mum's lap! Nearly all our pets loved Mum's lap! Well the tortoise, the budgerigars, the goldfish and my mice were indifferent but for the other furry pets, it was large and squishy, warm and cosy, and safe. Laddie was not supposed to go into the bedrooms but occasionally he would sneak in there and hide in a far corner under one of the beds. When I went in to get him, I would peer underneath and he would give me a warning growl.

"Don't you growl at me!" I used to say as I hauled him out. He never, ever, bit anyone or anything. He was all show!

It was about this time that I broke one of Mum's favourite pieces of china. I wanted something out of the medicine chest that was high on the wall in their bedroom. I was not supposed to go there but I wanted to save Mum getting it for me. I climbed on a chair to reach the chest and knocked this figurine off the mantelpiece. There were only two rules in our house; one was always to own up to a misdemeanour and the second was never to tell a lie. So straight away I told Mum what had happened. She went very quiet and told me how disappointed she was that I had broken the rule about going to the medicine chest. Then she added that the figurine had meant a lot to her because it had belonged to her mother. It was part of a pair; one was a shepherd-boy and the other a shepherdess. It was not valuable (I do not think we owned anything that had a significant monetary value) but the sentimental value made it irreplaceable and the shepherd-boy was broken beyond repair. I was not punished but I felt terrible. There was nothing I could do to put the figure back together again and I would have done anything not to see my mother so upset. She was very quiet for days. The shepherdess survived my onslaughts over the years and sits now, sadly in lonely splendour, on my mantelshelf, a constant reminder of my carelessness.

This is a good example of my mother's form of discipline. She only had to say how I had disappointed her in some way and I was reduced to shame. I wanted nothing more than to please her. It worked with me;

alas not with Sheila! She was much more of a rebel; some would say she had more spirit, and they would be right for it was also around this time that Sheila had become really cheeky; always answering back and having to have the last word. One day she was really rude to Mum so Dad told her not to speak to her mother like that. She responded by being rude to him as well and then ran outside. Dad was livid so he chased her all the way down the garden path and raced straight across his precious rhubarb patch to catch her. Then he put her over his knee and walloped her hard with the flat of his hand on her bottom. Did she scream! Not knowing what had occurred indoors, I was horrified. I ran into Mum exclaiming, "Mum! Mum! Dad's hitting Sheila!"

Mum calmly replied, "Well I expect she deserves it!" and carried on with what she was doing. What made the whole incident so memorable, apart from the smack, was the rhubarb! Dad was constantly remonstrating with us for cutting off the corner of the garden by walking over the fruit and then we witnessed him running straight across it!

This was the only time Dad reacted physically to her, both he and Mum normally turned the other cheek. I was the only one who did not have their patience or forbearance. I refused to give in to her so we ended up fighting! Literally hand-to-hand combat! Neither of us can remember now how the arguments started, and it is not fair to say they were always her fault, but she excelled at "winding me up" and I always took the bait. For instance she might walk past me when I was quietly reading and snatch the book out of my hands. I should have ignored her but I would invariably chase after her and a simple argument would escalate into war in order to retrieve my book! She could be like this, on and off, all day. Always demanding attention. There was never any peace. Thinking about it now, as an adult, I suppose she was just not good at amusing herself whereas I was more of a solitary soul, content with my own company. I still am! And she still needs constant reassurance!

Despite the arguments, and the fights, we still played reasonably well together: games like five-stones, creeping Jenny, hopscotch and the tried and tested "Mothers and Fathers", "Doctors and Nurses". Ellita was invariably with us on these occasions and Sheila, being the youngest of the three of us, would be relegated to "baby" or "patient", while I would have the starring role of "father" or "doctor"! The garden-shed would be our "house" or "hospital". Our favourite game, however, was "Pirates". For this we would drag everything out of the shed that was suitable as a "prop": the old tin bath, a wooden bench, a sack or two, a pair of steps, a scaffold board. These would be placed strategically over the lawn and the idea was that in order to escape the "pirate", we had to race all over the props without "falling into the water" (i.e. touching the grass).

Sometimes we would go into the road to roller-skate or play marbles, but never on a Sunday! Although at this stage, Mum was not a regular church-goer, we had to attend Sunday-school and she recognised it as a special day by not allowing us to play in the road, never hanging out washing on this day and cooking a traditional roast dinner (usually roast shoulder of lamb), whatever the weather.

We came to bicycles quite late but even without transport, from a relatively early age, say my eight years to Sheila's six, we wandered everywhere. Providing we told Mum where we were going, she did not seem unduly concerned and must have thought we would come to no harm. If we said we were going to the beach, she would give us 6d (sixpence) for an ice-cream. Then, when we reached Pier Road (where Jemima Love had lived in the waterman's cottage), we would have to make up our minds whether to spend the sixpence on the ice-cream or use it to pay for the ferry-boat ride across the river to West Beach. Sixpence would not allow us to pay for both treats and although we could walk to West Beach via the swing-bridge, that added at least two miles to our trip.

Another day we might go to Black Ditch and collect tadpoles, or if there was a circus, or a fair, in town we would explore that. If St James' Church had a jumble sale, we were in our element. We would take our pocket money and come home with a load of old clothes for dressing-up. Mum was always horrified when she saw the tat we had brought back! And, of course, along with 99% of the nation's children, without fail, every Saturday morning was Saturday-Morning-Pictures-Day.   A highlight of our week!

Perhaps it was these Saturday excursions that encouraged us to provide our parents with our own home-grown entertainment and we spent hours learning the words and tunes for such erudite renditions as *"How much is that doggie in the window?"* and *"If you go down to the woods today ...."* (Teddy Bears' Picnic) and *"Sisters, sisters, there were never such devoted sisters!"*

And talking of "sisters", Mum did her best to help us to "bond" by dressing us alike. I hated it! I suppose I thought that being dressed in identical outfits, made me appear babyish! I remember one time, someone gave Mum some multi-coloured, striped material and she decided to have dresses made for us out of it. They were ghastly! We looked like a couple of walking deck-chairs! We both protested so much that the dresses were consigned to a jumble sale!

As always national and international news did not come to a halt, even if we were preoccupied with our own lives. Three years after the war ceased, de-rationing had begun, starting with flour in July 1948, followed by clothes in March 1949. 1950 saw rationing end for canned and dried fruit, chocolate biscuits, treacle, syrup, jellies, mincemeat,

175

petrol and soap. Sugar and butter had to wait until 1953, along with sweets and confectionery. But war-time rationing did not finally end until restrictions on the sale and purchase of meat and bacon was lifted in July 1954, fourteen years after the scheme had been introduced.

Also in 1954, Britain sponsored an expedition to find the *Abominable Snowman*. As far as I know they are still looking! This year also saw the launching of the first atomic submarine, a report declaring cigarettes could cause cancer, and Dr. Roger Bannister running a mile in less than four minutes.

In 1954, an Independent Television Authority (ITA) was given parliamentary sanction to provide a service financed from advertising revenue. It created a rival to the monopoly of the BBC and gave the UK populace a choice of two television channels; the BBC, still funded by the licence payer without advertisements, and the ITV with constant breaks for commercials. The popularity of "the box" precipitated a huge change in the entertainments industry, and the way people would spend their leisure time. A choice of two channels was just the beginning. Within two decades broadcasts of documentaries, soap-operas, quizzes, plays, sports programmes, singing spectaculars and the like, would keep people at home and result in the closure of dance halls and cinemas the length and breadth of the country, although many of the cinemas were converted into Bingo Halls. At first British film companies refused to sell their old films to the new TV upstarts but in the end they had to concede defeat. Nowadays a large proportion of the output of the UK film studios (at least those that did manage to survive the transition) is films designed specifically for television.

1954 was an eventful year and ended with a far-reaching medical breakthrough. On 23rd December, at a hospital in Boston, Massachusetts, the world's first successful kidney transplant was performed. Previous organ transplants had always failed due to the problem of "rejection" but this operation had been undertaken between identical twin brothers, thus reducing the risk.

Eventually surgeons would learn how to transplant all of the major body organs, and even arms and hands, faces and legs, thanks to improved techniques of micro-surgery and the development of anti-rejection drugs. But December 1954 remains the pivotal moment when another piece of science fiction became fact.

In 1955 Disneyland opened in Anaheim, California and, on 30th September of that year, the teenagers' heartthrob, James Dean, died in a car crash, aged just twenty-four years. He only made three films but was posthumously Oscar-nominated for two of them, although his status as a cultural icon is best embodied in his most celebrated film *Rebel Without a Cause*. Although best-known as an actor, he was also a gifted photographer, a sports car racer, an artist and, of course, he was the ultimate rebel.

Family-wise, as the last months of 1955 ticked by, Sheila joined me at "Brownies" and both Sheila and I changed schools; she went on to primary education at the old flint-stone school in East Street and I moved to the Junior School, which I believe, at that stage, was still at Elm Grove Road, right next door to the Infants School we had attended in our early years.

And one of the first things I did at my new school was to audition for the nativity play. I was chosen to be the Angel Gabriel, complete with a small speaking part. The angels wore long white robes, with golden halos made out of tinsel, and large cardboard wings fixed to our backs. Bare feet, of course. Naturally Mum came to the first afternoon performance, and later wanted to know why I was fidgeting with my toes all the way through.

"My wings hurt!" I complained. "I was trying to take my mind off the pain! Did it notice very much?"

"Well," she replied, "I certainly noticed. Perhaps you should ask your teacher to adjust them before tomorrow's performance?"

I decided there and then that it wasn't much fun being an angel!

The 27th September 1955 was Mum and Dad's Silver Wedding Anniversary. Dad bought her a cameo brooch of a white rose in a silver frame and to celebrate he took us all to Brighton Ice-Rink to see an ice-show. We had front row seats and we believe the "star" of the show was the singer, Bryan Johnson, brother of the more well-known Teddy Johnson who sang with his wife Pearl Carr. Alas we cannot remember much about the event after all these years but we recall very well that he directed one of his love songs to Mum (much to her embarrassment!) and then said she would look lovely if she wore a gardenia in her hair! Whether he had been primed that this was a silver wedding anniversary treat, I do not know, but looking back this seems quite likely and is the sort of thing Dad might well have orchestrated, without telling Mum of course!

1955 drew to a close with a simple act by a black woman changing the course of American history. Segregation had been declared illegal in the United States in 1954 but individual States still implemented old segregation laws. On 1st December 1955, in Montgomery, Alabama, Rosa Parkes refused to give up her seat on a bus to a white man and was subsequently fined $10. This sparked a massive bus boycott and launched a young preacher, by the name of Martin Luther King, into the limelight. On 20th December, the Supreme Court upheld the decision of a lower court to end segregation on Alabama's buses and Mrs Parkes stepped into history as an icon for the civil rights movement in the United

States. Dr Martin Luther King Jnr was destined to become its figurehead and one of the greatest orators, and indeed one of the greatest men, in American history.

CHAPTER TWENTY-SIX

From Pyromania and Panto' to Politburo
(1956)

By now, "family traditions" were well established and joining in the festivities of "Bonfire Night" was another one. As we know from a previous chapter, the town of Lewes is the centre of these Sussex celebrations but in 1952 certain citizens of Littlehampton founded their own "Bonfire Society", joining an elite club of some thirty or so other towns and villages, mainly in East Sussex. Indeed, Littlehampton is one of only two towns to represent the west of the county. Rye's Bonfire Society is the oldest, dating back to 1695, but most of the surviving Societies were formed in the nineteenth or twentieth centuries. All of them have a theme for their costumes, "smugglers" for Hastings, "pirates" for Eastbourne, "Saxons" for Battle, for example. Littlehampton chose to have "Red Indians" and on a Saturday night, close to November 5th, Indian chiefs, squaws and warriors, of all shapes and sizes, would set fire to their tarred, wooden torches and lead the way to the sea-front. Other Bonfire Societies would join in so we might have "Aztecs", "cavaliers", "monks" or "knights" joining the procession. There was (and is!) fierce competition between the towns to see who could produce the best costumes.

At the sea-front, a huge bonfire had been built on the "Green", which separated the houses from the beach, and this would be lit with great ceremony as a prelude to a large firework display. It was such an unusual celebration, that often the "Guildford Family" would join us for the weekend and, after all the excitement, we would adjourn to "Dad's Club" for "refreshments". I can remember this was where I had my first experience with tip-up seats, which were all around the walls. I must have sat too far back and the seat tipped-up with me in it! Dad had to come and rescue me!

But this was not our only bonfire celebration. As part of his duties at *Dorset House School*, Dad had to build a bonfire, complete with a guy sitting on the top, and organise a firework display for the pupils and staff. We were also invited, and, although more modest than the later Bonfire Society effort, this would have been the first time we oohed and aahed at giant Catherine wheels, and rockets exploding their brightly coloured stars. Even this was not an end to our "pyromania" for at home we always had a few sparklers, at least, on the night of 5th November. A Sussex celebration indeed.

By the time of our parents' Silver Wedding Anniversary (in 1955), going to a pantomime over the Christmas/New Year period had become another family tradition. For some reason, we usually went to see one on ice at Brighton Ice-Rink. It followed the same format as a stage production but perhaps had more scope for visual effects than a theatre.

The history of the English pantomime can be traced back to 1716 and appealed then to a mainly adult audience. Modern pantomimes are performed in the winter months and are aimed predominately at children, with participation by the audience as an important part of the show. Everyone is encouraged to boo the villain whenever he appears on stage and offer advice as to his whereabouts, for example, "*He's behind you!*" They will join in to challenge a statement such as, "*I'm much prettier than you!*" with an "*Oh no you're not!*" The story-lines are based on well-known fairy tales, the most popular being *Cinderella, Mother Goose, Aladdin, Dick Whittington* and *Jack and the Beanstalk* although *Sleeping Beauty, Babes in the Wood, Peter Pan* and *Snow White* also attract large audiences.

There is always a "principal boy", played by a girl in knee-high leather boots and fishnet tights, and a "principal girl" who is the prettiest female in the cast. The "Dame" is usually related to the principal boy in some way and is always played by a man in drag. Her entrances are more extravagant and exaggerated than any other character.

There are "Goodies" and "Baddies", such as the *Fairy Queen* and the *Demon King*, and animals like the pantomime horse or cow. Many a famous pantomime "great" began their career by playing the back legs of a panto' horse and many, many years ago, at the Stockport Hippodrome Theatre, the front end was a young man by the name of Charlie Chaplin.

Pantomimes are as popular today as they have ever been, whether they are played in the top theatres by "star" names or performed at the local village hall by an amateur dramatic society. They have become as much of an English tradition as roast beef or warm beer.

We always went to a matinee performance and when the show was over Dad would go and buy us all a takeaway fish and chips supper. This was another family tradition; after any day-out he would end up in the fish and chip shop and bring us back our delicious meal wrapped in newspaper. In common with most working-class families, we rarely ate out, in a restaurant that is, except regularly once a year when we went to Portsmouth for our Christmas shopping. We took a large, empty suit-case and Dad would wait outside the shop, puffing away on his hand-rolled cigarette, while Mum, Sheila and I went into the shop picking out presents for everybody. Once purchased, into the case they went and onto the next shop we would go, with Dad guarding the case and contents. If there was one chore Dad hated it was shopping! I think it was the lesser of the evils to wait outside rather than fight his way around the various counters. When lunch-time came, we would adjourn to the first floor cafeteria at *British Home Stores (BHS)* and endeavour to get a table near the railings so we could look down on all the milling crowds, still feverishly shopping, in the store below us.

At this restaurant meal, the first person to choose what she wanted, and then to clear her plate, was Sheila. She was never any trouble to feed! I was the faddy eater. I could not stand any fat on meat or bacon, nor would I try anything a bit out of the ordinary. If I found an insect wrapped in the leaves of a Brussels sprout, for example, I would not eat any of them, which annoyed Dad greatly if it was a home-grown vegetable.

Before we came home Dad would treat us all to our favourite confectionary: Toasted coconut squares for him, liquorice allsorts for Mum, fudge for me and hot, roasted, salted peanuts for Sheila. In those days they were all sold loose by the ounce, as were biscuits. Very little packaging in the 1950's, or the years before!

On Saturdays in the season, often Dad would bring home winkles for tea that he had bought from the fishermen along the quay, adjacent to the River Arun. They would be served with brown bread and butter and the three of them would sit at the dining room table, pin in hand, pulling the flesh out of the sea-snail and gobbling them all up with relish. I thought it was disgusting! To this day I have never eaten any kind of snail, land or sea, or any kind of mollusc come to that. My loss probably!

For some reason Sheila preferred the legs of a chicken or a turkey and insisted on having both of them, although not at one sitting! A chicken in those days was a rare treat, probably eaten at Easter and perhaps only two or three times the rest of the year. A turkey would only be eaten at Christmas. Luckily the rest of us preferred the white meat, so it was no real loss if she had the legs, but I did get fed up that she always got her own way, even with a chicken leg! So one day I casually asked Mum why she did not buy a four-legged chicken so Sheila could have four legs instead of two. Mum told me not to be so silly but Sheila believed me and said, " Ohhh yes, Mum! Why don't you buy one with four legs?" She was quite young at the time and very gullible but undoubtedly this jest would have drawn a sharp retort from Mum for me not to tease her. One of my mother's pet hates was to witness a child being teased, by another child was bad enough, but especially by an adult. She regarded it as a form of bullying and would often leap to our defence if she thought an adult's "joke" had gone too far. She also had a strong dislike of sarcasm, reminding us that "it was the lowest form of wit!"

By the summer of 1956, I had been a "Brownie" for about three years but the "2nd Littlehampton Brownie Pack" had never been away together. This was the summer that this changed, thanks to the Herculean efforts of our lovely "Brown Owl", Marjory Hickford, and our "Tawny Owl", Mrs Ellen. The Girl Guide Movement prohibits "Brownies" sleeping under canvas so they had chosen to take us to a large house in Lanrick in East Sussex. The only two incidents I can remember about the holiday are having to have a bath with my sister (no different than at home!) and burying some dead animal in a grave! We made a cross, gathered flowers and held a little service! But this holiday marked the beginning of an annual week away from our parents as Pack Holidays, and later Girl Guide Camps, became a regular feature of our summer vacations.

One of the most evocative memories of our childhood has to be the dreadful reek of potato peelings, and sundry vegetable matter, being boiled up in a large saucepan for the chickens. The stench was truly disgusting! When it was cooked it was mixed with meal and crushed sea-shells and while the smell was awful for us humans, the chickens loved it! However, the odour of the cooking process is an aroma that anyone who has kept chickens will never forget.

Mum tried to cook up this fowl feast on a day when all the kitchen windows and the door could be kept open but even so the stench seemed to pervade the whole house. It was for this reason that she decided to invest in one of the new-fangled pressure-cookers. They were defined as a saucepan with a lockable lid, that created steam-heat in a vacuum within the pot, thus speeding up cooking times, using less fuel, and tenderising the meat. The first commercial pressure-cooker had its debut in America in 1939 and was promoted as producing a tastier, healthier meal. Subsequently they became very popular in Europe in the post-war years. Even Auntie Kathleen had one, and swore by it, so Mum duly followed all the instructions and placed the "goodies" inside the large pan. She placed it on the stove, adjusted all the weights, turned on the electric hotplate, and then left it to heat up. Suddenly she heard an almighty bang and raced back to the kitchen. The lid of the pressure cooker had blown off and the contents of the pan had exploded into the kitchen. The disgusting mess had stuck like glue to every surface; the windows, the door, the curtains, the units, the floor and the ceiling were festooned with vegetable matter. The kitchen looked as if it had been hit by some deadly disease. It took ages to clear up the mess entirely. The ceiling was the worst to deal with and we had bits of potato dangling down like weird Christmas baubles for weeks, until Dad could find the time to clean it all off and re-decorate. Needless to say the pressure-cooker was never used again and was relegated to the dark recesses of a kitchen cupboard in eternal disgrace. I suppose, because it was new, Mum could not bring herself to actually throw it out. However, after I was married, I wanted a saucepan for jam-making so Mum dug out the offending pan and the bottom was ideal for my purpose. I did use it for years but the useless lid was eventually thrown away.

(I feel I ought to add that the design and manufacture of pressure cookers have been improved greatly over the years. Although no longer sold in America, they are still popular in parts of Europe and Asia where the cost of fuel is a significant factor in the household budget.)

An explosion of a completely different kind happened in 1956. The previous year, a white Southerner, hailing from Memphis, Tennessee, had achieved his dream of becoming a professional singer. Then, in 1956, he appeared on American television and his career accelerated like a rocket. He was unique. The world had never witnessed anything quite like it and, love him or loathe him, the birth of a legend bombarded all the airwaves. Elvis Presley was the first ever rock and roll star but he also sang the blues, laced with country music, with a bit of gospel thrown in for good measure. Not only was it a wide musical spectrum, but he brought together music from both sides of the colour divide and he performed with a natural, hip-swivelling sexuality that made him a teen idol. He was repeatedly dismissed as vulgar, incompetent and a bad influence but he had a vocal range the envy of many a professional opera singer and a musical talent that made him a role model for generations of future rock 'n rollers. Even Mum, with a little encouragement from teenage daughters, later came to appreciate some of his music and had to admit he was very sexy! She used to say at least you could understand every word he sang.

During his career, he had 94 gold singles, three gold EP's and over 40 gold albums, more than any other single artist before or since. His later movies grossed over $180m and millions more were made by the merchandising of "Elvis" products.

Sadly "The King", as he was known, was not destined to die of old age, for on August 16th 1977, aged 42 years, Elvis Presley was discovered dead in his bathroom at his mansion in Memphis, called Gracelands. The cause of death was attributed to heart failure but it was determined later that addiction to prescription drugs may have been a contributory factor. Nevertheless he was a true legend in his lifetime and the biggest influence in "popular music" in the 20th century. The King" is dead but the legend, and his legacy, live on.

On 19th April 1956, another "star" made the headlines. The American movie actress, Grace Kelly, daughter of a wealthy industrialist, married the "world's most eligible bachelor", Prince Rainier III of Monaco. They went on to have three children before Princess Grace, as she became known, was killed in a car crash on 14th September 1982.

In the autumn of 1956 Queen Elizabeth II opened the first ever nuclear power station at Calder Hall in Cumberland but this historic event was overshadowed by the sorry saga of the "Suez Crisis". It had begun in July when the American and British Governments withdrew their promised financial support for the construction of Egypt's Aswan Dam. In retaliation Colonel Nassar announced that in order to pay for the dam, Egypt would nationalize the Suez Canal, thus threatening the main source of oil supply for Britain and France. Negotiations failed, so, with the connivance of Israel, in November Britain and France concocted an excuse to invade Egypt and they seized the Suez Canal. The US, USSR and the UN all condemned the British and French military action and the Prime Minister, Anthony Eden, was forced ignominiously to call a ceasefire and withdraw the troops.

The "Suez Crisis" was one of the most controversial events of British post-war history, for it divided the nation and marked the end of Britain's role as a world power. In future British foreign policy would be conducted in concurrence with American diplomatic support. In January 1957 Anthony Eden was forced to resign and Harold Macmillan replaced him as Prime Minister.

On 23rd October 1956, while tempers and tensions flared in the Middle East, a spontaneous nationwide revolt against the Government, and its Soviet-imposed policies, burst forth in Hungary. This was the first uprising Russia had encountered by one of its European satellite countries. At first Russia announced a willingness to negotiate but the Politburo changed its mind and moved to crush the revolution. By 10th November the fighting was over. An estimated 2500 Hungarians had died and over 200,000 had fled as refugees, many of them eventually settling in Britain. The Soviets set about ruthlessly suppressing all opposition and, by January 1957, not only had they regained control of Hungary, but they had strengthened their control over the whole of central Europe. It seemed communism was both irreversible and monolithic.

CHAPTER TWENTY-SEVEN

The Fifties End
(1957-1959)

On 25th March 1957, *The Treaty of Rome* was signed establishing a "European Economic Community", also known in the UK as "The Common Market". It was an international organization founded to ensure economic integration between France, West Germany, Italy, Luxembourg, Belgium and the Netherlands. It was to have far-reaching effects for the whole of Europe, although the French President, Charles de Gaulle, vetoed initial British membership, fearing that it was a *"Trojan Horse for United States influence."* It would be 1973 before the UK became a member of this now-not-so-exclusive club.

Meanwhile, by 1957, the United Kingdom was enjoying a post-war boom. High employment and increased production in major industries such as steel, coal and motor cars had led to a rise in wages, export earnings and investment. Most men had jobs; they could expect to buy (or at least rent) decent housing; they and their families could obtain free medical and dental treatment and they would receive a pension at the end of their working life.

Children under five years of age, received free health benefits, such as cod liver oil and orange juice. Along with free education, the older ones got free school milk and subsidised lunches and the brightest of the young adults might even be entitled to free university education.

Access to modern conveniences, such as gas or electric stoves, washing machines, refrigerators, vacuum cleaners, radios and televisions, was now readily available; many people would now be able to afford a car or a motor-bike and to go on holiday. The only modern conveniences lacking from most homes, including ours, would be central heating and a telephone.

All this must have been what prompted the Prime Minister, Harold Macmillan, to remark on 20th July 1957, *"Most of our people have never had it so good."* He went on to suggest that the history of this country had never witnessed such a state of prosperity. Sadly it would not last and these words would come back to haunt him in the years ahead.

September 1957 was the time for us to change schools, yet again. At this time, state secondary education was divided into three systems: grammar, secondary modern or technical. Which pupil went where was decided by an examination called the *11-plus*, whose name derived from the age group taking the exam'. It was introduced in 1944 and consisted of a mental arithmetic test, writing an essay, and a test of general knowledge and logic problems, mainly to assess the ability of pupils to apply logic to solve simple problems. Pupils achieving the most number of marks would be steered towards a more academic education at a grammar or "high" school and the rest would go to a secondary modern or technical school. However the latter were few and far between and generally available only in cities. What percentage of pupils went onto grammar schools varied greatly throughout the country. In some counties, as many as 35% would attend a grammar school; in others it was less than 10%. There was still mainly single-sex schooling and fewer grammar school places for girls.

(In the 1960's, the Labour Government decided the *11-plus* was unfair, arguing that all children, of both sexes, should have an equal opportunity in education. Thus they gradually turned most secondary schools, including grammar schools, into large, mixed-sex "Comprehensives". The *11-plus* is still held in some counties on a voluntary basis, and normally used as an entrance test for a specific group of prestigious schools or for streaming purposes when a pupil arrives at a "Comprehensive". Only 164 grammar schools remain in England today.)

I passed the *11-plus* and went onto secondary education at a grammar school in Worthing while Sheila started junior school at Connaught Road. I had only been at my new school for a matter of weeks when I complained that I could not see the blackboard properly. Spectacles became a necessity, as they are to this day. I did not know it then, but virtually all of my (known) biological family need help with their vision, unlike Mum and Dad who only ever needed glasses for reading.

By this time I had *"flown-up"* from Brownies to Guides and had attended my first Girl Guide camp. Despite our disastrous family experiment with an outdoor life in North Wales, I loved camping! I loved curling up on the hard ground in my cosy sleeping-bag and the camaraderie of my patrol members; I loved fashioning "furniture" (like wash-stands) out of a few sticks of wood and a bit of string; I loved cooking on open fires, despite the smoky flavour and ash as a condiment. Even the camp chores did not seem like chores, although I never did master the art of peeling a potato with a pen-knife! And the camp-fires every night and the camp-fire songs and the mugs of cocoa! Rain or shine, I just loved it all! I have many more happy memories of Guides and Guide camps than I do of school.

In those days we travelled to our camp-sites in an open, tail-back lorry. All the equipment was loaded first, then our kit-bags, and then we piled in on top, attempting to find a comfortable spot without a billy-can digging in our backs. It was such fun bouncing along in the lorry, singing away. A wonderful start to a real adventure. On more than one occasion we travelled all the way to Devon, which must have taken about five hours in those pre-motorway days, but the time flew by. Then, on the return journey, as soon as we crossed the county-line back into our own territory, we would sing:-

"Good old Sussex by the sea,
Good old Sussex by the sea,
You can tell by the smell
And you know darn well
It's Sussex by the sea!"

An irreverent, and not very truthful, reference to all the seaweed on the Sussex beaches!

Girl Guides are grouped into "Companies" and in those days we called our adult leader "Captain". We were so lucky with our "Captain", Winifred Burgess, our "Brown Owl's" sister as it happened. We were not much of a Company for accumulating badges but "Captain" and our patrol leaders were what made our hours with the Movement so special. When we were not camping, they used to organise hikes and "cook-outs" at the weekends. We would trudge off to Amberley, Arundel or Angmering with a knap-sack containing wet weather gear, a frying pan, lard, sausages, an egg, baked beans, bread and the like, and on arrival we would attempt to light a fire so we could cook our lunch. Our parents did not give active support to the Movement, but Mum was always there to cheer us on at a concert, or bake cakes for a fund-raising, and Dad and his car were always on hand when muscle or transport were needed.

It was not until 1957 that the family acquired our first camera. Actually to be precise, I acquired a camera. It was only a cheap *Kodak Brownie* and I cannot remember whether it had been a gift, or I saved up and bought it with my birthday money, but it is from this time that family photographs suddenly proliferate. Previously we had had to rely on the generosity of others donating their snapshots to us.

By this time Dad had become something of a leading light in Littlehampton's *United Services Club* for his prowess with a snooker cue. Clubs in the Bognor and Littlehampton area had decided to form a snooker league and compete against one another for a main trophy and individual cups and shields. At some stage Dad became Secretary of this league and would spend hours every pre-season drawing up a timetable of which club would play where, and against whom. He was also responsible for notifying the local paper, *The Littlehampton Gazette,* of the results of each match and at the end of the season he would have all the trophies, shields and cups engraved and then deliver them to the winning clubs. It was a lot of work and, because he had so much checking-up to do, he started to go to the Club on Sunday evenings as well as Saturdays.

Dad's other "hobby" was doing the weekly football pools coupon.

Before the UK lottery came into being in November 1994, the "Pools", and betting on horses, were the only legal forms of gambling. The "Pools" involved trying to guess what football teams would "draw" in their forthcoming matches and the score. If you managed to guess correctly, it was possible to win hundreds of thousands of pounds, perhaps even the magic one million. Millions of people doing their weekly "Pools" coupons generated huge business for the two main companies, *Littlewood's Pools* and *Vernon's Pools*. They employed part-time collectors who called door-to-door collecting the completed forms (called "coupons") and the stake money.

Dad would spend at least an hour every week poring over his "Pools coupon" trying to decide, for example, if *Arsenal* would win, lose or draw against *West Ham*. The same thought, and considered opinion, went into every single match listed on the form. He took the exercise very seriously and heaven forbid that we should interrupt this important weekly ritual! I am sure this was repeated in many other homes throughout the country, although sticking a pin in a number would probably have served just as well. In all the years he undertook this weekly chore, I can only remember him winning a few pounds, a few times, but the hope of netting the big prize was always there. When he did win, he always shared the money; half went to Mum and we were given extra pocket money.

Dad's football playing days ended when he left the army but he did love to watch all sport on television, especially football. I cannot remember whether he had a favourite team for he seemed to enjoy any game, but woe betide us if we disclosed the score on a match that had been played in the afternoon but was not broadcast until the evening. If the score was likely to be announced in the sports section of the news, Dad would sit there with his eyes closed and his hands over his ears so as not to see or hear the result!

I think the whole country would have liked to close its eyes and ears to the news that came through on 6th February 1958. A chartered 'plane, carrying the Manchester United football team back from a European cup match in Belgrade, crashed after refuelling at Munich Airport. There were 44 people on board including all the team, its staff, eleven journalists and photographers, miscellaneous passengers and six crew. Twenty-three people died, eight of them Manchester United players. The team was known as "*The Busby Babes*", after their manager, Matt Busby. He survived the crash but was the most critically injured. The average age of the team had been just twenty-four years, hence "*Babes*".

At first pilot error was blamed but ten years (and a lot of legal argument) later, it was established that the build-up of slush on the runway had prevented the 'plane taking off. New safety limits were introduced but it was too late to bring back those who had died and the whole country was saddened by the loss of some of its top players.

With some of its best players gone, Manchester United struggled to complete the season but did manage to reach the FA Cup Final, only to be beaten by Bolton Wanderers. Eventually Matt Busby built a second generation of "Busby Babes" including George Best and Denis Law. Ten years later, on 29th May 1968, Manchester United became the first English club to win the European Cup. Bobby Charlton and Bill Foukes were the only two crash survivors who took part in that match.

On 4th October 1957, the Russian space programme had taken a giant leap forward with the launch of Sputnik 1, the first ever man-made object to orbit the earth. On 3rd November of the same year, Sputnik 2 was launched. This had carried a little dog called Laika and thus she became the first earthling to orbit the globe. Laika actually died a few hours after the launch (from stress and over-heating due to a malfunction of a temperature gauge) but this was not made known until decades after the flight. Despite this, the experiment had proved that eventually it would be possible for a human passenger to be launched into space, endure weightlessness and live to tell the tale. Thus Laika's sacrifice paved the way for human space flight.

But the Americans were mortified that the Russians had beaten them to it in the race for control of Space. The surprise launches of Sputniks 1 and 2 galvanised them into speeding up their own space programme with an increase in spending on scientific research and education. On 29th July 1958 NASA (National Aeronautics and Space Administration) was created. The Space-Race between the two "Super-Powers" had begun, with the Americans using the technology they had acquired after the end of the war from the German rocket programme. They had also acquired the brains behind the technology, Wernher von Braun. He became a naturalized citizen of the United States after the war and is today regarded as the father of the United States space programme.

In 1957, Boris Pasternak's novel "Dr Zhivago" was smuggled out of Russia and published in Italy. In a matter of months it had been translated into many other languages and in 1958/59 the American edition spent 26 weeks at the top of the New York Times' bestseller list. In October 1958, Pasternak was named as the winner of the Nobel Prize for Literature. At first he telegrammed the Swedish Academy that he was "Immensely thankful, touched, proud, astonished, abashed." but four days later another telegram arrived saying "Considering the meaning this award has been given in the society to which I belong, I must refuse it." Reading between the lines of the second telegram, it is clear that he declined the award out of fear he would be stripped of his citizenship if he were to travel to Stockholm to accept it. The Swedish Academy announced, *"This refusal, of course, in no way alters the validity of the award ..."* (even if) *"... the presentation of the Prize cannot take place."*

In 1965 *"Dr Zhivago"* was made into a film of epic proportions starring Omar Shariff and Julie Christie. It became a worldwide blockbuster but the novel was not published in Russia until 1988 and the film was not released there until 1990.

Although Pasternak is best known in the West for this novel, in his home country he is most celebrated as a poet, not a writer. His *"My Sister Life"*, written in 1917, is arguably the most influential collection of poetry published in the Russian language in the 20th century. Sadly Boris Pasternak would not live to see *"Dr Zhivago"* published in Russia, nor the film, for he died of lung cancer on May 30th 1960, aged 70 years.

As I mentioned in a previous chapter, in 1949 I was a bridesmaid for my cousin Geoff and his wife Pam. On 6th December 1958, his brother, Derek, married Barbara Butcher in St Catherine's Church, Littlehampton and this time both Sheila and I would be bridesmaids. We wore identical, ankle-length, pale blue dresses with a full skirt that made a complete circle if laid out flat on the ground. Even though I was nine years older than last time around, I can remember very little about the day except how cold it was!

The photographs show us both with short hair (and me with glasses!). Throughout our childhood we had had to have our hair cut fortnightly (yes, fortnightly!) by a lady living in Stanhope Road. I think she was a war widow and Mum felt sorry for her. Neither of us was then at an age to actually rebel against this, although we both complained every time we had to go, and both of us grew our hair long as soon as we could. The only good thing about the frequency of these hairdressing appointments was that her house was very near to the sweet-shop! Since Mum's days of living in Stanhope Road, the sweet-shop on the corner had been turned into a general store (later it would become a Chinese takeaway) and so another of the occupants of the road, Mrs Slaughter, had turned her small, rather dark, front room into a den of delight for those with a sweet tooth. The multi-coloured confectionary was sold from huge, glass jars lined up on shelves behind her, brightening up the otherwise dull and drab interior. We were not the only family members to pay the shop regular visits; Dad was a frequent customer because he was addicted to *Fox's Glacier Mints* and always had a few of them stuffed into various pockets. And, of course, he regularly brought home boxes of chocolates, or liquorice allsorts, for Mum. It is no wonder we all needed the services of the dentist in later years!

Apart from Barbara and Derek's marriage, 1958 also had seen the first *"Lego"* toy bricks come onto the market, hula-hoops becoming very popular and the *"Hope Diamond"* being donated to the Smithsonian Museum. In 1959 Fidel Castro became dictator of Cuba and *"The Sound of Music"* opened on Broadway.

In September of that year Sheila moved onto secondary education. This time she would not be following in my footsteps for she had not passed the *11-plus* exam'. Instead she would be attending the nearby secondary modern school and, from that time on, her behaviour deteriorated. She always seemed so angry, with the world in general but with us in particular. Nothing was right; everything warranted a disagreement. Although the two of us did not come to blows anymore (it had become too painful!) we argued instead, about anything and everything. I am sure Mum did not have this in mind when she dreamed of having a sister! She and Dad still gave in to Sheila most of the time, for by now it had become a habit, but Mum also knew from where Sheila was coming. She was jealous of me. Life seemed to have dealt her a poor hand; apart from the polio' and her gammy leg, I was thin and she was fat. Where I seemed to have no difficulty in making friends, she did not seem popular. And now, to cap it all, I had passed the *11-plus* for grammar school and she had not. She could not verbalise the hurt; it just ate away at her and manifested itself as anger and unhappiness.

I did not see the jealousy and I did not see the pain. I only heard the abuse, the constant demands for attention, the need always to "score points" and to have the last word. I had had enough of being her whipping-boy (or girl) so I asked if I could have the front room as a bed-sitting room, where I could escape and do my home-work in peace and quiet. Sheila stayed in the back bed-room and turned that into her own little den. But we were drawing further and further apart. I hated having a sister and I hated having this sister specifically. Mum, ever the peacemaker, would say, "One day you'll be glad you have her!" And I thought, "Yea! Right! Pigs might fly!" Have you seen any flying pigs lately? Because Mum was right. I cannot imagine life without her now. But a lot of water was to pass under this particular bridge before I could admit that!

Grand-dad Benjamin Clement Oakley.
Taken when he was working as a thatcher.
(Note the knee-pads and ladder against the wall!)
Probably taken about 1935.
Unfortunately this is the only photograph we have of him.

Clement Benjamin Oakley, circa 1923

Dad's brother Edward, known as Ted. Assumed to have been taken c1920 when
he would have been seventeen years of age

Dad's sister Blanche Oakley. Assumed to have been taken c1925

Dad's sister Ellen, (known as Nellie), c 1930

Dad's brother John (known as Jack), c1930

Elsie and Blanche Okley, c1940

Dad's maiden aunts, Mabel and Bertha Pilkington. Pier Road,
Littlehampton, c1935. The river Arun is in the background.

198

Clem Oakley in India, c1920

Clem Oakley and Friends in India, c1920

Clem Oakley, c 1926

Three generations of "Loves". Mary Martin and Anne Martin with Jemima Love.
Taken at the Martin house in Stanhope Road, c1925
This is the only photograph we have of Jemima Love.

Tom and Mary Martin, c 1925

Anne Martin, c1925

Mum's brother William (Bill) Martin, c1927

The youngest of the Martin clan, Richard, known as Dick. c1925

Grandad Tom Martin (in the trilby) with his work-mates, c1930

Clement Benjamin Oakley and Annie Elizabeth Ellen Martin
on their wedding day, 27 September 1930

Mum and Mary Martin in the High Street, Littlehampton 1930

Mum's brother Tom and his son Geoff, 1932

Tom's wife Myrtle with Geoff and Derek, 1932

211

Mary and Tom Martin withgrandson Geoff.
Stanhope Road, Littlehampton, c1934

Evelyn Dodson and her sister in law, Ellen, known as Nellie. Evelyn's daughter Joan is in the pushchair which Nellie is pushing

Clem Oakley and Bill Roberts, c1939
(Bill Roberts later became my Godfather)

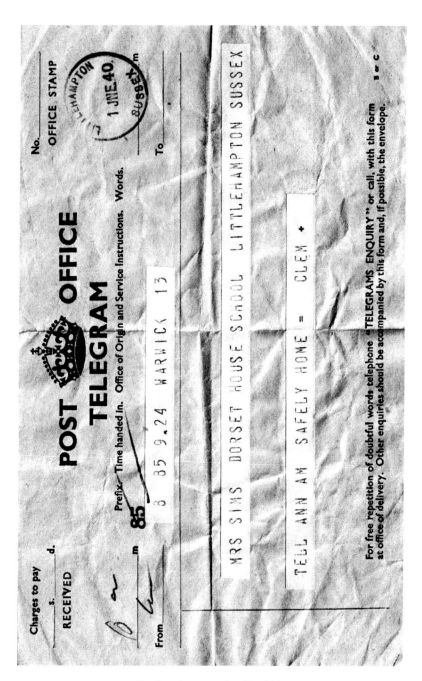

Dad's telegram after Dunkirk

215

Mum's father, Tom Martin, standing outside the extension
he built for them. c 1941

Mum and me on my Christening Day, 21 April 1946.
Taken in our back garden.

Cousin Geoff Martin's wedding to Pam, June 1949.
(Geoff's mother, Myrtle, is standing behind me, (aged 3).

"Uncle" Ted Standage's wedding to Kathleen, c1951

Me, Andrea, Dad, Peter and Sheila. Hotham Park, Bognor Regis. c1951

28

Family Picnic at Goodward, c1951
Dad has Sheila on his lap with me next to him. Mum is in the foreground holding a cup of tea. Gerald Roberts' wife is next to her. Gerald, son of dad's Army pal Bill Roberts, is behind her and to his left his mother Linda.

Camping in Wales, c1952
L–R Terry (Uncle Ted's eldest son), Uncle Ted's friend, Uncle Ted (in cap) Ivan
standing up. The other two boys are the friend's sons. L-R girls; Ellita,
Gwendoline, me.

29b

Me aged about six years, outside our home in Littlehampton.
(Note the gate we used to swing on.)
30

Sheila Oakley, aged 5 years

Sheila's Bithday Party, 1st July 1953 taken in our back garden.
Front row, L-R; NK, Sheila, Ellita, me. Middle row; NK, NK, Peter Starte, Lesley Steer. Back row; Phyllis Moore, Kathleen Beech, NK, Joyce Moore.

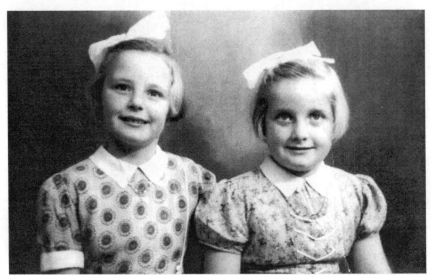
Sheila and me aged about six and eight years. Sheila is on the right.

On Littlehampton's East Beach, c1955
Gwendoline, Yvonne, Ivan, me, Sheila. Mum behind us in deck chair. (Note the fashionable ruched swimsuits.)

Cousin Derek's wedding to Barbara Butcher in December 1958 at St Catherine's Church, Littlehampton. From L-R; Uncle Tom, Auntie Myrtle, Sheila, Geoff Martin, unknown bridesmaid, Derek, Barbara, me. Mrs Butcher, Mr Butcher and Barbara's brother Christopher.

Dad, Sheila and our pet dog, Laddie at Beachy Head, c1963

Sheila's wedding to Eric Vernon "Mac" Carpenter in1972. Taken outside Mac's parents house. L-R Me, Janet Haddon (Sheila's friend), Gerry Brough (Mac's neice), John Barradell (best man), Mac and Sheila

Group photograph of our family at Sheila's wedding taken outside Mac's parents house, Hythe House, Hythe , Southampton.
L-R; Mum's brother Les and his wife Dorie, me, Bryan and Mum and Dad

"Mac", Russell, Vernon and Sheila Carpenter, c1974

Vernon and Russell at their beach-hut in Calshot, c1978

Mum and Dad arriving for their Golden Wedding Anniversay Party,
30th Sepetember 1980

227

Mum and her bridesmaids at Golden Party.
Mum in middle. L-R; Violet Martin, Edith and Carrie (nee Starte), Blanche Oakley

Mum's niece Andrea (daughter of Bill and Violet) with Mum's brother Dick. Taken at my parents Golden Wedding Anniversay Party, 27th September 1980

Dad's sister Blanche with their sister-in-law Daisy (widow of brother Jack). Taken at my parents Golden Wedding Anniversay Party, 27th September 1980

Sheila Carpenter and her sister Sheila Robinson, 1981

Sheila, her half-sister Sue and biological mother, Phyllis.
Taken at the Family Picnic, August 1982

Mum's 80th birthday celebration take at the family picnic August 1985.
L-R; Uncle Ted (Standage), Russell, Sheila and Mum.

Me, Mum and Sheila on Cliff Walk, Newport, Rhode Island.
Taken on holiday in March 1988

231

Mum and her brother Bill, c1987.
Taken at the ancient (smuggling) town of Rye, Kent.
(Note the cobblestones. One of the few places in the UK to have retained them.)

Mum and Dad on their diamond wedding day 27th September 1990, in our "back-room" of the family home in Littlehampton.

Vernon and Dad on his 90th birthday, 8 October 1991.

Russell Carpenter, 1993

Vernon Carpenter 1993

Vernon and me. Taken on his High School Graduation Day, June 1993.
(Note the painting of Mac on the wall behind us, hanging crookedly,
unfortunately!)

Russell Carpenter, Carpenter Close, Hythe, Hampshire, England

My sister and me, Newport, Rhode Island, 1993

CHAPTER TWENTY-EIGHT

Saints and Sinners
(1960)

As we entered the new decade, destined to become known as the *"Swinging Sixties",* I was coming up to fourteen years of age and Sheila would be twelve in July. We had stopped going to Sunday School some years before but we went instead to the main communion service. At that time we had a very pro-active vicar, Father Barry. If a regular churchgoer did not attend a service for more than a couple of weeks, he went around to his/her house to see what was wrong and he also made regular home-calls to all his parishioners, just for a chat. I think it must have been on one of these visits that he persuaded Mum to start going to church. Dad was a lost cause but at least he did take us there and bring us back!

Father Barry was responsible for "St Mary's" becoming a "high" church, modelled on Roman Catholic places of worship. Thus we had incense swinging about on special occasions, regular "confessions" were encouraged and we called priests, "Father". But he was a very sincere, caring man who took his duties to his "flock" very seriously.

I was confirmed into the church in 1960 and Mum and Sheila were confirmed together a couple of years later. Both Sheila and I stopped going to church in our late teens (Father Barry had left by then!) but Mum carried on going every week virtually until the day she died. But she was not just a "Church Christian"; she brought her faith into every aspect of her life, without ramming it down anyone's throat. I always think fondly of Dad being the "Sinner", where Mum was the "Saint"!

Some time around 1960, Father Barry was joined by a young curate, Father Patterson, who made a special effort to reach-out to the town's young people. Towards this end he set up a youth club in the Church Hall and installed a darts- board, table-tennis and a coffee bar; they also played records and held dances. (I suppose they would be called disco's now!) He organised hikes, bicycle rides and camp-fires. Despite his best endeavours, it was not really my scene. Apart from an increasing amount of home-work, in the autumn of 1960 I obtained a Saturday (and holiday) job with *Woolworth's,* on their sweet counter as it happened! I had to wear a hideous, white overall, several sizes too large for me, and a silly, little hat on my very short hair but at least I had more pocket money. I was trying to save for a school trip the following year to Venice and Switzerland. Mum and Dad had agreed to pay for the actual holiday but I had to save for new clothes and my own spending money. I was also a patrol leader in my Guide Company by this time and was organising my own hikes and cook-outs as well as helping out with a Cub Pack in East Preston, so I had little time for other outside interests but Sheila joined the Church Youth Club and loved it. She became a very good table-tennis player and later on she joined the local Badminton Club and went on to represent them in matches against other towns. She also used to baby-sit for the Patterson family which gave her a little extra pocket money.

But back in 1960, not yet twelve years old, one evening she left the Church Youth Club to walk home. It was 8.30pm and she knew she was expected to be back at home by 9pm at the latest. It was pouring with rain, so when our postman pulled up in his van and asked her if she wanted a lift home, she did not really hesitate. After all, he was well known to all of us, especially Dad because he was also a member of the *United Services Club*. To her surprise, however, he drove off in the wrong direction and then, to her consternation, they ended up in a deserted car-park. By this time she was very frightened but we had always been told to be polite to adults so she did not know what to do without seeming rude. At that very moment a face appeared at the driver's window and a fist rapped on the steamed-up glass.

"Who's this young lady then?" it enquired. It was a policeman who had pulled up on his bicycle.

"It's all right, constable" replied the driver. "It's my niece."

The policeman must have been satisfied because he pedalled off but the comment alerted Sheila that something was definitely not right. Then he ran his hand up her skirt and forced his fingers under the elastic of her knickers. She froze in sheer terror but then gathered her wits and had the presence of mind to open the passenger door and get out as fast as she could. The driver put out a hand to restrain her but she slammed the door shut, catching his fingers in the jamb as she did so. She ran off as fast as her legs could carry her.

All the way home she expected this man to catch up with her, but even as she fell in our front door, her troubles were not over. She was late and tried to explain what had happened but Mum did not believe her and accused her of telling lies. In tears she protested that it was true. Dad took over the inquisition. "C'mon, duck. It's OK now. Just calm down and tell us what happened." Between tears, Sheila related the story and Dad promised, "It's over now, duck. He won't bother you again. You just leave it to me."

The next day he confronted the postman on his round. The postman denied even offering her a lift.

"Why are your fingers bandaged then?" asked Dad. "Got caught in any car doors lately, have you?" His 5-foot 4-inches squared up to the man's taller height and with his face pushed firmly into the man's space, and his index finger repeatedly poking the man's chest, he warned venomously, "If you EVER touch my daughter again, so help me, I'll swing for you." (We still had hanging then for capital offences.) "You're nothing but a perverted bit of slime," he added.

The postman was never seen on our round again and he stopped going to "Dad's" club. Luckily Dad was a man of the world where something like this was quite beyond my mother's comprehension.

During the summer of 1960, Sheila and I went on a Girl Guide camp to Lympstone in Devon. It was at this camp that I met my first "boy-friend". The camp had been flooded out and we had had to be rescued by the local villagers, including the Boy Scout Troop! One of the Venture Scouts had taken a shine to me and we kept in touch by letter after the camp had ended. Indeed eventually he travelled all the way to Littlehampton to see me, staying in a local guest house. Unfortunately I had cooled by this time. (I was only fourteen years of age, after all, to his seventeen.) I did not have the experience to end the relationship in a civilised manner so I behaved in a very offhand manner! Not surprisingly, he cooled too. My parents thought him a lovely young man, which he was, and he deserved much better treatment from me. I hope my parents' innate good manners, and honest hospitality, helped to make up for my decided lack of both. I still feel bad about it nearly fifty years later and my sister still delights in reminding me how horrible I was!

It must have been around this time that I attended my first dance. We were on holiday in Guildford, as usual, and the local Sea Cadets had arranged a social evening. Uncle Ted's eldest son, Terry, and his fiancée (another Sheila) were organising it. I cannot remember now whose suggestion it was, but I was invited to go along as Ivan's partner. I did not have a suitable dress to wear, so Auntie Kathleen very kindly offered to make me one. It was a rush-job and only finished with minutes to spare. The dress itself was fine but the waist was miles too big and we had no belt to go around it. I remember spending the whole evening feeling so self-conscious that I must have made a very poor "date" for my cousin!

Returning to school after the summer holidays, I started my GCE "O" level (General Certificate of Education at Ordinary level) syllabus in earnest. I had to decide whether to do "Domestic Science", "Art" or "Needlework" as a "recreational" subject (instead of all three). I could not decide which one to choose, for I enjoyed them all, so I sought Mum's advice. She thought "Art" of no use whatsoever, and "cooking" she said I could get out of a recipe book. "Needlework" however was difficult to learn on your own and she had always regretted not being able to make her own clothes. "Do needlework", she recommended. So I did and thus it was that I ended up eventually making clothes, not only for myself, but for the whole family. I do not think Mum was aware when she gave me this advice, that my biological grand-mother had been a seamstress. It was a good choice; not only did it give me hours of pleasure over the years but, like my less than perfect eyesight, it was probably already lurking in my genes.

It was around this time that Mum suffered a nasty accident. She used to walk to the town-centre shops via a wide footpath we called *The Green Lady*. It ran alongside the playing-field of Connaught Road School and came out right opposite "Winterton Lodge" in East Street, which was then part of the Dorset House School complex where Dad worked.

On this particular day some young lads thought it would be amusing to tie a piece of twine across the path, a few inches above the ground, and watch for some poor soul to trip over it. The poor soul was our mother. Luckily she did not break any bones but her knees were cut and bruised, her stockings torn, and she was badly shaken. The lads ran off laughing while Mum managed to stagger across to Winterton Lodge and seek help. Dad was summoned and he fetched the car to take her home.

Mum was very fortunate in that none of her varicose veins ruptured but she was so unnerved by the incident that she began to develop agoraphobia. I started to do the shopping for her but, after a few weeks of staying indoors, she knew she could not go on like this indefinitely. She forced herself to walk to the shops again, forever after being extremely careful there were no hidden hazards in her path.

The first true laser was made in 1960 from a synthetic ruby, although the idea of "Stimulated Emission" (on which the modern laser is based) was first proposed by Albert Einstein as early as 1917. LASER is an acronym for Light Amplification by Stimulated Emission of Radiation and the uses to which this invention can be put seems almost limitless. Indeed, the early pioneers would be truly astounded to see the multitude of ways lasers are now used. The most well-known applications these days are bar code readers and laser printers but by far the largest single exploitation is in optical storage devices, such as compact discs and DVD players. Lasers are also used in manufacturing for such tasks as bending and welding; by the military for range finding and target designation; in medicine for surgery, diagnostics and therapeutic reasons, amongst many others, and it all began in earnest in 1960.

1960 also saw film director Alfred Hitchcock's *"Psycho"* released and Brazil's capital moved from Rio de Janeiro to a brand new city, Brasília.

On 23rd June 1960, the Federal Drug Administration (FDA) in America approved the use of the first oral contraceptive. It became known, both sides of the Atlantic, simply as "the Pill" and provided a reversible method of birth control that was almost 100% effective when taken as directed. However, in America, it was not available to married women in all States until 1965 and not prescribed universally throughout the country to all unmarried women until 1972.

Things were a little different in the UK for we did not require pre-marketing approval of drugs until the mid-1960's. Thus the Family Planning Associations (FPA's) conducted trials of the new contraceptive pill. It added it to its list of approved methods of birth control in October 1961 and on 4th December the Health Minister, Enoch Powell, announced that *Conovid* could be prescribed through the NHS at a subsidised price of 2s 0d (two shillings) per month to any woman who wanted it, married or not.

For the first time women were free to enjoy spontaneous sex without the fear of pregnancy (but at the risk of sexually transmitted disease!) and the Pill was to play a major role in the sexual liberation of women that began (for better or worse!) in these "Swinging Sixties".

It is probably hard for young people today to understand why the "Sixties" are remembered with such fondness by "oldies" of my generation. In these days of universal, high-tech, computer-generated "musak" and a proliferation of goods and entertainment aimed solely for their delectation and delight, it is difficult to imagine that youthful needs were not always of prime consideration. But it was not always so. By the early 1960's, the "baby boomers" of post-war years were becoming discerning teenagers, with spare cash in our pockets. We wanted more than our parents had accepted as the "norm". So clothes, music and clubs, solely for young people, suddenly exploded onto the market. Everything was so new, so different. The world was our oyster, it seemed. We felt there was nothing we could not achieve. We were shaking off the yoke of convention and many people claim that nothing today can match the absolute excitement of living as a teenager in the "*Swinging Sixties*".

One of the principle contributors in putting the epithet "Swinging" to "Sixties" was a pop and rock group from Liverpool, *The Beatles*. Formed in 1960, they are credited with leading the mid-1960's British invasion of pop music into the US and are one of the most commercially successful and critically acclaimed bands in the history of popular music. They have sold more albums in the US than any other band and had more number one albums in the UK than any other group in UK history.

Even though the group disbanded in 1970, to pursue solo careers, in 1985 their record company estimated that they had sold over one billion records world-wide. Even as late as 2004, the "Rolling Stone Magazine" ranked *The Beatles* number one in its list of 100 Greatest Artists of All Time. They put their home city of Liverpool on the world stage and their influence on popular music, clothes, hair styles and social awareness reverberate to this day.

The *Beatles* were very much "mainstream" and, despite *Beatlemania* amongst their teenage fans, their smart clothes and clean bobbed hairstyles appealed to an older generation as well. Not so the *Teddy Boys* who were now disappearing from the streets of Britain to be replaced by the equally dubious (in the minds of parents at least) subcultures of *"Mods"* and *"Rockers"*. Both were products of working-class British youth and each represented opposite tastes with regard to clothing, grooming, music and their preferred modes of transport.

"Mods" portrayed an image of being "stuck-up", snobbish and phoney. They dressed in suits, narrow trousers and pointed shoes. The girls displayed a boyish image and both wore their hair cut short to suit a unisex type of culture. The first *"Mods"* adopted the modern jazz music of Black America as their preferred "signature tune" but later they sparked a nationwide enthusiasm for Rhythm and Blues music, as played by such bands as "The Rolling Stones" and "The Kinks". However the band most closely identified with the *"Mods"* was the "High Numbers", later re-named "The Who". Their violence on stage personified the aggression inherent in *"Mod"* subculture. *"Mods"* consumed "Purple Hearts" (a mixture of amphetamine and barbiturates) and their preferred transport was a *Lambretta* or a *Vespa* motor-scooter.

"Rockers" were a British version of the Hell's Angels motorcycle gang. They wore jeans, boots and black leather jackets with lots of studs. They despised any fashion and all had the same shaggy hairstyles. With their scruffy, masculine, bad-boy image and anti-authority beliefs, they portrayed the very epitome of an easy-rider, nomadic, anti-establishment figure. They rode *Triumph* or *Norton* souped-up motorcycles at very high speeds, so they kept away from all drugs. *The Ace Café,* on London's North Circular Road, was the preferred haunt of the *"Rocker"* and his music was, of course, Rock 'n Roll.

It seems as if there is an innate desire in some young people to be part of a subculture, or gang, for it confers status, acceptance and even power. Gangs have always been with us but it was in the late 50's and early 60's that they first received the oxygen of mass publicity through newspapers and the new medium of television. Thus the rivalry between *Mods* and *Rockers*, fuelled in part by the media, was perhaps inevitable, culminating in a fight between the two groups at Clacton on an Easter weekend in 1964. In truth there was very little damage, apart from some broken windows and the destruction of some beach huts. But it occurred in a week of little newsworthy material and thus the national and international press, including the "New York Times" and the "New York Herald Tribune", reported the incident with such headlines as "hell-bent for destruction". As a result of the exaggerated media reports, the general public became outraged at their behaviour and perceived both groups to be social deviants. The days of the *"Mod"* were numbered. *"Rockers"* survived a little longer but they were never as popular as in the heady days of the early 60's

Indeed even as the "Mod" and "Rocker" declined in popularity, so another "cult" surfaced and it was one that would have a huge influence on Western society for decades to come: the age of the "Hippie" was upon us. Originally they were a San Francisco youth movement known as "Beatniks" but their name changed as their influence spread around the globe.

They created their own communities (or communes); listened to psychedelic rock music (i.e. music played under the influence of mind-altering drugs); embraced the sexual revolution of "free love"; created so-called "flower-power" and the "peace movement"; and used drugs, such as cannabis and LSD, to explore alternative states of consciousness.

By the end of the decade the Woodstock Music Festival on the East Coast of America, and the summer pilgrimage of "New Age Travellers" to free music festivals at Stonehenge in the UK, were well established. Hippie fashions and values were to have a huge effect on culture by influencing dress, hairstyles, music, television, film, literature, the arts and politics.

The legacy of the hippie movement continues to permeate Western society. Thanks to them most people today consider public political demonstrations to be legitimate expressions of free speech. Thanks to them unmarried couples of all ages feel free to travel and live together without society's disapproval. Thanks to them frankness regarding sexual matters have become common and the rights of homosexual, bisexual and transsexual people have expanded. There is more tolerance for religious and cultural diversity and a greater interest in natural foods, herbal remedies, vitamins and other nutritional supplements, all of which can find its roots in the hippie movement. They are also credited with the rise in the popularity of "ethnic" clothes and the decline of the necktie, which had been an essential part of a man's dress prior to this era. It is even claimed in some quarters that the development of the *Internet* can find its roots in the anti-authoritarian ethos promoted by the movement.

On the downside, of course, the increasing lack of moral values; the huge rise in drug addiction, teenage pregnancies, abortions and divorce; the selfishness and greed of a society that says "anything goes" and "I'll do what pleases me, irrespective of how if may affect you!"; and a total disregard for the observance of religious strictures, might also be said to have their roots in this movement. There is truly no gain without pain.

CHAPTER TWENTY-NINE

More Sinners than Saints!
(1961)

The 2nd April 1961 saw the start of a highly controversial and much publicized trial. It was controversial because the defendant had been kidnapped from Argentina in May of the previous year by the Israeli Intelligence Service, "Mossad", and then smuggled to Israel to face charges of "crimes against humanity". It was much publicized around the globe because the defendant was Adolf Eichmann, one of the most feared and hated Nazi leaders of the Second World War. He was "Chief of Operations" and responsible for deporting millions of Jews to the Nazi concentration camps. At the end of the war he escaped from an American internment camp, fled to Buenos Aires, and there he lived, under an assumed name, until "Mossad" tracked him down. The trial ended on 14th August with the inevitable verdict of "Guilty". Eichmann was sentenced to death and executed at Ramleh Prison on 31st May 1962. "Mossad" spent the rest of the century continuing to hunt down Nazi war criminals but this was by far their most spectacular coup in this regard.

On 12th April 1961, the Russians once again beat the Americans in the "Space-Race". Major Yuri Gargarin was launched into the stratosphere and orbited Earth for 108 minutes, the first human being ever to do so. He became an international icon but in 1968 he was killed in a 'plane crash, just outside Moscow, in what some people believed were suspicious circumstances.

On the 13th August 1961, the Soviet-backed government of East Germany began the construction of a wall separating East and West Berlin. On 24th August, Gunter Litfin became the first person to be killed trying to cross this wall to freedom in the West. Indeed there were to be no less than fifty deaths in the first year of its existence, such was the savageness of the ideology "The Berlin Wall" represented. Over the years the barbed wire was re-inforced with concrete; watch towers and anti-tank traps were added; attack dogs, floodlights and 1.6million mines installed. The Wall lasted for twenty-eight years and became a potent symbol of the "Iron Curtain" and the "Cold War". Official figures confirm 133 people died trying to cross the Wall but a victim's support group maintain at least 200 people perished.

1961 was the year the "Thalidomide" tragedy hit the headlines. *Thalidomide* was a drug first marketed in West Germany in 1957 but soon exported to at least 46 other countries under many different brand names. It was a sedative that gave great relief to pregnant women suffering from morning sickness. Unfortunately it was not realised that molecules of the drug could cross the placenta wall and affect the foetus, causing severe birth defects such as deafness, blindness, internal problems and the disability most associated with the drug, phocomelia, or deformed limbs. It was withdrawn from the West German and UK markets by December 1961 but this was too late for the estimated ten to twenty thousand babies who were disabled as a consequence of their mothers taking *Thalidomide*. Never counted, and never to be known, are the numbers of babies miscarried, stillborn or aborted because of the drug.

Over the next decade families around the world sued the drug and distribution companies and many were awarded substantial settlements. There are approximately 5000 survivors still alive today.

Thalidomide is still prescribed, though never to pregnant women, and only under strict supervision. Nowadays it is used to treat such ailments as certain types of cancer, leprosy and rheumatoid arthritis. Drugs chemically similar to *Thalidomide* are being investigated as a treatment for many other disorders.

While all this international news was taking place, the spring of 1961 began a year of teenage rebellion for me. I cannot remember the sequence now but I think the first occasion must have been a romance of which my mother disapproved heartily. I cannot recall that she ever met the young man concerned but his, and his family's, reputation must have preceded him. At twenty-two years of age he was seven years my senior, and he did come from a fairly "rough" background, but he was always very kind and generous to me. With the benefit of hindsight, and somewhat sounder judgement, it was becoming much too serious, much too quickly, at far too young an age. Mum, of course, could see this where I could, or would, not and she tried to persuade me to end the relationship.   With typical teenage pigheadedness, the more confrontational and desperate she became, the more determined I remained. It reached the stage where we were barely speaking.

One day Dad met me at the top of our road. "I wanted to have a word with you, duck. Away from home," he began. "It's about this boyfriend of yours. I know how important this young man is to you but do you realise you are making your mother ill with worry? She can't sleep, she can't eat....."

"But I love him, Dad!" I wailed.

"Yes, I know you do, duck. But you are very young. Would you not agree to stop seeing him just for a few months? For your Mum's sake? Then if you still want to go out with him after a break, and he with you, we won't stand in your way. After all you have your whole life ahead of you....."

Tears started pouring down my face. "Is Mum really that worried?"
"Yes, duck, she is. But she doesn't know that I'm speaking to you. This is just between you and me."

I ended the romance. I was heartbroken for about a week but in less than a month I went out for the first time with someone I was destined to marry ..... but not for many years and then only after a very on-off courtship! Such was the fickleness of youth! As for the young man, he was married within the year, so he was not exactly devastated either. I have no idea if Dad ever confessed to Mum that he had intervened but I thank my lucky stars that he did.

Having just recovered from this disagreement, Mum and I headed straight into another one. My school-friend, Jenny, and I missed the train to school one day. We caught the later one but knew we would have to do a detention for being late for assembly. So when we arrived at our destination, instead of going through the school-gates, we carried on walking and walked all the way home, about ten miles! We thought if we caught the train back to Littlehampton, the station-masters might report us!

When I got home I blithely asked Mum if she would write a sick-note for me. I could not really believe it when she replied, "No. I won't. I will not lie for you and I will certainly not tempt fate by making illness an excuse for you when it is not true."
"But Mum," I pleaded, "I'll get into terrible trouble! Jenny's mum is going to do it for her!"
"I don't care what Jenny's mum is going to do. I will not write a note for you with a lie. You should have thought of that when you skipped school!"

The thought of having to own up to a day of truancy was more than I could bear (and it never occurred to me to forge a letter) so I appealed to Dad when he came home from work.
"PLEASE Dad", I begged. "Will YOU write me a note?"
He agreed to do it, under protest, but for this time only, with a promise extracted from me that I would never play truant again. I never did and what is more I have never, ever, claimed I was ill when I was not. This incident had a profound effect on me for the rest of my life and I came to have a great respect for my mother for sticking to her principles.

I must have looked as guilty as sin when Jenny and I handed in our "sick" notes the next day. It was obvious our form-master did not believe us but at least we did not have to do a detention. Mind you the amount of work we had to catch up on, for this day of absence in an "O" level year, was unbelievable. Was the day of truancy worth it? Definitely not!

The holiday to Venice caused another confrontation. By now I had grown my hair and in the Spring of 1961 I had bleached it, against parental advice! Of course eventually it had grown out darker at the

247

roots and I have to admit it looked awful. I tried to dye it but the bleached ends went a bright red. I thought it was an improvement but my mother was of the opinion that it looked worse than ever and vowed she would not allow me to go to Venice looking like that. She insisted I had it dyed professionally. As she said she would pay for it, I was forced to agree. So in a matter of weeks I was a blonde, a redhead and a brunette!

I have never tried to dye my hair since, although a year later I decided to try and perm' it! I do not know whether I was just unlucky with my attempts at DIY hairdressing but the resulting head of frizz made me want to fall off the edge of the planet until it grew out! It was many, many years before I would risk another perm' and then only if it was professionally executed.

The last argument I can remember having with Mum was over clothes. I had made myself a very tight, pink and white cotton, straight skirt with very fashionable "Charleston" pleats around the hem. I suppose it came just above the knee as this was before Mary Quant and her mini-skirts came into fashion. (That was 1965.) With a tight, white top and my up-to-the-minute, white, winkle-picker, stiletto-heeled shoes, I thought I looked very sophisticated. Mum did not agree. She thought I looked "like a tart"! We had our worst row ever, in fact our only real row ever, and I ended up shouting angrily, "Well no doubt I get that trait from my mother!"

"Oh, Maureen!" she replied sadly. "You don't know what you are talking about. Your mother wasn't a tart!"

"Well what was she then?" I retorted. "You don't tell me anything about her!"

So she told me that my mother was in her forties when she had given birth to me and that she had worked in a laundry. She said she had been courting a Canadian soldier during the war and had been misled into thinking they would get married.

"If you want to know more, I will tell you everything I know when you are twenty-one," she added.

I still did not know that our Uncle Bert was my mother's brother nor that she too was deaf. In fact the "Canadian soldier" bit deflected further queries about my mother. How exotic my paternity sounded and I wanted to know more about him instead but of course Mum knew very little else in that regard, other than what she had already disclosed. By the time I was twenty-one, I was too busy with my own life to worry about the past and it would be many years before the subject surfaced again.

CHAPTER THIRTY

Out in the Big Wide World
(1962-1965)

1962 started off well for the United States for in February the Americans caught up with the Soviets in the space-race. On 20th of that month, astronaut John Glenn became the first American to orbit the earth in the rocket, *"Friendship 7"*.

Later that year, on 5th August, the screen icon, Marilyn Monroe, was found dead in bed at her Los Angeles home with an empty bottle of *Nembutal* sleeping pills by her side. Her death was recorded as "possible suicide" but many of her friends felt this verdict to be highly unlikely. They thought an accidental overdose was the more feasible explanation. However others have suggested a third party might even have administered the drug. The truth will probably never be known but what is certain is that her romantic life, like her death, was the subject of much gossip and speculation, for her name was linked with the then-President of the US, John F. Kennedy.

In October 1962, reconnaissance photographs, taken by an American spy-plane, revealed Russian missile bases being built in Cuba. Along with the *"Berlin Blockade"* of 1948, the *"Cuban Missile Crisis"* ranks as one of the two major confrontations of the "Cold War" and is regarded as the moment in which the two "Super Powers" came closest to a nuclear war. Fortunately, on 28th October, the President of the United States and the United Nation's Secretary-General, U Thant, reached an agreement with the Soviets for them to dismantle their missile bases in Cuba in exchange for an American no-invasion (of Cuba) agreement and the secret removal of US missile bases in Turkey. The threat of a nuclear holocaust had been averted.

1962 was also the year I left school. I debated whether to stay on for G.C.E. "A" (Advanced) levels as I had a vague notion of going into the teaching profession, but the thought of five more years of study was more than I could face, so I became a bank-clerk instead.

The winter of 1962/63 was the coldest over England and Wales since 1740 and the coldest in Scotland since 1879. From Boxing Day 1962 to early March 1963, much of England was continuously under a blanket of snow. Unlike the winter of 1947, however, 1962/63 was sunnier and the snowfall was less but mean temperatures were well below freezing almost everywhere. Extremely low temperatures were recorded across the length and breadth of the country but Braemar (in Scotland) took the record, on 18th January, with a minimum of minus 22.2°C.

Lakes and rivers froze, ice formed in harbours on the south and east of England and patches of ice were even formed on the sea. Huge blocks of ice were formed on beaches where waves broke and the spray froze. Coastal marine life suffered severely. As in 1947, roads were blocked by huge drifts and where railway lines were clear, the electric points were frozen so rail links were unpredictable at best and often non-existent. Once again supplies were dropped to isolated villages and farms by helicopter and once again farmers were unable to reach their livestock and thousands of animals perished in the cold.

Milder weather and rain reached the south-west of England on 4th March and, by 6th March, there was no frost anywhere in the British Isles. With the thaw came flooding but nothing like the floods of 1947.

On 23rd January, while Britain was enduring this bitter winter, one of the UK's most brazen spies, fearing discovery and arrest, fled to the Soviet Union. Harold (Kim) Philby was known as the "Third Man" of a Cambridge University spy-ring. In 1944 he had been employed by Britain's intelligence agency, MI6, in charge of "Soviet Affairs". From this exalted position he was able to protect other soviet agents such as Guy Burgess and Donald Maclean, also recruited while undergraduates at the university, and both of whom defected to the Soviet union in 1951, just before they were due to be interrogated by MI6. Later it came to be accepted that Philby had tipped them off and that another member of the Cambridge spy-ring, Antony Blunt (the Fourth Man) used his position in MI5 to assist in the arrangements for their defection. (MI5 and MI6 are roughly equivalent to the Central Intelligence Agency (CIA) of the United States.)

As the UK reeled from the revelations of this spying scandal, another kind of scandal erupted. This involved a senior Cabinet Minister of Harold MacMillan's Conservative government and the Minister's dalliance with a high-class call-girl. Not in itself so very earth-shattering, even though the Minister was married and adultery was still considered politically unacceptable, but this was when the "Cold War" was at its height and the Minister was no less than the Secretary of State for War, John Profumo. To make matters worse, it was alleged that the call-girl, Christine Keeler, also had a relationship with Yevgeny Ivanov, a senior naval attaché at the Soviet Embassy and a known Russian spy. The ramifications of a possible breach in national security were obvious, especially coming along so soon after the Philby debacle.

In March 1963 Profumo stated in the House of Commons that there was "no impropriety whatever" in his relationship with Keeler but in June he was forced to confess that he had lied in his testimony and misled the House. On 5th June he resigned his cabinet position and his parliamentary seat. It is said the scandal, known as the "Profumo Affair", helped to topple the Conservative Government and contributed to the victory of the Labour Party in the 1964 general election.

Profumo was a wealthy man and after his resignation, he devoted his energies to voluntary work. He began by cleaning toilets at Toynbee Hall, a little-known charity based in the East End of London, and eventually became their chief fund-raiser. Clement Attlee and William Beveridge are two famous names who were influenced by the work of Toynbee Hall, which was founded in 1884 as part of the "settlement movement" and remains a centre for social reform to this day. Similar "settlement" houses are in existence throughout England and the US, all countering social deprivation and under-achievement. The "Workers' Educational Association" and the "Child Poverty Action Group" were founded at Toynbee Hall, for example.

John Profumo was awarded the CBE in 1975 for his work with the charity and he died in 2006, aged 91, his reputation restored.

Sheila left school in July 1963, and also started work in an office. Mum had promised herself that once we both left school, she would give up her job in the kitchens and she was true to her word. So, as both Sheila and I joined the working masses, our mother bowed out of the rat-race. She had worked for the *School Meals Service* for ten years and had done well to last that long for she had suffered dreadfully with her hands while she worked there. Not only were they always sore and chapped but, on more than one occasion, she contracted a severe nail infection which necessitated pushing an ointment of some kind right down behind the nail. It still makes me shudder to think of it but she never complained.

Giving up her job meant Mum had more time to pursue other interests, so over the next few years she joined the *Mothers' Union,* the *Townswomen's Guild* and the *Women's Section of the Royal British Legion* which met at "Dad's club", the *United Services Club.* She thoroughly enjoyed the camaraderie of all the meetings, especially when they had a speaker or went on an outing. On several occasions, she and her friends, Carrie and Edith, went to see the *Royal Tournament* at Earls Court in London, organised as a regular yearly excursion by the British Legion.

The Royal Tournament was the first, the oldest and the biggest military tattoo in the world. It was first held as an Army pageant in Islington, London, in 1880 but over the years it grew in size and popularity until, in 1950, it moved to the Earls Court Exhibition Centre. By then all the Armed Services were involved and the acts included military bands, re-enactments of battles, musical rides by the Cavalry Regiments and musical drives by the Royal Artillery. The Royal Signals

Motor Cycle Team was a regular feature as was the Royal Marine Commandos' Assault Course, the Royal Navy's Field Gun Competition and Continuity Drills from the Royal Air Force. It was a fantastic show-case for the Armed Services and was a regular item in the summer schedule of BBC television. Sadly it ended in 1999 (after 120 years) as a cost cutting measure in the National Defence Budget.

Meanwhile Dad was still heavily involved in his snooker activities at the club. As well as the League Secretary, he was now the official captain of the United Services snooker and billiards team.

On the 8th August 1963, what came to be regarded as the most audacious UK robbery of the 20th century took place at Bridgego Railway Bridge at Ledburn in Buckinghamshire. Forever known as "The Great Train Robbery", it was undertaken by a gang of fifteen men, led by Bruce Reynolds and including Ronnie Biggs, Charlie Wilson and "Buster" Edwards. They robbed a mail-train of over two million pounds sterling (£2,631,784.00 to be exact!) in used bank-notes which were on their way to the Bank of England for destruction. This would equate to approximately £40m ($60m) at today's value and thus it was the largest robbery by value in British history at that time. The theft was supposed to be violence-free but one of the gang hit the train driver, Jack Mills, over the head to force him to move the train to their designated drop-off point.

The robbers fled to an isolated, rundown farm (near a village called Oakley, in Buckinghamshire!) but they only stayed long enough to divide the spoils. Five days after the robbery, a local herdsman tipped off police that they might have been there and eventually that trail, and further tip-offs, led to the arrest of thirteen of the thieves.

At their trial, the judge described the robbery *"as a crime of sordid violence inspired by vast greed"* and passed out sentences of an unprecedented thirty years on seven of the villains. Two of them, Ronnie Biggs and Charlie Wilson, subsequently escaped from their prisons. Biggs ended up in Brazil but in May 2001 he voluntarily returned to the UK to serve the rest of his sentence. He was released on compassionate grounds in 2009.

Charlie Wilson fled to Canada and was re-arrested there in 1968. He was released from prison in 1978 and found shot dead at his villa in Marbella, Spain, in 1990.

On his release, Roy James (another of the robbers sentenced to thirty years) became an accomplished silversmith and produced trophies for the Formula One World Championships, possibly thanks to his acquaintance with Bernie Ecclestone, the billionaire promoter of the sport.

Both of the two not initially apprehended (Bruce Reynolds and "Buster" Edwards) fled to Mexico. Bruce Reynolds was the last robber to be brought to justice, in November 1968. Following his release in 1979, he became a high-profile "former criminal" and wrote his autobiography in 1995, entitled, not surprisingly, *"The Autobiography of a Thief"*.

Ronald "Buster" Edwards voluntarily surrendered to authorities in Mexico and subsequently served ten years in prison. On his release, he became a flower-seller outside Waterloo Station. A comedy-drama of his life, called *"Buster"* and starring Phil Collins, was made in 1988. Edwards committed suicide in 1994.

The robbery spawned other films and books, and with the participants also regularly hitting the headlines, the robbery must be one of the most well-known heists of the 20th century.

On 28th August 1963, the "March on Washington for Jobs and Freedom" took place in Washington, D.C., USA. It was organised by the black activist, and committed Christian, Dr. Martin Luther King, Jr. and was attended by some 250,000 people. It was the largest demonstration ever seen in the nation's capital and one of the first to have extensive television coverage. It was also the venue where King delivered his famous *"I have a dream"* speech and there he raised the public consciousness of the civil rights movement and established himself as one of the greatest orators in American history.

In 1964, Martin Luther King, aged 35 years, became the youngest person to receive the Nobel Peace Prize for his work to end segregation and racial discrimination through civil disobedience and other non-violent means. In the coming years he would also focus on ending poverty and opposing the Vietnam War, both from a religious perspective.

But the most newsworthy event of 1963 has to be the violent assassination of the American President, John F. Kennedy, on Friday November 22nd 1963 in Dallas, Texas. He was fatally wounded by gunshots while riding with his wife in a Presidential motorcade. Initial Government investigations concluded that he was assassinated by Lee Harvey Oswald but later Gallup polls showed that the majority of the public disagreed with these findings. The assassination is still the subject of widespread speculation and has spawned numerous conspiracy theories over the years, none of which have ever been proved. Yet another conundrum that will probably never be solved.

In 1964 the boxer Cassius Clay, later to be known as Muhammed Ali, became the World Heavyweight Champion for the first time. He was a great self-publicist, claiming to be the "greatest" and to "float like a butterfly and sting like a bee" during his fights. There is no consensus among boxing pundits as to whether he was indeed the "greatest" boxer of all time but he certainly courted publicity along with the best of them for he was always a controversial figure, for example declaring he would refuse to serve if drafted into the US Army, publicly considering himself a conscientious objector. This decision was soon to result in the suspension of his boxing licence and the withdrawal of his World Heavyweight Title. But he came to be respected as a hero, and an athlete who stood up for his principles, and in 1970 he was allowed to fight again.

Another controversial stance he made at this time was aligning himself with the *Nation of Islam*, (or *Black Muslims* as it was also known) when mainstream America viewed the movement with suspicion at best, and often outright hostility. It was then that he changed his name from the Christian "Cassius Clay" to the Islamic "Muhammad Ali".

These days Muhammad Ali is a devout Muslim, having converted from the *Nation of Islam* sect to *Sunni Islam* in 1975. He is a social activist and peace campaigner, lending his name and presence to hunger and poverty relief around the globe. He is the winner of many awards, titles and honours, none of which have anything to do with boxing.

Sadly he has suffered from Parkinson's Disease since the early 1980's but despite his disability he remains a beloved and active public figure. He is said to be the most easily recognised American in the world... so perhaps he is the "greatest" after all?

By the time of Muhammad Ali's first title fight, and his conversion to Islam, the morally-corrupt system of apartheid was well-entrenched in South Africa. Indeed, ever since 1948, when a Nazi-sympathizing Nationalist government had taken power in that country, the indigenous people had been systematically robbed of their rights, disenfranchised and the different races segregated by law.

There was much opposition to the regime, both inside and outside the country. One of the chief opponents internally was a certain Nelson Mandela, a university-educated lawyer and son of a tribal chief. On 12th June 1964 Mandela was found guilty of plotting to overthrow the government by violence and sentenced to life imprisonment. He was incarcerated at Robben Island Prison, off Cape Town.

Despite his years in prison, Nelson Mandela's reputation grew steadily but he consistently refused to compromise his political position in order to obtain his freedom. He was widely accepted as the most significant black leader in South Africa and became a potent symbol of resistance as the anti-apartheid movement gathered strength.

Back on the mainland, one of his, and the movement's, main supporters was Father Trevor Huddleston, a monk from the order of the "Community of the Resurrection". Indeed Mandela remarked that he well-remembered Huddleston as the white priest, dressed in a black cassock and a large black hat, who regularly doffed his hat to his mother, a black cleaning lady, a gesture almost unknown in apartheid South

Africa.

While Mandela was in prison, Huddleston maintained a tireless crusade over the decades in advocating economic sanctions and sports and cultural boycotts of South Africa. In the 1980's he was supported, in no small measure, by the first black South African Anglican Archbishop of Cape Town, The Most Reverend Desmond Tutu. Their efforts, and Mandela's courage, resulted in the country becoming a pariah of the modern world but apartheid did not end in South Africa until 1990 and Nelson Mandela was not released from prison until 11th February of that year. In 1993 he was awarded the Nobel Peace Prize and on 10th May 1994 he became the country's first black president. Archbishop Desmond Tutu was awarded the Nobel Peace Prize in 1984.

Back once again to 1964, for this was the year "The Beatles" took the US by storm and the year that saw the toy firm *Hasbro* launch the first "doll" aimed specifically at boys, the "GI Action-Man" figure. It was also the year that saw Dad's accident with a starting-handle.

In the 1960's, vehicle manufacturers were beginning to think of ways to produce cars without starting-handles. These were universally unpopular for many women were now car drivers and many of them did not have the strength to turn the handle. The system was not liked by men either, for they had a lethal kick-back if the operator did not pull the handle out as soon as the engine fired, as Dad found to his cost one day in 1964.

His car would not start on the ignition, so he got out of the vehicle, inserted the handle, turned it, and the handle kicked back and hit him in the face, narrowly missing his eye. He came back to the house with blood streaming down from a bad cut to his eye-brow. It needed stitches and there was no-one else who could drive him to hospital, so he had to drive himself, as best he could, with one hand clamped to his "war" wound. This was the incident that gave me the impetus to learn to drive and I passed my driving test, at the second attempt, in 1964.

I had promised our pet dog, Laddie, that as soon as I could drive I would take him for a long walk in his favourite woods. Alas, this was not to be, for, only a few days after my test, he collapsed on his evening walk and Dad had to carry him home. His back legs were paralysed. Instead of taking him on a walk, I ended up driving him to the vet's, with Dad sitting in the back seat cradling our beloved pet.

The vet' thought he had contracted a virus that was prevalent in Tortington Woods at that time. Laddie stayed in the "pets' hospital" for a few days but he gradually deteriorated and the vet' recommended that we end his suffering. He was put to sleep on 9th October, just days short of his ninth birthday on 15th October. We were all absolutely heart-broken. Especially me. It was the first time I had lost something (someone) that I loved and it took me a long time to get over it.

One of the most well-known members of the *Nation of Islam* during the early 1960's had been *Malcolm X.* (Indeed it had been Malcolm X who had introduced the then-Cassius Clay (later Muhammad Ali) to the sect.) Previously known by the surname "Little", he was a streetwise, ex-hoodlum from Boston who had risen to become one of the most prominent African-American nationalist leaders at that time. Although Malcolm X was perceived by many whites to be a militant revolutionary, he also had the dignity, courage and self-respect to publicly align himself with the fight to win equality for all oppressed minorities, regardless of colour or gender. However by 1965 tensions between him and the leader of the sect, Elijah Muhammad, had reached a peak and he had left the movement to become an orthodox *Sunni Muslim* and human rights activist in his own right.

On 21st February 1965, 39 year old Malcolm X was assassinated, allegedly by agents of the *Nation of Islam.* At the time it was stated that one possible reason for the murder may have been simple jealousy: Malcolm X was becoming more well-known and more popular than the leader, Elijah Muhammad. He was also an outspoken critic of his rival about his extra-marital affairs. The subsequent conviction of the alleged perpetrators was suspect because the man who admitted firing the fatal shots maintained he was not an "agent of the Nation of Islam" and that the two other men convicted with him were not even present at the time of the shooting. Yet another enigma to be passed unresolved into history!

On 8th March 1965, the first American combat troops landed in Vietnam. Thus if you asked most Americans when the Vietnam War started, they would probably quote this date but in fact the US had sent military advisers to this part of Indochina from as early as 1950, as part of a strategy they called "containment". Their task was to advise and train the South Vietnamese Army, for America was concerned that North Vietnam (supported by its communist allies) would takeover non-communist South Vietnam and from there spread its doctrine all over the South Pacific. In 1959 fighting broke out between North and South Vietnam and US involvement escalated, until by 1964 a staggering 17,000 US military advisers were in the country. The deployment of the first combat troops in 1965 was just the beginning and would peak at 543,000 troops in April 1969.

The war had a major impact on US politics, foreign relations and culture and Americans were deeply divided over the justification for, and conduct of, the war. Opposition to the conflict contributed to the popularity and growth of the burgeoning "hippie" movement and in turn the movement influenced American policy over the war.

A year after the first combat troops had been deployed, the US Government lowered the minimum requirement of reading and writing skills needed to join the US Armed Forces, thus opening the door for many poorer, poorly-educated, young people (mainly black) to be eligible for the draft (including the boxer Muhammad Ali). This resulted in mass draft protests throughout America, bringing yet more pressure to bear on the Government to end their involvement in Indochina, for this was to become a brutal war where the enemy was unknown and often unseen, unpredictable and ruthless to the point of bestiality. A war in an alien and hostile environment, where a quick death was a welcome release and survival was a lottery. Probably it ranks as the worst conflict the US was involved in during the whole of the 20th century and unfortunately there would be no early, or easy, end to it.

Not all the fighting was in far-off shores, however. The American "Civil Rights Act of 1964" had been intended to herald a new era in race relations, giving equality to black Americans in housing, education and employment. In their wisdom, the State of California decided to block the legislation and this led to a great feeling of injustice and resentment among their black communities, especially those in inner cities.

In Los Angeles, in the middle of August 1965, this resentment flared into violence when a black man was stopped on suspicion of drunken driving. A crowd gathered around the car and soon began throwing bricks and bottles. It escalated from there with black youths rampaging through the streets, fire-bombing hundreds of white-owned businesses, churches, offices and other buildings.

The rioting lasted for six days. Some 18,000 National Guards were deployed to quell the unrest and nearly 4,000 people were arrested. At the end of the six days thirty-four people had died and about one thousand were injured. Over 500 buildings had been destroyed or damaged and the cost of repairs was put at $100m.

By 1965 electricity was part of everyday life in Europe and North America, and it was hard to imagine that there had ever been a time when the world managed to exist without it. Not only were electrical appliances of every description becoming prolific in homes, but shops, offices and factories also had been transformed by electricity. Elevators, air conditioners, electric typewriters, adding machines, even the budding computer industry, all ran on electricity. The demand on power stations, and the elaborate grid systems they had devised to meet the needs of all these consumers, was huge.

On 9th November 1965, at 5.27pm, the entire northeast area of the US and large parts of Canada were plunged into darkness. It was at the height of the "Cold War", the "Cuban Missile Crisis" was not long over, and many Americans thought Armageddon had arrived.

But it was not Armageddon! From Buffalo (on the shores of the Great

257

Lakes), east to New Hampshire and from New York City north to Ontario, a massive power outage had struck without warning. The worst effects were felt in the cities, especially New York. Trains suddenly stopped between subway stations; people were stuck in elevators; failed traffic signals brought traffic to a halt; and thousands of commuters were forced to sleep in their offices or hotel lobbies.

By 11pm some lucky areas saw their power restored but it was 6.58am the following morning, fourteen hours after the massive blackout had begun, before the whole of New York City was "electrified" once again. It took six days to locate the cause; a single faulty relay at a power station in Ontario had triggered a sequence of escalating overloads throughout the system. It was described as a "cascade effect", much like a row of dominoes falling one after another.

The Blackout forced Americans to reconsider their dependence on electricity, and caches of candles, batteries and torches became commonplace. The electricity supply industry also had to learn to plan for the unexpected and founded Regional Co-ordinating Councils and "Power Pools" to research and develop preventative measures so that a similar failure would not happen again. Ultimately producers and consumers throughout the world learned lessons from this "Night the lights went out."

Back in the UK every cloud had a silver lining, for Laddie's demise meant that Mum and Dad were free to go on holiday abroad for the first time. So in August 1965 Mum, Dad and Sheila loaded their equipment and clothes into the family car and set off on a camping (yes, camping!) holiday with Uncle Ted and his family, to Tossa de Mar, on Spain's Costa Brava coast. Sheila still remembers it well, especially the first day they arrived. The men got the tents erected and then disappeared to the local town for supplies and a beer, leaving the wives to unpack and the children to explore the beach and have a swim.

The camp-site was situated on the top of cliffs and all was well until a gale suddenly materialized from nowhere and blew the tents away! Luckily a German holidaymaker came to the rescue and helped Mum, Auntie Kathleen and offspring retrieve the tents, and anchor down the rest of the flyaway equipment until the men returned.

I think the holiday was doomed from that point on as far as Mum was concerned. Auntie Kathleen was pregnant again (Michael would be born in January '66) and was playing the part of pregnant invalid to perfection. Mum spent the whole fortnight waiting on Auntie Kathleen and thinking that at any moment they could all be blown to kingdom come! It was definitely the last time our mother would go camping!

It was also the one and only time Uncle Ted and Dad saw a bullfight. Unappreciative of the nuances of the matador's moves, the courage of man and beast and the beauty and artistry of the "suits of light", they saw only the cruelty and even Dad came away thoroughly disgusted and disillusioned.

While they were away in Spain, I was having my own problems. Almost as soon as the family stepped over the threshold for their Spanish adventure, I succeeded in giving myself food poisoning, from not re-heating a home-cooked pie properly. I have never been so ill, before or since! The pain was indescribable but somehow I managed to force myself off the toilet, my head out of a bucket, and go down the street to make a 'phone call to my employers. It was only the kindness of one of the girls at work, who came in to see me every day on her way home, which kept me going. I must have been off work for the whole week because I had to 'phone the doctor for a medical certificate. He chastised me thoroughly for not contacting him earlier saying, "You stupid girl! Don't you realise you could have died!" Well I certainly felt like I was going to die, that's for sure. I just wanted it to be quick!

While I was suffering indoors, a stray cat had had her kittens in a dark, out-of-the-way corner of our shed. When I was up and about again I started to feed her and then felt so sorry for them all, out there all alone, that I brought them into our sitting-room in a box and donated my wool dressing-gown as a soft bed. That night I opened the fanlight window in the scullery, so Mummy-cat could escape if she wanted to, and went to bed. I heard her jump out five times and thought, "That's it! She's taken them away!" But no, when I got up in the morning, there they all were; "Mum" plus five babies.

I was out when Mum, Dad and Sheila returned from their holiday so I left a note sellotaped to the sitting-room door: *"TAKE CARE! KITTENS IN HERE!"* It says a lot about my parents that they never complained about the waifs and strays, animal and human, that I brought home. It was not uncommon for me to turn up with a schoolmate whose parents could not afford to feed her, or a teenager who was without a bed for the night. I knew no-one in need would ever be turned away from our door.

Luckily everyone fell in love with Mummy-cat and her mischievous kittens. Of course they just loved to explore and one of their favourite places was to climb up inside Dad's fireside chair, so when he was in sitting in it he could feel kittens crawling up his back! I can hear him now grumbling away, "Those little b------ are inside my chair again!"

Thus it was that "Kitty" (duly spayed!) came to be part of our family, although the kittens were taken to Dad's sister Elsie's pet-shop in London to be sold to good homes. What a sad day that was when they finally had to go. Mum remained her usual dry-eyed, stoical self but Dad was openly tearful as he packed them all into a box for the journey for there was no way we could keep them.

Many years later, I asked Mum how she managed to hide her feelings so well, because by this time I knew she was as upset as the rest of us when sad things happened; she just did not show it as much. She replied that it probably stemmed from her upbringing. Her family were never the kind of people to show emotions in public, so she was conditioned to shed tears in private. Indeed this was the typical, public face of Victorian England where a "*stiff upper lip*" should be presented at all times. She added that she was also frightened that once she started to cry, she might not be able to stop and in any case she thought at least one member of the family should appear to be in control, hence the stoicism.

This unemotional response extended to happy events as well as sad. We were not brought up to be a tactile family, always hugging and kissing and telling each other how much in love we were! In fact I have great difficulty in remembering any physical contact, apart from the usual "*Let's kiss it better*" childhood scenario. Mum, and Dad to a lesser extent, showed their love in a myriad other ways but we had to become adults before we could truly appreciate the subtlety of this ..... and discover just how much we meant to them.

CHAPTER THIRTY-ONE

Home, Sweet Home
(1966)

Early in January 1966 I immigrated to Canada. It was not a sudden decision for the idea had been lurking around at the back of my mind ever since I had found out that my biological father was Canadian. However I had not really thought of making my dream a reality until someone rudely dismissed my vague intentions with the words, "*We all have our pipe-dreams that don't come to anything!*" I thought, "*Oh! Do we indeed!*" and immediately made plans to visit "Canada House", in London, for a comprehensive interview and a medical examination in order to obtain the necessary visa. In fact, because I wanted to stay there for a while, get a job and travel around, I actually had to formally emigrate. I do not think I had any intention of staying forever but by the time the implications of what I was about to do became a reality, as opposed to a far-off dream, I prayed that someone would beg me to stay, so I could change my mind and save face! No-one did! The only concession that was made to my forthcoming departure, was that my parents had a 'phone installed so that I could keep in touch and they could be contacted quickly in an emergency. So I gave up my job in the bank and, with great trepidation, I set off on my great adventure.

Affordable jet travel had begun in the 1950's but it was the first time any member of our family had ever flown. Mum, Dad and Sheila came to see me off from Heathrow and there were tears of farewell at the airport from Dad, Sheila (who would probably miss all the arguments we had!) and me. Even Mum had difficulty remaining her usual stoical self but it was too late for me to turn back.

I went to stay with Ellita and her family in London, near Toronto, Ontario. Ellita was the childhood friend who had emigrated with her parents many years before and had then become my pen-pal. I quickly obtained a job in the costing section of the accounts department at the local *3M* factory. In this section alone there were about sixty of us, all sitting in rows with a monster accounting machine in front of us. I do not think from the moment I started, to the moment I left, that I comprehended what on earth I was supposed to be doing! All day long I fed obscure, miscellaneous figures into the "monster" and then pressed various buttons, supposedly to ascertain the manufacturing cost of one *Scotchbrite* pad, for example. I hated it! I hated the feeling of being out of my depth, the size of the place, the noise, the strangeness of it all. The only saving grace were my colleagues who were kindness itself, including a lovely, motherly lady called Marie, who later used to invite me

261

to visit her family at the weekends. She had a daughter about my age and we would go out together sometimes, to the cinema or for a walk.

One of my other workmates was another *émigré* Brit, who joined the firm about the same time as I did. She was a middle-aged lady from Brighton, who had left the UK only under protest when her husband had insisted it was immigrate to Canada or divorce! The poor woman was so unhappy but she made herself very unpopular by prefacing every sentence with, "*In England we......*" and then proceeded to disparage Canada in some way. She also had a horrible, whining voice, which set my teeth on edge every time I heard her! Perhaps because I was aware how irritated the others were by this lady, and her constant references to England, I decided to take the opposite tack; I never spoke about "home" unless asked to do so and then kept my answers as brief as possible.

The factory itself was huge; thousands of people must have worked there, so we had our own nursing station and subsidised canteen. I saw the inside of the former first-hand when I stapled my thumb to a piece of paper and daily saw the latter. It was here I witnessed another colleague eating chips and gravy with gusto every single day. It was the first time I had seen anyone eat chips with this accompaniment and I thought it a revolting combination, although of course I would not dream of saying so!

After a few weeks of living with Ellita's family, Ellita started to make life very difficult for me. I think she resented having to share her room with me and was jealous of the fact I was working, with money to spend, while she was still at school. She was also going through a very rebellious period with her step-father, so all-in-all I thought it would make life easier for everyone if I moved out.

I found a room in a boarding-house where the tenants shared bathroom and kitchen facilities. Now I was truly on my own in a strange country and, without realising it, I became more and more depressed. But I covered it well. The only way I could cope was by imagining myself on a stage performing a part, and thus I buried the real sad-and-lonely-me and presented a coping, capable, sensible make-believe-me in her place. Apparently this is a classic symptom of someone heading for a nervous breakdown, but I did not realise this.

I did 'phone home occasionally, but economics required the calls to be very short, so mainly we kept in touch by letter and every week I wrote to the family with upbeat stories of all the new people I had met and the sights I had seen. I went to Niagara Falls one weekend, for example, and took in the sights of Toronto on another. I told them how on one day I had stood in a blizzard for twenty minutes, waiting for my lift to work, not realising with the wind chill factor that it was over thirty degrees below zero! Not something one ever does in those conditions, I was told in no uncertain terms when the lift finally arrived!   And how I had to have my carefully-grown, long hair all cut off because the air was so dry indoors, the static electricity meant I truly could not do a thing with it! Every week without fail, Mum wrote back to me, trying to think of tales to tell that would make me smile. Later, when I was safely home, she said she knew I was unhappy when I sent them one of those booth photographs of myself with my new hairstyle. She took one look at my face and read the sadness there, despite the brave smile. The offending photograph was duly tucked away in a drawer for she could not bear to look at it.

After I had been in Canada for about six months, everything came to a head one day at work. I was seated at my hated machine when I heard the whining voice of the Brighton lady starting her inevitable, "*In England we....*" and for no apparent reason, I started to scream, "NO! NO! NO!" at the top of my voice and collapsed in sobs on the floor. I was carted off to the nursing section for the second time and, on this occasion, a doctor was summoned.

"How old are you, my dear?" he asked.

"Twenty," I replied.

He shook his head. "Go home, little girl. Go home."

Thank God! At last! Someone was giving me permission to give up on my great adventure! I flew home a week later but decided to surprise the family with my return. All the way back on the train from London to Littlehampton, I was planning what I would do when I arrived. I decided I would take a taxi from the railway station and leave my suitcase in the porch. Then I would ring the bell and race round the back so I could creep up on Mum as she opened the front door. In the event she opened the door as soon as I arrived because she was cleaning the front bedroom and had heard the taxi pull-up! She looked overwhelmed with surprise, relief and happiness.

"Thank God you're home!" she exclaimed. "Thank God you're home!"

We fell into one another's arms. This stoical, non-tactile family was on the brink of change!

After the inevitable cup of tea, I told Mum I would borrow the car and go to see Dad at work. On my arrival at the school I had to ask the ladies working in the kitchen where I could find him. They said he was digging in the vegetable garden and gave me directions how to get there. Then there he was! Right over the far-side with his back to me. I called out to him and he stopped digging. With his foot still on the spade and his hands on the handle, he looked up at the sky and it was just as if he was thinking, "I can even hear her voice now!"

I called again, louder and more urgently, and he turned round. I shall never forget the look on his face: Sheer, unadulterated joy. He raced across his newly dug ground and hugged me like he would never let me

263

go. We were both in tears.

"You're back! You're back!" he cried. "I thought it was a ghost I heard! Have you seen your Mum?"

"Yes, Dad! And I've got your car!" I replied.

"That's good, duck. You keep it as long as you like. Oh! It's so good to have you home!"

Because my body-clock had still not adjusted to the different time zone, the following morning I slept in. What bliss it was to be back in my own bed in my own bedroom! I was awakened by a knock on the front door and I heard Mum telling our visitor that I had returned home unexpectedly. I listened intently to the voice of the visitor, trying to discern to whom it was that Mum was talking. It was a lady with a very broad Sussex accent and eventually I recognised it as that of my Auntie Myrtle! Until that moment I had not appreciated our local dialect could be quite so pronounced! Certainly I had not noticed it in my parents on my return, but perhaps I was just too used to their Sussex burr.

I have no regrets in going to Canada for I always say I grew up there, in the sense that I left any remnants of my childhood behind and came back as a fully-fledged adult. I do regret not seeing more of the country, however, for I had the intention of taking the train across Canada and through the Rocky Mountains to Vancouver ..... but this was not to be. At least I was thereafter always appreciative of what I had, and had so nearly lost, for it was not until this homecoming that I realised just how much my parents loved me and how much I had hurt them by going away. I vowed I would never leave them again.

Mum and I celebrated my return by going to Paris for a week and neither of us realised that this would be the first of many holidays we would take together. We also started a yearly ritual of going to London for the January sales and we often went to Worthing, Brighton or Portsmouth for the day. Canada was the catalyst; somehow we made an unconscious decision to enjoy one another's company; company that we had previously taken so much for granted. As Dad had been my hero in childhood, now Mum would be my mentor and my soul-mate as I entered my adult years.

After the break in Paris, it was time for me to look for another job. I did not want to return to the bank, so I reported to the local "Labour Exchange" (as it was then) in order to sign-on and claim unemployment benefit. In a matter of days, I found myself on the other side of the counter and thus began my career as a civil servant with the Ministry of Labour.

That summer Mum and Dad took their first package holiday abroad. Package holidays to the sunspots of the Mediterranean were now becoming very popular, thanks to jet travel and cheaper fares. With a flight, hotel and food included in the price, they offered incredible value for money, especially for families. And they almost guaranteed sunshine! But this kind of static holiday did not appeal to my father; he preferred to be on the move, seeing a different place every day, so they decided to do a coach tour of Italy, for Mum had always wanted to visit Rome.

This was to be the first of many such trips over the next decade or so and they ended up visiting just about every country in Europe, exploring the mountains of Switzerland and Austria, the rivers and forests of Germany, the canals and bulb-fields of Holland, the ancient ruins of Greece, and all places in between. When they had exhausted Europe, they travelled closer to home visiting the moors of Yorkshire, the Fens of East Anglia, the wilds of Cumbria, the lochs of Scotland and the peat-bogs of Ireland.

Mum's friend, Carrie, was now a widow and sometimes she accompanied them on these trips. Mum often told the tale of how Auntie Carrie went off on her own for a walk up a Swiss mountain, and got lost when a cloud suddenly descended! Mum was absolutely frantic thinking that she had fallen off the mountainside, never to be seen again, and was so relieved when her figure eventually emerged out of the mire, like a ghost surrounded by a swirling mist.

What she was not so pleased about, was that in the panic over her missing friend, she had left her treasured fruit-knife on the picnic-table. It was silver with a mother-of-pearl handle, not particularly valuable but it had belonged to her mother and thus had great sentimental attachment. Even years later, she lamented its loss.

Another story of their travels that we heard regularly was of a boat-trip they took in Yugoslavia. Apparently they sailed past a nudist beach and all the passengers tactfully averted their eyes. Except Dad!
"Cor blimey!" he exclaimed in a loud voice. "Look at that, Anne! Look! They've got no clothes on! Look! Look!" Mum said she wished the boat would open up and take her to the depths! No chance of fooling Clem Oakley with the story of the emperor's new clothes!

On one coach holiday they were in very prestigious company. Not only was "Annie Oakley" a passenger but so was a "Bob Hope" and a "Guy Mitchell". (As we know from a previous chapter, Bob's namesake was a very famous comedian and actor, born in London but a naturalized American. Guy Mitchell was a singer and, of course, Annie Oakley was world famous for her gun-toting prowess!) This Bob Hope was a widower and he and a widow became firm friends while on this trip, often joining Mum and Dad for meals and outings. After the holiday, their romance blossomed and Mum and Dad were invited to be witnesses at their wedding which took place a few months later. Even after Bob sadly died some years later, they kept in touch with Mary for the rest of their lives.

But all was not sweetness and light in the Oakley household. Dad had taught me to drive a couple of years before this period without too many problems, apart from the fact he told me I had to double-declutch when I changed down through the gear-box. I had a "proper" driving instructor for a few lessons before my test and she demanded to know what on earth I was doing when I changed gears.

"You don't need to do that with a modern gear-box!" she exclaimed.

I am not sure Dad was convinced of this when I told him on my return but I did not double-declutch again.

Nevertheless, it is thanks to Dad that I have no fear of stopping and starting on steep inclines. When it was time for me to learn this manoeuvre, he introduced an old Army technique into our lessons. We drove to the steepest hill he could find in Arundel, told me to park, and then put a match-box behind the back wheel. I had to pull away without crushing the box!

Anyway, Sheila was now of an age to learn to drive, so naturally Dad offered to teach her as well. He came back from their first lesson with steam coming out of his ears.

"That's it!" he raged. "It's impossible to teach her cos' she thinks she knows it all! She won't listen to a thing I tell her! If she wants to learn to drive she'll have to pay for lessons!"

And she did! And, like me, she passed at her second attempt.

1966 was an opportune year to learn to drive for, in theory at least, negotiating road junctions should be easier and safer. Traffic circles, as in the likes of the *Columbus Circle* in New York, had never really caught on in any country, and traffic lights were often slow and unreliable, but in the 1950's the UK introduced their own version of "traffic circles", called roundabouts. These were large round "islands", set at multiple road junctions, and they successfully slowed down traffic, but there were no hard and fast rules on how to negotiate them. Confusion reigned, but this did not matter too much when the roads were fairly empty. However, the 1960's saw a large rise in car ownership and thought was given on how to improve the safety and efficiency of the roundabout. In Britain it was decided to make a smaller island with wider entrances and in 1966 a law was passed requiring motorists "to give way before entry". Hundreds of roundabouts were then built and by the 1980's and 1990's, the system was considered so efficient that it was widely adopted by European countries. More recently Canada and the US have introduced the "roundabout" (called a "rotary" in the US), initially as an experiment, but they are proving so successful that many more are being built. Most countries now make a feature of their roundabouts, planting trees, shrubs, flowers and sculpture on the islands. A potential traffic hazard has become an opportunity for artistry.

But the argument between Dad and Sheila over learning to drive, was an indication that things between Sheila and the rest of the family had not improved over the years. For the most part she and I now went our separate ways with our own friends. Whenever we did come into contact, it only led to arguments and bickering. Mum and Dad still gave way to her on most occasions, in the hope of achieving a relatively peaceful life, but there was one argument with Mum that she did not win. Mum insisted that she should contribute a small part of her wages towards the household expenses. However, Sheila thought she should live at home for free because her friends apparently did. All these disagreements came to a head in the autumn of 1966 and Sheila decided to share a flat in Worthing with some other girls. However, Mum made it clear that, despite everything, her room would be kept open for her and she could return at any time. In the event she returned often for a meal and a visit, and perhaps stayed overnight, but she was never to live with us again on a permanent basis.

While 1966 produced its own trials and triumphs for our family, in April of that year two of the country's most infamous serial killers, Ian Brady and Myra Hindley, were brought to their own trial, a judicial one. Nearly fifty years later, their names still raise a feeling of revulsion and disgust in the minds of those of us who remember their infamous deeds. They were responsible for the kidnap, torture, rape, sexual abuse and murder of five children aged between ten and seventeen years, during the period 1963 to 1965. They were dubbed the "Moors Murderers" because all but one of their known victims were buried along the Saddleworth Moor, near Oldham in Lancashire.

In November 1965, just one month after they were arrested, the House of Commons voted that the death penalty should be suspended for a period of five years. The Act further provided that if each House of Parliament passed a resolution to make the effect of the Act permanent, then the death penalty for murder would be abolished. Thus it was that "two of the most hated individuals in British criminal history" were sentenced to life imprisonment and not forced to face the hangman's noose. Hindley died in prison in 2002; Brady is still incarcerated in an institution for the criminally insane.

There were no less than 34 serial killers convicted in the UK in the 20th century, although only ten, including Hindley and Brady, were convicted before the death penalty was abolished. I have not singled out the "Moors Murderers" for mention because their deeds were any more, or less, horrific than the others that went before or after them, but only because I can remember all the publicity at the time and the case was regularly regurgitated over the following decades as the bodies of their victims were discovered on Saddleworth Moor. The body of one of their victims, Keith Bennett, has still not been found.

Better news came on 30th July 1966. England won football's World Cup for the first time since the tournament began in 1930. They beat West Germany 4-2 in front of a crowd of 93,000 at London's Wembley Stadium. Geoff Hurst scored three of the goals, the only player to score a hat-trick in the history of the World Cup finals.

In October 1966, Dad was eligible to retire and draw his state retirement pension but he did not feel "old" and therefore elected to carry on working at the school. By this time *Dorset House School for Boys* had sold out to *Rosemead School for Girls* so although he was at the same place, he actually had different employers and had had to get used to seeing lots of girls instead of lots of little boys!

Two weeks after Dad's 65th birthday, on 21st October 1966, one of the UK's worst disasters occurred in a Welsh mining village called Aberfan. For generations the coal-waste had been piled-up on the mountainside in so-called slag-heaps, until they too resembled mini-mountains. Inadvertently one of these slag-heaps had been constructed over an underground stream and, after two days of heavy rain, it loosened and rushed down the mountainside like an avalanche. It destroyed a cottage, then engulfed more houses and raced on to bury the village school. 144 people were killed, including half the children in the school and some of their teachers.

A disaster fund was launched and over £1m was donated from all over the world to help the families. Some of the money did indeed go to the people; some was used to build new houses, a community centre and a new school but controversially some of it was spent on removing the remaining tips overlooking the village, because at that time the *National Coal Board* denied responsibility. This money was not refunded to the *Aberfan Disaster Fund* until 1997.

In 1966 the last of the British colonies in Africa, Botswana, gained its independence. Nigeria, Uganda, Kenya and Zambia had all gained their autonomy in the 60's and they were now members of the British Commonwealth of Nations, as opposed to being part of the rapidly diminishing British Empire.

1966 drew to a close with Rhodesia formally resigning from the Commonwealth on 22nd December. The British Government had refused to grant the country its independence because the white minority would not agree to give its black majority a fair share of power. Indeed on 11th November 1965, the Prime Minister of Rhodesia, Ian Smith, had illegally severed the country's links with the Crown and declared a *Unilateral Declaration of Independence (U.D.I.)*.

The British Labour Government (under Harold Wilson) refused to send troops to overthrow the Smith regime but trade sanctions were imposed and all financial aid ceased. However, thanks to the support of South Africa and Portugal, the "illegal" Rhodesian Government managed to survive until 1979 when Abel Muzorewa of the *African National Congress* became the first black Prime Minister of the newly-named Zimbabwe-Rhodesia.

(Robert Mugabe was elected Prime Minister of an independent Zimbabwe in 1980 under a new constitution. At the time of writing (in 2009), he is still hanging onto power and, under his leadership, this once prosperous, self-supporting nation declined to become one of the most impoverished and terror-ridden countries in the whole of Africa.)

CHAPTER THIRTY-TWO

The End of the "Swinging Sixties"
(1967-1969)

1967 was an eventful year internationally. It saw the *Torrey Canyon* disaster, Francis Chichester sail into Portsmouth, Stalin's daughter defect to the West, the "Six-Day War" in the Middle East, the death of Che Guevara and the first heart transplant.

The *Torrey Canyon* was an American super-tanker, under charter to *British Petroleum*, when it ran aground on rocks, between Land's End in Cornwall and the Scilly Isles, on 18th March 1967. Immediately it started to leak its cargo of 100,000 tons of crude oil into the sea. Seventy miles of beaches on the Cornish coast of Southern England and the Normandy coast of France were seriously contaminated, with threats that the slick could spread to the beaches of Devon and Dorset. Attempts to disperse the oil with detergents were only marginally successful, so it was decided to bomb the vessel. The crew had already been airlifted off the stricken tanker and, on 30th March, the wreck finally disappeared beneath the waves. The oil slick was eventually dispersed by favourable weather.

It was the world's first major, maritime, environmental disaster and the biggest problem of its kind that had been faced by any nation up to that moment. It cost the UK and French Governments tens of millions of pounds (and francs!) to attempt the clean-up. Apart from the cost to the marine environment, 20,000 sea birds were contaminated by the oil and the cost to the tourist and fishing industries of both countries was huge.

The American owners of the super-tanker initially offered just $50 (Yes! Fifty dollars!) in compensation. In the end, after much difficulty and years of litigation, $3million was paid, a tiny fraction of the clean-up costs alone.

A happier sea story occurred just two months later when, in May 1967, Francis Chichester stepped ashore (on famously wobbly legs!) from his ketch *"Gypsy Moth IV"*. He was the first person to sail solo around the globe (from Plymouth to Portsmouth) with just one stop-over in Sydney. His feat was all the more remarkable because he was in remission from cancer at the time. For this supreme act of endurance, he was knighted by the Queen in June, with the same sword that Elizabeth I had used in 1581 to knight another famous sailor, Sir Francis Drake, the first Englishman to circumnavigate the globe. Sadly his cancer returned and Sir Francis Chichester died in 1972.

However, he was to be the vanguard for a wealth of British sailing achievements over the next few years. In 1968 (Sir) Alec Rose followed his example and in April 1969 (Sir) Robin Knox-Johnston completed the first non-stop, solo circumnavigation of the globe. In 1970/71, (Sir) Chay Blyth defied sceptics to be the first to sail solo in a westerly direction, against prevailing winds and currents. Chay Blyth had already hit the headlines in 1966 when, with Captain John Ridgway, he had rowed across the Atlantic Ocean in a 20-foot dory, taking 92 days. Perhaps it is not surprising, as an island nation, that Britain should produce more than its fair share of remarkable sailors, and never more so than in the late 60's and early 70's.

Svetlana Stalin preferred to be known by her mother's maiden name of Alliuyeva. By 1967, she had been married three times, her third husband being an Indian Communist. When he died, she took his ashes to India to be buried and while there requested political asylum at the United States Embassy. She subsequently became a US citizen and on her marriage in 1970 to an American architect, William Peters, she changed her name to Lana Peters. However, this marriage did not last and, in 1984, she returned to the Soviet Union but went back to the US in 1986. In the 1990's Lana Peters settled in Bristol, England, but is now believed to be back in America and living in northern California.

A United Nations peacekeeping force had been stationed in the Middle East since the Suez crisis in 1957. In May 1967, Egypt's President Nasser expelled the force from the Sinai Peninsula and closed the Straits of Tiran to all ships flying the Israeli flag. He received strong support for his actions from the Arab countries of Jordan, Syria and Iraq. These countries, plus Saudi Arabia, Sudan, Tunisia, Morocco and Algeria, all contributed troops and arms in support of Egypt's decision.

On 5th June, Israel launched a pre-emptive strike against Egypt's Air Force. Jordan then attacked Western Jerusalem and Netanya. Israel retaliated and by 10th June had captured the Gaza Strip and the Sinai Peninsula from Egypt, the West Bank (including East Jerusalem) from Jordan and the Golan Heights from Syria. It was a decisive victory for Israel and the results of this "Six-Day War" affect the geopolitics of the region to this day.

Che Guevara must have one of the most well-known faces of the 20th century but quite why it should still adorn millions of T-shirts and posters in the capitalist West remains a mystery ... And a very lucrative one for someone, somewhere! He hailed from Argentina and was a revolutionary, communist icon in South America, champion of the downtrodden of oppressive regimes and a guerrilla fighter *par excellence*. In 1967, he was in Bolivia, trying to overthrow their President, Ren Barrientos. He was captured by Bolivian Special Forces near his guerrilla camp and executed by them on 9th October 1967.

On 3rd December 1967, the world's first ever heart transplant took place in Cape Town, South Africa, performed by Professor Christian

Barnard. Sadly, the recipient, Louis Washensky, succumbed to pneumonia after only eighteen days but his new heart beat strongly to the end, proving that a transplant of this major organ was indeed a possibility.

But, before I go onto news from 1968, I must not miss a personal event that took place in 1967. Apart from cementing my relationship with my parents, my absence in Canada had made another heart grow fonder and thus that was the year Bryan proposed to me, very formally, down on one knee! Of course, I said "Yes" and, according to a calendar hanging on his parents' kitchen wall, the motto for that day was *"Love is the triumph of imagination over intelligence."* Imagination was obviously in the ascendancy!

1968 was to prove no less newsworthy than its predecessor and major headlines began on 1st January with the UK government introducing colour television licences, despite the fact there were less than 100,000 colour sets in the country at that time. Television licences had been imposed since 1st June 1948 at an annual fee of £2. By 1968, the fee for a monochrome set had risen to £5. An additional £5 would now be added if a family wished to view in colour, making a total fee of £10. (As a point of interest, the standard fee today is £139.50.) Programmes in colour were actually only available at this time on BBC2 and then only on selected programmes in some areas. It was to be November 1969 before BBC1 and Independent Television (ITV) started to broadcast in colour. Then, in less than one month, around 200,000 colour televisions were suddenly in use, but it would be 1976 before there were more colour sets than there were black and white. Colour television was to herald the golden age of BBC broadcasting with documentaries such as *"Man Alive"*, televised classics like John Galsworthy's *"The Forsyte Saga"* and sitcoms such as *"Steptoe and Son"*, *"Porridge"*, and *"Fawlty Towers"*, just to name a few, for, at that time, the BBC had no equal in quality and quantity of output.

Back with international news for 1968. On 4th April, in Memphis, Tennessee, the prominent American civil rights leader, Dr. Martin Luther King, Jr., aged 39 years, was assassinated by a white extremist, James Earl Ray. Just hours earlier he had delivered what was to be the last speech of his life, now known as the *"I've Been to the Mountaintop"* address. Towards the end of this, he said that he had been to the top of the mountain and looked over and seen the promised land. He said he might not get there with the people who were listening to him but he was not afraid to die, for *"my eyes have seen the glory of the coming of the Lord."*

As news of his murder spread, civil unrest affected approximately 110

US cities, creating a wave of riots in at least sixty of them. Five days later President Lyndon S. Johnson declared a national day of mourning for the civil rights leader and a crowd of 300,000 attended his funeral later that day. Dr. Martin Luther King Jr. was posthumously awarded the Presidential Medal of Freedom in 1977 and the Congressional Gold Medal in 2004. The Martin Luther King Day was established as a national holiday in 1986.

One of the first politicians to inform the people of the death of Martin Luther King was Robert F. Kennedy, the Senator of New York and brother of the late President John F. Kennedy who had been assassinated in 1963. At the time, Robert Kennedy was touring America seeking the Democratic nomination for presidential candidate in the 1968 elections. As he passed on the news of King's death, little did he know that just two months later, on 5th June, he too would fall victim to an assassin's bullet, ironically at a celebration of his successful campaign in the Californian primary. The perpetrator was a twenty-four year old Palestinian immigrant, Sirhan Sirhan. As with his brother's death, Robert Kennedy's assassination, and the circumstances surrounding it, has spawned a variety of conspiracy theories, particularly in relation to the existence of a supposed second gunman. As before, nothing has been proved.

On 6th July 1968, the American petroleum industry hit the headlines once again when the North Sea oil rig, the *Piper Alpha,* exploded, killing 167 people. Only 59 people survived the conflagration and many of their rescuers received the *George Medal* for their courage and bravery. Thirty bodies were never recovered.

The rig was wholly owned by *Occidental Petroleum*, based in Los Angeles, California, and the company was subsequently found to be guilty of inadequate safety and maintenance procedures. Three weeks later, despite 80mph winds and 70-foot waves, the blazing remains of the platform were extinguished by the legendary firefighter, Red Adair, a world-renowned innovator in the highly specialised and extremely hazardous profession of capping blazing, erupting oil well blowouts, both land-based and off-shore.

Survivors and relatives of those who died went on to form the *Piper Alpha Families and Survivors Association,* which campaigns on North Sea safety issues. A memorial sculpture by Sue Jane Taylor, featuring three oil workers, has been sited in the Rose Garden within Hazlehead Park in Aberdeen as a permanent reminder to us all of the true price of oil and gas exploration and extraction.

In 1968 Britain was also in the international news for withdrawing from the Gulf, leaving the newly created United Arab Emirates in its place. They had already withdrawn from Aden; Marxists had taken over, renaming the area "South Yemen". Thus the British Empire, which once stretched around the globe, and covered one quarter of the world's land-mass, no longer existed in Asia, Africa or the Middle East. (However, many of the former colonies are, of course, members of the British Commonwealth of Nations. Currently only Canada, Australia and New Zealand (and a few isolated islands) still declare allegiance to the Sovereign and the British Crown.)

When Alexander Dubcek became Prime Minister of Czechoslovakia in January 1968, he began to implement wide-ranging democratic reforms. The re-birth of these social and political freedoms became known as "The Prague Spring". Unfortunately, these were not to the liking of its Soviet masters and, on 21st August 1968, Russia invaded Czechoslovakia. As with the invasion of Hungary in 1956, the West took no action, although, once again, the invasion drew condemnation from around the globe. The President of Czechoslovakia wisely offered no resistance to the onslaught of the Soviet war machine and all too soon, the "Prague Spring" gave way to a very long "Soviet Summer". Mr Dubcek and others were banned from office and his Government was replaced with a famously repressive communist regime that annulled or abandoned his reforms.

(The people of Czechoslovakia would have to wait until 24th November 1989 before the Communists were finally ousted from power and Mr Dubcek could make a triumphant return to Prague. He became Chairman of the new post-communist administration in what became known as "The Velvet Revolution".)

On 20th January 1969, Richard Milhous Nixon was inaugurated as the 37th President of the United States of America. He had successfully campaigned on a pledge of *"peace with honor"* (sic), for the war in Indo-China was still raging. He was the fifth President to have to deal with Vietnam and its problems.

In June 1969, Nixon announced his policy of *"Vietnamization"* of the war, in which the South Vietnamese Army would be trained and equipped to take over the fighting from the American troops. A phased troop withdrawal began immediately with 25,000 men being sent home – not a moment too soon, for morale and discipline was declining rapidly among the draftees serving involuntarily in Vietnam. Drug abuse had become rampant with nearly 50% experimenting with marijuana, opium or heroin, all of which were easily obtained on the streets of Saigon. By the end of the war, US military hospitals would have dealt with far more casualties of drug abuse than casualties of combat.

Taking 1969 more or less chronologically, one Saturday in the spring/summer of 1969, Mum received a telephone call from one of Dad's half-brothers. They said their father, Ben, was missing. A search party was being organised and they asked if Dad could participate. Dad was at work, so I drove the car as fast as I could to his workplace in order to collect him. (I remember the drive very well because I went around one corner on two wheels and realised there was not a lot of point in killing myself trying to arrive two seconds earlier!)

Granddad, at age 91, had been "forgetful" for quite a while but he had still been able to walk up to his "local", the *Spur* public house at Slindon, every day for a pint of beer before his lunch. This day he had gone up there as usual but had not returned. A check with the land-lord confirmed that he had left at his normal time but none of the regulars had seen where he went; they assumed he had walked home.

Rather to my chagrin, Dad did not think I would be of any assistance in the search, so he raced off to Slindon on his own, leaving Mum and me to wait for news. By the time Dad arrived at Granddad's house, the hunt was well under way. One search team had had the bright idea of using the family pet to look for him, but when the dog took them several miles along a track that no-one used much anymore, they began to think the canine believed he was just out for an unexpected, and very welcome, walk. However, the track led to a disused chalk quarry and, as they approached, the dog became more and more excited. They let him off his lead and he raced ahead, barking in a frenzy at the water's edge. A few feet in, hardly visible and up to his neck in sludge, was Granddad. As diminished as his poor old, grey cells were, he had had the sense not to struggle.

"I knew I'd go in deeper," he explained. "And I knew you'd find me eventually."

So he just waited, patiently, sinking very gradually, until his large and loving family, and dog, found him.

It was a miracle he was still alive and, when asked why he had wandered off, he said he was looking for his chickens! What chickens? He did not have any! And why in this direction? He could not say. His muddled old brain believed he was young and fit and logical. In truth, he was now none of these things. Once home and bathed, he was packed off to bed to recuperate. The doctor was summoned but there was nothing he could do; bed-rest was the only cure, but Granddad's days of going for a pint were over. Indeed, I believe he took to his bed on this occasion and stayed there, still trying to *"Live to be 100 or die in the attempt!"* His wife, Ada, her unmarried son from her first marriage who still lived with them, and Ben and Ada's children and grandchildren nursed him at home until the end. He died a few years later, aged 95, peacefully, in his sleep, in his own bed, trying to achieve the magic 100, right to the end.

History was made in 1969 when earthlings finally placed a man on the moon. On 20th July 1969, the American spaceship *Apollo 11* landed

Neil Armstrong, Edwin (Buzz) Aldrin and Michael Collins on the planet. The first man to walk on the surface was Armstrong and as he put his left foot down, he uttered the now immortal words, "That's one small step for man, one giant leap for mankind."

Mum and Dad remembered the feat very well for they were on holiday in Budapest at the time and they heard the news as they came down to breakfast. They were truly amazed that such an achievement should have happened in their lifetimes. Especially Dad. He insisted that at school he had been taught that the moon was a reflection of the sun, so it was quite hard to convince him that Neil Armstrong was not walking about on some kind of mirage! (I think what his teacher must have said was that the light of the sun reflects on the moon's dark surface, making it appear to glow. Dad misunderstood, or misheard, the concept and carried his erroneous impression regarding our lunar planet right into adulthood.)

Altogether six US missions landed on the moon and they returned a wealth of data and lunar samples. They also carried out numerous experiments on such things as lunar heat, wind, soil, magnetism and many others. However, these moon landings would prove to be the pinnacle of the "space race" and interest and investment in the space programme began to decline.

On 18th July 1969, the Kennedy family was in the news again. Once more somebody had died tragically, but this time it was not a Kennedy. Edward, (known as Ted), brother of the assassinated Kennedy brothers, John (Jack) and Robert (Bobby), co-hosted a party celebrating the Edgartown Regatta, taking place off Martha's Vineyard at Cape Cod, Massachusetts. The other co-host, Ted's cousin Joseph Gargan, rented a cottage for the partygoers to use on Chappaquiddick Island, separated from the Vineyard by a narrow channel and accessible only by a ferryboat.

It was decided to invite the ex-members of brother Robert's campaign staff as a kind of "thank you" for all the hard work they had put in behind the scenes before he had been killed. One of these was Mary-Jo Kopechne.

At some stage in the festivities, a very drunken Ted Kennedy offered to drive Mary-Jo back to her hotel. They crashed at the site of the ferry and the car disappeared beneath the water. Ted Kennedy managed to escape from the car but Mary-Jo drowned. It appeared that he made no attempt to rescue her and instead ran from the scene, seeming more concerned to save his own reputation than a young woman's life.

Less than a week after the accident at Chappaquiddick, there was a similar incident at Salem in Oregon. There, too, the passenger drowned while the driver swam ashore. This driver was charged with negligent homicide. However, the machinery of investigation and justice at Chappaquiddick crumbled under the weight of the power and prestige of the Kennedy family and no charges whatsoever were ever brought against Edward Kennedy, or any member of the ill-fated party.

On a lighter note, and back in the UK, one sport that greatly benefited from being broadcast in colour was snooker, not surprisingly perhaps with its cornucopia of coloured balls. "Pot Black" was first shown on BBC2 on 23rd July 1969 and its success was immediate and phenomenal. It became the second most popular programme on the channel and helped to transform snooker from a minority sport, played in smoky billiard halls, clubs and pub's, with just a handful of professionals, into one of the most popular sports in the UK, where every tournament is hotly contested and top players from all over the world earn millions annually.

The thought of being able to watch sport in colour, including his beloved snooker, appealed greatly to my father and thus a colour television set soon appeared in the Oakley household. Perhaps it was viewing "Pot Black" on the new television that inspired Dad to win the Littlehampton and District Snooker League's pairs and singles championships in 1969 ... and both on the same night! He was able to add the trophies from these events to the shield he had won in 1951 for being singles champion.

Some news items you would definitely not want to view at all, let alone in colour, began on 9th August 1969 with a series of horrific murders in Los Angeles. The actress, Sharon Tate, three friends and a local lad who was visiting their houseboy, were brutally murdered by multiple gunshot and stab wounds in Tate's rented home. Some of the bodies had been mutilated and blood was smeared everywhere, including the word "Pig" scrawled on the front door and "Death to Pigs" written on the living-room wall. The murders were made worse by the fact Sharon Tate was eight months pregnant and her unborn baby boy died with her. Her husband, Roman Polanski, was directing a film in Europe and returned home immediately on hearing the news.

Thirty-six hours later Leno LaBianca and his wife, Rosemary, were also brutally murdered and the crime scene was strikingly similar to that of the Tate murders.

In mid-October, clues left at another similar murder led police and FBI agents to Spahn Ranch, a ramshackle collection of movie-set buildings in the northwest of LA. There they arrested Charles Manson and his "Family", living a quasi-hippy existence.

Manson was an unemployed ex-convict who had gathered social

misfits around him and called them "The Family". Their activities included sexual orgies, hallucinogenic drug trips and frequent sermons from Manson on the meaning of Beatles' music. Manson dominated the lives of "The Family" and no-one questioned his authority. He even encouraged them to believe he was a new Christ. It was at Spahn Ranch that he conceived his murderous "Helter Skelter" plan, a term he took from a Beatles' song of the same name.

There cannot be a more insane motive for murder than that outlined in Manson's "Helter Skelter" plan. Manson thought that a series of bloody murders of wealthy families in LA would erroneously be blamed on African-Americans and would thus trigger a revolution of blacks against the white establishment. Then when (not if!) the blacks proved unable to govern, they would turn to Manson and his followers for leadership.

Although Manson himself never took part in the actual murders, he was convicted through the joint-responsibility rule of conspiracy. After one of the strangest trials in Californian history, Manson and three of his followers were found guilty and sentenced to death. However, after California abolished the death penalty in 1972, the sentences were commuted to life imprisonment. Manson is currently an inmate of Corcoran State Prison and is eligible for parole in 2012.

Of all the unlawful killings that have taken place in the US in the 20th century, the Manson murders remain among the most infamous. It is a cruel irony that they will forever be associated with a "Hippy Movement" that had strived to protect individual freedom, promote "flower-power" and "love and peace" and was at the forefront of the protests against a savage and brutal war in Vietnam. These bloody and senseless murders, and the conviction of Manson and his "Family", marked the beginning of the end of the "Hippy Movement". The murders would henceforth be regarded, by the establishment at least, as the dark face of "hippy-dom".

1969 was a busy year for the UK government. For one thing, they lowered the voting age to 18 for all British people, the argument being that if a young person was old enough to fight (and die) for their country, they ought to be old enough to vote in it.

They also sent British troops to Northern Ireland as a peace-keeping force, for the Nationalists and the Unionists were now openly fighting one another. The root of the strife was the partition of Ireland in 1923. Although the southern (mainly Catholic) part of Ireland was now an independent country, it was not enough for Catholic nationalists in the north who wanted independence for the whole of Ireland. The chief protagonists for the Nationalists were the Provisional Irish Republican Army (the IRA) and for the Unionists, the Ulster Volunteer Force (UVF). The IRA had also begun a campaign of terrorism in the province that

278

would eventually kill more than 2000 people.

And, last but not least, the UK government finally abolished the death penalty for murder. (Although never applied, hanging remained on the statute book until 1998 for certain offences such as piracy, treason and mutiny, and for espionage until 1981.)

At one time, England had the dubious reputation of being the country with the highest number of crimes punishable by death; 220 in all for such diverse offences as "being in the company of gypsies for one month" or "strong evidence of malice in a child aged seven to fourteen years of age". Indeed in *"The Black Act of 1723"* no less than fifty capital offences were added to the statute book, in one foul swoop, for various acts of theft and poaching. The tide had to turn but it was 1908 before the Children's Charter prevented juveniles under the age of 16 being executed. Then, in 1923, a new offence of "infanticide" was introduced to prevent the execution of women who had killed their babies less than one year of age. In 1933, the minimum age for execution was raised to 18 years. Over the years, Parliament tried several times to abolish the death penalty altogether but it was not a measure that met with the approval of the majority of the electorate.

Then, in the 1950's, a series of convictions for murder, and their subsequent executions, were suspect. Indeed Timothy Evans and George Kelly, both hanged in 1950, Mahmood Hussein Mattan, hanged in 1952, and Derek Bentley hanged in 1953, were all eventually granted posthumous pardons. In addition, the double execution of Edward Devlin and Alfred Burns in 1952 also raised serious concerns. They were convicted of killing a woman during a robbery in Liverpool but maintained they were elsewhere, on another robbery, at the time. Felons involved in their robbery supported their statement but the Home Office rejected their evidence and the two were hanged.

The execution of Ruth Ellis in 1955 was also extremely controversial. There was no doubt that she had killed her lover but she had been physically and emotionally abused by him for years and many members of the public felt leniency should be shown. It was not. At aged 28, she would enter the record books as the last woman to be hanged in Britain. Two teenagers aged 18 and 19 were also hanged in 1960 but perhaps the case that gave the most unease was that of Derek Bentley in 1953. He was a 19 year old, mentally retarded youth who accompanied 16 year old Christopher Craig on a burglary. Craig shot and killed a policeman but because he was under age, he served only ten years in prison. Derek Bentley paid the ultimate price for a crime he did not actually commit.

The Ruth Ellis case, and that of Derek Bentley, were the two executions that really forced the public, and Parliament, to re-think their commitment to hanging as a punishment, and thus, in 1969, it was officially abolished for murder, although the last execution in Britain actually took place five years earlier, in 1964.

1969, and the end of the "Swinging Sixties", was to herald the beginning of one of the most far-reaching discoveries of the twentieth century, for what we now know as the "Internet" was born. It had been conceived as early as August 1962, in a series of memos by J.C.R. Licklider. Previously data communication was based on one dedicated circuit being linked to a single party (or so-called "packet") on the other end of the circuit. Licklider thought it was possible to link one packet with more then one machine, and that each packet could be routed independently of other packets on the network. Based on his ideas, in 1969 the "Advanced Research Projects Agency Network" of the US Department of Defense (sic) developed the world's first operational packet switching network and called it, not surprisingly, *ARPANET.* Their development contained almost everything that the *Internet* is today.

For our immediate family the decade ended on a happy note when Bryan and I were married in a very quiet, low-key ceremony at Worthing Registry Office. I had wanted to get married on 27th September, my parents' 39th wedding anniversary, but my best and closest friend, Lesley, whom I had known from schooldays, "pipped me to the post" and arranged her wedding that very day. She asked me to be her bridesmaid, so I tempted fate by ignoring the old wives' tale, *Three times a bridesmaid, never a bride!*

Only close family members were present at our wedding and Mum hosted a delicious lunch at home afterwards. I had made a two-tier wedding-cake for the occasion (inexpertly iced!) so all the relatives and friends who had very kindly still sent presents, could at least be thanked with a decent slice of home-made fruit-cake. I also made my wedding-dress. Mini-skirts were all the rage so I made a fitted, white mini-dress in a crinkly, crimplene (!) material. With a white, wide-brimmed hat and a posy of small red roses, it looked wonderful on the day, but a word of advice to anyone reading this and planning a bridal outfit. Don't go for fashion! Wear a traditional outfit, for when you come to look at your photographs thirty (or forty!) years hence, you may see only "ridiculous"!

Bryan and I had spent months house-hunting and eventually had chosen a brand-new, detached bungalow on a new housing estate that was being built on the outskirts of Bognor, not far from where Bryan's parents lived. In fact, it was the estate that Bryan and his father were working on but the price was not reduced for us! However, the developer did agree to get the sub-contractors to build a honeycomb brick-wall around the back garden free of charge.

We put all our savings into the deposit in order to reduce the mortgage commitment, which turned out to be a prudent move because

Bryan and his dad were made redundant only a few weeks after our marriage. They both spent the winter unemployed and took great delight in attending the local auctions to see what bits and pieces of furniture they could pick up for our new home at a reasonable price!

Bryan always says these few months of unemployment helped him to adjust to the rigours (!) of married life and, in truth, it helped me too, for while I was at work, he prepared the vegetables for the evening meal and did some of the housework. Indeed before we "tied the knot", he told me he did not mind what I asked him to do as long as it did not involve shopping! He HATED shopping. He still does and it is still the one chore I never ask him to undertake.

Having used most of our savings on the bungalow, we spent the next few years saving up for curtains, carpets, etc. Indeed, it was several years before we finished covering all the bare floorboards with carpet! Obviously, we could not afford a washing-machine so Bryan got into the habit of going down to the launderette every week, with his dad, and there they would sit, chewing the fat and watching the sheets and towels slosh around in the soapy water.

We soon established a routine of going to my in-law's' house on Saturday evenings for a fish and chip supper, which I had to purchase from the shop across the road. I had strict instructions to wait while it was freshly cooked so we could eat it piping hot! Afterwards we spent the evening with them watching television, for this was another appliance Bryan and I did not own, this time from choice. In fact, we did not own a TV for the first nine years of our marriage, preferring to listen to the radio or just sit and talk. I feel to this day that our communication skills were honed in those years of "no box" and we learned to be at ease in one another's company without the stimulus of instant visual entertainment. These were the years when I became an avid *Archers* fan and came to appreciate BBC radio plays, discussion programmes and the *World Service*.

Meanwhile Bryan and my dad set about bringing our building-plot of a garden into some sort of order. As was, and is, normal with new houses, the front garden had been turfed but the estate was open-plan and we wanted some kind of boundary between our garden and the pavement, so Dad planted a privet hedge on two sides. By the time we sold the property some thirty years later, this little hedge was about 15feet (5m) high and about 6feet (2m) thick and took Bryan three days to cut with an electric hedge-trimmer. Dad also made a border on our side of the neighbour's fence and planted rose bushes, which he subsequently kept pruned for us.

Over the coming months (and years) Bryan would lay a concrete drive in the front garden because we did want to buy a car (well a minivan actually!) as soon as possible. At the back, he laid a large patio and then built a retaining wall with steps in the middle and piled all the excess rubble and soil behind it. This made the final rear-end of the garden higher than the patio and, at first, we tried to grow vegetables here but it was not a success so we decided to turn this into a lawn as well. By this time, Bryan was employed again so Dad undertook to turn this last piece of wilderness into our lawn. He chopped down all the weeds, piled the vegetation into one huge heap, and then set light to it. As we turned the corner into our road (in our new minivan), we thought our house was on fire! There was a huge pall of black smoke hanging over the roof with red sparks and flames shooting into the sky. All the kids in the neighbourhood were peering through the honeycombed holes in the brick-wall watching with glee our garden literally go up in smoke! Dad just LOVED a bonfire, the bigger the better!

So the 1970's were the beginning of a new era for us, with Bryan and I adjusting to married life, Sheila courting her first real boy-friend and Mum and Dad settling down to a *Darby and Joan* existence ..... Well that was the intention!

CHAPTER THIRTY-THREE

Black and White
(1970-1972)

The New Year, and the new decade of the 70's, did not start well for Sheila. The first blow was breaking her "polio" leg while out horse-riding. She could not manage all the stairs at the flat she still shared in Worthing, so she returned home to recuperate.

No sooner was she literally on her feet again, than her boyfriend, the supposed love of her life, told her he did not want to see her anymore; he had found someone else. In her mind, his new love was bound to be slimmer, prettier, sexier and smarter, and what little self-confidence and self-esteem she had, plummeted. She thought she would never find anyone else she could love as much as she had loved him, nor would anyone else ever fall in love with her. She was heartbroken. It was another rejection. She could not sleep; she could not eat; she could not stop crying. Eventually Mum persuaded her to see the doctor. He prescribed anti-depressants and referred her to the local psychiatric hospital as an out-patient.

Gradually over the coming months, with the help of the drugs and counselling sessions, she rallied and realised that living and loving, was not at an end. She began to put her life, and its disappointments, into perspective. Perhaps for the first time, she tried to appreciate her many blessings, including that of her supportive, loving family; even if they were not her "real" family, and did not always agree with her, at least they were always there for her.

Eventually she was able to return to her job at the garage in Angmering where she worked as a secretary/receptionist and unofficial car salesperson. Then a girl-friend asked her to share a flat in Worthing and once again she left home.

As the new decade dawned, it was not only Sheila who was in a state of turmoil for the whole world seemed ill at ease. Not only was America still embroiled in the Vietnam War but these were the years when terrorism truly became global. Of course acts of terrorism had always been with us; for example, Guy Fawkes and his Gunpowder Plot of 1605 could be said to be act of terrorism, but now nationalist guerrilla fighters would routinely hold the rest of the world to ransom. Thus this was probably the decade most people would remember as the time terrorism truly began to affect us all, indirectly if not directly.

Before we move on to the events of the 1970's, a little background information might be helpful, although any attempt to simplify these complex and convoluted problems are almost impossible without doing some injustice to one side or the other. Take the Middle East for example. Perhaps the seed for some actions in the latter part of this twentieth century could be said to have been sown in 1916 with the fall of the Ottoman Empire, when the zone of "Palestine" (today's Jordan, Israel and "West Bank") was mandated to British rule.

The Jews had actually begun mass immigration to the area in the 1880's and their efforts to convert this land of swamp and mosquito attracted an equally large number of Arab settlers, taking advantage of the increased prosperity and the better living conditions that the Jews had introduced. But no peoples had ever established a national homeland in "Palestine", at least not since the Jews had done so over 2000 years before, so it seemed feasible to the British that a Jewish state could possibly be created there. However, this proved to be no easy matter for Palestinian-Arab and Palestinian-Jew would need to co-exist. The British tried to maintain order between the warring factions but once oil was discovered in other parts of the Middle East, it became increasingly impossible.

Then the Second World War came and when it was over the Western Powers began to look again at Palestine, thinking this might solve the problem of all the Jewish refugees that were scattered over Europe. Meanwhile the British continued to attempt to keep the peace in Palestine but the situation became so fraught that in 1947 they asked the United Nations to intervene.

Finally the UN decided to "bite the bullet" and divide Palestine into a Jewish-Palestinian State and an Arab-Palestinian State. The Jews accepted the proposal but the Arabs did not. Although the Palestinian-Arabs may not have established the land as a "homeland" to the satisfaction of Western criteria, they had lived on it, and wandered through it, for centuries and they most certainly did not want a permanent Jewish settlement in their midst. But on 14th May 1948 the Palestinian-Jews went ahead and declared their own State of Israel. The very next day they were invaded by seven neighbouring Arab armies and the war between them lasted for nineteen months. At the end of it, Israel was slightly larger than before but nearly 85% of the old "Palestine" was still in Arab hands, mainly as the new territory of Jordan.

Soon Jews started to arrive in huge numbers from war-torn Europe and many of the remaining Palestinian-Arabs still living in Israel, sought refuge in neighbouring Arab states. Over the years, most of those that remained were pushed further and further east until they were sandwiched between the new Israelis to their west and Jordanians on their east. They co-existed uneasily for a decade or so but the Palestinian-Arabs always felt the Jews, with the connivance of the Western Powers (mainly Britain and the USA), had stolen their land.

On 28th May 1964, the Arab states of Egypt, Syria, Jordan and Iraq created the "Palestinian Liberation Organization" (the PLO), mainly to channel Palestinian nationalism in such a way that the Palestinian refugees living on their soil would have a focus for their hopes and dreams and not destabilize their own regimes. The leader of this newly-created PLO was Yasser Arafat and, publicly at least, he stated that the twin goals of his organization were the liberation of Palestine and the establishment of a secular democratic state for Arabs and Jews.

In 1967 the Six Day War took place in which Israel captured the Jordan-occupied West Bank of the Jordan River, where many of the Palestinian-Arabs had settled. Thousands of them were displaced yet again, across the river into Jordan itself. The more militant of them formed a para-military, nationalist-Palestinian organization, under the umbrella of the PLO, called the "Popular Front for the Liberation of Palestine", the PFLP, with the declared aim of destroying Israel and restoring Palestine to the Palestinian-Arabs, by whatever means they could. Historians and journalists cannot agree as to how much control Yasser Arafat exerted over the PFLP and its activities, but it is well known that democratic means were not part of PLO tactics.

The PLO and the PFLP became an increasingly autonomous challenge to the monarchy of the young King Hussein and his Jordanian Government and between 1968 and 1969 no fewer that 500 violent clashes occurred between Palestinian guerrillas and Jordanian security forces. In June 1970, an Arab mediation committee intervened in order to halt serious fighting between the two sides but just three months later King Hussein and the Government of Jordan were catapulted into a huge international incident, precipitated by the PFLP. The incident came to be known as the "Dawson's Field hijackings" and this set the stage for the global terrorism that was to be so much a part of the coming decades.

On 6th September 1970, four jet aircraft, bound for New York City, were hijacked over Western Europe by members of the PFLP who were demanding the release of three of their comrades held in a Swiss jail. One of the jets was a TWA flight from Frankfurt, another a Swissair jet from Zurich-Kloten and two were outward-bound from Amsterdam. The TWA jet (from Frankfurt) and the Swissair 'plane (from Zurich) were forced to land at a remote desert airstrip in Jordan, formerly used as a British Air Force base and known then as Dawson's Field. The hijacking of an El Al (Israel) flight from Amsterdam was foiled when passengers and crew overpowered the hijackers. In the ensuing struggle one hijacker was shot and killed and a crew member was seriously injured. The hijacker's female partner, Leila Khaled, was subdued. The 'plane diverted to London and there made an emergency landing where Khaled was handed over to British authorities. Two more of their cohorts had been prevented from boarding this 'plane at Amsterdam but they had managed to board a Pan Am flight and hijacked this instead. This fourth 'plane was a Boeing 747 and was too big to land at Dawson's Field so it was diverted to Cairo (via Beirut).

A fifth 'plane, owned by BOAC (now BA) and flying from Bombay, was hijacked on 9th September and also brought to Dawson's Field.

The majority of the 310 passengers were transferred to Amman and freed on 11th September. The empty 'planes were blown up by the PFLP and only the Jewish passengers and the flight crews (56 people in total) remained as hostages. However, before negotiations could be completed for their release, the PLO, once again, attempted to seize control of Jordan from King Hussein. The King and his forces prevailed and the PLO was finally expelled from Jordan. This came to be known as "Black September" because Arab was fighting Arab, instead of fighting the common enemy, Israel.

Incensed at their defeat and treatment by Jordan, militant members of the PLO and PFLP would now join forces with others determined to take revenge on King Hussein, his government and the Jordanian army, as well as Israel and the Western Powers, and they would call themselves "The Black September Organization", in memory of those who had died in Jordan. Their base would now be the Lebanon and Libya.

The conflict had nearly triggered a regional war involving Syria, Iraq and Israel with potentially global consequences. Swift Jordanian victory, however, enabled a deal to be brokered where, on 1st October 1970, the remaining PFLP hostages were exchanged for Khaled and the three PFLP members held in the Swiss jail.

Therefore it seems that terrorism "won" in this instance but the authorities must have been in no doubt about the ruthlessness of the perpetrators for, prior to the Dawson's Field incident, the PFLP had achieved notoriety for several similar events and indeed on 21st February 1970 the PFLP had bombed a Swissair flight bound for Israel, killing 47 people.

In every one of these cases, the hijackers boarded the aircraft carrying concealed weapons on their persons, for airline security was almost non-existent. Not only was luggage not x-rayed, and only searched spasmodically, but metal detectors were not used to screen passengers. Aircraft hijacking was becoming almost commonplace and thus methods would be developed that would eventually lead to the ongoing security checks that are now standard procedures at all international airports.

However it would not be accurate to blame all terrorist acts of the 70's on the PFLP or "Black September", for it seems as if almost every country from Thailand to the Philippines, Korea to Pakistan, South America, Germany, Italy and Britain had their own brand of home-grown terrorist. Indeed there were more than thirty Islamic terrorist groups alone. Some groups were nationalistic, some religious, some Marxist; some committed their acts of violence within their own frontiers; many others took their "fight" into other lands.

But 1971 began with a tragedy that had nothing to do with terrorism. On 2nd January, the Ibrox Football Stadium in Glasgow was hosting a match between Celtic and Rangers. It had been a rather lacklustre game and thousands of supporters decided to leave just before the end of the match. Crush barriers on one of the stairways gave way, blocking the exit, and, as the game ended, thousands more poured into the stairway with no way to proceed. The fans just piled up, one on top of the other, causing compressive asphyxia to those at the bottom of the heap. 66 people died and another 200 were injured.

This was the third time the Ibrox Stadium had been involved in a tragedy. On 5th April 1902, during a match between England and Scotland, a newly-built stand collapsed, due to heavy rainfall the previous night. Hundreds of people fell up to 40-feet to the ground below. 25 fans died and 517 were injured.

Then, in September 1961, there was another crush on a stairway and two people were killed. But it was not until after the 1971 incident that the Ibrox was converted to an all-seater stadium and subsequently awarded UEFA five-star status. It was another thirty years (in 2001) before a monument was unveiled at the stadium commemorating every one of the 93 fans who had died in these three tragedies.

But it was not long before terrorism hit the headlines again. On 12th January 1971, a group called the "Angry Brigade" exploded two bombs at the home of a UK government minister, Robert Carr. This was just one of 25 acts carried out by this group between August 1970 and August 1971 and prompted the Government to set up a "Bomb Squad", based at Scotland Yard, specifically to target the group. The "Squad" was successful and the "Angry Brigade" was apprehended in August 1971.

The newly-formed "Bomb Squad" was not founded a moment too soon, for on 30th October 1971 the IRA brought their terror campaign to mainland Britain when they exploded a bomb at the Post Office Tower in London. It caused extensive damage but no one was injured.

Fortunately there was other news apart from terrorism. The decade would see the first introduction of various statutes regarding discrimination, beginning with the "Equal Pay Act of 1970" (and later amendments) which aimed to give equal opportunity to male and female employees in relation to terms, opportunities and conditions in the workplace. It introduced the concept of equal pay for work of equal value.

The 12th February 1971 was the day the UK and Ireland switched to decimal currency. Gone forever was the old pound, made up of 240 old pennies, with twelve pennies making one shilling, and twenty shillings thus making one pound. Gone too would be words like "tanner" (sixpence), "half a crown" (two shillings and sixpence), a "bob" (shilling(s)) and "halfpenny" (pronounced hape-knee). The farthing (a quarter of a penny) had been discontinued in 1960.

Gone too would be the complicated formulae, not only for adding up but for working out multiples of money. Now tourists might be less confused but the rest of us converted the new currency back into £ s d (pounds, shillings and pence) for years before it made any sense! (Indeed some of us, like my husband, still say things like, "Ten bob for a loaf of bread!")

1971 was also the year a prominent landmark moved from the cold and grey of London to the desert of Arizona. London Bridge was originally erected over the River Thames in 1831 but by 1962 it was not sound enough to support the increased load of modern traffic. In the mid 60's it was sold to the chairman of McCulloch Oil Corporation to serve as a tourist attraction for a new retirement real estate development, modelled on an English village, at Lake Havasu City.

Each stone of the bridge was carefully disassembled and numbered and shipped to the US. The original stone was used to clad a concrete structure, so in fact the bridge is no longer the original on which it is modelled, but despite that it was a popular tourist attraction for the city. Sadly, in recent years, the large amount of development nearby has caused a decline in the desirability of the area and one would have to look hard now to see anything which resembles "an English village", although the bridge is still there.

In September 1971, free school milk for children aged seven to eleven came to an end as a cost cutting measure in Edward Heath's Conservative Government. The controversial, and highly unpopular, decision had been made by the then Education Secretary, Margaret Thatcher, and earned her the nickname *"Thatcher, Thatcher, Milk Snatcher."* Free school milk for secondary schoolchildren ended, without fanfare, in 1968, under Harold Wilson's Labour Government and was stopped for ages five to seven in 1980. Currently it is still available to the under-fives.

In October 1971 Dad was seventy years old. By now he had given up full-time work at the school in order to qualify for his retirement pension but he still worked there part-time. Which was just as well because every Christmas he still made his wreaths and needed access to the holly bushes he had nurtured for forty years, not to mention the laurel hedge and the fir trees. Strange to say, his place at the school was taken by one of the boys into whose garden we had crawled to play all those years ago.

It was around this time that Dad had given up something else: his beloved coal-fire! Even he had got fed up with all the work involved so he and Mum decided to have gas central heating installed and his coal fires became gas ones. Mum was still too nervous to cook with gas but she decided modern piped-gas was worth the "risk" for a nice warm house.

It was in October 1971 that I was promoted for the first time. I was to become a specialist employment officer, helping handicapped people find work and training. At that time it was quite unusual for someone so relatively new to the Civil Service to be promoted so soon and, at age 25, I was also one of the youngest so-called Disablement Resettlement Officers (DRO's) ever. A daunting privilege but privilege it was. I was based in Worthing but also covered my old office of Littlehampton. As well as interviewing people, visiting employers, attending committee meetings and writing endless reports, at one stage I even had to organise a reception at Arundel Castle! There was never a dull moment and I loved every minute. My photograph appeared in the local paper, along with a feature on me and my new job, and to hear my parents (especially Dad!) you would have thought I was being appointed a Permanent Under-Secretary at least! They were so proud of me, although, in truth, I had barely stepped off the bottom rung!

Late 1971 also saw Sheila on the move. She had had enough of working at the garage, and living in the flat, and felt a need to see fresh faces and places. When she was offered a job in another garage/car-sales in Hythe, near Southampton, in the neighbouring county of Hampshire, she decided to take it. She asked her new employer if he knew anywhere she could stay until she found a flat-share again and he recommended a friend's small hotel/guest-house, not far from her job. It was called *Deanslake* and was situated in a very rural area, on the edge of the New Forest, close to Southampton Water and standing in several acres of its own grounds. There were fifteen bedrooms in the main house and four in an annexe and the proprietor offered very generous terms for a long-let. His name was Eric Vernon Carpenter, known as "Mac" to all his friends ever since he had been a small boy, dressed in tartan trousers. Someone had remarked that he looked like "Mr MacTavish" and the "Mac" part stuck.

Mac had recently been widowed, his wife of thirty years having been killed in a car crash. Despite the twenty-nine year age difference, he and Sheila found they had a lot in common. They shared a love of the automobile and driving; they liked music, dancing and entertaining: cooking (and eating!) and literature. And they were both lonely. They talked for hours. Within weeks Sheila knew she was in love again and, to her amazement, so was Mac. By Christmas he had met the family and in the New Year they were engaged.

Everyone liked Mac; he was well-travelled, well-read, well-educated and well-off! He was extrovert, gregarious, generous, confident and, best of all, there was no "side" to him. Peasant or peer, he could talk to them all. He had always wanted a family but his first wife had suffered only miscarriages. He was anxious to have a second try at family life, while he was still young enough to enjoy it, so he and Sheila were married, after a very short engagement, at Hythe Parish Church in 1972.

It was a fairy-tale ceremony with all the trimmings: pony and trap, top-hat and tails and the bride looked absolutely stunning in a long, white, embroidered dress and matching veil and train. Dad looked so distinguished in his morning-suit as he gave her away and Mum was pride personified in a royal-blue, silk dress and matching coat. I was matron-of-honour, with two other bridesmaids, and Bryan, looking so handsome in his hired morning-suit, was an usher.

The reception was held at Mac's parents' house. It was almost a mansion by our standards with a very large, landscaped garden complete with marquee on the lawn and a string quartet. The sun shone on the bride and groom all day, completing a wonderful, wonderful day. And the complete opposite to my own wedding, but each to his, or her, own. I hate the limelight; Sheila revels in it!

The newlyweds honeymooned in London for a few days where they had a night out at the famous "Talk of the Town" cabaret restaurant. In 1958 the venue had been converted from the old "London Hippodrome" and, until its closure in 1982, it featured many famous popular artists of the time including Frank Sinatra, Sammy Davis Jr, Cliff Richard, Stevie Wonder, Tom Jones, Eartha Kitt, Shirley Bassey and many more!

Oh that all the news of 1972 was as happy as my sister's wedding day! Although on a light note, computer floppy discs had by now been introduced (1970), VCR's were now being manufactured (1971) and pocket calculators had been invented (1972).

Now for the not-so-light news of 1972. When British troops arrived in Northern Ireland in 1969, as a peace-keeping force, they were initially welcomed by the minority Catholic population but all this changed after the events of 30th January 1972, known, for reasons that will become obvious, as *Bloody Sunday.*

To this day it is not entirely clear what on earth went wrong but members of the 1st Battalion of the British Parachute Regiment opened fire on unarmed civil rights protesters. Twenty-seven civilians were shot, thirteen died immediately and one died several months later from his injuries. Of those who died, several people were shot in the back as they tried to run away and several more were killed as they went to the aid of comrades, at least one of whom was waving a white handkerchief. Tragically seven teenagers were amongst those who were slaughtered.

An enquiry was held, which cleared the soldiers of any blame, and thus was immediately labelled a whitewash. Many years later, in 1998, the then Prime Minister, Tony Blair, initiated a new inquiry. After interviewing 900 witnesses over a seven year period, the report is currently still being written. It is due to be published in 2009 at an estimated cost of a staggering £155 million. (NB It was finally published in 2010 at a cost of £200 million and it found that the civilians had been "unlawfully killed". One cannot help but wonder why it took nearly forty years, and this huge sum of money, to admit this tragic fact.)

The rights and wrongs of the incident may not yet (if ever) be known but it certainly put back any peace process for years and severely dented the public's faith in the impartiality of the "peacekeepers". The anger of the event was exploited by the IRA and increased not only the number of their recruits but the amount of money they received to support their campaign, especially from IRA sympathizers in the US.

Just two weeks later, on 12th February 1972, the IRA took their revenge. Their target was the headquarters of the Parachute Regiment in Aldershot but, unknown to them, most of the intended victims were stationed abroad. Nonetheless, seven people were killed by the car bomb they had placed in the car-park outside the officers' mess. They were an elderly gardener, five kitchen staff who had just left the premises and a Roman Catholic army chaplain who had just arrived. Nineteen people were also injured. This was the first time that the IRA claimed lives in their terror campaign of mainland Britain, and sadly it would not be the last.

But it would be incorrect to think that all the lives lost by IRA attacks this year were in England, for 1972 probably ranks as the worst year for the numbers of deaths, and the numbers of bombs, in Northern Ireland. The IRA killed 100 British soldiers and wounded 500 more in this year alone and in July the most devastating example of their commercial bombing campaign took place in the city centre of Belfast. In just a few short hours they exploded no less than twenty-two bombs, killing nine people and injuring 130. The day came to be known as *Bloody Friday.*

In May *Black September* hijacked another jet, a *Sabena Boeing* flying from Brussels to Tel Aviv, and took 100 hostages. Twelve Israeli soldiers, disguised as maintenance staff, stormed the 'plane and freed the hostages, killing two of the male hijackers in the process. The two female hijackers were found to have explosives packed into the lining of corsets they were wearing and they were also carrying a pistol and a grenade concealed in cans of talcum powder. They were jailed for life but were lucky to escape the death penalty.

In retaliation for killing the two hijackers, *Black September* recruited three Japanese gunmen from the "Japanese Red Army" terrorist group and on 26th May they opened fire on crowds at Tel Aviv Airport, killing 26 people and injuring dozens more. Two of the gunmen died; the survivor was tried and sentenced to life imprisonment. He spent thirteen years in jail before being released in a prisoner exchange with the Palestinians. He was given asylum in Lebanon, where he converted to Islam and was feted as a hero.

On 28th May 1972, the Duke of Windsor died in Paris, aged 77 years, from throat cancer. As we know from a previous chapter, Edward VIII would forever be known as "the King who was never crowned", and had chosen to marry Wallis Simpson rather than give up his throne. Apart from a few years serving as Governor of the Bahamas, he and his wife had spent their years of exile living in Paris. The Queen gave permission for his body to be returned to England for burial in the family plot at Frogmore, in the grounds of Windsor Castle.

(His widow survived him for another fourteen years, dying in April 1986, also in Paris, at the age of 89 years. She was laid to rest under a spreading plane tree, alongside her husband.)

In August 1972 Uganda was destined to sink into yet more chaos. Ever since Idi Amin had seized power in a military coup some nineteen months previously, conditions in the former British colony had deteriorated rapidly. Eventually his despotic rule would become infamous for its human rights abuses, political repression, ethnic persecution, extra-judicial killings and torture. So much so that he would become known as the "Hitler of Africa".

On 7th August 1972, he announced that all Asians who were not Ugandan citizens, must leave Uganda within 90 days. He claimed the Asians were "bloodsuckers" and accused them of milking the country of its wealth. Asians were in fact the backbone of the Ugandan economy; many had lived there for two generations and thought of the African country as their home.

On hearing of Amin's ultimatum, some fled to nearby Tanzania and some returned to an alien India, but up to 50,000 were British passport holders and about 30,000 of them sought asylum in the "mother country".

Hundreds of flights had to be organised to carry out the evacuation and the sudden influx of tens of thousands of refugees was a severe headache for the UK authorities. Most arrived virtually penniless, having been expelled without compensation for businesses and property. Some were robbed of their money and few possessions as they made their way to the airport.

Some families had been able to make their own arrangements for accommodation but most had not, so old army and RAF camps were re-opened to offer basic shelter. It was not ideal but they were fed and housed and they were safe. Although initially there were many objections to the arrival of so many Ugandan Asians, their resettlement came to be viewed as a success story for British immigration.

Idi Amin became increasingly erratic and outspoken. Foreign journalists considered him a somewhat comical, eccentric figure but the US ambassador described his regime as "racist, erratic and unpredictable, brutal, inept, bellicose, irrational, ridiculous and militaristic." Gradually every country in the Western world broke off diplomatic relations with him. In 1979 he was overthrown and went to live in Saudi Arabia until his death in 2003. The number of people killed as a result of his eight year regime is unknown but estimates from human rights groups say it could be as high as 500,000.

1972 was the year of the Munich Olympics, when the American swimmer Mark Spitz won a record seven gold medals. Alas his achievement is overshadowed by the incident for which the Games are now best remembered. On 5th September *Black September* kidnapped nine members of an Israeli Olympic team from the Olympic Village, demanding that 200 Palestinian prisoners held in Israel should be released in exchange for their safety.

The tough Prime Minister of Israel, Golda Meir, refused to negotiate with terrorists but the West German Chancellor offered to pay any price for the release of the athletes. He was told by the guerrilla leader that he cared for "neither money or lives" (sic), but he did accept the offer of helicopters to take the terrorists and hostages to Fürstenfeldbruck where they would be flown out.

Almost as soon as the helicopters landed, a gun battle commenced and all the hostages, one policeman and five of the eight terrorists were killed. To this day controversy reigns as to what exactly happened, for the events have never been fully explained. What is certain, is that the three terrorists who were captured, were later released by West Germany following the hijacking by *Black September* of a *Lufthansa* airliner.

Israel responded to the massacre with "Operation Spring of Youth" and "Operation Wrath of God", a series of air strikes against *Black September* and the PLO. The Israeli Secret Service, *Mossad*, formed a special unit that hunted down and killed two of the three surviving Munich terrorists.

The Israeli and Egyptian teams withdrew from the Games but, after just one day of official mourning, the IOC President, Avery Bruridge, announced, "The Games must go on."

CHAPTER THIRTY-FOUR

All Change!
(1973-1975)

By the time 1973 arrived, Sheila was already pregnant with her first child. I am ashamed to admit that when we first learned of her pregnancy, I was so envious that I could not bear to hear her name mentioned or learn anything about how her "bump" was progressing. Mum watched with growing concern for jealousy was not normally part of my nature. I told Mum how I felt and said how much I had wanted it to be me that presented her with her first grandchild.

"It might come between us," I exclaimed, "for you'll have a baby to love now."

"Yes," she replied, "and so will you! This isn't like you. You'll miss so much joy if you can't be happy for her."

Of course Mum spoke from experience. She was the only person who could understand where I was coming from and what it was like to have baby-dreams regularly shattered. With her love, support and quiet empathy, common-sense prevailed and I realised that the ability to love is not finite. Additions to a family, be it adult, baby or even pet, come with their own store of love which they scatter like fairy-dust over all who can open their hearts and minds to receive it.

So, in the end, far from coming between us, Sheila's pregnancies brought us closer, for Sheila was always generous with her sons and never tried to keep them for herself, which I confess I might have done! Mac was very tactile and under his influence Sheila encouraged her children to hug, kiss and cuddle and to say "*I love you*" at every opportunity. Between them they would help to break down the reserve that had been such a part of our family structure. It did not happen overnight but the births of Russell Scott Carpenter in 1973 and Vernon Scott Carpenter in 1974 were the beginning.

On 1st January 1973 the European Community (founded in 1957 and consisting of France, West Germany, Italy, and the three Benelux countries of Belgium, the Netherlands and Luxembourg) opened its doors to Denmark, Ireland and the United Kingdom. The main aim of this united Europe was "to preserve peace and liberty and to lay the foundations of an ever closer union among the peoples of Europe". It also called for a common customs tariff, a common policy of agriculture, transport and trade and an eventual enlargement of the EEC to include the rest of Europe.

Many of Britain's politicians had been keen for the country to join the

EEC right from the beginning but the French President, Charles de Gaulle, was not so sure. His first concern was that Britain would want to negotiate special terms for tariffs with its Commonwealth countries and this was unacceptable. Then in 1963, after years of talks between the then Lord Privy Seal, Edward Heath, and EEC members, de Gaulle once again vetoed Britain's membership, this time fearing that Britain's alliance with America would seriously damage the balance of power in Europe. Britain tried again in 1967 and once again de Gaulle issued his veto. It was not until Charles de Gaulle ceased to be President of France that Britain's membership was finally accepted.

By 1973 Edward Heath was now Prime Minister and he had always been a strong advocate for this "Common Market". Even though the *Treaty of Rome* had been signed and Britain was officially now a member, there was still strong opposition to his decision to join from those who felt Britain's independence and democracy would be lost in a European superstate. The battle for membership was not yet concluded.

By now peace negotiations had been taking place for years in order to end the conflict in Vietnam and on 27th January 1973 "Peace Accords" were at last signed in Paris. The parties agreed to an immediate cease-fire and withdrawal of the remaining US troops. President Thieu of South Vietnam was a reluctant signatory, labelling the terms "tantamount to surrender" but in a secret despatch, President Nixon had assured him that "swift and severe retaliatory action" would be taken if North Vietnam violated the terms of the treaty.

On the same day that the treaty was signed, the American Secretary of Defense (sic) announced an end to the draft in favour of voluntary enlistment. He assured the American people that in future the US army would be smaller but better equipped, totally professional and with better trained officers. Lessons had been learned the hard way in this brutal conflict.

On 29th March 1973 the last remaining American troops withdrew from Vietnam and America's longest war, and its first defeat, ended at last. A total of 2.59million Americans had served in the war and 47,244 of them had been killed in action, including 8,000 airmen. There were 10,446 non-combat deaths and 304,000 wounded, 153,329 seriously, including 10,000 amputees. 591 American POW's were released but over 2,400 American POW's/MIA's were unaccounted for. The North Vietnamese suffered ten times as many dead and their casualties were estimated at 15 million.

In June 1973 the US Congress passed the Case-Church Amendment which forbids further US military involvement in S.E. Asia. The Amendment would pave the way for North Vietnam to break the Accord and wage yet another invasion of the South, without the fear of US intervention and despite President Nixon's reassurances to President

Thieu.

On 14th March 1973 the space-race was back in the news with the launch of the American "Skylab". This was the first experimental space station designed to allow humans to live and work in space for extended periods. It would expand our knowledge of solar astronomy well beyond earth-based observation and become the site of nearly 300 scientific, technical and medical experiments.

By the end of the 70's the assignment was curtailed due to lack of funding and interest and when "Skylab" re-entered the atmosphere in July 1979, it was destroyed, scattering debris over the Indian Ocean and the remote desert region of Western Australia.

On 3rd April 1973, "*Motorola*" manager, Martin Cooper, placed a cellular 'phone call to *AT&T*. This simple act began the era of handheld cellular mobile 'phones.

On 10th October 1973 Spiro Agnew became the only Vice President in US history (to date) to resign because criminal charges had been filed against him. He was under investigation by the US Attorney's office in Baltimore, Maryland, for extortion, tax fraud, bribery and conspiracy. Eventually, however, he was allowed to plead "no contest" to a single charge that he had failed to declare $29.500 of income received in 1967, on condition that he resigned the office of Vice President. He had served under Richard Nixon and was the first Greek-American to serve in that capacity. He was succeeded by Gerald Ford.

In October 1973, Bryan's father died, suddenly, from a massive heart attack. He was only 67 and still working full-time, and was such a vibrant and pivotal part of Bryan's family that his death left us all devastated. Bryan made the comment that he felt rudderless, like a cork bobbing about on the ocean, just drifting with wind and tide. His mother and sister felt the same, for it was hard to believe the centre of the family had really gone. It was the first death of a close family member that either of us had had to face. One of Bryan's biggest regrets was, "*I never told him how much I loved him.*" This just was not done in either family but his words had a profound effect on me and I vowed I would learn to say those words to my own parents before it was too late.

Sheila's father-in-law had died too, a year earlier on 7th November 1972, Mac's 53rd birthday. Percy Carpenter, known to all as "Carp", was nearly eighty years old so his death was not quite so surprising but it too was relatively sudden and unexpected. Cancer had been diagnosed and he was dead just five days later. Sadly he never lived to see his latest grandchildren.

Mac's mother made arrangements to sell the "mansion" and move to a smaller property. The old house was on a large plot of land so it was demolished and a small estate was built in its stead. The Council decided the road should be called "Carpenter Close".

By the time Vernon was born in 1974 Sheila and I were becoming closer, although we still had a tendency to bicker which exasperated parents and husbands! I was still a bit wary of her and could not completely trust her protestations of love and loyalty, less it back-fired on me as it had done so many times in the past, but at least she came to regard me as her confidante.

She told me that Mac was causing her problems. He treated her more as a recalcitrant child than a wife, and certainly not as an equal partner. He had started to "invest" in all sorts of things from silver to vintage cars in need of restoration: chess-sets, glassware, sets of books. One of his favourite outlets was *Franklin Mint* that specialised in commemorative ware such as plates, dolls and thimbles. It was like a mania but the more Sheila tried to persuade him to be a little more circumspect, the less notice he took. She discovered that the staff at *Deanslake* felt his first wife had been the financial brain of the business, for she had been quick to put the brake on his spending and his more outrageous ideas for expansion. They knew that he had resented this but now the brake was gone, he could "invest" in whatever took his fancy. But as yet there was no cause for alarm. They still had a flourishing business and a lifestyle that was beyond her wildest dreams.

Meanwhile Mac confided to Bryan that Sheila was still moody; she always insisted on having the last word and was a past-master at "winding him up". He made the comment that sometimes it was like living with *Jekyll and Hyde*; she could be a holy terror one minute, yet charm-personified if a visitor arrived. It drove him mad, as it had me, so it seemed her deep-rooted problems had only transferred onto someone else and not disappeared.

But it was around this time that any problems they were having were forgotten as they united to fight for the life of their eldest son. The baby, Vernon, was about two months old and Russell an unsteady toddler just fourteen months his senior. Things started innocuously enough, with Russell suffering what appeared to be a minor stomach upset. Mac took him to the doctor who said it was nothing to worry about and implied they were paranoid parents, worrying unnecessarily.

"He'll be fine in a day or two," he assured them airily. "Just give him plenty of fluids."

Mac stayed up with his son the next couple of nights, trying to persuade him to sip a few drops of water, and Sheila did the same during the day as Mac caught up on a few hours of fitful sleep. But there was still another baby to look after, and a business to run, so when an equally worried Nana offered to come immediately and help with the children, Mac and Sheila gratefully accepted. By now it was Saturday and the one and only time Mum travelled by train to visit them.

That night Mac sat up with Russell as usual, but by now Russell could not even keep a few sips of water in his tummy. Overnight he deteriorated rapidly and early on Sunday morning he was barely responsive and his skin was grey and seemed loose and flabby. A frantic, and somewhat angry, parent 'phoned the emergency surgery and demanded that a doctor attend immediately. (This was in the days when home visits were still undertaken by your own GP, or a member of the same practice, at least.) The emergency doctor arrived forthwith, even though it was still not 7am, took one look at the toddler and said, "Drive to Southampton General straight away. I mean NOW! Go as fast as you can and shoot red lights if you have to. We can't even wait for an ambulance. Your son is in a very critical condition."

Leaving Vernon in the safe and loving arms of his grandmother, Sheila and Mac raced off to the hospital with a nearly comatose Russell.

When they arrived, the medical team was already waiting for them in the reception area and they rushed Russell to the paediatric intensive care unit. There they attempted to insert a drip into his veins, but his little blood vessels had already collapsed. Eventually they succeeded but, as the fluids revived him, he put his thumb in his mouth and pulled out the drip. Our Russell was a compulsive thumb sucker and after several "disconnections" the staff had to tie his arm to the side of the cot, which distressed his mother even more. I suppose his left thumb just did not offer the same level of comfort but having had such difficulty finding a vein, the staff did not feel they could put him through any more distress trying to insert the drip into his other hand.

Sheila and Mac were so relieved that Mum was there to care for Vernon. Sheila expressed her milk so that Mum could feed him and this meant she and Mac were able to spend many hours at the hospital with Russell. There they learned that there was an epidemic of this gastro-enteritis virus. Most people recovered in 24 hours; only the very young and elderly frail were considered to be at risk.

Then, just when they thought the worst was behind them, a permanent resident of the hotel reported to Mac that she thought his mother-in-law had collapsed in a bathroom. Somehow Mac accessed the room to find Mum semi-conscious on the floor. Luckily she was just coming round and with Sheila and Mac's help, was able to get back into bed. The doctor was summoned, yet again, confirmed that she had the virus and recommended bed-rest and plenty of fluids. She quickly recovered and was back to her old self the next day.

Fortunately only Russell and Mum were affected by the bug, although Russell was in the ICU for a week and when he came home he had to learn to walk, talk and feed himself all over again. But there was no long-term damage and Sheila and Mac felt truly blessed that their son had been returned to them.

In the summer of 1974, it was Dad's turn to have his photo' and write-up in the local newspaper. The United Services Club had invited two big names from the snooker world to give an exhibition match and to play two of the Club's best snooker players. Dad was one of these. This was one of the rare occasions when we went to "Dad's club" *en famille* to offer our support.

It was a huge turnout, for the invited guests, Rex Williams and Eddie Charlton, were well known to everyone for their exploits on the popular television programme *"Pot Black"*. Dad was a pretty good amateur player but up against Eddie Charlton it was no contest and his fellow club-mate, Bill Burnett, fared no better against Rex Williams.

On 9th August 1974, problems again haunted the White House. The scandal is known as "Watergate" and began in June 1972 with the arrest of five men for breaking and entering the Democratic National Committee Headquarters. Investigations revealed that this burglary was only one of many illegal activities and abuses authorized and carried out by President Nixon's staff, including campaign fraud, political espionage and sabotage, improper tax audits and illegal 'phone tapping.

Many of the offences could be confirmed by tape recordings that had been secretly made in the offices of the President, and with his authorisation. After a court battle, the US Supreme Court unanimously ruled that Nixon must hand over these tapes. With impeachment in the House of Representatives and a conviction in the Senate looming, Richard Nixon resigned from office, the only US President ever to do so. His successor was Gerald Ford and subsequently he issued a controversial pardon for any federal crimes that Nixon may have committed while in office.

1974 was the year the Terracotta Army was discovered by farmers drilling a water-well in the outer suburbs of Xi'an, Shaanxi Province. It was near the mausoleum of the First Qin Emperor of China and is a form of funerary art that was buried with him in 210BC.

The whole site has still not been excavated and may contain much more than has so far been discovered but the figures that have been unearthed, have already been enough to be called the Eighth Wonder of the World and to be declared a UNESCO World Heritage Site.

The Terracotta Army is in three pits and consists of 8,000 soldiers, 130 chariots, 520 horses and 150 cavalry horses. Each of the figures has individual facial features, making them all look different. The detail on each figure is truly remarkable and includes warriors, officials, acrobats, strongmen and musicians. Originally each figure had a coloured lacquer finish and was equipped with actual weapons and armour but the weapons were stolen shortly after the creation of the Army and the colouring faded over the centuries. The remains of the craftsmen working in the tomb were also found; it is thought they were sealed alive in the tomb to prevent them passing on information about the project. It is said the Terracotta Army is one of perhaps only three historical artefacts that can draw a crowd simply on its reputation. (The others are the *Titanic* and *Tutankhamun*.)

Despite a brief experiment in "power-sharing" in Northern Ireland in 1974, the year was still one of the worst for Provisional IRA terrorist attacks on the mainland. On 4th February eight soldiers and four civilians were killed in a coach bombing on the M62 motorway. On 17th June they exploded a bomb at the Houses of Parliament, causing extensive damage and injuring eleven people. On 5th October they killed four off-duty soldiers and one civilian at a public house in Guildford. On 22nd October another bomb exploded in London, injuring three people and 21st November saw the so-called Birmingham pub' bombs where twenty-one people were killed and 182 injured.

On 8th January 1975 the worst fears of South Vietnam's President Thieu were realised when his country was invaded by twenty divisions of the Soviet-supplied North Vietnamese Army. Almost immediately President Ford confirmed that the US was unwilling to re-enter the war and thus the South Vietnamese Army virtually gave up before any fighting began.

By 9th April the NVA were only 38 miles from the capital of Saigon and then, for the first time, the SVA fought back. But it was too little, too late. Realising defeat was only a matter of days away, a bitter and tearful President Thieu resigned. He condemned the "Paris Peace Accords", the US peace negotiator, (Henry Kissinger) and the US in general saying, "*The United States has not respected its promises. It is inhumane. It is untrustworthy. It is irresponsible.*" He was then ushered away to exile in Taiwan, aided by the CIA.

100,000 North Vietnamese troops then advanced on Saigon, which was overflowing with refugees. On 29th April President Ford ordered *Operation Frequent Wind*, the helicopter evacuation of 7,000 Americans and South Vietnamese citizens stuck in Saigon. Frantic South Vietnamese civilians swarmed the helicopters at Tan Son Nhut air-base so the evacuation was switched to the walled-in embassy compound, secured by US Marines in full combat gear. But thousands of civilians then attempted to get into the compound. I do not think anyone who has seen the newsreel footage, or later movies of the incident, can fail to be moved by the desperation of the poor people who were left behind to face the wrath of the advancing NVA.

Three US aircraft carriers stood by off the coast of Vietnam to handle incoming American and Vietnamese refugees. Many South Vietnamese pilots also landed on the carriers, flying American-made helicopters, which were then pushed overboard to make room for more arrivals.

300

On 30th April 1975 at 8.35am, the last Americans, ten Marines who had been guarding the embassy, flew out of Saigon. The US presence in Vietnam was over. North Vietnamese troops poured into Saigon and by 11am the red and blue Viet Cong flag flew from the presidential palace. President Thieu's successor, General Duong Van Minh, broadcast a message of unconditional surrender. The war was over. The Philippines, Indonesia, Malaysia and Singapore managed to stay free of communism but in 1976 North and South Vietnam were united to become the Socialist Republic of Vietnam.

Meanwhile in neighbouring Cambodia, and just two weeks earlier on 12th April, a similar airlift had taken place at the US embassy in their capital of Phnom Penh. It was less dramatic than the airlift from Saigon but a fleet of thirty helicopters had taken 276 people to safety, including 159 Cambodians who had worked for the Americans.

Cambodia was now in the control of the communist despot, Saloth Sar, better known as Pol Pot. He was head of the Cambodian Communist Movement (the Khmer Rouge) and he had a vision of an agrarian utopia. Over the coming months and years, he forced thousands of people to leave the urban areas and become farmers. His reforms led to the death of an estimated 1.7million people. Some were executed but many (ironically) died of starvation and disease. His activities concerning the extermination of 20% of the Cambodian population inspired the award-winning movie "*The Killing Fields*".

(In 1979 Vietnam invaded Cambodia and Pol Pot's *Khmer Rouge* fled. The country collapsed into civil war which was not ended until the United Nations brokered a peace deal in 1991.)

(In 1997 Pol Pot was convicted of treason by a "people's tribunal" and sentenced to life under house arrest. By this time he was already suffering ill-health and he died, aged 73, on 15th April 1998.)

As we know from an earlier paragraph, Britain had joined the EEC in January 1973 but there was still a considerable amount of dissent to this decision. In his general election manifesto of October 1974, the Labour Party leader, Harold Wilson, had promised the electorate a referendum on the issue, in order that the people could decide for themselves whether Britain should stay in, or leave. Wilson won the election so, on 5th June 1975, we all went to the polls to answer the question *"Do you think the UK should stay in the European Community (Common Market)?"*

Our own families were split by this conundrum. Bryan's family (including me!) voted *"No"*. The Oakley's and the Carpenter's voted *"Yes"*. Mum and Dad made their decision in the hope it would prevent another European war. We voted *"No"* because we did not want to be dictated to by Europe. In the event just over 67% of voters supported the campaign to stay in. So committed to a "Common Market" the country might have to be, but the Government would not agree to Europe's 1978 proposal of a European Monetary System.

By the time June 1975 arrived, Mac had sold *Deanslake*. He had been running the guest-house/hotel for over twenty years and he felt he needed a change. Also it involved very long hours, seven days a week, and he wanted to spend more time with his new family. He was very much a hands-on father and there was nothing he would not do for their care.

Deanslake was on a large plot of land and, like his parents' house, it was quickly snapped up by a firm of developers who intended to build a block of flats on the site. Mac got a good price for it and re-invested some of the money in a large house in Hythe which he intended to turn into a smaller bed and breakfast establishment.

Moving was a nightmare for he had so many "investments" to transfer to their new abode, from collectibles to cars, cutlery to clocks, huge silver tureens to a giant *Scaletrix* train-set, and furniture, rugs, curtains, sheets, towels, photographs by the thousand, books by the hundred and so much more. Not only was he a "collector" but he was a sentimental squirrel to boot! Nevertheless, somehow they managed to squeeze the precious possessions into the new house, garden and garage and they began to look forward to their new business venture and to having more time together.

Of course Mum and Dad lived too far away to play an active part in their new house but from day-one Mum had become their primary baby-sitter. If Sheila and Mac were going to be out late for a business function, or Lord Montagu's ball at Beaulieu (I kid you not!), Mac would drive all the way to Littlehampton, either with babies in tow or to collect Mum so she could stay with them for a few days. If either of the children were unwell, Mac would be despatched to fetch the "oracle". There was no-one my sister would trust with her precious babies except Mum (or perhaps me!).

1975 was the year *Microsoft* was founded and it also saw the African-American Arthur Ashe win the singles title at Wimbledon. He was the first black person to win the title at the world's most famous and prestigious lawn tennis club.

The mid-seventies probably offered the peak of employment opportunity in most parts of the UK, for a new industry, and all its spin-offs, could be added to the UK job descriptions. Oil! The first commercial oil-field was found in the North Sea in 1969 but it was not until the giant *Forties Field* was discovered the following year, that the true potential was appreciated. Oil, and gas, from the North Sea was first piped ashore in 1975 and would eventually lead to a mammoth gas conversion programme for all domestic and industrial users. This was not the only change, for economies of the North-East of England and Scotland were transformed by the discovery and the direct and indirect effects, like the gas itself, permeated the whole country. The British economy had been suffering from a continuing balance of payments problem, exacerbated by rapidly rising oil import bills; now it would be an oil exporter and its economy should flourish .... or not, as only history will reveal!

CHAPTER THIRTY-FIVE

Home Is Where the Heart Is
(1976-1978)

1976 got off to a flying start when the supersonic jetliners called *Concorde,* built as a joint project between France and Britain, began their transatlantic service on 21st January. The first ever supersonic passenger 'planes, they flew regularly from London's Heathrow Airport, with the *British Airways* logo, and from Paris' Charles de Gaulle Airport, sporting *Air France* colours, to New York's JFK and to Washington Dulles. They took less than half the time of conventional jet aircraft and were therefore very popular with business people.

Only twenty *Concordes* were ever built, and then only thanks to a heavy subsidy from both governments. As a result of its one and only crash (on 25th July 2000), world economic problems (as a result of the "9/11" attacks in 2001) and other factors, the last flight of this magnificent 'plane took place on 26th November 2003 but it remains an icon of aviation history.

1976 was the year of the Montreal Olympics, where the Romanian Nadia Comaneci was given an unprecedented seven perfect tens for her gymnastic performances. Four were given for the uneven bars and three for the balance beam. Not surprisingly she won gold medals in these two disciplines and another for the individual all-round event. The Russian gymnast, Nelli Kim, also received two perfect scores, on the vault and on the floor exercise, in the all-round team event. These were the first perfect scores any person, male or female, had received in any Olympic gymnastic discipline.

1976 was also the year the *Commission for Racial Equality* was established in the UK as part of the "Race Discrimination Act". It was a statutory body charged with trying to stem the ever-increasing rise of racial discrimination. Britain's non-white residents now numbered 1.4million and numbers were still increasing, even though immigration was now greatly restricted. Despite the cutbacks, some 83,000 immigrants from Commonwealth countries had settled in the UK between 1968 and 1975; a considerable number of them Ugandan Asians of course.

This Act against racial discrimination was the last in a series of statutes against inequality in the 1970's. As we know from a previous chapter, the first was the "Equal Pay Act" of 1970. This was followed by the "Sex Discrimination Act" in 1975. The "Disabled" would have to wait until 1995 for discrimination against them to be made illegal and laws against discrimination regarding "Age" and "Gender Re-assignment" would not follow suit until the new millennium.

On 8th September 1976, the Chairman of the Communist Party of China, Mao Tse Tung, died at the age of 82 years. He is still regarded as one of the most influential figures in modern world history, despite several "misjudgements". Initially his victory over Chiang Kai-shek and the Kuomintang, in the civil war that ended in 1951, brought relative peace and prosperity to China and the Chinese peasant, but it was not to last. In the late 1950's, Mao introduced the *"Great Leap Forward"* that had every one of his 800-million population making steel, often literally in their backyards. The result was that virtually no food was grown and in 1961 there was a widespread famine, killing up to 35-million people. This weakened his power and influence within the Party and the country, and he feared his position was threatened by a growing professional and middle class. In 1965 Mao decided they had to be removed by a violent class struggle he called *"The Cultural Revolution"* and he chose the Chinese youth to carry out this "cleansing" on his behalf. They formed so-called *Red Guard* units throughout the country and they set about zealously persecuting, torturing or killing almost everyone who had any skill above that of the average peasant. Many managers and professionals who survived the initial attacks were sent to rural labour camps but it is still estimated that up to 80-million people died in these purges.

People were not the only target. Theatres, schools and universities were closed and the *Red Guards* set about destroying China's rich cultural heritage, considering it "elitist". Books and ancient manuscripts were burnt in their millions, antique porcelain, pottery, paintings and ornaments were smashed beyond repair, ancient buildings and temples were torn down. Even plants were uprooted and ornamental trees destroyed. Pets were banned, exotic birds exterminated and even grass was uprooted. The only thing that proliferated (apart from violence and loss of reason) was Mao's "little red book" which was printed in the hundreds of millions and contained thousands of his sayings ....many of which are quite meaningless.

It was not until the death of Mao, and the subsequent downfall of his infamous *"Gang of Four"*, that the unbridled madness of the *Cultural Revolution* could be brought to an end. In 1978 Deng Xiaoping assumed leadership of this vast country and then, at last, China could begin its journey to become the huge economic power that it is today.

The only piece of family news my sister and I can recall for 1976 is Mac's mother dying. Ethel May Carpenter, known as "Jane" for some reason, was 73 years of age and died suddenly of a heart attack. She had been suffering from (type II) diabetes for some years but nevertheless her death was unexpected.

305

In 1976 Dad was still working part-time at the school, still playing snooker and running the league, and still driving his car, although I drove them if they were going any distance. Mum was still going to her "clubs" and thoroughly enjoying being a "Nana". Both parents seemed full of energy and both were growing older very gracefully, while remaining staunchly independent and young at heart. They still enjoyed their holidays, the family picnics and visits to and from relatives and friends.

Kitty, the cat, was long gone by now and had not been replaced. "No more pets!" my mother had insisted! However, a neighbour's cat visited most afternoons while its owners were at work, so it was still not unusual to see a furry presence on Dad's armchair or sitting on Mum's lap. A strange turnaround for, in her final years, Kitty had taken to visiting an elderly house-bound lady who lived next door and spending the afternoons curled up beside her on her bed. It was a useful contact because the husband would feed Kitty while Mum and Dad were on holiday.

1977 was the year of Queen Elizabeth's Silver Jubilee. It was celebrated on 6th June, beginning with a procession to St Paul's Cathedral for a service of thanksgiving. The golden state coach was used and more than 1million people lined the streets of London to see their sovereign pass by. Millions more watched the spectacle on television.

Among the 2,700 specially selected guests for the service were (US) President Jimmy Carter, many other world leaders and all the living former Prime Ministers. Afterwards they all attended a lunch at the Guildhall, hosted by the Lord Mayor of London.

Later the Queen and her family appeared on the balcony of Buckingham Palace, facing a sea of people stretching all the way up *The Mall,* waving Union Jacks and singing *God Save the Queen* with gusto. That evening the Queen lit a bonfire-beacon at Windsor Castle and its light joined a chain of other beacons throughout the country.

Of course not everyone thought it was an occasion for celebration. This was the era of *Punk Rock,* with its spiky, multi-coloured hair, heavy eye-liner, body piercings, tattoos, torn clothes held together with safety-pins, and with chains and studded dog-collars completing the ensemble. Sid Vicious and his Sex Pistols was the best known band of this new musical movement and Vivienne Westwood designed some of the more outrageous outfits. The lyrics of the songs, the clothes and the accessories were all supposed to shock and spread the message of anarchy and anti-establishment.

The Sex Pistols, Vivienne Westwood and sympathisers decided to try and upstage the Jubilee celebrations by hiring a barge to sail up the River Thames with the band playing their controversial version of the

National Anthem. This was made into a single and although radio stations were banned from playing it, it still managed to reach number two in the charts, indicating there was more than a little discontent with the Royal Family within the population. However, despite their best endeavours, they received very little publicity for their stunt and the overwhelming majority of the populace joined in the spirit of the occasion by staging huge street parties and parades with many people taking the day off work.

(The Sex Pistols broke up in January 1978 and Sid Vicious went on to pursue a solo career. On 2nd February 1979 he died of a drug overdose in New York. Vivienne Westwood became an icon of the fashion industry, if a somewhat controversial one. In 1992 she received an OBE from the Queen and in June 2006 she was made a Dame. Apparently her anti-establishment, anarchic views did not extend to refusing to accept these very royal honours, even if she did wear a badge sporting an image of Che Guevara at one of the ceremonies. *Punk Rock* as a popular sub-culture has long gone but its legacy of multiple body piercing, tattoos and torn clothes (especially jeans) remain.)

The Jubilee celebrations received the "icing on the cake" early in July when Virginia Wade, one of the most successful British tennis players of all time, won the Wimbledon Ladies Singles Final. For the first time ever, the Queen was actually at Wimbledon to watch the match and presented Virginia Wade with her trophy.

At that time, Bryan and I always had our annual holiday during Wimbledon fortnight and we usually hired some kind of motor-home so that we could tour the country and stop where and when we pleased. We can remember the excitement of Wade's match against the American Betty Stove to this day, for we were parked on the shores of Loch Lomond in Scotland and listened to the match on the car radio.

Celebrations for the Jubilee were still not over for, soon after Wimbledon, the Queen and Prince Philip embarked on a three month trip to many of the Commonwealth countries.

12th September 1977 saw the death of Steve Biko, one of the founders and current president of the "Black Peoples Convention" in South Africa and a thorn in the side of the white-supremacist South African Government. He had been arrested some days before under their anti-terrorism legislation and had been taken for interrogation at the security police headquarters in Port Elizabeth. There he was tortured and, after slipping into a coma, transferred to a Pretoria Prison in the back of a land-rover, rolling around on the floor. A few hours after his arrival, he was found alone and naked, lying on the floor of a cell. He had died from brain damage, caused by a severe beating.

Initially the government suggested that he had died as a result of a hunger strike but a post-mortem revealed the truth. There was a worldwide outcry about the treatment of black, political prisoners in the oppressive apartheid regime for Steve Biko was the twentieth person to die in police custody in the previous eighteen months. Steve Biko became a martyr for the cause of freedom and a potent symbol of the black resistance movement. His contribution to the anti-apartheid movement is often placed as second only to that of Nelson Mandela. Many years later five policemen admitted being involved in his death but no-one was ever prosecuted.

In 1987 Steve Biko's life story was immortalised in Richard Attenborough's film *"Cry Freedom"*. It starred Denzil Washington as Steve Biko and Kevin Kline as Donald Woods, the white editor of the newspaper *Daily Despatch* who befriended Biko and had to flee South Africa. The film was nominated for three "Oscars".

1977 was the year Mum's brother, Les, died, at just 74 years of age. He had suffered a series of strokes that gradually took his mental and physical health. On his retirement he and Auntie Dorie had moved to Norfolk to be near their eldest daughter. It was too far to travel for the funeral but the following year I drove Mum and Dad up there for a short holiday with Dorie. Perhaps spurred by her brother dying, Mum wanted to visit her brother Bill and his wife, Violet, who were now living in Folkestone, having moved from the general store in Romney Marsh many years before, and we journeyed there several times in the following years.

By now I was working part-time. The Civil Service was innovative in introducing part-time work and job-sharing and I decided to take advantage of the new schemes, for the death of Bryan's father had made me realise that there was more to life than a stressful career and loads of possessions. This meant I had more time to spend with my parents and to be with Bryan's mother who was still struggling to come to terms with her husband's death. Also I had time to do some kind of voluntary work but I did not know what to choose. Then fate took a hand.

Mum lived near the *Littlehampton and District Commissioner for the Girl Guide Movement* and one day she told Mum that my old company was in danger of folding because they could not find a Guider to run it. Thus 1977 saw the second phase of my involvement with the Girl Guide Association (GGA) begin, this time as an adult, and it was to last for the next twelve years.

Mum and Dad supported me wholeheartedly in this new venture of Guiding, once again helping out with cake-baking and transport for our never-ending, ongoing, fund-raising activities.

As well as running the company, with help from a lovely lady, Beryl Hart, who was to become a very good and life-long friend, from 1978 we took the girls to camp every year. The Movement insists on a lot of training and various qualifications before you can do this, so I found myself going to First Aid classes and later life-saving lessons, as well as a lot of in-house training sessions run by the GGA. For our first camp, Beryl was to be our QM (Quarter-Master, head cook and bottle-washer, in other words!) and Sheila agreed to come as another adult helper, as we had to have at least three adults. She brought her two sons, then aged six and five years. The boys loved it and the girls loved having them. They attached themselves to one of the patrols and joined in all the chores, the games, the cooking and the camp-fires. I have such happy memories of watching them trudge off "wooding" in their little red Wellingtons, hand-in-hand with the girls.

But another not-so-happy memory is having to punish Russell for playing with the QM's fire! He would just not leave it alone and was always poking sticks into it, despite Beryl and Sheila constantly telling him off. Beryl had brought up three sons of her own and she suggested that we introduce a punishment she had used when her boys were small … a naughty corner! So I roped off a square in the corner of our camp-site, installed a picnic-chair and told Russell if he played with the fire again, he would have to spend time here.

Well, of course, he just could not resist the lure of the flames so I had to banish him to the punishment zone. It was only for five minutes but you would have thought he had been hurled into Dante's Inferno! He sat in the chair and sobbed and sobbed with humiliation. It was awful! The girls begged me to release him, which I did after he promised to leave the fire alone. And he did!

That night Beryl and I kept the next-door tent awake by talking into the wee small hours. I agreed that the girls could decide our punishment, and Beryl and I were banished to the naughty corner for an hour. What a treat! Sheila brought us a cup of tea and we were able to sit and do nothing for the duration! Russell, however, was overjoyed that we appeared to have shared the same punishment.

Sheila, Russell and Vernon came with us every year until, under GGA regulations, Russell was deemed to be too old (at the grand old age of ten years) to be with girls of his own age. Despite all the hard work, by then these "holidays" had worked their magic. Not only had they given me the chance for "quality time" with my nephews, they brought Sheila and me closer in a joint fun endeavour.

I was dreading telling Bryan's mother that I was off to Guide camp in the summer of 1978 and leaving her beloved son to fend for himself! In truth he was more than capable of doing this and was very supportive of my camping ventures, even to the extent of visiting us during the week. In the event I never did have to confess my heinous intent, for on 21st February 1978, she died. She had been suffering from cancer for several months and in the end her death was a happy release. My parents were much the same age as Bryan's (his had been born just a few months after Mum in the early months of 1906; Mum of course had been born in August 1905) and I felt so lucky that mine were still alive, whereas both of Bryan's parents were now gone.

Around the time we all set off on our first Guide camp, science, once again, scored another "first". On 25th July 1978 Louise Joy Brown was born in Oldham, England. For gynaecologist Dr Patrick Steptoe and physiologist Dr Robert Edwards, it was the successful culmination of years of research and experimentation, for Louise was the world's first, successful "test-tube" baby. Conceived in a test-tube outside her mother's womb, using her mother's egg and her father's sperm, her conception and safe delivery were heralded as a triumph for medicine and science. It also gave hope to thousands of couples unable to conceive a baby normally because of the woman's blocked fallopian tubes. Today "in vitro" fertilization is considered commonplace and utilized by infertile couples around the world, although, sadly, not always successfully.

On 16th October 1978, a new Pope was elected by the Roman Catholic Church. Born Karol Wojtyla, Pope John Paul II was the only Polish Pope ever appointed and the first non-Italian since a Dutch pontiff in the 1520's. He was the youngest Pope of the 20th century and destined to become the second longest pontificate, serving for almost 27 years. He is widely acclaimed as one of the most influential leaders of modern times and credited with being instrumental in bringing down communism in Eastern Europe. He was one of the most-travelled world leaders in history, effectively circling the globe twenty-seven times, and fluent in nine languages. He significantly improved the Church's relations with other religions, but was criticised by some people for his traditional views on such matters as divorce, contraception, abortion, the ordination of women and homosexuality. In 1981 an attempt was made on his life as he drove through crowds in St Peter's Square and he was seriously wounded. After a long recovery, he famously visited, and forgave, his would-be assassin, a Turkish fanatic. The last years of his life were dogged by ill-health and he died, aged 84, on 2nd April 2005.

Perhaps one of the oddest incidents of the century came on 18th November 1978. It is called the "Jonestown Massacre" but perhaps it should really be known as the "Jonestown Mass Suicides". An Indianapolis preacher, called James Warren Jones, set up a cult based on a combination of religious and socialist philosophies. Known officially as the "People's Temple", it relocated to California where it continued to grow until it became the subject of an IRS (Internal Revenue Service) investigation. Wishing to escape the scrutiny of "American capitalism" (and criticism) Jones urged his congregation to join him in a new isolated community, called Jonestown, in the middle of a South American jungle in Guyana. Relatives of the cult members became concerned about the living conditions there and believed their loved ones were being brainwashed by Jones.

In November 1978, a Californian congressman, Leo Ryan, arrived in Guyana to survey "Jonestown" and interview the cult members. When his life was threatened by a Temple member, he decided to return home but he and four members of his party were killed as they tried to board the 'plane. Jones told his followers that it was now impossible to carry on living together in the commune and said they should make the ultimate sacrifice, their lives. A deadly concoction of a purple drink containing cyanide, sedatives and tranquillizers was prepared and all 912 followers swallowed the deadly brew. Jones apparently shot himself in the head.

By the summer of 1978, I knew that Uncle Bert (the deaf man) was indeed my biological uncle. Sadly he had died some years before so I never got to greet him as a blood relative but now that I knew my parents had known my mother before I was born, I would occasionally ask Mum to tell me something about her. Thus one day around August 1978, as Mum and I were walking back to the car from a shopping trip in Worthing, I posed yet another innocuous question about Nellie, the colour of her hair or her height for example. I cannot remember what the query was now but I do remember Mum's reply.

"Oh, Maureen! I can't remember now! It was a long time ago!" Then she added, "Would you like to meet her and see for yourself?"

I was completely taken aback because this suggestion was totally unexpected. I thought for a few seconds then blurted out, "Wouldn't you mind?"

"Mind? Why should I mind?"

"Well she might come between us," I suggested. Mum laughed.

"Maureen!" she exclaimed. "Nothing and no-one will ever come between us!"

"Well then, if you are sure you don't mind.......Yes!.... I think I would. Do you know her address?"

"No. I know she still lives in Guildford but I don't know where. I can write to Auntie Margaret (*Uncle Ted's sister, the lady who had lived with my Uncle Bert after his wife died*) and see what she thinks. I believe she is still in touch with her. I think Nellie is married now, so be prepared that she may not want to meet you." Then Mum added, "If you do want to go ahead I need to tell you two things."

"Oh no! That sounds ominous! Good news or bad news?"

"Both not good, I'm afraid." I steeled myself for what was to come.

311

"First of all Nellie is deaf. Not as bad as Bert because she can speak but she is deaf."

"Oh! That means it's hereditary? Oh, Mum! You should've told me. What would you have done if I hadn't lost the baby?" (*I had been in a traffic accident some time before and miscarried.*)

"Worried enough for both of us!" my beloved mother replied and went on to explain what Dr Waddington had said about deafness only affecting every seventh generation.

(Incidentally this is the only thing about my upbringing that I would criticise; I believed then, and I believe now, that I did have the right to know about this handicap, at least before I was married. But what you could never fault about our mother, was that she never reached her decisions lightly and that in the end she always did what she thought was best for us.

"What's the second thing?"

"Nellie has breast cancer and I don't know how bad she is. If you do want to see her, we may need to ask fairly soon."

(I believe now that Mum may have engineered this conversation to give me the opportunity of meeting Nellie before it was too late. This possibility did not occur to me at the time but it would have been typical of her selflessness.)

Mum wrote to Auntie Margaret straight away asking if Nellie would agree to meet me. The reply came back within the week, but not from Margaret. It was from Nellie's sister-in-law, Connie. She confirmed Nellie was very ill but said she would love to see me. She also mentioned that Nellie was married now and had just celebrated her silver wedding anniversary. Her husband, another Bert, was totally deaf, without speech, but he knew all about me and also was looking forward to meeting Nellie's daughter.

We made arrangements to visit through Connie and, one day in September 1978, Mum, Dad and I, accompanied by Connie, made our way to Nellie and Bert's council flat in Guildford. Connie was a regular visitor, so when we arrived she pressed the flashing door-bell and we all walked straight in.

As an adopted child, you tend to fantasise that if you met your parent(s) by chance, some sort of telepathic message would flash in your brain and you would know instantly that you had a close biological connection. Not so! My first thought was that I could have passed this woman a million times in the street and not realised she was my mother. She was about my height and build and she wore glasses but other than that, I could discern no likeness to me. Before I had the chance to think anything else, she struggled to her feet with her arms outstretched and hugged me tight. Her first words to me were, "Forgive me. I had no choice. Forgive me."

312

"There's nothing to forgive," I assured her. "You gave me two wonderful parents. I could'nt have asked for more."

"Yes. I knew you'd be alright with Annie and Clem." Then turning to Mum and Dad, she hugged them and said, "Thank you, Annie. Thank you, Clem." Then she looked at me again. "My goodness!" she declared. "You're the dead spit of your father!"

By this time we were all in tears as we were introduced to her husband. Nellie turned to him explaining in sign language that I looked like my father. He shook his head and made a sign with one hand, cutting his face in half. The top part is you, he signed to Nellie.

From then on, Mum and I travelled up to Guildford several times to see Nellie and Bert and, every time we went, Nellie was progressively weaker. Dad did not come up with us again and nor did Bryan ever join us. He had made it clear from the outset that, as far as he was concerned, my parents lived in Littlehampton and he had no interest in meeting another mother, or father.

Communication was not that easy, for Nellie was profoundly deaf with impaired speech, and I did not have any formal sign language, but with gestures and writing things down, I discovered a little about my family background. Ellen Jane Dodson (known as "Nellie") had been born at the end of 1902 so she was 43 years old when she gave birth to me, her one and only child, in 1946. By this time, her mother had been dead for some years and Nellie lived with her sister and her father. She adored her father and said one of the reasons she was keen for me to be adopted was so that I would have a dad. Her sister seems to have ruled the roost for she was the one who would not allow Nellie to bring me home.

"No bastard is going to come into this house!" as she so succinctly put it! Nellie's father was old and frail but he desperately wanted to see the baby. He asked Nellie to bring me home just once for a visit but Nellie told him she could not do that; it would make it even harder to part with me. I was named Ruby Kathleen by her, in memory of two sisters who had died.

I also learned my father's name, Walter Capon, but she could not seem to remember many details about him, where he had lived in Canada, for example, nor did she have any photo's of him. Not surprisingly, she had torn them up in disgust!

She told me that she had written to the Colonel of his regiment when Walter left her literally "holding the baby", albeit an unborn one! The Colonel had interviewed him but he denied having any "intimate relations" with her and said she must have "gone" with someone else. I think of all the things he did to her, this remark caused her the most pain and anger because she was made to feel like a trollop. She assured me they had been together throughout the war and she had truly believed that they would get married. It was the Colonel who broke the news that Walter Capon had a wife and children in Canada and it was the Colonel who arranged for me to be born in the Military Hospital in Aldershot.

Nellie had married her Bert about seven years after I was born and he had wanted her to try and get me back but, of course, this was not possible. Once you sign away a baby, there is no way of reversing that decision.

It was comforting to know that Nellie had tried so hard to make sure I would be well-looked after and loved. And so, so sad to know how much she had suffered in having to part with me. I did not really have enough time to get to know her well but there was one facet of her character that was completely at odds with my upbringing. Nellie made some comment about making sure I "repaid" my parents for all they had done for me. If there was one thing that Mum had impressed on us from an early age, it was that we owed them nothing! She felt very strongly about this "pay-back" attitude some parents had to their offspring. She said children had not asked to be born (or adopted, I suppose, in our case!) and felt they should be free to do what they pleased and go wherever they wanted, without worrying about how their parents would cope without them. She stressed time and time again that if the time came when they needed care, we should have no compunction at all about putting them in a nursing home. She just asked that we always kept in touch and visited when we could. Anything we did for them had to be because we wanted to, and not because we had to out of some kind of misplaced duty. So had we some "debt" we had to repay? No, we did NOT!

One day in June 1979, I received a 'phone call from Connie to say Nellie had been admitted to a hospice. Mum and I went up to see her. She was very weak but conscious and she knew whom we were. Once again her first words to me were, "Forgive me. Forgive me," and then she thanked Mum again.

"No", Mum insisted. "It is I who should thank you. Thank you, Nellie, from the bottom of my heart, for the gift of your daughter. God bless you, Nellie."

Ellen Jane Cannon, neé Dodson, died later that night, 29th June 1979, nine months after I had been re-united with her, which struck me as sadly ironic.

The chapel at her cremation service was packed and Bert insisted I sit in the front pew with him. It was a beautiful service and the first time I had seen one that was conducted in sign language as well as sound. Connie thought it wise if I did not introduce myself to Nellie's sister, the one who had refused to allow her to bring me home. Apparently I was never allowed to be mentioned again in her company. Now she was the only surviving sibling out of eight children, four of whom had been born profoundly deaf. She did not appear to be curious just who this new face in the congregation belonged to, and no-one enlightened her.

One of Bert's brothers and his wife hosted "the wake" and it was obvious they all thought the world of him. He had been one of eleven children but, unlike Nellie's family, the only one to be born deaf. He was a lovely man and I was pleased Nellie had found happiness with him for the latter part of her life, for they were true soul-mates who seemed to be able to communicate without the need of the spoken word. Mum and I carried on visiting Bert until he died and he always introduced me as his daughter, which caused no offence to my parents but might have caused confusion to anyone who did not know my background!

Some time after Nellie died, I took myself off to St Catherine's House in London. This building is home to the central register of all births, deaths, marriages and wills in England and Wales. I felt very strongly that my bio-father was probably not born in Canada but born in England and then immigrated to that country in the 1920's. I had no proof of this; it certainly was not something that Nellie had suggested but it seemed logical. I wanted to see what I could discover, if anything, about the elusive Walter Capon.

The records are stored in huge, hand-written ledgers, every quarter of every year has its own ledger; births, marriages and deaths recorded separately. The only way to conduct a search is to be methodical. I knew my father was about 40 years of age in 1940, so I started my birth search in 1890 and finished in 1910. I found only one "Walter Capon" in this period, born in Camberwell, London, on 18th December 1899. On his birth certificate, strange to say, his father's occupation was listed as "Gardener".

Then I looked for a marriage for him and found that he had indeed married on 24th October 1921 to a "Florence Hall". At that time he was employed as a "Ship's Steward". Their first child, a boy called Ronald, was born about five months after the marriage, by which time Walter had changed jobs and was now a "Tea Merchants Dock Clerk". Then in 1924 a girl, Patricia, was born. Then nothing. I could find no more records for this Walter Capon or his family. Did they immigrate to Canada around 1926, as the General Strike and the Great Depression hit the UK? Was this even "my" Walter Capon? I think it is but I have never been able to prove it.

Then, some years later, Auntie Kathleen mentioned that she had met Wally (as he was known) several times during the war. (Kathleen was the lady who had married Uncle Ted after his first wife died.) Apparently, as a young teenager, she had been evacuated to Leapale Lane and she remembered him coming to visit several times with Nellie. (Nellie's brother, Bert, had lived at Leapale Lane. This was the address from which his wife, Evelyn, had written to my parents asking if they wanted to adopt me.) I had had no idea that Kathleen had any connection to the family at such a young age. She very kindly offered to search through her old photographs to see if Walter Capon had been included in a group picture, but alas there was nothing. The only thing she could remember about him was that nobody liked him very much! They all thought him very big-headed!

Some time after that I wrote to the authorities in Canada and asked if they could tell me anything about the Walter Capon who had served in the Canadian Army during the war but they replied that it was impossible to trace records of any particular soldier without knowing the regiment in which he had served.

The final effort (so far!) was to make use of the *ancestry.com* website that my sister was using as a research tool for this book. This too drew a blank for she was inundated with "Capon's" at that time and could not sort out the most likely culprit! I just hate to think, for Nellie's sake, that he was able to disappear without trace, maligning her reputation and breaking her heart. A true "chicken" from the beginning and it would give me great satisfaction to pop-out from the woodwork and say, "Here I am!" Of course he, and any of my half-siblings, are probably dead by now but my sister has not given up on searching through *ancestry.com* records and they have started to publish lists of passengers who sailed on emigrant ships in the 1920's, so who knows? I may yet trace his descendants at least.

CHAPTER THIRTY-SIX

A Turbulent End to a Troubled Decade
(1979)

When William Shakespeare penned the words *"Now is the winter of our discontent...."* (circa 1591), even the great bard himself surely could not have foreseen that nearly four centuries later the current Prime Minister would borrow this phrase from his *"Richard III"* masterpiece to describe the winter of 1978/79.

In truth James Callaghan could have applied the epithet to the whole of the decade, for rising prices, high interest rates and runaway inflation were fuelling huge demands for higher wages, reinforced by numerous strikes. The masses were "discontented" indeed and strikes, by the miners and dock-workers in particular, were causing huge headaches for successive governments in these years.

The current problems could be traced back to 1967 when the then Labour Prime Minister, Harold Wilson, was forced to devalue the pound. This was still not enough to "balance the books" and in 1976 the pound collapsed. By then, Harold Wilson was back in power and he was forced to ask the *International Monetary Fund* (IMF) for a £3.9billion loan. He promptly resigned and his deputy, James Callaghan, became Prime Minister in his stead.

Part of the conditions for lending the money was that the Government should cut public spending and peg wage rises but this not sit well with the unions. However they agreed to co-operate with a wage freeze and by 1978 inflation had been halved.

The unions then expected pay limits to end but when they did not, strikes began in earnest, culminating in a "Day of Action" on 22nd January 1979 which marked the greatest stoppage of labour in the UK since the General Strike of 1926. By this date, tanker-drivers had forced petrol stations to close, striking grave diggers had left bodies unburied, and rubbish had accumulated in the streets as dustmen withdrew their labour. Car-workers, railwaymen, ambulance drivers and even nurses (traditionally loathe to take industrial action) were also among those who had joined in at some stage. By the end of February, after weeks of negotiation, most of the strikes had ended with a total of 29,474,000 working days having been lost.

The minority Labour Government was already only able to operate by entering into an agreement with the Liberals and the Scottish Nationalist Party. When the SNP withdrew their support and called for a vote of "No Confidence", the Government lost the vote and was forced to call a general election, to be held in May.

No sooner had the general election been announced than the Provisional IRA and the Irish National Liberation Army (INLA) decided to show their contempt for the democratic process. On 30th March they attached a bomb to the underside of the car belonging to the Shadow Northern Ireland Secretary, Airey Neave, while it was parked in the House of Commons car-park. It exploded as Mr Neave drove up the exit-ramp and he died in Westminster Hospital from his injuries. The 63 year old Conservative MP was well-known for his tough line on anti-IRA security and was a close adviser to the Conservative Leader, Margaret Thatcher. The INLA claimed he had been targeted because he was engaged in *"rabid militaristic calls for more repression against the Irish people".*

Apart from the "sympathy vote" that Airey Neave's death may have evoked for the opposition party, the economic catastrophes seen in recent years and the industrial chaos that the "Winter of Discontent" had so recently witnessed, James Callaghan's election campaign had at least two more disadvantages to overcome. One was the fact he wanted to go ahead with more devolution to Europe by adopting their metric weights and measures systems, despite widespread disenchantment with this proposal from the electorate. Secondly he was up against a prolonged assault on his party's record in Government, and their manifesto, from the tabloid newspaper *The Sun,* which supported Margaret Thatcher and her Conservative Party.

The unions and the working masses were traditional supporters of the Labour Party and their preferred daily newspaper had been the Labour-supporting *Daily Mirror.* However the circulation numbers of the *Daily Mirror* had been seriously eroded by *The Sun* since 1969 when the latter started to feature a full-page picture of a bare-breasted beauty on page three every day. This was enough to titillate the testosterone of many a working man and encourage him to change his "reading" preference! Thus he, and the other *"Sun"* subscribers, were also fed a subtle diet of Tory propaganda, as opposed to their normal fare of pro-socialist editorials. (To be fair *The Sun* had a very popular crossword as well, one of the first tabloids to run this feature.)

The Sun was responsible also for one of the major disinformation features of the campaign. On returning from an economic conference in the West Indies, James Callaghan had been asked how he was going to deal with the problem of ongoing strikes. He replied, "*I don't think people in the world share the view (that) there is mounting chaos."* *The Sun* reported the interview with the headline *"Crisis? What Crisis?"* implying that this was the Prime Minister's response to all the disruption.

It was all enough to contribute to his downfall and, on 3rd May 1979, Britain's first female Prime Minister swept to power. Margaret Thatcher had fought the election on a manifesto pledge of controlling inflation and reducing the increasing power of the Trade Unions, who had supported the mass strikes that she felt had brought the country to its knees. Her Government's free-market policies would come to include deregulation and trade liberalisation and sweeping privatisation of nationalised industries. As well as breaking the power of the unions, they would focus on the individual and the creation of an enterprise culture. Her critics would argue that her "reign" (and that of her great friend and ally, the soon-to-be-elected US President, Ronald Reagan) would pave the way for greed and self-interest to become the "norm" but for good or ill, *Thatcherism* would prove to have a profound, and lasting, economic and social impact on Britain.

The Soviet Union would come to refer to her derisively as the "Iron Lady" but she bore the "insult" with pride and would tolerate no weakness in herself or her colleagues. She would go on to win another two elections, becoming the first PM ever to serve three consecutive terms and, despite many controversial decisions, is now generally considered to be one of the best peace-time prime ministers of the 20th century.

The public sector and large firms were not the only casualties of a chaotic economy for many small businesses also found themselves caught up in the downward spiral. One of these was Mac's latest enterprise.

Mac's decision to open a "Bed & Breakfast" (B&B) establishment had not been successful and on top of that he had been hit by a massive tax-bill. He had been led to believe that by buying a similar business, some of the capital gains profit from selling the hotel, could be offset against the cost of buying the B&B. The taxman thought differently and demanded the full 40% of the money he had received from the sale of *"Deanslake"*.

So, by the time 1979 arrived, Mac had sold the B&B to help pay the taxes and had moved his family to a bungalow in a nearby village. From thinking that they could live comfortably without cash concerns, now Mac believed he needed to start another business to generate an income. He made the fateful decision to invest in two village toy and model shops, just as the economy took a nose-dive.

Meanwhile, within the first months of Margaret Thatcher's election victory, the IRA struck again. This time the target was the Queen's cousin, Lord Louis Mountbatten. On 27th August 1979 he was enjoying his traditional summer holiday at County Sligo in Ireland with his family and was about to embark on a day's fishing. The fishing party had just set off in his boat from the village of Mullaghmore when a bomb was detonated, blowing the boat to smithereens and hurling all seven occupants into the water. Earl Mountbatten, one of his twin grandsons (aged 14) and a local boat-boy (aged 15) were all killed. The Dowager Lady Braborne (aged 82) died the next day although the other passengers survived. A local man, Thomas McMahon, was later convicted of the murders but released from prison in 1998 under the "Good Friday Agreement".

While the country was still in shock from this latest atrocity, a surprise of a different kind was just around the corner and this concerned another of the Queen's cousins, albeit a very distant one this time. On 16th November, in a speech to the House of Commons, Margaret Thatcher named Sir Antony Blunt as the "Fourth Man" in the Cambridge University spy-ring, which had first come to light in the 1951 defections of spies Guy Burgess and Donald McLean and the 1963 defection of Kim Philby.

She went on to confirm that the Establishment had been aware that Blunt was a spy for the Soviet Union as early as 1964 but he had been given secret immunity from prosecution in exchange for a full and frank confession, although one has to wonder if his connection to Queen Elizabeth the Queen Mother (they were third cousins) had anything to do with the cover-up! Be that as it may, he was allowed to remain as art adviser to the Queen, the Establishment maintaining that the security services did not want to lose his co-operation by forcing him to resign.

In the light of the public disclosure of his betrayal, Buckingham Palace announced that he would be stripped of his knighthood, which ironically he had been awarded in 1956 for his work in MI5. He said he had come to "bitterly regret" his spying activities but at the time he had done so out of idealism. He died in disgrace three years later with rumours persisting that there was still an undiscovered "Fifth Man" involved in the spy-ring. (Indeed there probably was. In 1990 a KGB defector named him as John Cairncross who died on 8th October 1995.)

(An autobiographical memoir, written by Blunt and held in the British Library, is due to be released in 2013, thirty years after his death.)

In March, while the UK was embroiled in its "Winter of Discontent", an election campaign, IRA atrocities and tales of espionage, America had endured an amazing co-incidence that could have had catastrophic consequences. Earlier that month a movie called "The China Syndrome" had been released. It featured the actress Jane Fonda as a news presenter at a Californian TV station and the actor Michael Douglas as her cameraman. In the story-line of the film, they were supposedly at a nuclear power plant where she was trying to raise public awareness of how unsafe it was. A subsequent, fictional near-accident in the film stems from a plant operator overestimating the amount of water in the core.

By a very weird co-incidence, just twelve days after the film's release, fiction became fact, on 28th March 1979, when there was a partial meltdown at the Unit 2 of a nuclear power plant at Three Mile Island in Dauphin County, Pennsylvania. The cause was later found to be an operator's focus on a single misleading indicator measuring the level of water in the pressurizer. A few simple water level gauges in the reactor vessel might have prevented the potentially fatal oversight..

It was the most significant accident in the history of the American commercial nuclear power generating industry but despite the release of radioactive krypton and iodine:131, no deaths or injuries to plant workers or members of the nearby community were said to be attributed to the near-disaster. Unit 2 was de-commissioned and the accident marked the end of further investment in the US nuclear power industry, though not necessarily solely because of this event, nor due to the adverse reaction from "The China Syndrome". Cheap natural gas was now available and Federal policies on air pollution were becoming more tolerant of coal-fired stations. There are still approximately 450 nuclear power reactors in the US; the licence to run Unit 1 at Three Mile Island expires in 2014, with a possibility that it will be extended to 2034.

1979 also witnessed Mother Teresa of Calcutta receiving the Nobel Peace Prize for her humanitarian work among the sick and dying on Calcutta's streets. She was an Albanian Roman Catholic nun who founded the "Missionaries of Kolkata (Calcutta)", in India, in 1950. She ministered to the poor, sick, orphaned and dying for 45 years and, by the time of her death in 1997, her "Missionaries of Charity" operated 610 missions in 123 countries, including soup kitchens, orphanages, schools, hospices and homes for people with HIV/AIDS, leprosy and tuberculosis. In 1980 she would receive India's highest civilian honour, the *Bharat Ratna* and following her death, on 5th September 1997, she was beautified by Pope John Paul II and given the title "Blessed Teresa of Calcutta". She had her critics but she still remains one of the most remarkable women of the 20th century.

While history was being made elsewhere, 1979 would see Iran, and their arch-enemy Iraq, undergoing changes that would reverberate through the coming decades. In 1953, the CIA had helped to topple Iran's democratically elected government and place the autocratic Shah Mohammad Reza Pahlavi in its stead. By 1979, the Shah was deeply unpopular and in January his government collapsed, thanks to the Shiite Muslim leader, the Ayatollah Ruholla Khomeini, who had orchestrated the revolution from his exile in France. Now it was the Shah's turn to flee with his family into exile, while the Ayatollah returned to Iran in triumph. In February he won a landslide victory in a referendum to find a new leader and declared Iran the world's first Islamic republic. He became its political and religious leader for life, presiding over a brutal and repressive regime until his death in 1989.

The Iranian people were already highly suspicious of America and its allies and relations with America deteriorated even further when the exiled Shah was allowed entry to the US for treatment for cancer. The Ayatollah's rabid denunciation of American interference and influence came to a head in November when militant Islamic students stormed the US embassy in Tehran and took over 60 hostages.

Thirteen female and black hostages were released after two weeks but fifty-two US diplomats and embassy staff were still detained for, despite pleas and threats from Washington, the militants adamantly refused to release them.

Meanwhile, in neighbouring Iraq, on 16th July 1979, Saddam Hussein became President of that country. He had been vice-president, under the ailing General Ahmed Hassan al-Bakr, since a coup brought their revolutionary Ba'ath Party to power in 1968. After spearheading Iraq's nationalization of the Western-owned Iraq Petroleum Company, he went on to cement his authority with repressive security forces to control the ongoing conflict between the government, the armed forces and his opponents.

We were thus destined to enter the 1980's with both Iran and Iraq very much to the fore and the embassy siege still unresolved. What a turbulent and conflicting decade the 70's had proved to be! Perhaps not surprisingly, these years had given birth to films of pure escapism such as "Star Wars", released in 1977, and "Star Trek: The Motion Picture", premiered in December 1979 and based on the highly successful "Star Trek" television series. Captain Kirk, Mr Spock and the Starship Enterprise spawned a new cult phenomenon.

A more terrestrial kind of fantasy was provided by John Travolta's highly popular 1977 film "Saturday Night Fever", followed by the musical "Grease", which made its debut in 1978, starring the man himself and Olivia Newton-John. The song "Summer Nights" from this movie was a massive hit in the UK, spending seven weeks at number one, although it only peaked at number five on the "Billboard Hot 100" in the USA.

The fashions of the decade were equally diverse. Easy-wash, polyester fabrics became popular and we had flared trousers and bell-bottoms, hipsters and hotpants, crop-tops and skinny-ribs, skirts gathered into tiers and shirt-waister dresses, baseball jerseys and T-shirts with messages, platform shoes and "bovver" boots. Men started to wear 3-piece suits again with multi-coloured, wide ties and large knots, and footballers began to become celebrity fashion icons, like Kevin Keegan, for example, who began the trend of having his hair permed in a so-called bubble-cut. And the actress Farrah Fawcett, a sex-symbol from the television series "Charlie's Angels", was hugely responsible for promoting one-piece bathing costumes with high-cut legs. The decade was like a giant pendulum swinging from chaos to calm, flared to narrow,

322

long to short, fact to fantasy, rags to riches, good to evil.........and everything in between.

CHAPTER THIRTY-SEVEN

Golden Threads
(1980)

1980 began with the US hostage situation in Iran still at stale-mate. In an attempt to force Tehran to release the fifty-two Americans, US President Jimmy Carter ordered sanctions to be imposed and the freezing of all Iranian assets held abroad. The Iranian Government still refused to give in, so, in April 1980, President Carter ordered a dramatic rescue mission. But the effort had to be aborted after a sandstorm damaged some of the helicopters and a troop carrier that were to be used in the evacuation. Eight American servicemen lost their lives and the hostages were no nearer to being released. This failure did not bode well for Jimmy Carter, for it put him at a distinct disadvantage in the ongoing presidential campaign.

But not everything was going the Iranians' way. On 30th April, six armed Iranians stormed their own embassy in London and took twenty-six hostages. Most were embassy staff but they also included a number of tourists, two BBC employees who had called in to pick up visas, and a police-constable who was with the diplomatic protection squad and happened to be there on duty at the time.

The six gunmen called themselves the *Democratic Revolutionary Front for Arabistan*, their name for the oil-rich province of Khuzestan. They were protesting against oppression by the Ayatollah Khomeini and, amongst other things, were demanding the release of 91 political prisoners held in jails in Iran. They threatened to execute all the hostages and blow up the embassy if their demands were not met.

Over the next five days, six of the hostages were released but by the sixth day the terrorists became convinced that their demands would not be met and executed one of the hostages, an Iranian press attaché who was said to be a keen supporter of Khomeini.

His death meant the siege would have to be brought to an end by force. The elite *Special Air Service (SAS)* had been on stand-by right from the beginning of the siege and, less than twenty minutes after the body of the press attaché was thrown onto the pavement, they stormed the embassy. Television news stations from around the world had been monitoring the event, so the SAS mission was conducted in the full glare of publicity as TV cameras relayed live pictures of the rescue, and all of it during peak time on a Bank Holiday Monday.

One of the SAS team had his life saved by the imprisoned police-constable. As the soldier appeared at one of the windows, one of the militants took aim but before he could fire his weapon, he was rugby-tackled by PC Lock, giving time for the soldier to kill the gunman. PC Lock later received the George Cross Medal for his action.

The nineteen hostages were released unharmed but, controversially, five of the six gunmen were killed. The survivor was later jailed for life for his part in the siege but was paroled in 2008. He was not deported back to Iran but, with Government support, went into hiding in the UK.

The SAS normally prefer to operate in secret, but the very public demonstration of the courage and ability of the team had shown to the world that they were one of the best special forces of any country around the globe.

While the UK was glued to its television sets watching the Iranian siege unfold, Washington State, USA, was undergoing its own "siege" by a natural adversary, for Mount St Helens was about to erupt. The first signs of volcanic activity were a series of small earthquakes that began on 16th March. By 17th May more than 10,000 earthquakes had been recorded and the shape of the mountain had visibly changed.

On 18th May 1980, at 0832 local time, Mount St Helens exploded. It triggered an earthquake measuring 5.2 on the Richter scale. Avalanches of hot ash, pumice and gas poured out of the crater at 50-80 mph and spread as far as five miles to the north and fifteen miles into the atmosphere, turning day into night. Over the course of the day, prevailing winds blew 520 million tons of ash eastward across the US and caused complete darkness in Spokane, Washington, 250 miles from the volcano. The blast cloud travelled seventeen miles north and the landslide travelled fourteen miles west down the North Fork Toutle River.

2000 people were evacuated but despite having time to leave the area, 57 people died. In addition it is estimated that 7000 big game animals (deer, elk and bear) perished, as did all birds and most small mammals. Of the 32 species of the latter thought to be living near the volcano, only 14 are known to have survived. About 12million salmon fingerlings in hatcheries perished.

150 square miles of forest, containing 4 billion board-feet of timber (enough to build 300,000 two-bedroomed homes) was destroyed, as were 27 bridges and 200 homes. The depth of the channel in the Columbia River was reduced from 40-feet to 14-feet, leaving 31 ships stranded upstream. Spirit Lake, at the foot of the mountain, was wiped out by the massive force of the explosion and the mountain itself was 1314-feet lower after the eruption. It had the power of 500 atomic bombs and was the largest of its kind in recorded US history.

Seismic activity has continued ever since but scientists believe the chances of an imminent eruption as huge as that of 1980 are low.

Meanwhile the Embassy hostages in Iran had still not been released but 1980 was the year our parents would celebrate 50 years of marriage so while "sieges" of various kinds were hitting the headlines, Sheila and I planned a "siege" of our own ...... a surprise Golden Wedding Anniversary Party which could take place on the actual day because the 27th September 1980 fell on a Saturday. We decided to try and invite every person, relative or friend, who had played a role in their lives, young or old, rich or poor, significant or not, recent friend or lifelong pal. To this end I surreptitiously borrowed Mum's address-book and ended up sending out 75 specially-printed invitations. Everyone was sworn to secrecy and I told them their presence, not presents, were important but if they did want to mark the occasion with a gift, perhaps they would like to contribute to a "Golden Holiday" in Jersey? This was one place Mum and Dad had never visited but one Mum had always wanted to see.

Sheila still lived in the Southampton area so it was easier for me to organise the venue and the caterers while Sheila arranged the entertainment and booked the holiday.

The ideal place to hold the party would probably have been Dad's United Services Club but I could not be sure this would remain a secret, so I eventually settled on our old school premises in East Street as the best venue. At this time, it was no longer a school but used mainly as a meeting place for young people and called the "The Flintstone Centre". Mum, Sheila and I had all spent part of our school years there so it had memories for all of us and even though it was not the most upmarket location, it had the advantage of being easy to find, with loads of parking in the old school play-ground. There was a large main hall with several smaller (ex class) rooms also available with equipment like pool and table tennis tables that could keep the younger guests occupied.

The weather on the day was beautiful. Sheila drove up from Southampton in the morning to meet Bryan and me at the Centre where we prepared the main hall with decorations, laid out the tables and chairs and the stage for the band, checked the toilets and generally got everything ready. Beryl, the very dear (Guiding) friend of mine had volunteered to do all the floral arrangements and "Guiding" connections had also provided the caterers, the photographer, child minders and baby sitters! Mac closed his shop early and arrived in the afternoon with the boys to organise the bar.

While Bryan and I went home to get ready for the evening festivities, the "Carpenters" would remain at the Centre, change into their party gear and be ready to greet the guests as they arrived. Some of them had made long journeys and had wanted to arrive early so they could have more time to chat with relatives and friends, many of whom they had not seen for years. In all 150 people had said they would be there, including all the helpers, nine teenagers, fourteen children, six toddlers, five babies and one dog!

Mum's brother, Bill, his wife Violet and eldest daughter, Barbara,

326

travelled all the way from Folkestone. Their youngest daughter Andrea and her family were travelling from their home in Surrey. Sadly Mum's brother, Les, had died but his widow, our Auntie Dorie, was making the journey from her home in Norfolk, courtesy of her daughter, Peggy, and her family who were picking her up as they journeyed from Nottingham. The widow of Dad's old Army pal (Bill Roberts, my godfather) was making the trip from Aylesbury in Buckinghamshire, thanks to her two sons and their wives who were all sharing one car. Several friends, (including Mary Hope, widow of Bob Hope whom Mum and Dad had met on holiday) were travelling by train from London. Many had car journeys from Surrey, including all the Guildford clan and the daughter of Dad's first Dorset House employer, Rosemary (née Sims) and her husband.

Of course, there were also many guests who lived locally, including the Oakley clan. Sadly Dad's brother, Jack, had died recently after a very brave fight against lung cancer but Uncle Jack's widow, our Auntie Daisy, and all their children (and their children) had decided to attend. Dad's sister Elsie had also died by this time and another sister, Nellie, was too ill to come but sister Blanche was there.

We had tried to invite as many of their friends as possible and of course Carrie and Edith (née Starte), Mum's friends from when she first started in service, headed our guest-list. This meant all of Mum's bridesmaids would be in attendance: Carrie, Edith, Blanche and Vi. Neighbours, who had also become friends over the years, were going to join us, as were the vicar and his wife and Dad's new employer from Rosemead School. I had truly tried to include everyone I could think of and to this day it amazes me that the party remained a secret. We had even gone to the "Family Picnic" as usual and no-one had breathed a word.

I had led Mum and Dad to believe that we were meeting Sheila, Mac and the boys at a restaurant for a celebratory meal, so Bryan and I arranged to pick them up in all their finery at about 7pm. While en route to this non-existent restaurant, I told Mum I needed to pop into the Flintstone Centre to check it out for a Guiding venue and wondered if they would like to see what the old school now looked like? Thus it was that we lured them into the hall, completely unsuspecting as to what awaited them.

This, of course, was before mobile 'phones were readily available, so Sheila plunged the hall into darkness at 7pm and everyone just had to wait until we arrived. No-one uttered a sound. Then as Mum and Dad came through the door to the main hall, someone switched on the lights, the band struck up the tune of "The Anniversary Waltz" and all the guests started to cheer, clap their hands and stomp their feet. Luckily our photographer-for-the-night caught the look of absolute amazement on Mum's face as she stepped over the threshold. They truly had no idea that this had been planned.

It was a wonderful, wonderful night and Mum said it was one of the best memories of her life. The food was superb and the "Oakley" and "Martin" clans, with sundry friends, danced the evening away to live music provided by the "Blue Diamonds" dance band. Mac acted as the Master of Ceremonies and there was a help-yourself bar of wine, beer, soft drinks, tea and coffee. About half-way through the evening Mac gave a little speech and presented Mum and Dad with their "Golden Holiday" in Jersey, plus some spending money, on behalf of all their friends and relatives. Then they cut the three-tier "wedding" cake I had made, once again inexpertly iced, but this time I had decorated it with artificial flowers which helped to cover the worst of the flaws!

By this time they were both very close to tears but for Mum the night was also special for a very personal reason. Soon after her marriage, her two new sisters-in-law, Myrtle (married to Tom) and Ethel (married to Dick) had fallen out. Mum could not remember what the upset had been about but Auntie Myrtle could be a little forthright and rather tactless, although there was absolutely no malice in her opinions. Auntie Ethel, on the other hand, tended to be hypersensitive and rather unforgiving, so I suppose they were bound to clash sooner or later. Anyway whatever the problem had been, Ethel resolved never to speak to Myrtle again, and had not done so for nearly fifty years.

When I sent out the invitations I did not know whether both would attend, each guessing that the other might also be there. But attend they did and during the evening Mum glanced across and saw them sitting together and talking ..... for the first time in nearly five decades. Mum's heart soared with happiness for she hated dissent and disagreement, especially in families, let alone her own! She told me I had brought about a miracle, which was perhaps a bit of an overstatement, but she insisted it was the best present anyone could have given her.

We had secretly arranged for Uncle Bill, Auntie Vi, their daughter Barbara and Auntie Dorie to sleep at our parents' house that night. At some stage in the evening Peggy and her husband slipped away from the party in order to pitch a tent in the back garden. (I think Peggy must also have offered to make up the beds while she was there!) Sheila and Mac and the boys were also staying overnight in Littlehampton, in their VW caravannette which they parked in a nearby cul de sac. Ten other guests were booked into local hotels.

On Sunday morning, everyone who was still in Littlehampton descended on Mum and Dad's bungalow and the party continued. Sheila and Mac set up a running canteen in Mum's kitchen providing them all with a breakfast of bacon, eggs and fried bread. Dad made endless pots of tea and I arrived in time to organise a picnic lunch. Auntie Vi wrote to me afterwards to say she almost enjoyed Sunday in the garden more than the Saturday party! It was truly a weekend to remember.

For Mum and Dad the celebrations were not over for they still had their holiday in Jersey to take. The following Thursday, Bryan and I drove them to Southampton Airport and there we met Sheila, Mac and the boys in order to give the "golden couple" a good send-off. Sheila had been in touch with the *Montfort Hall Hotel* and told them this was a "Golden Anniversary" holiday for a very special couple and asked them to lay on some unexpected treats. The hotel did us proud. They arranged for fruit, flowers and champagne to be in their room when they arrived and that night, at dinner, the chef carried in a special cake, compliments of the hotel, which was shared amongst the guests. Mum said that for the whole of their four day stay, they were treated like royalty.

At the end of the holiday Mac collected them from Southampton Airport and drove them home. To her dying day Mum never forgot the pleasure these celebrations of their Golden Anniversary had brought ...... which made it worth every penny and every second of effort.

For me the effort was still not quite over. I had kept all the acceptance cards, the letters people had written to me, a blank printed invitation, one of the serviettes I had had printed with their names, a brochure of the hotel, and stuck everything I had into a scrap-book. I presented this to them some weeks after the event, along with a photograph album, so that they would have a permanent reminder of their "Golden Day". Little did I realise that these would be an invaluable aid in writing this some thirty years later!

Although we were far too pre-occupied with our party plans to find time to play games, there were two which came onto the international market in 1980 that were destined to become very popular. One was the 3-D mechanical puzzle, the *Rubik Cube,* actually invented in 1974 by the Hungarian Ernö Rubik. It is widely considered to be the world's best selling toy, some 350million now having been sold worldwide.

The other game was *Pac-Man.* It is among the most famous of arcade games of all time and became a land-mark in video-game history. It is the most easily recognised videogame character in the world and appears in more than thirty officially-licensed game spin-offs as well as numerous unauthorised clones and bootlegs.

"Beatles" fans would say one of the dates they will never forget is 8th December 1980, for this was the day John Lennon was assassinated. He was shot by a deranged fan, Mark David Chapman, at the entrance to the building where he lived in New York. Five bullets were fired; one missed but all four of the remaining bullets inflicted severe wounds and he was dead within minutes.

Since the break-up of the band, John Lennon had pursued a successful solo career. Many would claim Lennon was the most talented of the famous four and he was also well-known for his political activism and his attempts, with his wife Yoko Ono, to spread "love and peace" wherever he went.

Chapman pleaded guilty to second degree murder and was sentenced to twenty years to life. He has been denied parole five times and remains in prison.

Jimmy Carter lost the US presidential race of 1980 and the year came to a close with the US Embassy hostages still held in Tehran. However, on 22nd September 1980, Saddam had invaded Iran, following a long history of border disputes. Perhaps not surprisingly, as Iran was hardly their favourite country at that time, the US Navy backed Saddam and Iraq, despite Saddam's treatment of the majority Shia population and the residents of Kurdistan.

With a war to fight on its Iran/Iraq border, and with the Shah having died in July anyway, the Iranian captors were finally forced to give up the hostages but not until the new US President, Ronald Reagan, had agreed to unfreeze Iranian assets. In a final snub to the outgoing-President Jimmy Carter, the prisoners were not released until minutes after the new President's swearing-in ceremony. So on 20th January 1981, after 444 days in captivity, the US hostages were finally on their way home, and were greeted at an American Air Force Base in Germany by .... Jimmy Carter!

However, several British hostages were still held in Iran and the first of them was not released until a month later following the intervention of the Archbishop of Canterbury's special envoy, Terry Waite. This would be the first time Waite made headline news, but it would not be the last.

(The war between Iran and Iraq would drag on for eight years, until 20th August 1988, without any significant gains being made on either side, although at the end of the conflict both countries claimed victory. But it came at a great cost in lives and economic damage, with half a million people killed and many more injured and wounded. The last prisoners of war were not exchanged until 2003. Sadly this would not be the last we would hear of Iran, or Iraq, nor of Saddam Hussein.)

330

CHAPTER THIRTY-EIGHT

In Pursuit of Dreams
(1981)

On 1st January 1981, Greece had become the tenth member of the European Economic Community (EEC). On 2nd January one of Britain's most prolific serial killers was apprehended.

Peter William Sutcliffe was dubbed *The Yorkshire Ripper* for murdering thirteen women and attacking several others, most of whom were prostitutes. The murders took place in a five year period, from 30th October 1975 to 17th November 1980, but because he has only ever confessed to nine of them, there are suspicions in some circles that there might have been two *Yorkshire Rippers*. On the other hand, another school of thought maintains that he killed more than the thirteen with which he was charged. Be that as it may, later in 1981, he was convicted of the murders, jailed for life and sent to Broadmoor Hospital for the Criminally Insane.

On 30th March 1981, an attempt was made on the life of the new US President Ronald Reagan by John Hinckley. He succeeded only in wounding his target and injuring three others. Thus it was that Ronald Reagan became the only serving US President (so far) to survive being shot in an assassination attempt. Hinckley was found not guilty by reason of insanity and ordered to be detained indefinitely in a secure psychiatric facility.

14th April 1981 saw the "most significant outbreak of civil disorder in 20th century London" with riots breaking out in Brixton. Tensions in the area were already at boiling point between the police and the black, Afro-Caribbean population, who made up approximately 25% of the residents at that time. The main reason was because the police were operating the highly unpopular and controversial "*sus*" law, where a person could be stopped solely on suspicion that they might be intending to commit a crime. The police were exempt from the "Race Relations Act" and it seemed to many in the Brixton area that the "*sus*" laws were targeted only at black youths.

When the police tried to arrest a man, violence erupted. Within hours the streets had become a battle zone; buildings were set on fire and petrol bombs were thrown, then looting began. By the time hostilities had subsided, over 360 people had been injured and 82 arrested: 28 premises had burned to the ground, 117 buildings damaged and looted and 100 vehicles (including 56 police vehicles) vandalised.

Following the riots, a police enquiry was held under Lord Scarman. His subsequent report was heavily critical of the Metropolitan Police and prompted the creation of the "Police Complaints Authority" and a new outlook on police recruitment and training.

Despite this, many said his report did not address the root causes of the disturbances, such as the decline and decay of inner-city areas, the institutionalised racism, the feelings of rejection and alienation felt by the residents, and the crucial issue of accountability. Perhaps not surprisingly therefore, serious violence broke out again on Brixton's streets in 1985, 1991 and 1995.

Of course disturbances did not (and do not!) happen only in Brixton. Many parts of East London erupted into violence in 1981, as it did in parts of Bradford and Toxteth, in Liverpool. Not all of these could strictly be called "race riots", however, with the implication that it was one ethnic group against another. Many of the riots were of one group against the police as symbols of authority, albeit the police were mainly white. And not all the participants were of Afro-Caribbean descent. Incidents of violence in East London from as early as 1969, for example, were between white skinheads and Asians, the main protagonists being the skinheads, egged on by racist/fascist groups such as The National Front, amongst others.

On 5th June 1981, the US "Center for Disease Control and Prevention" (CDC) published an article in their *"Morbidity and Mortality Weekly Report"* about five previously healthy men in Los Angeles who were exhibiting symptoms of something that looked like pneumonia and which was usually only seen in patients with severely weakened immune systems. The men were later recognized as the first reported cases of *Acquired Immune Deficiency Syndrome,* AIDS. By the end of 1982 CDC officials concluded the cause was a new infection spread by sexual contact.

In 1981 the diagnosis was a death sentence and more then half a million people would die from it over the next two decades. However, thanks to high-profile support from many Hollywood film stars, and a subsequent, massive injection of money for research, a drug "cocktail" is now available for patients afflicted with the virus and AIDS is no longer synonymous with terminal illness.

On 12th August 1981, the computer industry took a giant leap forward when IBM released their new computer, renamed from *"Acorn"* to the *"IBM PC".* PC stood for "personal computer" and thus IBM were responsible for introducing a new "word" into the language and popularising the term PC. Less than four months after IBM introduced the PC, *Time Magazine* named the computer "Man of the Year"!

But the most newsworthy event of 1981 had taken place two weeks before this PC launch. It was the marriage of Prince Charles, aged 32 and heir to the throne of the UK (and what remains of its Empire!) to Lady Diana Spencer, aged 20 and daughter of Earl Spencer, one of the oldest aristocratic families in Britain. They were married at St Paul's Cathedral, on 29th July, before an invited congregation of 3,500 and an estimated global television audience of 750million, making it the most popular programme ever broadcast. Another 600,000 people lined the streets of London in the hope of catching a glimpse of the newlyweds.

The public had been fed the image of a fairytale romance for months and when Diana walked up the aisle in her *Emmanuel*-designed gown of ivory taffeta and antique lace, with a 25-foot train trailing behind her, it seemed dreams really do come true.

Less than a year after the marriage, their first son, William, was born, followed by Harry just over two years later. But by this time Prince Charles had re-established a relationship with an old flame, Camilla Parker-Bowles and more than a decade later, Diana, Princess of Wales, would publicly remark that there had always been "three people in her marriage" and the nation would grieve along with her, as her marriage, and her dreams, disintegrated.

Sheila was very proud of the fact she shared her 1st July birthday with the Princess of Wales and, while Diana was pursuing her dreams, Sheila decided to chase hers by endeavouring to find her biological mother. She had known her mother's maiden name, Phyllis Ridgers, for many years, for Mum had presented her with all her adoption papers on her 21st birthday in 1969. These had included her original birth certificate, with her birth-name of Mary Ridgers, but finding her natural mother was going to be a lot more difficult than it had been for me. Whereas my adoption had been a private one, with a birth-mother known personally to the family, she had been "official", through the local Social Services department, and our parents had only ever met her birth-mother once, very briefly at the court hearing. The only thing Mum said that she could remember about Phyllis was that she had been a nurse.

Knowing so little, Sheila decided to consult a solicitor and see what he could discover on her behalf. He suggested engaging a private detective but it all ended up costing her a lot of money, which she could ill afford, and got her nowhere. So she resolved to contact Social Services and see if they could provide any more information.

When the Adoption Act of 1976 gave permission for adopted children to try and trace natural parents, one of the stipulations was that the "child" should go through official channels, not only to obtain information that may not be on available documents, but to make sure they were of "sane mind" and aware of all the pitfalls before they began the search. Fortunately, when Sheila attended her Social Services interview, they found her mentally competent to pursue her investigations but, unfortunately, there was nothing new that they could tell her, other than to wish her success in her quest.

Sheila felt she had reached another dead-end so she asked me to accompany her to the main registry of births, marriages, and deaths at St Catherine's House in London to see what we could discover for ourselves by delving through official archives. We decided to go up by train from Littlehampton and as we were clattering along in the carriage, Sheila turned to me and remarked, "You've never seen my official birth certificate, have you?" and she thrust it into my hands. I took one look at it and pronounced, "Oh heaven help us! There's more than one of you!"

"What do you mean?" she demanded indignantly.

"Your birth certificate has a time on it. Only multiple births in England and Wales have the time recorded. You're probably a twin!"

"No, I'm not!" she gasped incredulously.

"Oh yes, you are!" I replied pompously, in my best big-sister voice. "At least you were," I added as an afterthought.

"How on earth do you know about times on birth certificates?" she asked.

"Bryan's mum's a twin and she told me," I answered.

To say she was astounded is an understatement. She did not really believe me until we arrived at St Catherine's House and checked the records. She was indeed a twin. Another girl, who had been given the name Sheila Ann Ridgers, had been born minutes before her. So their biological mother had named her first-born twin SHEILA! What an amazing co-incidence, and then Ann as well! It just made the whole thing seem more surreal.

We decided to 'phone Mum from a pay-phone in the lobby, thinking that she would not believe what we had discovered. Wrong! Her first words were, "Oh! So you've found out then!" She went on to say she had known from the beginning that Sheila was a twin but had thought it was kinder all round to say nothing. She was able to confirm that the twin also had been adopted and told us how sad she had felt at the time to learn that the babies had been separated. She had even offered to take them both but the other baby had already gone to its new home, so this was not possible. She knew nothing more about the twin, her adoptive parents, nor what her new name might be.

We felt like a couple of deflated balloons; we could not believe our beloved Mum had kept secrets from both of us: genetic deafness for me, now having a twin for Sheila. Once again I think Mum was wrong not to tell her, but once again she had done so with the noblest of motives, so Sheila, like me, was not upset with Mum for long.

We went back to the archives to see what else we could discover. It was impossible to ascertain anything else about her twin, so we turned our attention to her mother and discovered that she had married three years after the twins' birth. So now we had a married name, the name of the church where her wedding had taken place and the area where she had been living. We decided we had had enough excitement for one day and returned home.

Sheila resolved to return to Social Services and ask them if they could tell her anything about her newly-discovered twin. This time she had an interview with the Director and at first he refused to acknowledge that there had been another baby. Sheila pushed their birth certificates across the desk and he was astonished.

"I can't believe it!" he frowned. "You were my first adoption so I remember it very well. I should have been told there were two babies," he added angrily. "I will track down the midwife and investigate this!"

It later transpired that the first baby was a private adoption and had been passed to an acquaintance of an acquaintance, as arranged. The second baby had come as a complete surprise but was also offered to the couple. They felt they could not manage two babies, so baby "Mary" was handed over to Social Services for official adoption. In any case, in those days, it was common practice to separate twins destined for adoption, even when both were handed over to the same official body.

Although this was very interesting, it did not help Sheila in her searches for her twin and for her mother. Sheila thought if she found her mother, perhaps this would lead to her twin, even though she had not kept her.

With this in mind, Sheila had the brilliant idea of writing to the vicar of the church where her mother had married and amazingly he 'phoned her as soon as he received her letter. Even more amazing, he confirmed that he remembered marrying her mother and knew where she was now living. He asked if Sheila would like him to act as an intermediary and visit her mother on her behalf. Of course, Sheila gratefully accepted his offer and later that day he 'phoned back to say Phyllis had agreed to meet her.

So, in July 1981, Sheila found herself nervously driving to Surrey. Mac had offered to go with her but this was something she had wanted to do on her own. As Sheila pulled up at the address, she saw a lady peering anxiously out of the front window. Her mother was looking out for her and, as Sheila parked her car outside the house, Phyllis walked down the path to greet her. No hugs, no kisses, just a big smile with the words, "I knew you'd find me eventually!" as she invited her in for a cup of tea.

Sheila told her a little about her life and family and Phyllis said she was now a widow but she had another daughter living nearby called Susan and a stepson from her husband's first marriage who now lived in Ireland. In a short while, Phyllis took Sheila to meet Sue, her husband, Derek, and their two children, a boy and a girl. It was a lovely surprise to discover she had an unexpected half-sister, and a nephew and a niece about the same age as her two sons, but it was not the same as meeting her twin. To Sheila's consternation, Phyllis could not remember by whom her twin had been adopted, nor could she remember much about Sheila's biological father. But the meeting had gone well and Sheila would form a bond with Phyllis and Sue and her family over the coming months and years. And it was great that, at long last, Russell and Vernon had cousins of their own age, and vice versa, for Derek had been brought up as an only child and Sue did not see much of her step-brother's offspring.

But Sheila was still no nearer to finding her twin, so in desperation she decided to write to all the tabloid newspapers and ask if they could help in her search. "The Sun" responded immediately, and in their edition of Tuesday 4th August 1981, the headline "*FIND MY TWIN*" appeared in huge capital letters followed by an article about her. It was accompanied by a picture of her, forlornly holding their birth certificates and a photo' of herself aged about one year (with me torn off the other side!)

Almost as soon as the 'papers plopped through the country's letter-boxes, "The Sun" started to get a response. In all they received thirteen 'phone calls, all claiming to know the elusive twin and all relating to different people. One of the contacts was an anonymous call claiming the twin was a friend who lived in Borden in Hampshire, only 50 miles from where Sheila lived. "The Sun" thought this the most likely candidate and asked Sheila if she was willing to accompany them to the address they had been given, without being able to say for certain that this was the person she had been seeking. Sheila agreed to go with the reporter and, when they arrived at the address, Sheila just knew instinctively that she had found her twin. Alas there was no-one at home so she and the reporter de-camped to a local café for some refreshment, intending to go back in an hour or so.

By the time they returned to the house a car was parked outside, so they assumed the home-owner was now there. The reporter knocked at the door, explained the purpose of his visit and disappeared inside, leaving Sheila sitting very nervously in the car. A short while later he came out and declared, "Your instincts were right. This is your twin and she's shown me her original birth certificate. Fortunately you are not too much of a shock as she has known she had a twin from childhood and had tried to find you herself some years ago. Are you ready to meet her?"

They walked up the garden path and the reporter pushed open the front-door. Her twin was walking down the hall towards her and they both stopped, fixed to the spot, just looking at each other. The reporter broke the silence. "Aren't you going to hug or something?" he asked. In unison they replied, "We're not like that!"

Her name was still Sheila. By a remarkable co-incidence not only the birth-mother but both sets of adoptive parents had chosen the same

Christian name for their new baby. And the same name was not the only co-incidence. Both had married men a lot older than themselves, both had polio' at a young age, both loved ball-room dancing and reading, both were rather impetuous and strong-willed. At one stage in their lives they both did similar office work in garages only one mile apart and both had been involved in youth work. They were both smokers, claustrophobic and terrified of mice and snakes. They had both been "difficult" children, both had suffered emotional problems in their early twenties and both had been adopted by a loving family. They also looked and sounded very alike, although at this stage we did not know officially if they were identical twins.

Sheila Robinson was brought up as an only child but both Sheilas had children, although Sheila Robinson had three (two boys and a girl) to our Sheila's two boys. Suddenly her sons had yet more cousins and all the cousins, including Sue's children, looked very alike.

It was a successful result for "The Sun" newspaper and the very next day, on Wednesday 5th August, on their front page no less, they carried the headline, "WE FIND THE LONG LOST TWIN" with the sub-heading, "It's joy at last for the two Sheilas" and a picture of the two hugging each other!

The "Family Picnic" was only days away so Sheila invited Sheila R to come with her husband and family to meet us. She had already invited Phyllis and Sue and her family, so it would also be an opportunity (albeit a rather public one!) for Sheila R to meet her biological mother and family for the first time as well.

Rather surprisingly (to me!) she agreed. Our Sheila says she can remember Phyllis arriving first at the picnic with Sue and her family. Before she even had time to introduce anybody, the children scampered off with their newly acquired cousins to climb trees and Sue and Derek were soon talking very animatedly to her and Mac. Phyllis seemed a little "out of it" but before Sheila could say anything to include her in the conversation, Mum approached, introduced herself and invited Phyllis to sit with her. In less than five minutes they were chatting away like old friends while Dad made everyone a cup of tea on the primus-stove. Thus began a friendship that would last until Mum died. Sheila said she was so proud of our parents in that moment, and realised how special they were and what huge and loving hearts they had.

When Sheila R and her family arrived, her adoptive parents were with them and we were immediately struck with how similar they were to our Mum and Dad, in looks, build and background. Indeed it came out in conversation that her father had also been in the Army. Once again Mum did her open-arms-greeting routine and once again Dad re-lit the primus-stove.

Phyllis, Sue, Derek and family were destined to come to the "Family

Picnic" for several more years but Sheila R and her family would move to the north of England and would not come again. The physical distance then between the two Sheilas meant that they could never really become emotionally close but the bond that developed with Sue and our Sheila (and me) has lasted to this day.

A couple of weeks after this get-together, Sheila and I went off to guide camp, accompanied by Russell and Vernon as usual. At some stage every day, Sheila would make a quick trip to a public telephone-box to contact Mac and after one such occasion she returned very excited. Mac had received a 'phone call from someone called John Stroud. He was the Assistant Director of Social Services at Hertfordshire County Council and in his spare time he specialised in finding pairs of twins separated at birth and re-uniting them in middle age. Indeed since 1960, by painstaking detective work, he had re-united twenty-six pairs of twins. Obviously his efforts in this regard were too late for Sheila but Mac said he had another proposition for her and would she contact him as soon as possible to discuss it. What he suggested was beyond her wildest dreams.

Apparently John Stroud was in touch with a Professor Thomas Bouchard of the University of Minnesota in Minneapolis. Professor Bouchard and his team were conducting research into the old conundrum of "Nature versus Nurture" and were using separated twins to aid them in their study. Separated identical twins were especially useful because they had the same genetic make-up and therefore medical, psychological, physiological and intelligence tests might help to ascertain if, and how, they differed from each other by having a different upbringing. In other words, are we are, what we are, solely from our inherited genes? Or does nurture play a part? If so, to what extent? These were the sort of questions Professor Bouchard was trying to answer but put very simply and in layman's terms! Mr Stroud wanted to know if Sheila and her twin would be prepared to take part in the study and, if so, on behalf of Professor Bouchard and his team, he was offering them, and their husbands, an all-expenses-paid trip to Minneapolis.

Sheila Robinson took a bit of persuading because she was anxious about leaving her children but when the University agreed to pay for them to accompany her, she finally acquiesced. Our Sheila needed no such inducement and jumped at it. Mum agreed to go down to Southampton to look after the boys while Sheila and Mac were away for the week. (They were at school during the day so at least she would be able to have some respite from them!) So in October 1981 Sheila and Mac, and Sheila and her husband and children, flew off to the "Twin Cities", so called not because of its twin associations but because it is really two cities in one; Minneapolis on one side of the river and St Paul's on the other.

There all the adults were subjected to a total of 15,000 questions, in a battery of tests, interviews and endless filling-in of psychological questionnaires with inane, unanswerable questions like "Do you prefer black dogs or brown dogs?" It is the sort of question that you really want to answer, "Well, it depends...."! But the idea is that you become brain-numbed and just respond instinctively, without really thinking about the answer. Even the husbands underwent some of the tests, including the questionnaires, as part of a control group. The children spent their days on the campus, in the swimming-pool or in the gym', under the watchful eye of a volunteer student. At the end of the week the team concluded that the two Sheilas were not identical but were the closest fraternal twins they had ever come across.

They were the 168th set of multiple births (including triplets and even two sets of quads) who had taken part in the Bouchard investigation and it elevated them to unexpected levels of publicity. Soon the Sheilas, sometimes along with other twins or triplets, were the subject of many a magazine article and were featured in the "Mail on Sunday", "The Times" and the "Sunday Times Magazine". While they were in Minneapolis, they even took part in a short feature for the famous *Phil Donahue TV Show*. My Sheila was the more outgoing twin and on their return she appeared on several UK television programmes and was invited by several women's organisations to raise money for the NSPCC (National Society for the Prevention of Cruelty to Children) by giving talks on her adoption and twin experiences. Fame at last!

Fame too for Dad in 1981, although not on such a grand scale. On 8th October he was 80 years old. He was still working part-time at the school and driving his car but he decided the time had come to hand over the paper-work of running the *Littlehampton and District Billiards and Snooker League* to a younger pen. In celebration of his birthday, and in recognition of the decades of service he had given to the League (and thus to all the snooker clubs in the area), they presented him with a gold watch. His own Club, the United Services, also wished to mark the occasion and register their own appreciation. He and Mum were invited to a special ceremony where they presented him with a gift of a tankard and a certificate of honorary life membership. Mum was delighted to be given a huge bouquet, perhaps in recognition of all the hours her husband had spent away from home, wielding his billiard-cue.

Fame again for Dad just one month later. Phoebe Somers was a well-known local author, broadcaster and artist, particularly interested in the dying crafts of rural Sussex, especially those that had used working horses. As well as giving a regular series of talks on local radio on *"West Sussex Men and their Horses"*, she wrote a weekly article in the *West Sussex Gazette* on the lives of people who remembered the old ways. I do not know how Dad came to be chosen but she interviewed him one day in October at home, and then drew a pencil sketch of him, both of which were featured in the 12th November edition of the newspaper. The headline was *"Carter boy start to a long working life."*

The year came to an end with me taking my very first trip to Mallorca with Bryan's sister. Iris was very familiar with the island and the tales of the holidays she had taken there had made me very much want to see it. We had a great time and the holiday is memorable for many reasons: the beautiful Caves of Arta that just took my breath away: a horse-ride where the stirrup broke on Iris' old nag and it took off at a gallop with her clinging to the mane for dear life: me getting tipsy on sangria. But the one memory neither of us will forget is the 'plane trip. The pilot made a bad landing in Palma and burst a tyre. We slewed out of control across the tarmac, racing at a great rate of knots towards the terminal building, with the pilot fighting for control. The shuddering of the aircraft was unbelievable. The overhead lockers burst open, spewing their contents of coats, bags, bottles and books all over the passengers sitting below, the toilet doors were wrenched off their hinges and the side panels of the seats fell on the floor. But the passengers uttered not a sound until we finally came to a halt, only yards from the terminal building, then everybody cheered!

We were told to remain in our seats and await instructions. This was 1981 and Palma Airport was not the sophisticate it is today but their fire-service appliance was sent out to meet us......A man on a moped with a bucket of sand swinging from his handlebars! It did not put me off Mallorca or flying and I still love both. Iris and I had survived to enjoy many more holidays together and I knew Mum would fall in love with the island too. I determined that it would not be long before she too would enjoy a Mallorquin experience, preferably without a bumpy landing!

CHAPTER THIRTY-NINE

Memories
(1982-1983)

1982 would see the birth of *"Star Wars"*, the nickname given to US President Ronald Reagan's *"Strategic Defense Initiative"*, intended to shield the whole country against "incoming intercontinental ballistic missiles." Always controversial, many claimed it would be unworkable and indeed a less complex and less extensive system, called *"Son of Star Wars"*, evolved in the Bush administration in 1999.

This new *"Iniative"* is not designed to defend the US from a massive attack but it would be effective against powers with a limited missile programme. Britain played (and plays) a key role in the operation of both systems as early-warning radar equipment is based at RAF Fylingdale (also known as RAF Flyingdale!) in Yorkshire. However questions remain as to whether the missiles would be used to defend Britain and Europe, or just the US.

Defence was very much in everyone's thoughts in 1982 for that was the year Argentina invaded the inhospitable and windswept Falkland Islands, some seventy miles south-east of Cape Horn, situated at the very southern tip of the Americas. Sovereignty over the Islands had been disputed ever since Britain seized them from Argentina in 1833 but the inhabitants were of British stock and proud to be so.

Argentina had been ruled by a military *junta* since 1976 and the country had sunk into economic and social chaos, notorious for its human rights violations. The government, headed by General Leopoldo Galtieri, sought to divert public attention from the problems at home by seizing the Falklands from British control and thus, on 2nd April 1982, 3000 Argentine troops landed at Port Stanley. Their commander, Admiral Jorge Anaya, appealed to the Falklands Governor, Rex Hunt, to surrender but he refused and 80 members of the Royal Marine Regiment, stationed on the Island, plus 20 local civilians were mobilised to fight off the invaders. But they were heavily outnumbered by the Argentine forces and Governor Hunt was forced to surrender.

Galtieri did not expect Britain to respond with any more force as their only naval presence in the area, *HMS Endurance*, had been withdrawn a year earlier. In this he grossly underestimated Prime Minister Margaret Thatcher's resolve. Although initially taken by surprise at the attack, she immediately cut diplomatic ties with Argentina and started to assemble a large naval taskforce to reclaim the Islands. Commercial passenger liners were commandeered and brought into service as troop-carriers and hospital-ships, while destroyers and aircraft-carriers sped to the scene.

The conflict would last 74 days, until 14th June, and cost the lives of 255 British soldiers, sailors and airmen and three civilian Falklanders. 649 Argentineans also died.   There were 777 non-fatal British injured and 1188 injured on the other side.   Some of the wounded would die later, mostly from burns received when ships received a direct hit.

It was a resounding victory for Margaret Thatcher and is said to have helped to secure her re-election the following year.   There was one political casualty; the Foreign Secretary, Lord Carrington, resigned in response to his department's failure to anticipate the war. He was to be the last UK government minister to resign for a failure in his department. Sadly these days a lack of integrity and responsibility are all too common in (British) politics.

The hostilities (strictly speaking it should not be called a "war" as "war" was not declared by either country) marked the end of the Galtieri regime and he spent three years in prison for "military incompetence", although it was to be July 2002 before he was arrested on charges relating to the abduction, torture and death of thousands of opponents to his military regime. He died in January 2003 before coming to trial.

In October 1983 Argentina returned to civilian rule but it was 1990 before full diplomatic relations were restored with Britain. Argentina has still not lost the hope that the Falkland Islands will one day return to Argentine sovereignty but now says that the use of force can never again be contemplated to achieve this aim.

1982 and Mac's finances were getting worse. One toy-shop had closed and the remaining one was struggling to pay its way. Sheila's offer to return to work was gratefully accepted as a way of paying the household bills, so in May she began secretarial work for a local engineering firm. Fortunately, Mac had always been a hands-on parent so he was more than capable of looking after their sons when they came out of school, as well as keeping an eye on the shop. The arrangement worked well and, in truth, I think Sheila was glad to escape the problems at home for a few hours each day.

Over the next few years, as the struggling shop gobbled up their savings, they would downsize to a terraced house and, as the business went from bad to worse, eventually they would be reduced to living in a makeshift apartment above the shop. Sheila's secretarial earnings were still not enough to pay the bills and any possessions of value had to be sold just to keep their heads above water. Throughout it all, despite their early differences and arguments, Sheila supported Mac 100% and went up in my estimation a thousand-fold. At last, Sheila was considered an equal partner in the marriage and a strange conversion gradually took place; Sheila became a "nicer" person. She grew in self-confidence and was no longer so argumentative or riddled with jealousy. Far from adversely affecting their marriage, as their finances deteriorated, their relationship improved. And this decline in their family fortunes would also prove to be one of the major turning points in our relationship.

1st July 1982 would be the future wedding anniversary for at least 2075 couples, for they were all "blessed in marriage" on this day by the Reverend Sun Myung Moon, in a giant ceremony at Madison Square Gardens in New York City.

The Reverend Moon is a self-proclaimed "sinless messiah" from Korea who personally matched the couples, many of whom had never even met before the ceremony. Once upon a time, his Unification Church was derided by the American media as a sinister cult but by clever marketing, skilful use of funds, paying big-name celebrities and politicians to give talks to his organisation and his stress on family values, fidelity and sexual abstinence before marriage, his church is still flourishing. Indeed, he claims he and his wife have "blessed" 360million couples in marriage worldwide.

But a "Moonie" marriage does not come cheap. It is said couples in Japan pay $29,000 for the privilege of a group blessing while the same ceremony in America comes at a "bargain" $2,000. Perhaps not surprisingly, therefore, he has offered his "blessing" to people of other faiths, even if they do not support his views on family values, and to couples already married.

After an eight month lull, on 20th July 1982, the IRA was at it again by exploding two bombs within hours of each other. The first was a nail-bomb, left in a parked car in Hyde Park, and it was detonated by remote control, just as members of the Household Cavalry rode by. Three soldiers were killed instantly and six died later from their injuries. The survivors were all badly injured and shrapnel and nails, sprayed into the tourists standing nearby, caused many additional casualties. Seven horses were killed, or so badly injured that they had to be destroyed.

The second bomb was hidden weeks in advance under the bandstand in Regents Park and detonated by a timing device, set to go off as the band from the Royal Greenjackets Regiment was entertaining a crowd of 120 to music from "Oliver". Here, too, the audience was hit by shrapnel causing dozens of injuries. Seven bandsmen were killed outright and all the rest were badly injured.

In 1987 Danny McNamee was sentenced to 25 years imprisonment for the Hyde Park bomb but always protested his innocence. He was released in 1998 under the "Good Friday Agreement". His conviction was overturned the following year, however, because fingerprint evidence implicating others was withheld from his original trial. No other arrests were made.

11th October 1982 and the skeletal remains of the *"Mary Rose"*, flagship of King Henry VIII's navy, rose from the depths of the Solent after 437 years. In her heyday, the *"Mary Rose"* had been the pride of the British fleet and one of the earliest purpose-built warships. She began her fighting life in 1510, able to fire a full broadside of cannons and eventually upgraded to carry 91 guns. She had a complement of 200 sailors, 185 soldiers and 30 gunners. When she sank, with the loss of all hands, off Portsmouth Sound in 1545, the enemy French fleet assumed it was thanks to their cannons, but naval historians now believe that it was simply bad handling.

She was only 50-feet beneath the waves but the task of raising so fragile a wreck was beset with technical problems. In the end she was brought up in a specially-crafted, air-cushioned cradle and, as the first timbers broke the surface, a cannon was fired from the ramparts of Southsea Castle in her honour.

She is a unique relic, bridging the gap between the medieval "floating castles" and Elizabeth I's navy galleons. 10,000 well-preserved items had already been excavated including weapons, clothes and even a backgammon set. These artefacts, and the ship itself, are now part of the naval museum at Portsmouth Historic Dockyard, alongside such worthies as Admiral Nelson's flagship, *HMS Victory,* and the world's first iron-hulled, armoured warship powered by steam as well as sail, *HMS Warrior 1860.*

I cannot close 1982 without mentioning *Cabbage Patch Kids,* for mass-production of these highly popular dolls, with large, round, plastic or vinyl heads and cloth bodies, began in this year. Originally created by Debbie Morehead and Xavier Roberts in 1978, they were then all cloth and sold at craft shows. Now they are still in the list of "best selling toys" and sold around the world.

1983 and it became compulsory in the UK for car-drivers and front-seat passengers to wear seat-belts. The Government had been trying to persuade us to do this voluntarily for years and the extrovert DJ, Jimmy Savile, was chosen to "front" the huge publicity campaign. His slogan *"Clunk-Click Every Trip"* remains with many of us to this day. Jimmy Savile is famous for his support of various charities and fund-raising events, especially Stoke Mandeville Hospital and the London Marathon. He has received many awards for this work and was knighted in 1990. He is probably the most well-known, and the most-loved, of all British eccentrics.

February 1983 and, at last, I was going to show Mum Mallorca. Sheila had decided to come with us, so it was going to be a "girls" only holiday, leaving Dad, Bryan, Mac, Russell and Vernon to cope without us for a week. We hired a car and were delighted to discover that February is the month when the almond trees come into flower and the island was covered in pink and white blossom.

One of the first "must-see" places on our tourist itinerary was the *"Caves of Arta"*. Having heard me wax lyrical about the attraction, Mum was determined to see them for herself and struggled up the long, stone stairway, leading to a dark hole halfway up a sheer rock-face. An elderly Spanish guide came out to greet us and fussed over Mum while she recovered her strength. The caves were in darkness, guarded by a steel door. The guide opened the door and threw a switch, suddenly illuminating the whole of the interior. Nothing I had said had prepared Mum for the sheer majesty of the sight that met her eyes. The first impression was of a huge natural cathedral, with coloured lights playing on the rock formations inside.

The guide took charge of Mum, insisting she hold onto his arm for the whole of our tour, much to her consternation, while Sheila and I trailed along in their wake. The four of us travelled down into the eerie lower chambers, into the *"Room of a Thousand Columns"* and on past the *"Queen of Stalagmites"* rising to an incredible 70-feet. Then on over stone bridges, up and down stairways and through tunnels to *"The Theatre"*, *"The Lamp Room"*, *"The Flag Chamber"* and then into *"The Inferno"* where we stood on a platform and gazed into a pit where coloured lights played over strangely-shaped rock formations, while the music of the Danish composer, Rued Lauggaard's *"Dante's Inferno"*, assailed our ears. Then on through *"Purgatory"* into *"Paradise"*, where an "organ" and "angel's wings" could clearly be seen. Finally the shadowy form of a stone "ghost" bade us farewell. The caves had surpassed Mum's expectations and she said it was well worth the struggle up the many steps, even with her bad legs.

Later in the week we visited the *Caves of Drach,* stalagmites and stalactites once again very cleverly and colourfully illuminated, though Mum declined the boat-trip over the underground *Martel Lake*. Nevertheless, she was still able to enjoy the haunting music of Frederic Chopin's *Polonaise* as it serenaded the rest of us across the dark, mysterious waters, believed to be at least 438-feet deep.

The *Monastery of Valldemosa* was also on our list, where we toured the rooms in which Chopin had stayed with his (female!) lover, the famous French author George Sand, and viewed his piano and death-mask. It was here he wrote his famous *"24 preludes"*, including the *"Polonaise"* . The view from his terrace was stunning, though apparently it rained for most of the time he was there so one can only hope he had the opportunity to appreciate it. He was at Valledemosa trying to recover from tuberculosis; the weather did not help and sadly his efforts to fight the disease were, eventually, to be in vain.

On another day we swapped our motorised transport for a quad-cycle, the kind with four wheels, a front and back seat and with a "surrey" on top. Mum sat in the back in regal splendour while Sheila and I pedalled furiously in the front, all the way along the promenade. We decided to return along the side streets, which proved not to be such a good idea as we found we had a small hill to climb. Try as we might, we could not pedal the wretched machine uphill, so poor old Mum had to get out and walk while we pulled it behind us, huffing and puffing, and falling about with laughter all the way back. Happy memories!

By the time we returned from our Mallorquin break, the newspapers were full of the arrest of serial killer Dennis Nilsen. He is known to have murdered at least fifteen men and boys between 1978 and January 1983, seven of whom have never been identified. His victims were often foreign students, homeless young people or male prostitutes. His killing spree only came to an end when he tried to dispose of some of the remains of his latest victim down his toilet and succeeded in blocking the drains. Other victims were found dismembered and hidden in various places in his flat.

At the time of his arrest he was working as a civil servant in a London Jobcentre. One of his colleagues later transferred to the office in which I was working and Dennis Nilsen was a talking point for many weeks. I can remember her saying how "ordinary" he seemed and how he was always bringing curries he had cooked into the office for the staff to eat. They were delicious but later, hopefully without foundation, they would speculate what kind of meat they had been eating!

He was sentenced to a minimum term of 25 years, although the Home Secretary recommended he should never be released. However if the *Court of Human Rights* in Strasburg outlaws life imprisonment as a violation of human rights, he could be freed on life-licence almost immediately. This only goes to confirm my belief that the powers-that-be have lost the plot!

Lebanon was back in the news on 18th April 1983 when a bomb, packed into a delivery van, was driven into the US embassy compound and exploded at the very front of the building, causing massive damage and killing 64 people: 32 Lebanese employees, 17 Americans, 14 visitors and passers-by and the suicide-bomber. A pro-Iranian group calling itself the "Islamic Jihad" claimed responsibility, adding that they would "keep striking at any imperialistic presence in Lebanon".

Following the attack, the US embassy was moved to a supposedly more secure location in East Beirut. However on 20th September 1984 another car-bomb exploded at this embassy killing 20 Lebanese and 2 American soldiers.

But the attack in Beirut that claimed the most casualties was on 23rd October 1983 when a truck loaded with six tons of TNT, ploughed into the four-storey barracks where more than 300 US troops, from a UN peacekeeping force, were sleeping. It is claimed to be the largest non-nuclear bomb in history and it killed 241 Americans, mostly marines. Minutes later a bomb at the compound of the French peace-keeping force killed another 58. Three months later President Ronald Reagan pulled the American troops out of Lebanon and the peace-keeping efforts were in tatters.

Once upon a time, Lebanon had been a peaceful enclave in an unstable Middle East but all this changed when the PLO was thrown out of Jordan and fled there. They attracted Christian and Muslim militia into the country and it descended into chaos and infighting. Israel invaded in 1982 hoping to crush the PLO but failed. It was in exchange for Israel's withdrawal that the UN had sent in the peace-keeping force. Now this too had failed and civil war returned to Lebanon for the next seven years, until a settlement left Syria firmly in control. The failure would also pave the way for a tiny guerrilla movement, the Iranian-and-Syrian-supported *Hezbollah*, to grow into a military and political Goliath. The man who is believed to have controlled *Hezbollah* is said to have masterminded the 1985 TWA hijacking of flight 847, en route from Athens to London's Heathrow Airport on 14th June. The 153 passengers and crew endured a three-day ordeal during which one passenger, a US navy diver, was murdered. Some passengers were then released but dozens were held hostage for up to two weeks. He is also said to have inspired a certain Osama bin Liden.

Happier news on the 18th June 1983 when Sally Ride became the first American woman (and the youngest American at age 32) to enter space in *Space Shuttle Challenger 7*. However the Soviets can claim the world record for the first women in space: Valentina Tereshkova in 1963 and Svetlana Savitskaya in 1982. Sally Ride would go on to complete 343 hours in space in various *Challenger* missions.

1983 and Dad had completed fifty years of employment with Dorset House and Rosemead Schools. He and Mum were invited to a short ceremony at the school where he was presented with a matching clock and barometer, mounted on a plaque of polished wood with the following inscription:-

Presented to Mr C. Oakley (Clem)
By the staff of Rosemead School
With gratitude for long and loyal service
July 1983

Sadly the clock no longer works but the gift still hangs on my wall, another constant reminder of my beloved parent.

More trouble on 1st September when the Soviets shot down a commercial Korean airliner, KAL 007, en route from New York to Seoul via Amsterdam. The Soviets claimed it had strayed into its air-space, over a very strategically-sensitive area, without navigation lights and that it had not attempted to contact Russian air traffic control. They had thought it was a spy-plane.

The Americans said the 'plane had suffered navigational problems and that Soviet fighter 'planes had fired at it without warning. This was one of the tensest moments of the Cold War and the opposing points of view over the incident have never been resolved.

Wherever one apportions blame, the fact remains that all 269 passengers and crew, mainly Americans, were killed. President Reagan ordered the US military to make the GPS (Global Positioning System) available for civilian use, so that errors like that of KAL 007 could never happen again. This was the beginning of the availability of the GPS we use today for all types of navigation, surveillance and tracking, in the air, at sea and on land.

November 1983 and Mum and I headed off to Benidorm on the Costa Blanca coast of Spain. Benidorm had the downmarket reputation of a "fish and chip" resort for working-class Brits but we liked it, out of season at least. It has a beautiful, long, sandy beach and there is plenty to do and plenty to see. This time we decided not to hire a car but to take some of the trips the hotel was offering, so one day we journeyed inland with one coach party to view the fortress village of Guadalest and watched the Spanish ladies sitting in the sun making traditional lace and crocheted shawls for the tourists.

On another day, I fancied a donkey-ride into the lemon-groves and when Mum learned she could go by jeep instead of beast, she was keen to join me. The donkey-riders enjoyed a very pleasant, gentle ride through the groves towards a makeshift bar where "entertainment" was laid on.

The jeep-riders arrived a little later having sped through the groves at a great rate of knots, bumping over the rough terrain like they were training for the Dakar rally. Mum said she wished she had chosen the donkey instead! Despite her protestations, I quietly complained to the tour-guide that a little more consideration for its elderly passengers would be much appreciated. The jeep-ride back to the coach was conducted at a snail's pace!

To add insult to injury, the "entertainment" was abysmal. The sort of thing where you are supposed to get up and make a fool of yourself for the delight of your companions. Definitely not "our cup of tea", and not the most successful outing, but as I have said before, even at 78 years, Mum was game to try anything!

One of the advantages of us going abroad, as far as Dad was concerned, was that we came home with our full allowance of duty-free tobacco on his behalf. Every time we returned he would chuckle, "One in the eye for Maggie!" Delighting in the fact the exchequer (and Margaret Thatcher!) was being denied a bit of revenue!

Later that month, on 26th November, six robbers broke into the "Brinks Mat" warehouse at Heathrow Airport to steal £3m in cash but instead of cash they found 3 tonnes of gold bullion, worth £26m. The security-guard in charge of the warehouse was related to one of the robbers and it did not take long for the thieves to be apprehended but they were found without the gold. The two ring-leaders were sentenced to 25 years imprisonment and the security-guard to six years.

But the story does not end there. Some of the gold had been passed to a certain Kenneth Noye and he melted it down for re-sale. However, the sudden movement of large sums of money through his bank account, alerted the Treasury, who told the police. Noye was placed under surveillance and, in January 1985, he killed an undercover police officer he found lurking in his garden. At the resulting trial he pleaded "self-defence" and was found not guilty of murder.

A year later he was tried for conspiracy to handle the Brinks Mat gold and sentenced to 14 years in prison. He served eight years and was released in 1994, but the story continues! In 1996 Noye murdered a motorist in a road-rage incident and fled the country. He was tracked down to Spain, extradited, and in 1998 was tried and convicted of murder. He received a life sentence.

The gold from the Brinks Mat robbery was never recovered and, it is claimed in some circles, that anyone wearing gold jewellery purchased in the UK after 1983, is probably wearing "Brinks Mat".

It is hard to believe that a group of people, whatever their grievances with the establishment, can plant a bomb in a crowded place, knowing it will blow-up innocent people. It is even more unbelievable when so-called Christians plant a bomb deliberately to target Christmas shoppers. But this is what happened on 17th December 1983 when a car-bomb was detonated in a side-street near *Harrods Department Store* in Knightsbridge. The streets were crowded with pedestrians shopping for the festive season and the blast was so strong it blew the car onto the roof of a nearby five-storey building. Chaos and panic ensued as a pall of black smoke enveloped the area and glass from *Harrods* display windows, and miscellaneous debris, showered down onto the shoppers. Ninety people were injured; some were treated on the spot and others were ferried to hospital by ambulances and army vehicles. Six people died; three were Metropolitan police officers sent to inspect the suspect vehicle and three were passers-by, one of whom was an American citizen. Another policeman died from his injuries on Christmas Eve and yet another lost both legs and a hand.

Members of the Provisional IRA claimed responsibility, although the leaders of the organisation said they had not authorised the attack. *Harrods* re-opened three days later, despite the damage, its owners saying "they would not be defeated by acts of terrorism." A memorial to the fallen officers now marks the spot where they were killed. A sad and sorry end to 1983.

CHAPTER FORTY

Skating into 1984
(1984)

The Winter Olympics of 1984 were held in Sarajevo, Yugoslavia (now known as Bosnia and Herzegovina). Jane Torvill and Christopher Dean, from Nottingham, England, performed a free dance interpretation of Ravel's *Bolero* and made double history. They scored an unprecedented perfect score of 6.0 for artistic impression from all nine Olympic judges, and were the first non-Russian duo in Olympic history to win the gold medal in an ice-dancing competition. Ice-dance was never the same again. They revolutionised the sport but were building on the achievements of John Curry, another British figure-skating champion who was the first to combine ballet and modern dance in competitions. He won an Olympic gold medal in 1976 in Innsbruck, followed by Robin Cousins who won a gold in Lake Placid, New York, in 1980. These were truly the golden years of ice-dance for the UK.

1984 and the UK Prime Minister, Margaret Thatcher, was determined to meet the unions head-on. In February she announced that a union presence would be banned from GCHQ in Cheltenham. This is the "Government Communications Headquarters", our "spy" centre in other words! It is responsible for providing signal intelligence to government departments and military commands and some of its work is highly classified. All the employees are civil servants and she said they would be offered £1000 to give-up their rights to union membership.

The TUC (Trades Union Council) called for an afternoon of action against the proposal, so Tuesday 28th February 1984 saw me out on strike, for the one and only time of my life. The national response from union members was mixed. Most DHSS (Social Security) and Tax Offices closed early in solidarity for their fellow civil servants but most other industries stayed at work. Only British Rail backed the TUC in any great numbers, with Bognor Railway Station being one of the worst-hit areas of the UK because most of their guards had failed to turn up for work.

Locally there were about 120 of us at a meeting held in a local public-house and we were all incensed that a union member should be regarded as less patriotic, and thus, by implication, more likely to betray the nation's secrets, than a non-union member of staff. How insulting! Of course our action made no difference whatsoever and GCHQ lost its union representation.

Next in Margaret Thatcher's sights was one of the strongest unions in the country, the NUM (National Union of Mineworkers). In 1983 the PM had appointed Ian MacGregor as Chairman of the (nationalised) Coal Board. He had come to his new job with the reputation of turning *The British Steel Corporation* from one of the least efficient in Europe, to one of the most efficient, but at a cost of halving the workforce in the space of two years. The miners feared he was going to decimate the coal industry and early in March he proved their fears true by announcing his intention to close twenty uneconomic pits, putting 20,000 miners out of work. They knew this would be just the beginning.

This is what precipitated a year-long strike but it is arguable that the only people who suffered during it were the miners themselves. Most homes had oil or gas central-heating and the railways had long since converted from coal to diesel or electricity. The only sector still dependent on coal was power-stations and Thatcher had made sure that they had secretly stock-piled enough supplies to see them through a prolonged miners' strike.

The President of the NUM, Arthur Scargill, did his best to mobilise the workforce with the use of "flying pickets". Violent confrontations at pits between pickets, police and non-striking miners became commonplace. Often striking miners had to face baton-wielding police in riot gear and mounted police charging lines of men with truncheons drawn. Six pickets died.

The decision of some miners not to support the strike was seen as a betrayal by those who did strike and in some cases this led to attacks, not only on the working miners but their property, families and pets. One taxi-driver was killed by a concrete block falling on his car from a bridge as he took a non-striking miner to work.

In addition, welfare benefits were cut to striking miners' families and they had to rely on donations from charities, the EEC Food Mountains, sympathetic supermarkets and communal kitchens, in order to survive. Three children were killed as they scrabbled about on a colliery waste-heap seeking pieces of coal.

The integrity of some of the NUM leaders was brought into question with allegations, for example, that Scargill had met Libyan leaders in Paris and that he diverted money donated from Russian miners. Despite the smear campaigns, he was perceived as a militant hero by the union ..... and a Marxist thug by most of the mainstream press, 75% of which was owned, at that time, by just three men.

The strike formally ended on 3rd March 1985, with not only ten people dead, but with the miners' defeat and the political power of the NUM broken forever. Closures and job losses continued and where there had been 170 working mines in 1983, by the time privatisation came in 1994, there were only 15 major deep mines left. Now, in 2009, only four remain.

Many mining communities have become ghost towns and in 1994 the

EU classified Grimethorpe, in South Yorkshire, as the poorest settlement in the country and one of the poorest in Europe. Many others are officially classified as areas of deprivation. Recovery in the places where there was a more varied industrial base has been much better and some of these areas are even more prosperous than they used to be. Coal mining is now a very small industry in the UK but, as of 2003, it is more productive in terms of output per worker than the coal industry in France, Germany and the US.

The UK miners' strike was a defining moment in British industrial relations and its defeat severely weakened the British trade union movement. The dispute exposed deep divisions in British society and caused considerable bitterness, some of which has still not healed. But it was a major political and ideological victory for Margaret Thatcher and her Conservative Party and changed the face of our nation forever.

The Thatcher Government was now able to steam ahead, almost unchallenged, with its "free market" programmes and its privatisation, not only of coal, but of all the utility industries. Also it began the process that would eventually see the privatisation of the railway but, for good or ill, it did not have enough time in power to achieve the privatisation of the National Health Service.

Alongside its privatisation programme ran its de-regulation of the City. Bankers, commodity brokers, investment managers and the like prospered as never before, while thousands more found their jobs and dreams disappearing. A new word came into the language, "Yuppie", an acronym for "young, upwardly-mobile, professional". Sadly the word would also become synonymous with greed, self-interest and a disregard and disinterest in the fate of others. It might even be argued that the collapse of the banking system in 2008/9 began in these get-rich-quick years.

On 17th April 1984, 25year old WPC Yvonne Fletcher was on crowd patrol duty outside the Libyan Embassy. There were two factions demonstrating; one protesting about the execution of two students who had criticised the leader of Libya, Colonel Gaddafi, and the other which was in support of him. They were kept apart from each other by strategically placed crowd-control-barriers. At 10.18am shots from a sub-machine gun were fired into the group of protesters, striking eleven people, including Fletcher. She died approximately one hour later.

The shots were believed to have come from inside the embassy and it was immediately surrounded by armed police. The siege lasted for eleven days, the longest police siege in the country's history. Eventually the Government allowed the embassy staff to leave and then expelled them from the country. The embassy was closed and Britain broke off diplomatic relations.

In 1997 doubts surfaced that Yvonne Fletcher had been killed from the second floor of the Libyan Embassy, as had been suggested. A television programme claimed it was highly possible, even probable, that someone in the penthouse above No 8 St James Square, may have been the shooter and support for this theory came from three highly respected sources: George Stiles, the senior ballistics officer in the British Army: Hugh Thomas, the consultant surgeon at the Royal Victoria Hospital in Belfast (who had seen more bullet wounds that anyone else in Britain): Professor Bernard Knight, the Home Office pathologist. It was suggested that elements of MI5, America's CIA or Israel's Mossad Intelligence could have been involved, with the intention of bringing Colonel Gaddafi and his regime into disrepute.

However, just to confuse the issue even further, in 1999 the Libyan Government accepted "general responsibility" for the murder of the young police officer and paid compensation to Yvonne's family. Her mother, Queenie Fletcher, is still trying to ascertain the truth and to bring her daughter's killer to justice.

In September 1984, Sheila left the engineering firm and started work for an American multi-millionairess, Elizabeth Meyer. Elizabeth was a keen sailor and was renovating a J-class racing yacht, which had originally been left to rot on a Southampton mudflat. The *Endeavour* was one of only ten J-class sloops built between 1930 and 1937, six in America and four in Britain. She was commissioned by sailing legend Tommy Sopwith and built at *Camper and Nicholson's Yard* at Gosport. She was launched in 1934, specifically to race for the America's Cup. She did not win but came closer than any other contender by winning the first two races and was generally accepted as the faster boat. *Endeavour's* 130foot-long construction had been a work of art, with a rig that towered 165 feet above the water and supported 8000 square feet of sail. To race effectively, she had needed a minimum crew of 30 people.

The Second World War saw the end of J-class racing and *Endeavour* was sold in 1945 and taken to America. In 1972 she was sold to the British Maritime Trust and taken to *Souter's Yard* at Cowes, in the Isle of Wight. There she became a pathetic sight, a rusting hulk unrecognisable as the magnificent racing machine she had been before the war. In 1978 she was bought for just £10 by John Amos, whose intention it was to restore her to her former glory, but this had proved impossible with his limited resources.

In 1982, Elizabeth was in England, researching J-class yachts for a magazine article, and she saw the vessel by pure chance. Despite its impoverished condition, it was "love at first sight!" and Elizabeth felt it was her destiny to restore the yacht. Sheila felt herself extremely fortunate to obtain the job with Elizabeth, and privileged to be involved with such a prestigious project. She had been recommended for the position by a friend who was already working for Elizabeth, but the friend had to move out of the area. The job was fascinating; a mixture of PA, business manager, trouble-shooter, secretary, and liaison with suppliers, craftsmen and shipyards. She was also responsible for the day-to-day accounting and at first this was a constant source of concern, for she was never confident with figures. However, before going into the hotel business, Mac had worked for ICI in East Africa as an accountant, so he told her to bring the books home and he painstakingly taught her the intricacies of profit and loss, debit and credit, bank reconciliation, tax returns and PAYE. Elizabeth paid well but she was a hard task-master and I doubt Sheila would have stayed the course if it had not been for Mac's help, support and his enduring confidence in her abilities.

The project would take four years and cost a massive $10million. The original riveted hull was replaced by stronger and more durable welded steel; the aluminium mast was fabricated from four longitudinal extrusions and, at seventeen storeys high, was to be the tallest mast in the world; massive hydraulic winches would control the rig, allowing it to sail with a far smaller crew. The inside resembled a gentlemen's club, with interior panelling of American cherry and fittings of solid brass. The floor was pine and there was even a working, Victorian-style fire-place. There are only three surviving J-class racing yachts, the *Valsheeda,* the *Shamrock* and the *Endeavour.* It was Elizabeth's dream to see them race again and this would eventually be fulfilled when she and the yacht went home to Newport, Rhode Island.

The news on breakfast television on 12th October 1984 shocked the nation. The Conservative Party was holding its annual conference in Brighton and we awoke to see horrific images on our TV screens confirming that a bomb had torn apart the Grand Hotel where members of the Cabinet were staying. Prime Minister Thatcher and her husband, Dennis, narrowly escaped injury and I doubt anyone will forget the sight of a pyjama-clad Trade and Industry Secretary, Norman Tebbit, being carried out of the rubble on a stretcher. His wife, Margaret, was permanently paralysed from neck injuries received in the attack. Five people died and 34 were injured.

The IRA claimed responsibility and declared that the target had been the PM, adding, *"Today we were unlucky. We only have to be lucky once; you have to be lucky always."*

The bomb had been planted several weeks earlier by Patrick Magee, who had checked into the hotel under a false name. He was caught and sentenced to 35 years but released in 1999 under the "Good Friday Agreement".

Firemen said the death toll would probably have been higher had it not been that the basic construction of the Victorian building was so sound, for despite the central section of eight floors collapsing into the basement, much of the hotel itself remained standing. The conference went ahead as planned.

India was in the news on 31st October 1984 with the assassination of its Prime Minister, Indira Gandhi. She was highly respected by many of her people for her battle against famine in rural areas but, despite this, she was shot by Sikh extremists who were protesting at the storming, in June, of their sacred shrine, the Golden Temple of Amritsar. The Sikhs in the northern state of Punjab thought they were being discriminated against by the Hindu majority and had occupied their temple in protest, disobeying a 36-hour curfew the Government had imposed. The Government ordered troops to the area and they tried to forcibly evict the protestors. By 12th June more than 1000 people had died; 800 militants and 200 soldiers. The Government later admitted that they had underestimated the strength of feeling of the Sikhs regarding their temple and that it was this that had started the chain of events that led to Indira Gandhi's murder.

Riots erupted in India following her death as Hindus took their revenge on Sikhs. Another 1000 people died as a result and the army was ordered into the cities to quell the violence. The election to find Indira Gandhi's successor was won by her son, Rajiv, in a landslide victory. He was himself assassinated by a suicide-bomber in 1991.

(Incidentally Indira Gandhi was no relation to her famous namesake, Mahatma Gandhi, but was the daughter of Jawaharlal Nehru, who became the first Prime Minister of India after its independence in 1947. Nehru, however, was greatly influenced by Mahatma Gandhi's policy of civil disobedience and peaceful protest, as was Indira.)

On 3rd December 1984, India was in the news again. In the early hours, a storage tank leaked 40 tonnes of highly poisonous methol isocyanate gas into the streets of densely-populated Bhopal. It came from the American *Union Carbide* pesticide plant, which had been cutting costs, training and maintenance at the factory for years. Most of the residents of Bhopal were sleeping; many woke up coughing or choking on the fumes. As they jumped from their beds, they felt their skin burning. Some fell to the ground in contortions of pain; others ran and ran but they did not know where to go. In the confusion, families were separated; children and adults fell to the ground unconscious and then they were trampled underfoot. It was a scene from hell.

Estimates put the numbers that died from immediate exposure between 3000 and 8000 and at least another 15,000 people have died since. Even today 120,000 people live daily with the effects from the gas, including blindness, extreme shortness of breath, cancers, birth deformities and early menopause. Chemicals from the plant have contaminated the water system and the soil, so the poisoning is ongoing.

In the immediate aftermath of the gas leak, the Chairman of *Union Carbide,* Warren Anderson, was arrested for multiple manslaughter but fled back to the US while out of jail on bail. Due to political issues, he has never been extradited to face trial and lives in luxury in the US. Although *Union Carbide* has paid some compensation to some victims, they deny liability, claiming the plant was sabotaged. To this day, the site remains contaminated while various officials argue over who should be responsible for the clean-up, and tens of thousands continue to suffer with no realistic hope of recompense.

CHAPTER FORTY-ONE

Going West!
(1985-1986)

January 1985 and Mum and I were off to Mallorca again. We were lucky in that neither Dad nor Bryan ever raised any objections to our regular disappearances! However, my nephews were green with envy that we were off again because they wanted so much to go on an aeroplane for the first time. We offered to take them with us and Mac asked if he could come too, so this time the old stalwarts and Sheila were the ones to be left behind.

We were going to stay at the same hotel, the *Bahia del Este* in Cala Millor, and once again we hired a car, although, much to my delight, Mac would do all the driving. One day, early in our stay, we woke up to find we had had two or three inches of snow overnight and the area was covered with a blanket of white. Russell and Vernon were delighted to see it, for even by 1985 this was a relatively rare occurrence in Southern England; on this coastal strip of Mallorca, the locals said it was almost unknown. So, after breakfast, Russell and Vernon raced off to have a snowball fight and to build a snowman on some waste-ground opposite the hotel. Not many people can claim to have gone on holiday to sunny Spain and to have built a snowman! Fortunately, or unfortunately if you are only eleven and twelve years old, the snow did not last long and, along with Mr Snowman, it soon disappeared on the coast when the sun came up.

We used the car a lot that week and travelled all over the island. The weather was no deterrent to Mac. When he lived in East Africa he had regularly taken part in the *East African Safari Rally* and was competent and confident in all road conditions. Indeed we came across a car that had become stuck in snow on the side of a mountain and he took great delight in showing the driver (and the boys and me) how to drive out of it.

We thought it would be educational, as well as interesting, to take the boys to see the caves in the area so we visited *Arta* and *Drach* (again) and also toured the *Cuevas de Ham*, although this time Mum (now in her eightieth year) was content to sit in the car while we did the exploring. Every cave system is different; the *Caves of Ham* reminded me of a fairy grotto, smaller than the other two but with lots of twists and turns and nooks and crannies; stalactites and stalagmites of all shapes and sizes again in abundance.

All too soon the week was over but the "boys" and I look back on this winter break with great affection and many happy memories. And I did not realise that it would be the last holiday Mum and I would be able to

358

take together without Dad coming with us for his brain's cognitive powers were beginning to go. The first signs were in his driving. Over the coming months his car handling ability would become more and more erratic: hitting kerbs, clipping wing-mirrors and misjudging turnings. We pleaded with him not to drive anymore but he would not listen. I knew I should take action to have his driving licence taken away but I prevaricated. I just could not find it in my heart to do that to him. Then one day he went right up a kerb, across the pavement and drove into a hedge. He guiltily admitted, "I could have killed someone." It was enough to make him give up car ownership immediately. At first, he went back to using his bicycle but eventually even this became too much and, with the loss of his transport, came the loss of his little part-time jobs, including the one at the "School". Sadly it also put paid to his weekend visits to the "United Services Club" and to his now-very-occasional games of snooker. Then Mum and Dad really did become "Darby and Joan"!

On 11th May 1985 the city of Bradford was hosting a football match between their home side and Lincoln City at their Valley Parade Football Stadium. It was a wooden structure and the roof was covered with tarpaulin and sealed with asphalt and bitumen. Forty minutes into the first half of a mediocre game, a glowing ember was noticed in the accumulation of rubbish below the floorboards in one of the stands. Combined with a strong wind, the glow erupted into flame and the roof and wooden stands became a fireball within minutes. Burning timbers and molten materials fell from the roof onto the crowd below and black smoke engulfed a passageway behind the stand where spectators were trying to escape.

It was the worst fire disaster in the history of British football, claiming the lives of 56 supporters and injuring another 265. The event was being televised and no one will ever forget the sight of one poor man staggering onto the pitch, alight from head to toe with boiling pitch. Despite the attempts of people to beat out the flames with their jackets, he died later in hospital. Half of those who died were under 20 or over 70 years. It was survival of the fittest.

However there were many acts of heroism that day. 28 police officers and 22 civilians were publicly documented as having saved at least one life, later receiving police commendations, or various bravery awards, including six people who were awarded the Queen's Gallantry Medal. Many others, perhaps equally deserving of praise and recognition, remained anonymous.

The cause was thought to be an accidental dropping of a match or a cigarette, which was fuelled by the debris below the stand and the wooden structure. As a result of the fire, the construction of wooden grandstands, at all UK sports facilities, was prohibited.

It was in 1985 that everyone became familiar with two Russian words: *Glasnost* (meaning "freedom of speech") and *Perestroika* (meaning "restructuring"). The Soviet leader, Mikhail Gorbachev, was determined to change the policies of his country when he introduced his plan of *Glasnost*. He succeeded in ways that must have been beyond even his expectations for it led to less censorship on an unprecedented scale. Suddenly hunger, poor housing, pollution, alcoholism and corruption could be openly discussed. Thousands of political prisoners were released from the Gulag, or the Russian penal systems, and books, plays and films that had been banned under the old regimes were made available.

Perestroika completely changed the Russian economy. It gave businesses and entrepreneurs more economic freedom to become self-financing, and to be allowed to decide for themselves what to do with the profits.

Glasnost and *Perestroika* had exposed the corruption of the previous dictatorships of Stalin and Lenin, and the shortcomings on the ideas of Karl Marx, and led to the eventual fall of the Communist Party in Russia and the rise of democracy.

As Mikhail Gorbachev was making "holes" in the Communist Party, in 1985 another hole was discovered: an ozone hole in the stratosphere above Antarctica. The ozone layer absorbs 93-99% of the sun's high-frequency ultraviolet light, which is potentially damaging to life on earth, hence its importance. Its existence was discovered by French physicists, Charles Fabry and Henri Buisson in 1913 but it was a British meteorologist, GMB Dobson, who invented an instrument to measure it. Between 1928 and 1958, Dobson established a worldwide network of ozone-measuring monitoring stations, which are still in use today.

By the 1970's it was thought that aerosol sprays containing chlorofluorocarbons (CFC's) were damaging this layer. In 1978 the US, Canada, and Norway banned CFC's in aerosol sprays but they were still used in other applications, such as refrigeration and industrial cleaning. When the hole in the ozone layer was discovered in 1985, international discussions were held to reduce CFC's and from 1987 the production of CFC was limited and phased out completely by 1996.

(In August 2003 scientists announced that thanks to the international ban on CFC's, the depletion of the ozone layer was thought to be slowing down. However, CFC's were replaced by HCFC's and these have also been found to have a negative impact on the ozone layer, so, now, they too are being phased out.)

On 1st September 1985, seventy-three years after it sank in the North Atlantic, a joint US-French expedition located the *Titanic*. The sunken liner was roughly 400 miles east of Newfoundland, lying at a depth of about 13,000feet. By the 4th September, the first pictures of the wreck were released, filmed by an unmanned submarine.

The following year, the leader of this expedition, Dr Robert Ballard, made eleven dives to the site in a three-man submarine. Many more have visited the wreck since, despite the objections of some survivors and some of the relatives who lost members of their family when the liner hit an iceberg in 1912. They felt it was desecrating the graves of the 1500 people who lost their lives in the tragedy.

Salvage experts say it would be impossible, at the present time, to raise the ship but, in 1994, a US court granted *"RMS Titanic Inc"* exclusive rights to the wreck, so who knows what may happen in the years ahead as technology improves.

Technology was already improving at a rapid rate in other directions, and the transition from old to new was not always received with equanimity. Rupert Murdock's *"News International"* empire owned four of the UK's major newspapers: *The Sun, The Times, The Sunday Times* and *The News of the World*. Since the 18th century, these and other newspapers had been printed in London's famous Fleet Street but Murdoch wanted to move his business to a new purpose-built site in Wapping, East London. The new, computerised technology installed in these premises threatened the livelihood of many of the printers and, on 24th January 1986, 5,500 employees decided to strike rather than move to the new site. Murdoch immediately sacked them all and employed members of the electricians union, the EETPU, to keep the printing presses running.

The print unions called for a boycott of all of Murdock's 'papers and organised regular marches and demonstrations at the company's new plant. Despite a large-scale police operation to protect the site and its workers, picketing was exceptionally violent with 1262 arrests and 410 police injuries. The strike lasted a year and, like the miners' strike of 1984/85, ended in ignominy and near bankruptcy for the unions.

News International did not lose one single night of production during the strike and its ultimate success broke the power wielded by the print unions over the newspaper industry. By 1988 all national newspapers had moved from Fleet Street to the newly-developed Docklands and adopted the new, cheaper, computerised printing technology. It was another victory for Maggie Thatcher's war on the unions.

On 28th January 1986, the world witnessed the worst space disaster and tragically it was shown live on television. Just over a minute into their flight from Cape Canaveral in Florida, the American space shuttle *Challenger* exploded. It killed all seven astronauts on board, including a school-teacher, and mother of two, Christa McAuliffe. The cause was later found to be a leak through a faulty seal in one of the rocket boosters. The disaster was a severe blow to the American space programme and no further manned flights were launched until September 1988.

Less than one month later, the Soviet Union launched the core module of their *Mir* space station. It was enlarged several times so that it would eventually accommodate a crew of up to six astronauts and, over the coming years, international teams would use the space station to conduct experiments. These would include the newly-independent countries of the former Soviet Union as well as Afghanistan, Bulgaria, France, Germany, Great Britain, India, Japan, Syria and the USA.

Mir was abandoned in 1999. In March 2001 it fell to earth, the largest spacecraft ever to decay, showering an estimated 1,500 fragments, each weighing at least 44lbs (20kg), into the Pacific Ocean, over an uninhabited area 120miles wide by 3,600miles long.

On 5th April 1986, "La Belle", a West Berlin nightclub, was bombed, killing two American servicemen and a Turkish woman. US President Ronald Reagan said he had irrefutable evidence that Libya was responsible, so he resolved to bomb Libya, arguing that America was exercising its right to self defence as defined by Article 51 of the UN Charter. He also wanted to send a strong message to Colonel Gaddafi that terrorism would not be tolerated and he hoped that the action would reduce Libya's ability to support and train terrorists.

The President wanted to launch the USAF bombing raid from American bases in Britain and the death of WPC Yvonne Fletcher outside the Libyan Embassy in April 1984, was a major factor in PM Margaret Thatcher's decision to allow this.

Thus, on 15th April 1986, USAF 'planes, based in Britain, bombed targets in Libya, narrowly missing the French Embassy in the capital, Tripoli. Some reports claim that at least 100 people died in the raids, including the adopted baby daughter of the Libyan leader. Just two days later, the Syrian-based terrorist group *Arab Revolutionary Cells* murdered three hostages, two British and one American, in retaliation for the attack.

Some time late in 1985, Sheila had been invited to a *"Twin Reunion"* in Hertfordshire, organised by John Stroud, with Professor Tom Bouchard as the guest of honour. Her twin was unable to go so she asked me to accompany her instead. We had a great weekend, staying a couple of nights in a nearby country pub' and it was fascinating to meet some of the twins, having read and heard so much about them. It was also an opportunity for Sheila and me to catch up on some of more of the "bonding" we seem to have sidestepped in our adolescent years.

Professor Bouchard was doing his best to chat with all those present and when he got to us, he told us that he had just received funding to extend his research to include adopted siblings of separated twins. They had compared many people from multiple births, both identical and fraternal, but now the time had come to compare adopted siblings with no common genetic input. He asked me if I would agree to take part in the study and if so I would be the first sibling to do so. He went on to say what a rare creature I was for very few of the twins who had taken part in the study had adopted siblings, at least within a specific age difference of ten years.

So, on 25th April 1986, I set off for Minneapolis, alone! The research grant for siblings did not extend to their spouses. The tests were fascinating but the questionnaires were tedious and never-ending! One of the physical tests was to check eye to hand co-ordination. The sort of thing where you run a loop along a copper wire and try not to set off an alarm bell. There were several similar ones to do and, to my absolute amazement, I scored the highest marks ever! Which is why I remember it so well! It should make me a good ball-player apparently but as I have no talent whatsoever in that direction, something has gone wrong somewhere!

At the end of it all, I asked Professor Bouchard what conclusions he had come to on the *"Nature versus Nurture"* conundrum. Needless to say, it is not straightforward! As I understand it, every facet of "personality" is subject to a different amount of input from our genes and from our upbringing. In some cases, that input could be almost entirely genetic, intelligence for example (not surprisingly) is almost all "heredity". In other traits, upbringing will be more important.

"There is one," he proclaimed, "that is almost entirely down to nurture: The ability to give and receive love." For me, that said it all.

When the week in Minneapolis was over, I did not head straight back home. I thought I might never go to America again, so while I was on that side of the Atlantic, I had decided to see a bit of the country on my own and then pick up a coach tour to see even more. The one place I had always wanted to visit was San Francisco, so from Minneapolis I flew to the Pacific coast.

San Francisco could not have been more of a contrast to Minneapolis. The landscape around the Minnesota *Twin Cities* is flat; San Francisco is surrounded by mountains. Minneapolis is inland, on the banks of the Mississippi River, in a State famous for its 10,000 lakes and its loons. San Francisco is in a bay on the Pacific Ocean and subject to earthquakes from the *San Andreas Fault* and famous for its trams, its steep streets, its *Golden Gate Bridge* and *Alcatraz*.

The architecture of Minneapolis was modern, skyscrapers of every colour, texture, shape, material and design. About as far north as you can go and still be in the US, Minneapolis in April was still chilly but all the major streets, stores and a huge shopping mall, were linked by a "sky-walk" system, tunnels high above the city traffic and covering some twenty blocks. It meant you could park your car in a multi-storey car-park and walk all around the city in a climate-controlled environment, winter and summer, without your feet touching the pavement.

The tallest sky-scraper in Minneapolis then was the *IDS Tower,* 774 feet and 57 floors high with an observation tower on top. I did not go there but Sheila and Mac did. They took the regular elevator to the top and the "express" to descend. They said coming down they left their stomachs somewhere around the 40th floor! The express lift alone was an experience not to be missed but the view from the top was fantastic. It was near the railway station and to this day Sheila can remember the sight of the freight-trains, hundreds of carriages long, streaking their way across the plains, looking like an elongated *"Dinky"* toy.

San Francisco mixed the old with the new, while retaining a real olde-world charm. Their new buildings had to be earthquake-proof so there were no sky-scrapers and their construction technology was constantly coming up with new ideas to counteract the effects of tremors, like building on ball-bearings so the edifice would roll with the shaking and not collapse. Sadly, only another earthquake will tell us if these ideas are truly effective.

Of course, I saw all the usual touristy attractions: Alcatraz: the "Crookedest Street in the World": toured USS Pampanito, a Second World War submarine: saw City Hall where the UN Peace Treaty was signed in 1948: visited Chinatown on a minibus tour: rode on a cable-car: went across "The Golden Gate Bridge" in a coach and underneath it in a boat: saw the giant redwoods in Muir Woods and a herd of buffalo in Golden Gate Park: toured the Conservatory of Flowers which is based on Kew Gardens and walked up and down Fisherman's Wharf where I saw street performers for the very first time and heard my first English accent for over a week! I loved SF and it lived up to every expectation I had of it.

After seeing all the tourist sights San Francisco had to offer, I travelled to Los Angeles and, after visiting *Disneyland, Sea World* and *Universal Studios,* I picked up my coach for my *Wonders of the Golden West* tour. En route, I would stay on the shores of Lake Havasu and see *London Bridge* in its new home, view the *Hoover Dam,* gamble in Las Vegas, walk the forest trails in *Yosemite National Park* and view one of the world's most spectacular sights, *The Grand Canyon.*

What an incredible place! We stayed there overnight so we were able to see the *Canyon* at sunset and again at sun-rise. The sight of the different colours of the gorge, over a mile deep, coming to life as the sun rose and hit each strata of rock, will stay with me forever. We were also there long enough to take advantage of a trip over the *Canyon* in a light aircraft. I did not realise that flying in a small 'plane is quite different to that in a jetliner and it did not occur to me, or my fellow passengers, to take anti-airsickness tablets. Almost as soon as we took off, we started to turn "green". I cannot remember now if anyone was actually ill, but all I could do was to aim the camera at the window and keep pressing the shutter. It is a testament to how amazing the place really is that every photograph turned out to be worth the effort. And what a tale to tell when I finally returned home!

Soon after I had arrived in America, the world had suffered its worst ever nuclear-power-plant accident, far worse than Three Mile Island in 1979. It was at Chernobyl, just north of Kiev, in the Ukraine, and was not acknowledged by the Soviet authorities until 28th April 1986, two days after it had happened. It emerged that design flaws had led to a power surge, causing massive explosions, which blew off the top of the reactor. The discharge of radioactivity was so great that by the time the fall-out reached Sweden, 1000miles away, it was still powerful enough to register twice the normal level of radioactivity in the atmosphere. Estimates on the number of people that have died, and could still die, from this exposure vary tremendously, from a conservative 9,000 to a massive 93,000, and the contamination spread right across northern Europe. In north Wales, sheep on some 350 farms still have to be tested for radiation before the meat can be eaten. An official exclusion zone around the plant still remains in place, extending for 30kms (18 miles). It is one of the most radioactive places on our planet.

It was in November 1986 that the "Iran-Contra" scandal surfaced. It was a scandal in two parts. One part was the disclosure that guns and other weaponry were being sold to Iran, by the US, in exchange for hostages. Many Americans were horrified to learn that guns were being sold to a hostile government with their known links to terrorism, whatever the reason. To make matters worse, they were to learn that profits from the sale of these arms were being secretly channelled to *Contra* guerrillas in Nicaragua, in direct violation to the wishes of Congress. The National Security Council was found to be the agency involved in the scandal, but it could not be discovered if President Ronald Regan was complicit.

The military aide to the NSC was Lt Col Oliver North, their adviser was John Poindexter, and many other high-ranking officials were also found to be implicated. In May 1989, Oliver North was found guilty of obstructing Congress but the conviction was overturned by the new President, George Bush. Poindexter was convicted on similar charges in 1990 and sentenced to six months in prison; his conviction was also overturned. Former Defense Secretary Casper Weinberger was indicted on five counts of lying to Congress. His conviction was pardoned. On Christmas Eve 1992, George Bush issued presidential pardons to all those involved in the Iran-Contra scandal. It was an early Christmas present to all Americans, for, by this time, they were heartily sick of hearing about the whole sorry charade.

For us Christmas 1986 was a bittersweet celebration. For one thing, Uncle Ted died on 13th December. His death would come to mark the demise of the *Family Picnic* for, although there were modest get-togethers in the coming years, we all seemed to realise that the picnics just could not be the same without him and thus the inclination to recapture the camaraderie that had existed at these gatherings, departed with him.

The other point of sadness that marred the festive season was that we thought it was probably going to be the last one that we would spend with Sheila, Mac and sons, for, some months before, Sheila had announced that her employer, Elizabeth, had offered her a job in America. The project of rebuilding the yacht in Europe had been completed; *Endeavour* was going to her new home in Newport, Rhode Island, and Elizabeth had invited Sheila to organise the charters that the yacht would now undertake.

Initially Sheila was not at all sure that she wanted to accept the position. It would mean uprooting her sons and it would mean leaving us. Mac, on the other hand, was ecstatic at the prospect. He had managed to avoid bankruptcy but only by selling virtually everything they had. He saw a move to the US as a chance to begin again. In addition, Elizabeth was not only offering a well-paid job but a lovely apartment. In the end, Mac and the boys were so keen to go that Sheila could not find it in her heart to refuse. Mum encouraged her to do what was best for the family and re-assured her that she and Dad would be fine without her. So while Sheila made the decision to leave for the US, with the boys, in the coming March, Mum put on her extra-brave face and wept her tears in private. She was devoted to her grandsons and the thought that she might not see them all again, nearly broke her heart. Poor old Mac, the one most keen to depart these shores, would be left behind temporarily, trying to sell what was left of the business. Little did he realise that this would take the whole of the coming year.

CHAPTER FORTY-TWO

A Traumatic Year
(1987)

1987 was going to be a traumatic year, in more ways than one. Not just for our family but southern England would experience a hurricane for the first time for nearly three-hundred years, *"Black Monday"* would see share prices plummet and London's underground would suffer a horrendous fire. But before all this would take place, the trauma would begin with Terry Waite hitting the headlines again. Terry Waite was the Archbishop of Canterbury's special envoy who had successfully secured the release of hostages in Iran, Libya and Lebanon. However, his integrity had been compromised when he was seen in public with Oliver North and then had secretly used an American helicopter to travel between Cyprus and Lebanon.

He was advised not to try to free any more hostages but he felt the need to honour his commitment to the cause, so he arrived in Beirut with the intention of negotiating with members of the Islamic Jihad Organization who were known to be holding Western captives. On 20th January 1987, he was promised safe conduct to visit some of them who were said to be ill, but the organization broke this promise, accusing him of being an American agent, a charge he strongly denied. They took him prisoner and Waite was to remain in captivity for 1763 days, nearly five years, the first four of which were spent in solitary confinement. He endured beatings, interrogation and torture but says his faith kept him going and he held on to the belief *"that his captors could try to break his body, they could try to bend his mind but they could not possess his soul."*

He was not released until September 1991, when the political climate had altered enough in Lebanon to allow the UN to negotiate his release. He still dedicates himself to humanitarian work and feels immensely fortunate, and privileged, to be able to do so saying, *"....... I like to think (my efforts) are doing something to help to heal our world."*

At the time Sheila and the boys went to America, in March 1987, Dad could still walk to the town every day and buy a few groceries. He could still grow a few vegetables, mow the grass, cut the hedge, but everything was taking longer and required more effort. Then one day he came back from the town with all the things on Mum's shopping list but no receipt for the 2lb bag of sugar. Mum realised he had put it into his shopping-bag by mistake, instead of the store's basket, and that he had, in effect, stolen it. She was beside herself with guilt and worry. We discussed what to do for hours! If I took it back and offered to pay for it, would they still charge him (or me!) with theft? Would they ban him from the store? Would it get into the local papers? In the end, she thought the best thing to do was to stop him going to the town. She would manage the shopping on her own and what she could not do, I would do on their behalf.

From this point on things went from bad to worse. Before the year was out, the vegetable patch was overgrown and Bryan was mowing their grass and cutting the hedge. Mum started to fret about the decorating Dad had never got around to doing, so we undertook that as well. Not in a very speedy fashion but we did keep "at" it ..... and it was NOT because we "had to" but because we wanted to!!

Mum still went to church most Sundays and she trotted off to her various clubs two or three times a month. Once a month her name would come to the top of the roster for cleaning duties at the church and off she would go to dust the pews or polish the lectern. Dad started to get very possessive of the time she spent away from home and Bryan still chuckles at the typical conversation that he overheard one afternoon as she was on her way out.

Dad :- *"I don't see why you have to go!"*

Mum:- *"I don't HAVE to go. I WANT to go!"*

Dad :- *"I can't see why! It's just a lot of old women gossiping about everyone else's business!"*

Mum, exasperated:- *"We do NOT gossip! And I'm going!"*

Bryan says that is the nearest he ever heard my parents come to having an argument! Indeed probably it was the nearest they ever got! While Mum was gone, Dad took to hanging over the garden-gate, pitifully waiting for her return.

Dad was not the only family member whose brain was deteriorating. His sister Blanche had retired to a studio-flat in Worthing some years before and she had regularly visited my parents. Now she would turn up unexpectedly and not be able to remember how she had got there. She would have no 'bus or train ticket to indicate how she had travelled and Mum was concerned that she would not be able to find her way back to her flat. So she would ring me in the early evening and ask me to run her back home. Having turned out, somewhat begrudgingly, for my two hour chore, Auntie Blanche never made the good deed pleasurable. I can remember collecting her on one occasion and her saying, "*Oh yes! I know who you are! You're the girl they took in, aren't you?*" She made me feel like some stray cat they had adopted!

More trauma on 21st April 1987 with the first death of one of Mum's sisters-in-law: Myrtle, wife of her older brother, Tom. They only lived a few hundred yards away and when Mum visited him some weeks later, she was horrified to discover that Uncle Tom was boiling a bacon joint every Sunday and making it last all week. Apparently his sons had offered to organise *Meals on Wheels* for him but he had stubbornly refused. He was also struggling to do his laundry without the aid of a washing-machine. Mum told him to pack up his laundry and bring it round to her. She would do his sheets and towels, and other bits and pieces, every week in with theirs. She also told him it would be no trouble if he was to come round every day for a decent meal, after all she was still providing Dad with his bacon roly-poly's, his steak and kidney puddings, his roasts, his stews and dumplings, his fish and chips, liver and bacon and such like, followed by his apple pies and custard, rhubarb crumbles, rice puddings, and so on! Thus if Bryan or I popped in on an afternoon after lunch, we would often find poor old Mum washing-up and two old codgers fast asleep in the armchairs!

I think Mum rather enjoyed looking after Uncle Tom. She said at least he was very appreciative, thanking her every single day, and he made a small contribution to the family budget. She also felt she was keeping the promise she had made to her mother all those years before when Mary Martin uttered her final words, *"Look after the boys, Annie."*

On 11th June 1987 the face of British politics changed forever when four non-white politicians were elected in the same General Election. However, equal representation requires at least 55 black MP's and, as there are currently (2009) just 12 non-white MP's in the House of Commons, there is still some "way to go", as they say.

1987 was going to see the face of forensic science change forever. On 21st November 1983, fifteen-year old Lynda Mann was raped and strangled. On 31st July 1986, another fifteen-year old, Dawn Ashworth, suffered the same fate. The modus operandi of each case was the same and semen samples taken from both victims revealed the perpetrator had type A blood with an enzyme profile that matched only 10% of the male population. The prime suspect, with the right type of blood and enzyme, was a local 17-year old kitchen porter, Richard Buckland. Under intense questioning, he admitted killing Dawn but denied the murder of Lynda.

In nearby Leicester University, Alec Jeffreys was developing techniques for DNA (deoxyribonucleic acid) profiling. Using this new technique, Jeffreys compared semen samples from both murders and conclusively proved that both girls were indeed raped and killed by the same man. Then he compared the semen samples to a blood sample from Buckland and there was no match. Despite his confession, Robert Buckland had become the first person to have his innocence established by DNA fingerprinting, as it also came to be known.

However, this left the problem of a double-murderer still at large. Therefore, Leicester Police and the Forensic Science Service (FSS) undertook a project where 5,000 local men were asked to submit blood or saliva samples. This took six months and no matches were found.

Then a local man was heard bragging that he had been paid £200 for providing a sample on behalf of his friend, Colin Pitchfork. On 17th September, Pitchfork was arrested and a sample from him matched that of the killer. He was to become the first criminal to be convicted for murder on DNA fingerprinting evidence and the first to be caught using mass screening. On 22nd January 1988, he was sentenced to life imprisonment, with a recommendation that he served a minimum of thirty years.

(In April 2009, he appealed for early release. He had used his time in prison well, achieving a high standard of education to degree level. He had also made himself a specialist in the transcription of printed music into Braille, a rare and intensely specialised skill and his work is used throughout the UK and abroad. In view of his "exceptional progress while in prison", his sentence was reduced by two years and he is now eligible for release in 2015, although it remains to be seen if his desire for freedom comes to pass.)

The first American to be convicted using DNA techniques, was a Florida rapist, Tommy Lee Andrews. He was convicted on 6th November 1987 and sentenced to 22 years in prison.

The first American to be sentenced to death through DNA testing was Timothy Wilson Spencer, also known as *The South Side Strangler.* In a series of trials between 1988 and 1989, he was convicted of raping and murdering five women and executed on 27th April 1994. In a bizarre twist, similar to that of Richard Buckland, a certain David Vasquez had been convicted of one of Spencer's murders. He had served five years of a 35-year sentence before becoming the first American to be exonerated based on DNA evidence.

I do not think any of us who lived in Southern England will forget the trauma of the night of 15/16th October 1987. By the time most people had gone to bed on Thursday 15th October, exceptionally strong winds had not even been mentioned in TV or radio weather broadcasts. However, as soon as Bryan and I had retired, the wind got up. We lay there listening to the elements rattling the tiles on the roof and blowing the dustbins over. Bryan got up and moved the car from the drive onto the grass, well away from the house, and then tried to secure everything that could move. Tiles were flying off the neighbours' roofs and crashing onto the concrete; fence panels were down and rubbish from the overturned dustbins was flying through the air. Then he came back to bed and we lay there listening to all the bangs and crashes as the wind became stronger and stronger, thinking that at any moment our roof would disappear.

At about 3am, we heard an almighty bang and got up to find the garden wall had crashed through our back-door. Broken bricks, shattered glass and the back-gate were now in our kitchen! I have never been so relieved to have a man in the house! And I will never forget the noise of the wind as it screamed through our broken back-door. It sounded like an express-train roaring through the kitchen. Luckily, Bryan had a piece of plywood in the shed that he could use to make temporary repairs to the door but there was nothing else we could do until daylight.

Hurricane-force winds and torrential rain battered the south coast from Dorset to Kent that night, leaving a trail of devastation in their wake. Roofs were blown off, walls were blown down, caravan parks were flattened, Shanklin Pier on the Isle of Wight was reduced to driftwood, yachts and boatyards were severely damaged and a *Sealink* ferry was blown aground. 15million trees were lost, hundreds of roads and railway lines were blocked. It was utter chaos but would have been so much worse if the storm had not come at night.

When dawn came, the wind had ceased. All the neighbours were out in the street surveying the damage and we began the massive clear-up. As soon as practical I 'phoned Mum.

"Did you have any damage from the storm last night?" I asked.

"Storm? What storm?" she replied.

They had slept through it all! I told her to check the house and ring me back. The greenhouse I had bought Dad for his eightieth birthday had been demolished and the felt from the shed-roof had been ripped off but otherwise all was well. I told her we would be over later and meanwhile to leave the clearing-up until we got there.

Later that day we went out taking photographs of fallen trees, roofless houses and flats, crushed cars and a demolished greenhouse. That weekend we would see a whole wood where the trees were literally cut in half, as if some giant had walked through snapping them off like matchsticks. Winds had been recorded at 110mph in the Channel Islands and at 94mph in London but officially the gusts, although hurricane-force in strength, were not sufficiently widespread to be called a "hurricane", so it is known only as "The Great Storm". (The last "storm" of a similar magnitude was in 1703.) It had cost a total of eighteen lives and an estimated £1billion in repairs and clean-up costs. Hundreds of people were injured and hundreds of thousands of homes were without power for more than 24 hours.

Naturally I made a claim on our house insurance for the damage we had incurred, the one and only time we have made a claim. As instructed, we obtained estimates to re-build the wall, ranging between £5,000 and £8,000, but the insurance company refused to pay as much as this and offered £2,000. We accepted and Bryan decided he would do the repairs himself.

A few days after our "Great Storm", stock markets around the world crashed, shedding a huge value in a very short time. It began in Hong Kong on Monday 19th October, spread west through international time zones to Europe and then to America. Debate as to the cause of the crash still continues, many years after the event, with no firm conclusions reached. This "*Black Monday*" marked the largest one-day percentage decline in stock market history, but taken over the whole calendar year of 1987, in retrospect, does not seem so bad. For example, the *Dow Jones Industrial Average* figure opened in January at 1897 points and was very close to the December closing figure of 1939 points. It was an August high of 2722 points that made the crash seem so much worse and this figure would not be achieved again until almost two years later.

18th November 1987 was the date of the fatal fire at Kings Cross underground station in London, which killed 31 people. The fire was found to have started in the pre-WW2 (Second World War) wooden escalator. The running-track had not been cleaned since its installation in 1940 and it was covered in grease, fluff and flume and miscellaneous debris. Although smoking was banned, the fire probably started when a commuter discarded a burning match and it fell down the side of the escalator onto the track.

But fire investigators wanted to know why the fire had spread so quickly. For the first time in fire investigation, a computer simulation of the station, including the escalator and the booking hall, was made. The results showed that the fire was depicted as burning horizontally to the 30° slope of the escalator. This was thought to be impossible and it was believed the programming was faulty, so a scale replica was made on farmland, with the same result.

It was found that the 30° angle was crucial to the severity of the incident and that the large number of casualties was an indirect consequence of a combustion phenomenon that was later named "the trench effect". This phenomenon was completely unknown prior to the fire and thus a new phrase would be entered in fire safety manuals.

As a result of the fire, all wooden escalators on London's underground stations were replaced with metal ones and smoking was banned throughout the entire system. As well as the 31 people who died, 60 received injuries ranging from severe burns to smoke inhalation. One of the fatalities was not identified until 22nd January 2004 when DNA evidence proved he was 73year-old Alexander Fallon, from Falkirk in Scotland. Six firefighters were awarded "Certificates of Commendation" for their actions at the fire, including one posthumously to Station Officer Colin Townsley who had died trying to help a woman with breathing difficulties. A memorial plaque was unveiled at St Pancras Church by Diana, Princess of Wales, and another was erected at Kings Cross Station.

Christmas 1987 was approaching and Mac despaired of ever selling the shop. He was planning to fly to America for the festive season, courtesy of a courier service (they pay your fare and you deliver their package) and he wanted so much to be able to take news of a sale with him. Then a Chinese Restaurant offered a price and he accepted. He had to return in the New Year to the UK to finalise the arrangements, settle his accounts and finish packing but at least 1988 was looking more hopeful.

CHAPTER FORTY-THREE

A Leap of Faith
(1988)

Having returned to the UK after spending the New Year of 1988 with his family in America, Mac was not expecting to leave the UK shores again until he emigrated. However, in February he received a 'phone call from his wife's employer to say Sheila had been admitted to hospital and was to undergo emergency surgery for a burst appendix. He was horrified to learn that Sheila was within one day of death from peritonitis! To her credit, Elizabeth had already arranged for Mac to fly to America and, by the time he got there, the surgery had been done, just in the nick of time. He stayed a couple of weeks while Sheila convalesced and then returned to Southampton to complete his packing.

There was much excitement in the Oakley household as the 28th March 1988 approached for Mum, Dad and I were flying to Boston for a holiday with Sheila, Russ and Vernon at their new home in historic Newport, Rhode Island, and, while we were away, Uncle Tom was going on his own holiday, to his son and daughter-in-law in Surrey.

At this time, both our parents were reasonably physically fit, considering their ages, now 86 and 82 years. Mum was still very mentally alert but Dad's short-term memory was almost non-existent. He was a sweet, gentle, old man who was just very forgetful but this made it quite nerve-racking to travel with him because if he wandered off, or we became separated, we could not be sure if he would know how to get back to us. Mum and I kept a very close eye on him but neither of them would allow me to ask for any "special favours", like priority boarding, insisting that they could manage.

On landing at Boston, we joined a long queue at Immigration Control and when we reached the desk, the officer scrutinised our passports, noted the ages of Mum and Dad and then promptly told me off for allowing them to wait in line and not asking for priority attention for them! Some days you just cannot please everybody!

Sheila had arranged for a friend to pick us up at the airport and she drove us to the *Carpenter* apartment, part of a large house in a tree-lined street, full of similar properties. It had the same house number as my parents' home, which seemed such a good omen. As we pulled up, we were amused to see a "Union Flag" flying from a flagpole attached to the building. Mac had put it there on his last visit. We were very impressed with their new home: a large lounge, dining area and kitchen, all open-plan, and four bedrooms. In the huge basement was a family-size washing-machine, a dryer of similar proportions and a proper utility area with a large double-sink.

Sheila said we could use her car while she was at work; the apartment was not far from Newport town centre but Mum and Dad would not be able to walk too far, especially as the house was on a small incline. Naturally we spent as much time as possible with the family, seeing where Sheila worked, where the boys went to school, the hospital where she had had her operation, meeting her new friends and so on, but we also toured the area enjoying the "touristy" sights, such as travelling down the ten miles of *Ocean Drive*, with its rugged views of the Atlantic Ocean on one side and glimpses of the regal estates of society's millionaires on the other.

It was in the 1750's that wealthy and prominent people started to come from the south to spend summers at Newport, developing the town as a centre of society and culture and making Newport America's first summer resort. But it was at the turn of the last century that the social elite of American society built spectacular summer residences in Newport, the most famous being *"The Breakers"*, constructed in 1895 for Cornelius Vanderbilt. *Bellevue Avenue* is also home to many of these mansions and here they back onto *Ocean Walk,* a footpath about two miles in length that meanders along the top of the cliff. Mum, Sheila and I walked along this one Sunday morning, enjoying the sound and sight of the waves and the ocean, the bird life, flora and fauna and, of course, the back view of the mansions and the huge expanse of lawn and parkland between us and them. Most of the mansions are now historical "white elephants" and the only people traipsing through the ballrooms and the bedrooms are the summer tourists, duly impressed, no doubt, at the sheer opulence of these extravagant symbols of a bygone age.

Newport is the main town on Aquidneck Island, situated about a mile offshore from mainland America, in the middle of Narragansett Bay, and nowadays linked to it by a bridge. It was originally the home of the Aquidneck tribe of Native Americans but was settled by Europeans in 1639, a small group of people who left neighbouring Massachusetts in search of religious freedom. Like many other European settlers, they would not have survived had it not been for the indigenous tribes who showed them what foods to eat and how to survive the bitter winters.

With its sheltered harbour in Narragansett Bay, Newport quickly became famous for its seafarers and pirates. Twenty-six of the latter were hanged here in 1723 but, over the centuries, many different kinds of seafarer have evolved; Newport was famous for hosting the classic *America's Cup* for many years and is home to the *Naval and Education Centre* and a large naval base. It has many wharves, boatyards and marinas and might justly be called the sailing capital of America.

The oldest surviving house, of more modest proportions than the mansions, was built in 1675 and the *White Horse Tavern* on *Marlborough Street*, has been selling alcoholic beverages since 1687, the oldest continuously-operated tavern in the country. Newport also has the oldest synagogue still standing in the US, dedicated in 1763, and one of the oldest Episcopal churches in continuous use, *Trinity Church* dating back to 1726 and whose graceful spire dominates the Newport skyline. The town prides itself on its history and new buildings have to be in keeping with its past. No skyscrapers here!

The symbol of Newport hospitality is a pineapple and many of the older houses feature a stone replica of the fruit. It dates back to when colonial sailing captains brought home pineapples from their voyages and placed them outside their homes as a sign that neighbours and friends were welcome to call. Another feature on some of the houses are so-called *widows' walks*. These are balconies, built at the top of the house and facing out to sea, enabling the wives of mariners to walk along the vantage points, watching and waiting for their husbands' safe return.

The commercial centre of Newport is situated on the cobbled *Thames Street* (pronounced *Thaymes* with a lisping "*th*" as in "*that*"!) Nowadays the establishments here are mostly upmarket craft shops, and downmarket souvenir outlets, for the thousands of tourists who visit Newport every summer for the sailing, to view the mansions, or just to enjoy a step back into history. As in every American town or city, the real shopping is done in out-of-town shopping malls and one day we set off across *Newport Bridge* to visit one of the biggest locally, the Warwick Mall.

When I mentioned that Mum, Dad and I were going to visit the Mall, Russell and his friend said they would come with us. Almost as soon as we got there Dad said he wanted to use the "bathroom", as the Americans euphemistically call the toilet facilities! I asked Russell to take him while Mum and I waited in the car. The boys soon wandered back, minus Dad. I could not believe they had returned without him! I screamed at them, "How could you be so stupid? You know he can't remember things!" Mum stayed in the car while we raced back into the Mall. There was no sign of him. I went back to the car and told Mum to stay put in case he came back, meanwhile the boys and I would go to look for him.

The boys soon gave up the search and eventually Russell's friend started to become anxious that he should be home by now.

"Tough!" I hissed. "'Phone your mother and explain why you're not!"

I searched the Mall on every level. I went in every store and asked them to put out a tannoy-call for him but Dad was so deaf, I could not be sure he would hear it, let alone understand the instructions. I contacted security and they started looking as well. I think it was worse for Mum.

She was just standing by the car, watching out for him and becoming more worried as every minute ticked by. At least I was doing something, even if I was like a headless chicken, racing off in all directions. I looked at the four-lane highway running alongside the Mall and had visions of him trying to walk home. Where was "home"? I doubted if he could even remember we were in America, let alone the town or address where Sheila lived. He had no money and nothing in his wallet to say who he was or where he was staying.

Panic, guilt, anger and sheer terror does not even describe how I felt. I was frantic with worry. In and out the Mall I kept going until I finally realised there was a small exit, tucked away in a hidden alcove, that in my panic and "headless chicken" routine, I had not spotted before. It led into another huge car-park, on the other side of the building, that I had not realised even existed. And then I thought I saw him. Right over the other side of this car-park, about as far away from the building as a person could get, was a small dot leaning against a car. I ran towards it and the dot gradually got bigger and bigger and metamorphosised into my beloved parent. The relief was indescribable! He had been missing for nearly two hours.

"Oh, Dad! Thank God! Are you all right?"

"Well I would be if I'd had my smokes!" he grumbled.

"Weren't you worried?" I asked, as we walked slowly back to the car.

"No, duck!" he retorted, "I knew you'd find me eventually and that the best thing to do was to stay put. I just wish I'd had my tobacco!"

"Never mind! We'll soon be back to the car. Do you know where you are, Dad?"

"I can't remember," he replied pensively. "Is it Scotland?"

"No, Dad. We're in America. We've come to see Sheila and the boys, haven't we?"

"America!" he chuckled. "Fancy that! We're in America!"

And he remembered that fact for about two minutes and then forgot it again. But ask him about pruning roses, the names of plants or people from the past and he was fine. It was just with recent events that he had problems.

As forgetful and illogical as he had become, like his father before him when he fell into the quarry-pit, he knew enough to stay in one place. I broke a golden rule and allowed him to puff away merrily in the car. And I apologised profusely to the boys for shouting at them. It was my fault, not theirs. At the very least I should have reminded them that they needed to play nursemaid and had I used a bit more rational thought, and not utter desperation, I might have found Dad sooner. As soon as we got home, I put his name, Sheila's address, telephone contact numbers and a few dollars into his wallet. As long as I live, I do not think I will ever forget that dreadful moment when we lost him, or the sheer joy and relief I felt when I saw him standing by that car.

We were in America for three weeks, and we had had a lovely time, but just a couple of days before we were due to fly home, Mum had a serious bout of diarrhoea. She had suffered episodes of this in the past but it usually disappeared within twenty-four hours. This bout seemed here to stay and poor old Mum dreaded having to return home with the problem. So we went to see Sheila's doctor who prescribed some tablets for her with the advice that if it happened again, she should see her own doctor when she returned to the UK. The tablets did the trick and we had an uneventful journey home. Once we got back it was great to be able to put real pictures to scenes that, before our trip, we had only been able to imagine. I do not suppose Dad was able to recall anything about the holiday, but it was one of the highlights of Mum's twilight years and she remembered it for the rest of her days.

Soon after we returned home, Mac travelled to the US; this time it was to stay. He was 68 years old now and was therefore able to "export" his retirement pension, which helped to augment the family finances. But he also found little cash-in-hand/under-the-table jobs to do, such as car deliveries and playing *Father Christmas* at a local *"7-Eleven"* convenience store. The boys made their own contribution as well. Now aged 15 and 14 years, they soon obtained paper-rounds, throwing the plastic-enclosed papers up the drives or paths in true American fashion, or placing the package into the mail-box. No letter-boxes in American front-doors; all post is delivered into some kind of metal box near the pavement, or perhaps I should say "sidewalk". They loved every minute of their new life and the family were happier, and more financially solvent, than they had been for many a long year.

It was not long before Mac fell in love with the basement of their new home, seeing it as a vacant void just waiting to be filled! The apartment was furnished but they needed things like book-cases, coffee-tables and chests of drawers. Mac discovered the *Salvation Army's* second-hand furniture store, run like our charity shops. It was a treasure trove for him and there he found many excellent bargains, including a full-size billiard-table complete with balls and cues. That soon found its way into the basement, but sadly not while we were there or Dad might have enjoyed a game or two!

Mac had been a freemason in the UK and now found a new lodge to join. He discovered American freemasonry is not the secret society that it tends to be in the UK. There they join the 'masons openly and even march publicly in parades on such occasions as "St Patrick's Day".

Every week since Sheila had gone to the US, Mum had religiously written an air-mail letter to her but she had seldom received a written reply, for my sister will be the first to admit she is not the best correspondent in the world, preferring to use the 'phone in these pre-email days. However as soon as Mac got there, he and Mum wrote to each other every single week. He would read Mum's letters out to the family and after Mum had read his to Dad, she passed them to me. I can see her now, sitting at the dining-room table, pen poised and the page of blue lying naked before her, lamenting, "What can I say this week?" But she always managed to fill the air-mail letter in her neat hand-writing and it would be the kind of missive you looked forward to receiving. She was actually a fantastic writer.

On 3rd July 1988, an American naval warship, the *USS Vincennes*, was patrolling in the Persian Gulf. The Iran-Iraq War was still ongoing and US warships had been escorting Kuwaiti tankers in and out of the Gulf as part of its undertaking to keep the Straits of Hormuz open, although this increased military presence antagonised Iran. On 3rd July the Iranians shot at a US helicopter. The *Vincennes* then engaged in a gun-battle with three Iranian gunboats. Less than an hour later, the crew from the *Vincennes* thought they were about to come under attack from an Iranian F14 jet-fighter. They warned the 'plane to keep away but when it did not, they fired two surface-to-air missiles, at least one of which hit the 'plane. But it was not an F14; it was an Iranian passenger-jet making a routine flight from Bandar Abbas in Iran to Dubai in the United Arab Emirates. There were nearly 300 passengers and crew on board, mostly Iranians on their way to Mecca. There were no survivors and the victims included 66 children and 38 foreign nationals.

Iran reacted with outrage, accusing the US of a "barbaric massacre" and vowing to "avenge the blood of our martyrs". It took four years for America to admit officially that the *USS Vincennes* was in Iranian waters when the skirmish with the gunboats took place. They have never admitted responsibility or apologised for the tragedy but in February 1996 the US agreed to pay Iran $61.8m in compensation for the 248 Iranians killed, plus the cost of the aircraft and legal expenses. It had already paid $40m to the other countries whose nationals had been killed.

If we discount all the unpaid hours Bryan had spent re-building our wall after "The Great Storm" of the previous year, you could argue that we had made a "profit" from our insurance claim. We decided to spend this "profit" on a villa holiday in Cala D'Or, Mallorca and this was to be the first of many villa and apartment holidays we would enjoy in Spain, and marked the end of our camper-van holidays in the UK. Of course this one was special, not only because it was the first, but it was all the more enjoyable knowing the insurance company had paid for it!

Thanks to Elizabeth offering to pay for their flights as a Christmas bonus for Sheila and a gift for the family, in the early hours of the 21st

December 1988, Sheila, Mac and their sons arrived at Gatwick Airport to spend Christmas and New Year with our parents. As well as presents, they came loaded with live lobsters that a fisherman friend of theirs had given to them as gifts for relatives and they distributed some of them to various family members on their way to our parents' home.

Mum and Dad were so excited at the prospect of having the family with them for the festive season but Sheila was determined to make it a rest for Mum as much as possible by issuing strict instructions that she and Mac would do all the shopping and cooking, not only when they arrived, but throughout their stay. When they got there, they added a tree to their shopping list, which the boys decorated. It was going to be so alien for Mum to sit down in her own sitting-room while other people waited on her! Meanwhile Uncle Tom was off again to spend his Christmas with his son and family in Surrey.

The next morning the Carpenter family awoke to the devastating news that a *Pan Am* flight had exploded over Lockerbie, in Scotland, the day before. At that stage they were too shocked to take-in whether it was an incoming or outgoing flight and the thought that they had flown transatlantic on the very same day, filled them all with a mixture of relief, terror, horror and extreme thankfulness. As the terrible news unfolded, it became apparent that *Pan Am Flight 103* was en route from London's Heathrow Airport to New York and that the explosion had occurred at approximately 7pm the previous evening. There were no survivors among the 259 people on board and it was later disclosed that another eleven people had been killed on the ground.

That Christmas the news media was full of the tragedy. The residents of Lockerbie would report that they had witnessed the sky lighting up and had heard a large deafening roar. Wreckage was strewn over 50 square miles with pieces of the 'plane and body parts landing in fields and gardens, on fences and on roofs. Fuel from the 'plane was already on fire before hitting the ground, turning the houses and fields below into an inferno. Twenty-one of Lockerbie's houses were completely destroyed, killing the residents inside.

179 of the 259 people on board were Americans; the rest were from twenty other countries. Immediately questions were raised as to whether this was in retaliation for the US bombing raid on Libya in 1986, or for the Iranian passenger-jet that the Americans had shot down only months before. Talk of retaliation was on everyone's lips, but did America have any more right to retaliate than the Arabs apparently had? There was little doubt that the shooting down of the Iranian 'plane caused as much horror and sorrow in that country as the explosion of *Flight 103* did in America and Britain.

Talk of retaliation gradually turned instead to investigation, and to bringing the perpetrators to justice. 15,000 people were interviewed: 18,000 pieces of evidence were examined: research was conducted in over forty countries. Eventually it was determined that the bomb had been made out of *Semtex* and hidden in a radio-cassette player, which in turn was placed in a suitcase. It was activated by a timing device. A tee-shirt was discovered in a forest near Lockerbie with pieces of the timer in it. Through these scraps of evidence investigators eventually felt confident that they knew who had bombed *Flight 103* but, by this time, the suspect bombers had fled to Libya and for many years Colonel Gadaffi refused to extradite them. Eventually relations between Libya and the West improved and, subject to certain conditions being met, the men were handed over to be tried for the bombing. It had taken nearly two decades but, on 31st January 2001, Mohmed al-Megrahi was found guilty of the bombing and sentenced to life imprisonment. Al Amin Khalifa Fhimah was acquitted.

(On 20th August 2009, al-Megrahi was released from prison by the Scottish government on compassionate grounds. He was said to be suffering from terminal prostate cancer and only had months to live. To date he is still alive but undergoing extensive chemotherapy treatment. He has always denied that he was involved in the Lockerbie bombing and has vowed to clear his name before he dies.)

It was a very nervous Carpenter family who returned to America after their 1988/89 Christmas and New Year holiday, and a very relieved Oakley clan who learned of their safe arrival.

CHAPTER FORTY-FOUR

Love Endures
(1989-1990)

On 16th January 1989, the second of Mum's sisters-in-law passed away: Dorie, widow of her brother Les. Dorie had lived in Norfolk for many years and therefore they had not seen her very often, but Mum was particularly fond of her and was very saddened at her death. All the more so because she did not feel we could travel all that way to attend her funeral and pay our last respects.

On 24th March 1989, a supertanker, the *Exxon Valdez*, left the Valdez oil terminal in Alaska, bound for Long Beach, California. The outbound shipping lane was covered with icebergs, so permission was given to sail out via the inbound lane. Just three hours into her journey, she struck Bligh Reef and spilt 10.8 million gallons of oil into Prince William Sound. It was not the largest oil spill in the world but it was considered to be one of the worst environmental disasters to occur at sea. The location was accessible only by boat and helicopter and severely taxed existing plans for a response.

What they did manage to achieve seemed to be fraught with difficulty. They tried dispersant but there was not enough wave action to mix the chemical with the oil in the water. A burning-explosion was relatively successful but had to be abandoned because of deteriorating weather conditions. Booms and skimmers were clogged by thick oil and kelp. High-pressure hot water cleaned the rocky coves but destroyed the microbial populations, such as plankton, bacteria and fungi, affecting the coastal marine food chain.

Nevertheless, the efforts eventually left little visual evidence of the event but thousands of gallons of oil still lodge in the sandy soil of the contaminated coastline. Thousands of animals died immediately including at least 250,000 sea birds, 1000 sea otters, 12 river otters, 300 harbour seals, 250 bald eagles and 22 Orcas, as well as the destruction of billions of salmon and herring eggs.

Even today, there are reduced numbers of various ocean animals, and sea otters and ducks show higher death rates from ingesting prey contaminated with oil and the ingestion of oil residues from grooming. There is still stunted growth in pink salmon.

Some scientists predict that some shoreline habitats will take many more years to recover, as will the economic effects from the loss of the public's perception of a no-longer pristine Prince William Sound. Of course, the livelihoods of the local indigenous people, who relied on the harvest from these previously unpolluted and prolific waters, were ruined; some of them would never recover.

Many recommendations were made after the oil spillage, including requiring two tugs to escort every loaded tanker sailing from Valdez through Prince William Sound. In addition, Congress has enacted legislation requiring all tankers operating in their waters to be double-hulled from 2015.

In 1994, the *Exxon* Company was sued and found to have been "reckless". They were ordered to pay $5.6billion in punitive damages. *Exxon* appealed, and appealed, and appealed. Eventually they offered $25million. It was refused. They have dragged their human victims through years of litigation with at least 6,000 plaintiffs having died awaiting compensation. To date the issue is still not resolved and *Exxon* have not even double-hulled their tankers working in the area.

Another 1989 event, still unresolved twenty years later, is the "Hillsborough Disaster", where 96 Liverpool fans were crushed to death at the Sheffield Wednesday Football Club Stadium. It was not the only tragedy to occur at a football venue in the 20th century but it was the deadliest stadium-related disaster in British history and one of the worst in international football.

The occasion was an FA (Football Association) Cup semi-final between Liverpool and Nottingham Forest. The date was 15th April 1989 and the crush occurred when thousands of Liverpool fans were inadvertently allowed entry to an already full stand. Improved security measures had recently been introduced to keep rival fans apart, and to keep hooligans off the pitch, and these contributed to the tragedy, for as the human stampede poured in, those fans already there were pushed forward and crushed against the new, high, wire-topped safety-fences.

The match was stopped as soon as the disaster became apparent but BBC television cameras carried on filming the on-going tragedy, resulting in a huge emotional impact on the general population. Thus, we were all horrified to witness Liverpool fans desperately trying to climb over the fences, children being thrown over them, bodies laid out on the pitch and members of the public, club officials and police officers frantically trying to give first aid to the injured.

Apart from the 96 deaths, 766 people were hurt, 300 of them requiring hospital treatment. Some of the survivors never fully recovered from their wounds nor the psychological damage.

A subsequent report declared that bad policing was the major reason for the disaster but it was 2002 before the two most senior officers were put on trial. One was acquitted and charges against the other were dropped when the jury could not agree on a verdict. Relatives of the victims are still demanding to be allowed to see the full report on the tragedy, which has never been fully explained.

New safety measures were introduced as a result of the "Hillsborough Disaster"; fences in front of fans were removed and the main stadiums were converted to become all-seated. Prior to the tragedy, it was traditional for most of the fans to be standing. Before this event, the worst sporting disaster of a similar nature in UK history was in 1971 when 66 fans were crushed to death at the Ibrox Stadium in Glasgow.

In May 1989, the Russian leader, Mikhail Gorbachev, visited China. This encouraged thousands of students to stage a peaceful protest in Tiananmen Square, situated in the Chinese capital of Peking, now more commonly known as Beijing. They were seeking similar democratic reforms to those that had been granted to the Russian people. They occupied the Square for seven weeks, refusing to leave until their demands were met. As the weeks passed, millions of people from all walks of life joined in, angered by the widespread corruption of the communist system. It was the greatest challenge to the communist state since the 1949 revolution and several attempts to persuade the protestors to leave peacefully failed.

Suddenly, late on 3rd June, tanks rumbled into the Square from several directions, randomly firing at the protestors. The ferocity of the attack brought condemnation from around the world. It is thought that as many as 4000 people were killed, although the precise number will never be known. The cry for democratic reform had been brutally silenced.

In August 1989, I took my Guide Company on my last Girl Guide camp and then resigned from the Movement. I felt I needed to spend as much spare time as I had helping my parents who were becoming more and more dependent on us. Bryan was now doing all their gardening and house repairs, and helping me with their decorating, while I was doing the shopping and the running around for them. Mum had stopped going to her clubs and had resigned from the church cleaning rota.

She was concerned now about leaving Dad on his own, for on one occasion he had answered a knock on the door, unbeknown to her, and invited the caller into the house. Fortunately she heard voices in the front room and went in to find Dad blithely showing a so-called antique-dealer (or "knocker" as they are more commonly called) all their bits of china and such like. Luckily, the man seemed genuine and polite but so many are not. Another time she answered the door to find two men telling her that two of her roofing-slates had slipped and enquiring whether she wanted them re-secured. She was not so easily conned but Dad could well have been.

In 1989 Bryan and I went to Mallorca again and, while we were there, we were astounded when a delivery-van pulled up at our out-of-the-way, rented villa and presented us with a huge bouquet. It was from Mum and Dad to celebrate our twentieth wedding anniversary. Earlier that morning we had opened our cards and our "china" gift from them, a small white vase with two swans, necks entwined, embossed on the surface. Most people are aware that major anniversaries are given special names, silver for 25 years, gold for 50, diamond for 60, for example, but in fact every anniversary from one to twenty is also associated with a different product from paper to copper, crystal to linen. On every anniversary, Mum had given us an appropriate gift: "flowers" for our fourth: carved "wooden" elephants for our fifth: "lace" tablemats, crocheted by her friend Mrs Reeves, for our thirteenth, and so on. Naturally, she did the same for my sister's wedding anniversaries.

On 9th November 1989, the East German Government announced that visits to West Berlin and West Germany would be permitted. Crowds of East Germans climbed onto, and over, the dreaded *Berlin Wall,* which had kept the city divided for so long. They were met by euphoric West Germans on the other side. Over the next few weeks, chunks of concrete souvenirs were chipped away from the *Wall.* Its days as a symbol of communist oppression were numbered.

Eventually bulldozers were brought in and the *Wall* was reduced to a pile of rubble. The fall of the *Berlin Wall* paved the way for Germany's re-unification, which was finally concluded on 3rd October 1990.

As 1990 and a new decade dawned, Dad was becoming even more forgetful and would repeat the same question over and over again. Mum commented that his most common enquiry was, "Is our Maureen coming over today?" Mum would respond, only to have to answer it again a few minutes later. Luckily, she had the patience of Job but even she was sorely tested, having to cope with him every day, all day. She never complained and dreamed up a coping strategy. It was to count up to ten, although she rarely went above five! One annoyance that always produced a count, was handing him a cup of tea. Without fail, Dad would immediately take a sip and say,"Cor blimey! That's 'ot, Anne!"
"One ..... Two .... Three ..... Four ......," Mum would respond. If we were there, it was amusing to watch, and even Mum was able to see the funny side. Poor old Dad would just sit in his armchair, with a confused look on his face, wondering what we were laughing at.
"It's you!" Mum would tell him. "Of course it's hot and you say the same thing every time!"
"Do I, duck?" he would chuckle in reply.
If he was not asking a question, or commenting on his tea, he would make the same statement over and over again, his favourite being, "Best day's work we ever did, wasn't it, Anne? Adopting our girls."
It was not long before he started to fall and could not get up. Mum did not know what to do except to 'phone for an ambulance. After about

three call-outs, the ambulance staff remonstrated with her. They told her a call-out of this nature was not part of their duties and that it was an abuse of the emergency system. Mum was mortified; a person less likely to abuse anything would be hard to find. So, if he fell over, he had to stay there until we could arrive or until a very kind neighbour could assist in getting him to his feet again.

Then Dad started to wake up about 6am and insist he had to get to work, unbelievably for his job as a milkman! Several times he managed to get out of the bungalow without Mum noticing. Fortunately, each time, a neighbour spotted him walking up the road in his pyjamas and brought him home. But Mum was becoming more and more exhausted with stress and worry. Something had to give.

On 2nd August 1990, Iraq invaded Kuwait, and thus the United States, the United Kingdom and Canada prepared for war. In the UK, over the coming months, all reserve forces were called up and hospitals were told to free-up surgical wards to cope with the expected casualties. As forgetful as he had become, Dad knew he had been on the reserve-list and thus he too expected to be called up any day! I know the country was desperate, but not that desperate, bless him!

27th September 1990 was Mum and Dad's Diamond Wedding anniversary; they had achieved sixty years of wedded bliss. Dad chuckled to think no less a personage than the Queen had remembered to send a telegram (!!) and he was thrilled with the card from Sheila, Mac and the boys. It had flashing coloured lights on the outside and played the anniversary waltz when he opened it up. I held it close to his ear so he could hear the tune and remember so well his lovely smile and cheeky chuckle, all recorded on a camcorder I had hired for the occasion in order that Sheila and family could share this special day. In the ten years since our parents' "Golden Anniversary", camcorders had become widely available but they were the sort where a cassette-tape had to be inserted. We were still some years away from digital camcorders and cameras. Mum was delighted with the cards too, of course, but Dad's pleasure was so innocently childlike that it just added something extra to the day.

Our card included a poem I had written for them, which was about finding a diamond, pulverising in into dust and the dust blowing into every crack. I likened it to their love which had penetrated every nook and cranny of our lives and it ended *"For love endures when diamonds blow away."*

I had organised a small tea party in the afternoon, with the inevitable, badly-iced fruit cake, this time in the shape of a diamond. Uncle Tom was there, his son, Derek, and his wife, Barbara: Auntie Dorie's daughter, Peggy, and her husband, Cyril (at this time they were living in Sussex): Mum's brother, Dick, and his wife, Ethel, and their son, Keith, and his wife, Rosemary: and Harry (a very good neighbour and friend who lived opposite). Lesley, the dear friend of mine who lived in Worthing, transported Auntie Blanche (again!) and the party was complete.

Eleven days after their anniversary was Dad's 89th birthday and, soon after that, Mum approached their GP about Dad's falls. Dr Owen had treated the family for years and realised Mum was exhausted. He arranged for Dad to go into Littlehampton Hospital for "observation" but in truth I think it was to give Mum a well-earned rest.

The hospital soon got fed up with Dad! They said he was "disruptive", refusing to stay in his bed. They provided one with bars at the side but he crawled out at the bottom! They managed to suffer him for two weeks and then sent him home. Dr Owen called to see Mum and gently suggested that Dad should go into care. She reluctantly agreed and a few days later two social workers visited to make the necessary arrangements.

It was decided that Dad would go to a council-run "Unit" for the *Elderly Mentally Infirm*, in Worthing. As heartbreaking as it was, we knew we had no choice; Dad could no longer be cared for at home. However, when Dad heard the word "Unit", he thought he was being re-called to his regiment to fight in the expected "Gulf War"! Thus, when the time came for him to leave his wife of sixty years, and his home of fifty-eight and a half years, he went off quite happily. It was Mum and I who were left bereft.

Soon after Dad's departure, I took Mum to see Dr Owen on her own account. The episodes of diarrhoea were becoming more frequent, more than she had even admitted to me, and she had begun to think something was amiss. The GP arranged for her to see a specialist who said she needed an urgent bowel operation. There was a tumour that needed to be removed and it was arranged to carry out the operation on Christmas Eve.

I 'phoned Dr Owen. I wanted to know if Mum had cancer. He replied that the specialist thought the tumour was malignant but he himself was not convinced because blood tests revealed that Mum was not making any cancer antibodies. He said we would not know who was right until after the operation.

Obviously Mum needed complete rest before undergoing this major surgery so I wrote to Uncle Tom's son, Derek, and explained that Mum had to go into hospital. I asked if they were able to make alternative arrangements for Uncle Tom until Mum was on her feet again. Immediately Derek and Barbara came down and took Uncle Tom to live with them in Surrey, at least until we knew what was happening.

By this time, it was late November and several things happened more or less simultaneously. All was not going well in America. Elizabeth had sold *Endeavour* and when the boat sailed off into the wide blue yonder, Sheila's job would go with it. Elizabeth offered to re-employ her in another capacity but this meant having to apply for a new work permit (the so-called *Green Card*) which would not necessarily be forthcoming and, even if it was, it could take months to organise. It looked as if they might all have to return to the UK while the problem was resolved. None of them wanted to do this and they lived in dread that this would come to pass.

Dad had settled in well at the *"East Tyne EMI Unit"*, although Mum could not face going to see him there. She was just about coping with her own problems and to have to visit him at the "Unit" was more than she could bear. Then suddenly I had a 'phone call from the Unit to say Dad had been admitted to Worthing Hospital. He had a severe attack of jaundice and he was not responding to treatment. They thought it might be hepatitis and warned us that we should expect the worst. Mum and I sat down and discussed Dad's funeral arrangements.

A few days later, I had a 'phone call from one of Mum's neighbours to say that Mum had been taken ill and the doctor had been called. I raced over to Littlehampton to find Mum had been diagnosed with fluid around her heart. She had been prescribed some tablets and bed-rest. Not only was she exhausted but also she was terrified. The pain had been so bad in her chest that she thought she was going to die.

"Maureen", she whispered, "I'm so frightened of dying! I'm ashamed to admit it but I am!"

How to comfort someone you love who is frightened to die? Mum was more "Christian" in her ways than almost anyone else I had ever known. A true saint, although she would hate to hear me say it! (Or write it, in this instance!) Her fear of dying was something I had not expected, but why not?

So I held her in my arms and said, "It's OK to be frightened, Mum. We're all frightened to die." I thought for a minute for something else to say, and then murmured, "Mum, I don't know where this quote comes from but I wrote it down years ago and I hang onto it when the going gets tough. Perhaps it will help you. It's *"Be not afraid, for I go before you always"*. That's the bit I like best but it actually continues with, *"Come. Follow me, and I will give you rest."* Just keep saying it and believe it, for I do believe it to be true. And when it IS time for you to go, know that you will never be far from me. You'll sit on my shoulder forever. I'll just have to turn my head and you'll be there. We'll NEVER be parted."

"Oh, Maureen," she cried, "You say the nicest things!"

"Well it's true! How about a nice cup of tea?"

I obtained compassionate leave from work and went to stay with her for the week. How strange it was to be sleeping in my old bed again! It no longer felt like our old bedroom for I thought of it now as the boys' room! With the tablets and the bed-rest, and possibly my company, Mum quickly recovered and, against the odds, Dad was making a slow but miraculous recovery too, proving the discussion on his funeral arrangements to have been rather premature! Eventually the hospital would determine that he had been allergic to a tranquilliser the Unit doctor had prescribed. He did not have hepatitis.

I already had a general "Power of Attorney" so that I could act on their behalf in all financial matters. Before she went into hospital, Mum suggested I invoke this and put their modest savings into my name. Then, if anything should happen to her, it would not be necessary to go to probate. They trusted me completely, not only to safeguard their assets, but to pass on my sister's share to her, when the time came. I asked Sheila if she was happy with this arrangement and she readily agreed.

Just before Christmas 1990, I drove a very nervous Mum to Worthing Hospital to have her dreaded operation. Dad was still there but she still could not summon up the resolve to see him. She was just about holding herself together; she said if she saw him, so frail and vulnerable, she would fall apart and so would he. So when I visited, I would drift between the two of them, seeing Mum first, then take Dad in a wheelchair for a coffee and a "stroll" around the corridors, then return him to his bed and go to see Mum again. Without fail, Dad would begin our conversations with, "Where's Mum?"
"She's not feeling too well today, Dad. She sends her love. I'll try to bring her next time."
"OK, duck."

Prior to her operation, Mum had to have the usual pre-op' checks and the nurse commented accusingly, "I can tell you're a smoker!"
"I've never smoked in my life," Mum indignantly replied. "But my husband's a heavy smoker."
"That's the answer then," the nurse responded, rather reluctantly acknowledging her erroneous assumption. "His smoking has obviously seriously affected your lungs."
Mum also had slight asthma, a condition that both my sister and I have developed in later years. Did our father's smoking habit affect all of us? Food for thought if you are a smoker and you read this!

Mum had her operation on Christmas Eve. She made a good recovery and Dr Owen was right; it was not cancer. I told her the good news on one of my early visits. It was the first time the "big-C" word had been mentioned between us. "Thank God," was all she said, but with great sincerity so I knew that this had been her greatest fear too. We only had one concern and that was that the hospital seemed to be rushing her recovery, trying to get her to eat before she felt ready for solid food. Of course all the hospitals in the UK were under pressure to empty the wards, for the hundreds of casualties they had been told to expect from the "Gulf War", although the efforts to remove the Iraqis from Kuwait had not yet even begun.

On one day of her convalescence, Mum told me the hospital chaplain had visited the ward and given Communion to the lady in the next bed. Screens had been placed around the patient to afford some privacy but Mum said she could hear every word and had mentally followed all the responses. I asked why she had not asked to join them.

"I didn't want to push myself on them," she responded.

"How about I get the chaplain to visit you then?"

"Oh, no! I wouldn't want to be a nuisance!"

Another day, I noticed her Christmas gift from the hospital's *League of Friends* was still lying unopened on her bedside table. The *League* was a charitable organisation, providing various comforts and facilities for patients and their families, such as a book service that toured all the wards, running a gift shop in the foyer, providing waiting rooms for families with comfortable armchairs, pictures on the walls and a television set. The *League* had also presented every patient with a small gift on Christmas Day

"Aren't you going to open your present?" I asked.

"No. I'll open it when I feel better."

On Friday 28th December 1990, I was preparing to go and visit Mum and Dad when our 'phone rang. It was Sheila to tell me that Mac had been admitted to the intensive-care-cardiac-unit at Newport Hospital, having suffered a heart attack. We could not believe it! What else could go wrong? Sheila was convinced the stress of possibly having to return to the UK, had been a major contributing factor. So far Mac was holding his own but the next few days would be critical. We made the decision not to tell Mum that Mac was ill; we had already decided not to tell her about the *Green Card* problem. Mum just needed to concentrate on getting better.

I visited Mum and Dad on Saturday and Sunday but told them I would not be in on Monday 31st December as I was working, and the roads might be busy with New Year revellers, but I would see them both on New Year's Day.........

CHAPTER FORTY-FIVE

Be Not Afraid

Early in the morning of 1st January 1991, Sheila 'phoned with some terrible news. Two minutes after midnight, USA Eastern time (5am GMT), Mac had suffered another massive heart attack and died. There was a very bright, full "blue" moon at the time and one of the last things he said to her was how beautiful it was. He was 72 years old but always so youthful in his outlook. Sheila was to be left a widow, at age 42 years, with her sons, aged 17 and 16, still at school.

I could not believe it! Mum and Dad were both in hospital in the UK; we had prepared ourselves to lose one of them but not Mac. How could fate be so cruel? Sheila was devastated. The boys were stunned. What a way to start a new year and a new decade! I could not go to them but her half-sister, Sue, flew out immediately. We decided not to tell Mum that Mac had died. She had not been told that he was ill, nor did she know about the *"Green Card"* problems, for we felt she needed to focus all her energies on her recovery. Also she and I had planned to visit them all in the spring and I wanted her to hang onto that dream.

I visited Mum and Dad in hospital later that day, as arranged. Dad was doing very well and there were plans to take him back to the "Unit" within the next few days. Mum was in reasonably good spirits but still very weak and a little tearful. We talked vaguely about our proposed holiday in America and I passed on all my news and my office gossip. That was one of the nicest things about my mother; even though she did not know half the people I talked about, she was always interested in anything I had to say and always remembered to ask after my friends and colleagues. I said if it was acceptable to her, I would not be in to see them on 2nd January because I was back at work but I would try to see them the following day. She said that was fine because a friend of hers was visiting the next day anyway.

On Thursday 3rd January I was at work when a colleague took a 'phone message from the hospital asking me to ring them back as soon as possible. My stomach did a somersault.
"What ward?" I asked, full of trepidation and wondering whether it was problems with Mum or Dad.

It was Mum's ward. The ward-sister told me that she had developed a temperature and fever overnight. It looked as if the internal wound was not healing properly and they were re-operating on her at that very moment. They suggested that I should come as soon as possible but I did not have our car at work so someone ran me home. Luckily Bryan was there, so I grabbed a few toiletries and we set off for the hospital.

When we arrived we were shown into a small, private waiting-room, nicely furnished with comfortable armchairs, pretty curtains and pleasant prints hanging on the walls, courtesy of the *League of Friends*. Eventually the surgeon arrived and sat down. He explained that the stitches had come adrift on the original operation. It happened sometimes when the patient was elderly and their tissues were weak. He said they had repaired the bowel once more and then added that the repair had gone well but there was now another problem.

"I'm sorry, my dear," he began, "But we cannot rouse her. We have tried for some time without success. I'm afraid there is nothing more we can do. I'm so sorry."

I asked if I could see her and he took me along to the recovery room. There my beloved mother lay inert on a trolley with some kind of airway-tube sticking out of her mouth. The surgeon stood on one side of her and I stood on the other.

"Try speaking to her," he suggested.

"Hello, Mum. It's me!"

And her eyes fluttered open.

"Good Heavens!" the surgeon explained in amazement. "She's heard you! See if you can get her to spit out her tube!"

"Mum! Can you hear me? Spit out your tube!"

She spat out the tube.

"Right!" gasped the surgeon incredulously. "At last! She's in there fighting now! Let's get her up to intensive care right away. We'll give her every chance to recover now!"

And he sped off to organise whatever he had to organise, leaving me with Mum.

"Hi, Mum. It's me again. You gave us quite a fright!" And her eyes flickered towards me. I stood looking down at her, holding her hand and stroking her hair.

"Do you know what I'm thinking as I look down on you now? That the roles have been reversed and it's my turn to say, "*I cannot believe you are not really mine!*" for I love you more than words can say."

The surgeon returned. "Young lady," he pronounced. "You have achieved a miracle! I have only seen a relative's voice revive a patient once before in all my years as a surgeon!"

"Well," I replied, "she'll fight for me like she'll fight for no-one!"

"I can see that!" he retorted.

The porters arrived, grabbed the trolley and raced off to the ICU with me racing along beside them. While they inserted all the tubes, and connected Mum to all the machinery, I made my way back to the waiting-room where Bryan was still sitting patiently.

"I'm going to stay with her," I declared, "for as long as it takes. I'll probably be here all night!"

"That's fine. But if you don't mind, I'll go home now and get something to eat and then I'll probably go to bed early. We haven't had a decent night's sleep for weeks and I'm shattered! Will it be OK if I turn off the 'phone until the early hours? All your relatives will be ringing for information this evening and I won't be able to tell them anything anyway."

"Yes. That's a good idea. At least one of us needs to get some rest. I'll give Sheila a quick call from here so she knows what's happening and I'll ring you in the morning. Say a prayer for us all……"

And as Bryan went back home, I made my way to the ICU to begin my vigil.

I do not know what time it was when I began my watchfulness at Mum's bedside. I know it was dark because one of the first things she asked me was if I had noticed the moon yet. She could not see it from that bed but she had seen it several days before and had commented to me that it was so bright, so full and so beautiful. Like Mac, she seemed fascinated with the same night sky.

"What on earth are you doing, lying there thinking of the moon?" I asked. "Are all sorts of thoughts running around in your head?"

"Yes," she whispered. "What does the moon look like tonight?"

I went off to find a window.

"You're right," I agreed on my return. "It is beautiful. It's still very bright with a sort of blue halo around it and it still looks like a full moon." I paused, thinking of Mac and how his last thoughts had been of the moon as well. I added, "It is strange to think that the same moon looks down on all of us. Us here and Sheila and the family all those miles away."

"And on Dad" she reminded me. "Don't forget Dad."

"No, Mum. I never forget Dad."

My vigil was broken every hour when a nurse would come and put her on a nebulizer for ten to twenty minutes to help her to breathe. For some reason this really distressed her. Since then, I have been on a nebulizer several times and there is nothing in it to cause distress, so whether the mask over her face and nose made her feel claustrophobic, I do not know.

Most of the time she seemed to be asleep but she knew I was there and occasionally she would open her eyes and she would murmur something. The nurses showed me how to moisten her mouth so I was able to do that for her but mostly I was just sitting, watching, waiting and praying.

After a few hours, the doctor called me aside and said things were not looking good. Despite all the drugs they had pumped into her system, they could not get her blood pressure to rise. If her blood pressure did not come up, her organs would gradually shut down. He was very sorry but now it seemed that it was just a matter of time before she faded away. I made another 'phone call to my sister to prepare her for yet more bad news.

At about 9pm the night-sister tried to persuade me to get some rest. I refused to leave Mum's bedside. She threatened to summon the doctor and have me forcefully removed.

"Call who you like!" I exclaimed. "I'm not going! And I'll make such a fuss, you'll wish you had left me alone!" Then I added, placatingly, "You don't know what this woman has done for me. If you knew our history, you would not ask me to leave."

"Well," she snapped. "Rest assured I shall review the situation throughout the night!" and then she stomped off.

At 9.30pm Sheila 'phoned the ward to enquire how Mum was. The nurse asked me if I would like to take the call. After I had passed on the news that there seemed to be little change, Sheila revealed, "There has been one bit of good news today. Vernon passed his driving test! With everything that has gone on, I'm really proud of him."

I returned to Mum's bedside and told her Sheila and the family sent their love and that Vernon had passed his test.

"Oh, good!" she whispered.

Just before 10.30pm, the nurse came to give her the dreaded nebulizer again. I asked, "Do you have to give it to her? Only she hates it so much." The nurse replied, "I'm afraid I do. Doctor's orders." But she turned it up so it was pumping out the drug-laden mist at a great rate of knots and she held it so far away from Mum's face, it was useless. It was all done in about five minutes but I decided I would see the doctor myself and ask him to cancel the wretched machine. If Mum was not going to make it, I could not see the point of giving it to her, especially as it distressed her so much.

So when it was over, and the nurse had removed the nebulizer, I turned to Mum and said, "That's it, Mum. It's over. I promise that you'll never have to have that horrible machine again." In the split second that I had uttered the words, I realised the statement had a double meaning. She opened her eyes, looked at me one last time with a questioning gaze and opened her mouth as if she was about to say something. At that very moment the heart monitoring machine flattened out, making that awful, continuous tone.

"Remember! Don't be afraid, Mum!" I cried out to her but I doubt whether she heard. Perhaps her soul did as it departed her body but she herself was gone. Our gracious, gentle, generous, patient and much-loved wife and mother was dead. She was 85 years old but there was still so much we wanted to do together.

The night-sister came over and switched off the machines.

"You see," I said. "I didn't have to leave her, did I?"

"No, you didn't have to leave her. Have you got someone who can take you home?"

"I think so. I'll go and make some 'phone calls and then come back and sit with her, if that's alright?"

No tears. I think I was in a state of disbelief. The tears would come later.

I 'phoned Sheila to tell her Mum had passed away and I think she was just numb, especially having to face another death so soon after Mac. Even though you have been warned to expect it, the news still comes as a shock. Thank goodness Sue was there to help her through the first few days.

As anticipated, my home 'phone was turned off, for I had truly thought I would be at the hospital all night. By now it was about 11pm and I knew my dear friend, Les, whom I had known since schooldays, would probably still be up, for she and her husband never went to bed very early. We had seen one another through a lot of trauma, and joy, over the years and she had been very fond of my parents. Living in Worthing had made her my ideal chief transporter of Auntie Blanche to our family parties! I knew she would come to my rescue if she could.

Les arrived about fifteen minutes later, leaving her husband in charge of the children. She asked if she could see Mum and we went into the ICU together. The bed had now been screened and the machines removed. Les whispered reverently, "She looks beautiful! Years younger. So peaceful and unworried."

I had asked her if she would mind if we popped up to see Dad before she drove me home, so we padded through the dimly-lit corridors until we got to his room. I stood in the doorway just looking at his shape lying on the bed. Suddenly he moved and said, "Is that you, duck? Is that my Maureen?"

"Hello, Dad. I didn't wake you up, did I?"

"No, I couldn't sleep. What are you doing here, duck?"

"I'm here with Les. We've been out together this evening and we just wanted to see you before we went home."

"That's nice, duck."

He did not seem to think that it was at all strange that we were wandering the hospital corridors, visiting patients, at nearly midnight! I gave him a kiss and Les and I said goodnight to him.

"Try to go to sleep now, Dad. I'll see you tomorrow. Love you!"

"I love you too."

The next day Bryan and I returned to the hospital to collect Mum's things and sign the paper-work. To my consternation, the clerk handed me Mum's wedding ring. Mum had once told me that she did not care what happened to any of her other possessions but she wanted her wedding ring to remain on her finger and to be buried with her. I explained this to the lady and she said it was hospital policy to remove all jewellery and hand it to the next of kin. She suggested it would be more sensible to hang onto it until the ashes were available and then place the ring into the casket. So, to keep it safe, I slipped it onto the wedding-ring finger of my right hand. It was a perfect fit and I have to confess that it remains there to this day for I could not bear to take it off! One day, in the not too distant future, I will bury it with her ashes, somewhat belatedly but I do not think she will mind.

I asked this clerk if making Mum eat too soon could have caused the wound not to heal properly. She said if I wanted questions like this answered, I would have to agree to a post-mortem and she had not thought I would want to go that route. She was right. I certainly did not want that. No amount of questions would bring her back, so I had to let the matter rest but to this day I still wonder.

Having discussed Dad's funeral arrangements with Mum, I knew exactly what Mum wanted for herself, so I arranged for her to be taken to *Reynolds Funeral Home* in Littlehampton Cemetery. As Mum's mortal remains left the hospital, so did Dad. Ironically he was taken back to *East Tyne EMI Unit* not only on that very same day but at about the same time.

Mum's funeral was arranged for Monday 14th January 1991. There would be a service at St Mary's Church, followed by another service at Worthing Crematorium and a wake afterwards, at their home, and ours, for so many years. Eventually her ashes would be interred into her parents' grave in Littlehampton Cemetery.

In the intervening days several strange things happened. Whether it was my heightened sense of awareness, plain co-incidence or an unseen spiritual force at work, I will leave you to decide.

I suppose the first would probably be Dad being awake at the time of Mum's death and then not being surprised to see me. Then "co-incidentally" leaving the hospital at the same time as she did, but perhaps co-incidence was all that it was?

The next strange event was the morning after Mum died. Despite going to bed well after midnight, I awoke at 6am, after a very fitful night, with such a feeling of joy! I just felt in my bones, that wherever she had been going, she had arrived safely and that all was well. A hymn kept popping into my mind! *"Rejoice! The Lord is King!"* I have no idea why on earth this should suddenly come to the fore as I had not heard it, nor thought about it, for years. Nevertheless we felt it could mean something, so we decided we would have it as one of the hymns at her funeral service.

A few nights later, I was lying in bed, thinking of Mum and shedding a few silent tears, when the moon suddenly shone full in my face, just for a few seconds before it disappeared behind a cloud. I felt as if she was sending me a sign that I, too, was never far from her thoughts.

I decided to wear yellow at Mum's funeral. It was not a colour any of us ever wore but she loved everything yellow, from daffodils to sunshine, baby ducks to yellow roses. She had chosen yellow tiles and yellow towels for their bathroom and yellow wall-paper throughout the house. She just loved yellow, saying it was a happy, sunny colour. So, on Wednesday 9th January, I set off for the shops at Worthing, in wild winds and a torrential downpour. Going to look for a summer-coloured dress, in the middle of winter, was a long-shot but I felt if it was meant to be, I would find it. As I parked the car, the sky turned blue, the sun shone down, and the first shop I went into had just one double-fronted coat-dress in yellow linen. It was a leftover from the summer, hanging on a back-rail, out of sight amongst the brown wools and the black, winter velvets. Over the past few months, I had lost quite a bit of weight, so although it was in a smaller-than-usual size, it actually fitted me. Unbelievable! ...... But perhaps not!

When I had finished my shopping, I went into the hospital and told them that any donations given in lieu of flowers at Mum's funeral, would be handed to the *League of Friends* because we had been so impressed at the efforts they made to give some comfort to patients and their relatives. Strange to say, it was Mum's wish not to have flowers at her funeral. She thought it was a dreadful waste of money!

Then I went to see Dad at *East Tyne*. The staff had suggested that I did not tell Dad that Mum had died. They said he would not remember anyway. For the time being I had decided to take their advice, but I hated keeping this so-important fact from him. The Manager of the "Unit" said they would take him to her funeral if I wished. It was another decision we would have to make.

After buying the dress, visiting the hospital and going to see Dad at *East Tyne,* the last item on my agenda for the day was to go and see Mum at the Chapel of Rest. However, when I arrived, the undertakers had not finished preparing her body for viewing, so I left a bunch of yellow freesias, her favourite flowers, and asked the staff to place it with her on my behalf.

That evening at home, I was telling Bryan about my day when a strong smell of freesia wafted towards me. He said I must be getting a whiff of one of Mum's presents, which were still unopened. I decided to open them and the one from the *League of Friends* was a flannel, a talcum powder and a moisturiser, perfumed with the fragrance of "freesia". Co-incidence? Again? I don't think so!

Meanwhile, Sheila was experiencing strange happenings on her side of the Ocean about Mac. It was a few days after his death, and she awoke from a deep sleep to see a bright light under her bedroom door. She thought she had turned off all the lights, so that seemed strange. She got up and opened the door and there stood Mac. He looked so handsome. He was slimmer, his beard had been trimmed, and he was dressed from head to toe in emerald green.

She blurted out, "What on earth are you doing here?"

"I've just come to say I'll always love you," he replied, and then he was gone.

When she woke up in the morning, she was convinced she must have dreamt the incident but Sue asked, "Who was that you were talking to in the middle of the night outside your bedroom? Your voices woke me up!"

By now a funeral service had been held for Mac at Trinity Church in Newport, where a piper had played *"Amazing Grace"* to a packed congregation. The Masonic Lodge had also insisted on holding a memorial service for him and they performed a song that the men sang to their wives on their "Ladies' Nights". It was called *"Here's to her health in a song"* and it reduced Sheila to uncontrollable sobs. America certainly had done Mac proud, but Mac was an Englishman first and foremost, and Sheila wanted his ashes interred with those of his parents in the churchyard where they were married. So Sheila and the boys were arriving back in the UK on Thursday 10th January, to attend Mum's funeral on the 14th, and then to hold a memorial service for Mac at St John's Church in Hythe, Southampton, on the following day.

I had already been over to our parents' home to get the bungalow ready for their arrival. I had dragged out Mum's old boiler to wash the sheets and dropped them in it to simmer away merrily while I hunted out more clean linen. I was searching through the drawers for pillow-cases and kept coming across ones with holes in them.

"Oh, Mum!" I wailed out loud in exasperation. "What on earth are you saving these for?"

Her reply came immediately into my head.

"You never know when they'll come in handy!" her silent voice replied.

A few minutes later I went back into the kitchen to find it was full of steam. I turned the boiler off and found I was paddling on a flooded floor! What on earth could I use to mop it all up? The old pillow-cases, of course!

When Sheila, Russell and Vernon arrived at the bungalow, everything was ready for them: beds made: refrigerator stocked: kitchen floor clean and dry! How strange it was to be there without Dad sitting in his armchair puffing away and without Mum bustling about making cups of tea. I left the family to settle in. The boys immediately went to their old room and started to unpack, leaving Sheila sitting quietly in our old sitting-room, shedding a few silent tears and no doubt twirling her wedding-ring around her finger, as she always does when she is under stress. Nothing would ever be the same. Suddenly she looked up and there was Mum, sitting in her armchair, where she always sat when they did the crossword together. She gave her youngest daughter her gentle smile ..... and then she was gone.

The next day Sheila had to travel to Southampton to make arrangements for Mac's memorial service, so it was Saturday before we could visit the *Chapel of Rest*. Having been thwarted in my attempt to see Mum on Wednesday, I was not at all sure that now I wanted to go, but Sheila wanted me to be with her. She thought Mum looked beautiful but to me she did not look "right". Then we went to *East Tyne* to see Dad. We had to make a decision whether to tell him that Mum had died and then we had to decide if he should come to her funeral.

Almost as soon as we arrived he asked his usual "Where's Mum?" I looked at Sheila and she shrugged her shoulders. Then she looked up and just behind me was a copy of a war-time poster saying *"Keep Mum!" Don't say a word!"* So we took this as a "sign", left him to his dreams and decided not to take him to the funeral.

The day of Mum's funeral, Monday 14th January, dawned with a heavy frost but the day turned out to be beautifully sunny with clear blue skies. I wore my sunshine-yellow dress with black accessories and both Sheila and I sported a yellow freesia on the lapels of our coats.

Although Mum had been a regular churchgoer at St Mary's for most of her life, the vicar had recently changed and thus the new one had never met her. He was genuinely upset that he had not known her, nor been told about her illness, and I was then full of regrets that I had not thought to suggest that he visit her at home, nor asked him to call and give her Communion at the hospital. My excuse is that I was just too pre-occupied thinking about everything else.

I was surprised at how many people had decided to come to the church as well as the crematorium. We had wanted lots of hymns because Mum loved her hymns, so as well as *"Rejoice, the Lord is King!"*, we had *"Come Down O Love Divine"* and *"Be still my soul, the Lord is on your side,"* because they were Mum's favourites. Also *"God be in my Head"* was sung as a solo and the choir sang the *"Prayer of St Francis"*. Russell read from *1 Corinthians, Chapter 13* and Vernon read from the *Gospel according to St John, Chapter 14, verses 1-6*. While Vernon was reading his piece, the sun poured through one of the windows, right onto Sheila and me. Even Bryan, more sceptical than most, remarked that when he saw the sun on us, he knew it was a message from Mum to us all.

We had yet more hymns at the crematorium. *"The Lord is my Shepherd"* (tune by Crimond) followed by *"Love Divine"* (my favourite) and *"Morning has Broken"* (Sheila's choice). Russell read the poem, *"Footprints"*. Both services were a grand and wonderful send-off, and a fitting tribute to an exceptional human being, whose quiet, selfless love touched all who were privileged to know her.

We all adjourned back to our family home in Littlehampton where Sheila had organised most of the catering. She had spent most of Sunday preparing it all but fortunately there is nothing she enjoys more than feeding people!

During the "wake", a neighbour approached me. "I never heard your mother say an unkind word about anyone!" she remarked, and then, perhaps not able to believe our mother could have been such a paragon of virtue behind closed doors, she added, "Did she ever say something derogatory about someone to you?"

I thought for a few seconds. Occasionally she would make a negative comment but normally the worst she managed to conjure up would be along the lines of, "That woman would try the patience of a saint!" She had never expressed a less than flattering opinion on a person's character out of spite, jealousy, or in retaliation for a thoughtless comment or deed. Up to this point, I had not appreciated how truly unusual this was! It was so much part of her character that I had taken it for granted.

"No," I replied, somewhat surprised. "She never did. Her grand-mother adopted the maxim "*If you can't find something nice to say about someone, then it is best to say nothing at all*", and I think she must have followed this example."

"That's amazing!" the neighbour said. "What a remarkable woman!"

"Yes, she was," I preened. "In her quiet, unassuming way she touched all our lives."

The final tribute. It was a fitting end to a great life. But life goes on.

CHAPTER FORTY-SIX

Come to Dust

On 15th January 1991 the memorial service for Mac was held at St John's Church, Hythe, the same church where he and Sheila had been married almost nineteen years earlier. The mourners walked into the church to *"Ave Maria"* and two of Mac's favourite hymns were sung: *"Morning has broken"* and *"Jesu, joy of man's desiring."* Both of his sons read a verse from Shakespeare's *Cymbelline* that begins:-
Fear no more the heat o' the sun,
Nor the furious winter's rages;
Thou thy worldly task has done, ...
And ends
The sceptre, learning, physic, must
All follow this, and come to dust.

After the service his ashes were interred in the churchyard, in the same plot as his parents, and Sheila and the boys returned to Littlehampton. The next day Russell and Vernon flew back to America, so they could return to school, while Sheila stayed on a little longer to help me decide what to do with our parents' possessions.

Unlike me, she is not a sentimental clutterbug, so she wanted very little in the way of personal items: a vase or two: a pewter coffee-pot both of us had always admired: an oil painting of her birthplace (Rustington): one of Dad's billiard trophies: some pieces of Mum's jewellery and two small, china book-ends that had never been used for the purpose intended, but had stood at either end of the mantelpiece in the front room for as long as we could remember. Sheila wanted them because they reminded her of Mac. Indeed he could have posed as the model for them, for not only do they look like him, they have the same build, thinning, white hair and a beard. Both figures are seated on a chair; one is reading from a book placed on his lap, spectacles falling down his nose, and the other is contemplatively smoking his pipe. Mum called them her "Little Men". Sheila calls them her "Little Macs". I do not believe they are very valuable but to Sheila they are priceless.

The bungalow had been placed in our names several years earlier so we were free to dispose of it, if we wished. Very reluctantly we decided this was the most sensible option, so, when the time came for Sheila to return to America, she had to say a fond, and final, farewell to our childhood home. Truly things would never be the same again.

On 16th January 1991, the day after Mac's memorial service, fighting began, at last, in the Gulf War. Since the 2nd August 1990's declaration of intent to expel Saddam Hussein's Iraqi troops from Kuwait, the combat zone had seen twelve countries send naval forces, four countries send combat aircraft, eight countries send ground forces. A total of 34 nations were massed against Iraq, which only had a few gunboats and small missile craft to match the coalition's naval armada. But Iraq did have greater strength on the ground, elaborate missile and gun defences and 750 fighter and bomber aircraft.

The overwhelming majority of the participating military forces were from the United States and they called their operation *"Desert Storm"*. Saudi Arabia, the United Kingdom and Egypt also made significant contributions. $44billion of the estimated $64billion cost was met by the Saudi's.

The war was a resounding victory for the coalition forces and fighting ended little more than one month later, on 28th February, but not before the retreating Iraqi army dumped 400million gallons of crude oil into the Persian Gulf, the largest oil spill in history. They also set fire to Kuwait's oil-wells, causing further huge ecological damage in the area. The legendary Red Adair and his team would be at the forefront of putting them all out.

Ironically for our family, the expected huge number of casualties never materialised, and thus all the hospital wards had been emptied in vain. Only 190 coalition troops were killed by Iraqi combatants but 379 died from "friendly fire" or accidents with munitions. The UK suffered just 47 deaths, nine of which were due to friendly fire. The USA suffered 148 battle-related deaths, 35 of which were due to friendly fire.

The exact number of Iraqi military casualties is not known. Some estimates put the number of these fatalities as low as 20,000, some as high as 200,000. Similarly the estimated numbers of Iraqi civilians killed during the war vary enormously, from 2,300 to 200,000.

The conflict raised many controversial issues including the allegation that thousands of Iraqi soldiers, in fortified trenches, were buried alive as anti-mine ploughs, mounted on tanks and earthmovers, bulldozed over the heavily fortified *"Saddam Line"*.

What is not in dispute is the sight of coalition aircrew, shot down over Iraq, being displayed on television with visible signs of abuse. Some were forced to make statements on camera against the war and later many alleged that they were tortured.

For thousands of returning military personnel the end of the war only brought a different set of problems as they struggled to cope with strange, debilitating symptoms and unexpected birth defects in their children. The phenomenon became known as *Gulf War Syndrome* and there has been widespread speculation, and disagreement, about its cause. Some of the possible culprits include depleted uranium, chemical weapons, anthrax vaccine and/or infectious diseases. As of the year 2000, the *Department of Veterans Affairs* declared that some 183,000 US veterans, more than a quarter of the US troops who participated in the war, have been permanently disabled by the war. Many others suffer an array of serious symptoms whose causes are not fully understood.

As the war raged in the Gulf, I fought my own battle with bereavement and came to know the meaning of the cliché *"it feels as if your heart is breaking."* I thought I had been broken-hearted in the past but never like this. The pain was almost physical. Every waking and sleeping moment, my thoughts were of my mother. It was as if I no longer had a brain of my own. I knew what people meant when they said you could go out of your mind with grief. I remember driving back from a visit to *East Tyne* and crying out loud, *"Please, Mum! Get out of my head! I feel as if I'm going mad!"*

One of my colleagues had recently lost her father. Her situation was much worse than mine because she was much younger than I was and was still living at home. To make matters worse, her mother had died some years earlier. We shared our grief and discovered we both felt as if we had been "taken over".

Then gradually I realised I had actually spent a whole five minutes without thinking of my mother. Then it was ten, then half an hour. Over the coming weeks, months and years, I thought of her less and less. And the thoughts became happy memories with profound gratitude that she had been part of my life. But it was ten years before I could go a whole day without thinking of her and even now I miss her. I miss not being able to tell her my news; I miss her gentle smile; her quiet commonsense, her unfailing support and her love. But this is not surprising, I remember how she used to tell me that she still missed her mother, decades after she had died.

I visited Dad at *East Tyne,* every Thursday and Sunday. Every time I saw him his opening gambit was, "Where's Mum?" After a few weeks I decided to tell him that Mum and Mac had died.

"What a disaster!" he replied. "But at least they are together."

So far, so good, I thought.

Then he added, "Who killed her?"

"No-one, Dad. She was not very well and just went to sleep. It was very peaceful."

I left him pondering Mum's demise, wondering if I had done the right thing in telling him.

At my next visit I was to seriously doubt the wisdom of my action when he opened our conversation with, "I wish I could get the person who murdered Mum!"

So much for not remembering anything, even if he was confused over the circumstances.

"She wasn't murdered, Dad! She just went to sleep and didn't wake up. It was very peaceful."

"I thought she'd been trapped in a fire and got badly burned!"

"No, Dad. Truly she didn't. She wasn't murdered and she wasn't in a fire."

I began to wonder what on earth I had done but the next visit we were back to "Where's Mum?" I breathed a huge sigh of relief and vowed never again to tell him that his beloved Anne had died.

When the weather was fine I would take Dad out in a wheelchair for a stroll around the streets, encouraging him to admire the gardens, stroke a friendly cat, pat a dog. Every other Sunday, the staff would have the use of a minibus. Each helper was permitted to take charge of two residents, so the staff encouraged me to go with Dad so I could take another person who would otherwise not be able to join us. We would pile in as many residents as possible and take them for a drive to the beach. After a walk along the promenade, we would stop for a cup of tea, or an ice-cream, in the café in the nearby gardens.

Our group attracted quite a few stares for it was obvious most of the residents were suffering from dementia. Some would shuffle along muttering to themselves, others would be hand-in-hand, one might go wandering off and have to be gathered back into the fold. I would be pushing the wheelchair with some poor, demented soul hanging onto the handles. The outings, and the "Unit" itself, were not everybody's "cup of tea". The very idea of the place had upset Mum; Bryan found it extremely depressing; Sheila found it upsetting and depressing. But luckily it, and the residents, did not bother me. Of course I felt sorry for them, lost in their own worlds, unable to make sense of anything or anybody. But perhaps because I had been used to dealing with physical and mental disabilities in my work, I only thought how lucky they were to be living in a place of safety, with good food and a private room, being looked after by a committed and caring staff. I felt it was a privilege to help on the outings.

Nevertheless, although I had no complaints about *East Tyne*, I did make enquiries to see if Dad could be transferred to their sister-unit in Pagham. This was only a few minutes from my home whereas *East Tyne* was an hour's drive away. I thought if Dad was closer, I would be able to pop-in and see him every day. But that "Unit" was on two floors and residents had to be able to use the stairs. Dad was no longer very mobile so my application was turned down.

In June 1991, Sheila's worst fears were realised. Her job with Elizabeth had ceased and the "Green Card" had not materialised. She had no option but to return to England. It meant she had to pack up her goods and chattels and ship them all back to the UK. Luckily most of the furniture could stay in the apartment but all the bits and pieces that Mac had acquired, including the billiard-table, had to go back to the Salvation Army's charity shop. The basement had been Mac's domain because he did most of the domestic chores while Sheila was at work, including the laundry. Thus when Sheila went down to clear out this area, she was exasperated to discover boxes and boxes of jam-jars under the billiard-table! For some reason, known only to himself, Mac had been unable to throw them away. It seemed his mania for collecting things had not completely deserted him during his time in America!

Vernon returned to the UK with Sheila but Russell, now aged 18, adamantly refused to go back. He still had a student's visa and was therefore legally allowed to stay in the US. Sheila arranged for friends to provide him with room and board in return for a nominal payment. With that and some part-time earnings, he survived, finished high school and graduated in 1992.

Fortunately by this time, I had sold our parents' bungalow. (I say "our parents' bungalow" because that is how we thought of it but, as it had already been signed over to us, legally it was "our bungalow".) In fact just one advertisement in the local paper had secured a purchaser. All their remaining personal effects had been dispersed, to charity shops, to auction, or to me. I now had more ornaments, vases, crockery, linen, and suchlike, than I knew what to do with!

I was therefore in a position to send Sheila her share of our "parents' estate" and with that she was able to assist Russell financially and to return to the UK in style. It had always been her dream to sail across the Atlantic Ocean in one of the "Queens" so she booked a passage for herself and Vernon on the flagship vessel of the Cunard shipping-line, the "QE2". Thanks to connections through a friend, they were even upgraded to first-class! It was a trip she and Vernon would remember for the rest of their lives. Another advantage was that there were no baggage restrictions so their worldly goods sailed with them.

When they disembarked, they made their way to a cottage Sheila had rented on the edge of the New Forest and there she tried to get her life in order. She managed to secure temporary work, which suited her just fine as she still hoped the "Green Card" would eventually be forthcoming. Vernon returned to the English education system and they settled down to await developments.

Although it had not been her choice to return to the UK, I think it helped us both with our grieving process, especially Sheila, perhaps, as she had to come to terms with two losses. Even though everyone was sympathetic, and many had travelled the same road before us, no-one could empathise or share memories, as we could. At last our sisterly bond was complete and Mum's prophecy that I would "be glad to have a sister one day" was proved true a thousand-fold.

At least once a month, Sheila would make the two-and-a-half hour journey from Southampton to see Dad at *East Tyne*. She hated it, but she came, and she tried to join us on an "outing" Sunday when at least we were away from the "Unit". We were truly blessed that Dad never forgot whom we were. So many of the other visitors were not recognised by their loved ones, which must have been heart-breaking.

On 8th October 1991, Dad celebrated his 90th birthday and we held a small party for him at the "Unit". Sheila and Vernon came, Bryan and me, my friend Les who lived nearby, and Harry, the neighbour who had lived opposite Mum and Dad for so many years. Dad saw Harry pull up in the car-park and exclaimed excitedly, without any prompting, "Here's Harry! He'll have brought Mum!"

We had to explain that Mum was not well enough to come.

"But it's my birthday!" he frowned uncomprehendingly, bottom lip quivering.

We changed the subject quickly and hoped the issue would soon be forgotten.

I had made a cake for the occasion (of course!). This time it was a square one covered with green icing to represent grass! In each corner I had placed a small memento of his life. There was a plastic horse and a soldier to remind him of his time in the Army: a football: a miniature billiard-table and, last but not least, a tiny garden gnome with marzipan vegetables. In the middle was "DAD", "90" and a candle. Dad blew out the candle and the cake was cut. I asked for the remainder to be cut up and given to the residents for their tea but I had to take all the plastic figures home with me in case they tried to eat them as well!

Just days after his birthday, Bryan and I went on holiday to Spain and Sheila stepped up her visits to every Sunday while we were away. I was so relieved to discover that Dad still knew me on our return. Indeed it was as if I had never been away.

CHAPTER FORTY-SEVEN

When Diamonds Blow Away

When Bryan and I returned from holiday late October 1991, Dad did not seem to realise we had been away. One day blended in with the next for him but I thought he seemed quieter, frailer, sadder, more "lost" somehow. I was sure the fact that he had not seen Mum on his birthday had penetrated his sub-conscious and that he had finally begun to realise that all was not well. He was not capable of verbalising his fears but it appeared that slowly he had started to give up.

On the afternoon of Thursday 14th November 1991, I went over to see him at *East Tyne* as usual. For the past few days he had been going to bed in the afternoons and that day he was very sleepy. A member of staff helped me to put him to bed and he was fast asleep within minutes. They told me he was not eating, or even drinking, very much.

When I arrived at *East Tyne* on Sunday 17th November, I found him slumped in an armchair, nearly asleep but he gave me his usual lovely smile and "Hello, darling!" greeting when he saw me. Once again I helped to put him to bed and once again, he was fast asleep within minutes. One of the carers said she had managed to persuade him to eat a few spoonfuls of mashed-up Sunday roast but he still did not want to drink anything, not even his much-enjoyed cups of tea.

I sat next to him as he lay in bed, quietly thinking about all he had done for us over the years, when he suddenly brought his arms out from under the covers and hugged an invisible body. He did this three times and the third time I said to him, "Is that Mum you're hugging, Dad? Is that your Anne?"

He turned his head towards me, opened his eyes and gave me a lovely satisfied smile, as if he was thinking, "Yes! Aren't I the lucky one!" I began to speak gently to him again.

"Yes! That's right. It's your Anne, isn't it? She's not far away now, Dad, is she? No. She's not far away."

I stroked his hair, gave him a kiss and told him that I loved him so very, very much but that it was all right to go and be with Mum.

"I know you're worried about leaving us. Don't worry about us, Dad. We'll manage without you. I know you want to be with Mum. I don't blame you. We all miss her. It's OK to go, Daddy. It's OK. We'll be all right. It's time now. It's time."

He seemed to understand every word but he made no attempt to reply.

When I got home I told Bryan that Dad had given up. Bryan said he was pining away, like an animal trapped in a strange place. He said I had done the right thing in speaking to him as I had, for he had read that some people needed "permission" to slip away.

The next morning I 'phoned *East Tyne* to see how he was. They said they had not been able to rouse him and suggested I should go over. I was supposed to be at work and had loads of appointments booked, but I did manage to visit on an extended lunch-hour. It appeared that Dad was fast asleep. He was just about rousable but it was obvious now that he was gradually losing his hold on life.

Sheila had been out of reach all weekend. She and Vernon had gone to her sister-in-law's Golden Wedding Anniversary celebration and I did not have the 'phone number, so it was Monday evening before I could speak to her. I told her Dad was fading away and we agreed to meet at *East Tyne* the following day, Tuesday 19th November.

The next morning she arrived before me, at about 11.45am. I arrived an hour later, once again on an extended lunch-hour. Sheila said she wanted to stay indefinitely but she did not want to stay alone. Luckily her hours of work were very flexible but mine were less so and there was no one who could take over from me at such short notice. I thought we should set up some kind of rota because I felt he could drift on like this for days.

"No," she stated decisively. "It's the 19th today. He'll go today. Things always happen to me on the 19th!"

Much to her chagrin, I had to leave at 3pm to give a seminar at work. I just could not let twenty people make the effort to be there, only to find me absent. I returned at about 6pm and Sheila said the care-staff and volunteers had been wonderful. They had popped in all afternoon to say "Hello" and to ask her if she wanted anything to eat or drink. I still thought we could go on like this for days but we agreed to sit out the night and review the situation in the morning. Meanwhile I had cancelled all my interviews for the next few days.

We took it in turns to sit at his head, holding his hand. While Sheila was at that end, I massaged his feet. Like my husband, Dad had loved having his feet massaged! The hours ticked by but, as his condition deteriorated, Sheila said she could not bear to be at his head any longer. Now even I accepted that the end was close. We both told him how much we loved him and thanked him for everything he had done for us. I carried on stroking his head, holding his hand and talking softly to him, about not being afraid, of being with his beloved Anne again, how lucky we had been. Sheila sat in a chair, sobbing quietly. She still could not bring herself to touch him so I chanted, "One stroke for Sheila, one stroke for me, and go, Daddy, go."

At 10.10pm I felt his hand release its grip and his whole body relaxed; his laboured breathing ceased. I felt for a pulse. There was nothing. I carried on talking to him while Sheila went to get the manager. I thought he looked like an angel, even with no teeth, his mouth open and his face all gaunt. I made this observation to the manager when she arrived and the look she shot me was of total disbelief!

"Well I think he looks like an angel!" I declared emphatically. "I think he's beautiful!"

While the staff did whatever they had to do, Sheila 'phoned Vernon and I 'phoned Bryan. At about 11.30pm we went back into his room. He looked so peaceful. We rejoiced that he had hung on long enough for us both to be there, and I felt doubly privileged to have been with both parents as they had taken their last breaths, but the main emotion we felt was relief. It was over but what a lovely death: so peaceful, so loving, so dignified.

When Sheila eventually arrived home in the early hours, there was a letter waiting for her from the US Embassy. Thanks to the Herculean efforts of Elizabeth, it was her "Green Card". She and Vernon could now plan to return to America. Like she said, everything happens to her on the 19th.

In the coming days and weeks there were many times when I would quietly weep for the loss of my father, thinking I would never again see his lovely smile, hear his cheeky chuckle, nor look into those twinkling, blue eyes and see all the love lodged deep in his soul. Never again to feel those strong arms encircling me, protecting me from harm; never again to hear his broad Sussex burr and his "'ello, duck!" I thought of all the times I had turned to him when I was in difficulties or in need, and how his quiet confidence would put my troubled world to rights. I remembered the hundreds of times he had delivered his home-grown vegetables and fruit to me; given us the choicest cuts off the Sunday roast; sacrificed his herring roe so we might have it! He was one of the most caring and unselfish people I would ever know. How doubly lucky we had been and he deserved these tears of sorrow and loss.

I had no "signs" or "co-incidences" from Dad until exactly one week after his death, when suddenly he came to me, late at night, or at least his spirit did. I felt his presence so strongly on my right-hand side. I asked if Mum was there as well and looked around for her. I expected her to be on my left but she was not. She was just to the right of Dad; they were separate but somehow joined. Then they were gone. I felt as if they had come to me to reassure me that they were now re-united.

We arranged Dad's funeral for Thursday 28th November at Worthing Crematorium. The United Services Club provided a trumpet-player to perform *"The Last Post"* and the "Rodgers and Hammerstein" tune *"You'll never walk alone"*, from their musical *"Carousel"*, was sung with much gusto by all those present. Since the 1960's, the song has been performed by a massed chorus of supporters at football clubs throughout the world, and the words seemed so right as a fond farewell for our football-loving father. The ever-popular hymn, *"Abide with me"*, was also sung with great enthusiasm. The first and last verses of this hymn have been sung before kick-offs at FA (Football Association) Cup finals since 1927, and at the Rugby Cup Finals since 1929.

After the service we all adjourned to a nearby hostelry, "*The Frankland Arms*" in the village of Washington. It seemed singularly appropriate that our beloved parent should have his send-off from a pub'!

Dad had very little to leave in the way of personal possessions, for these, along with so much else, had already been taken, and he had given his Army medals to his grandsons years before. At the suggestion of the "Unit", I had made a scrap-book for him and had stuck into it photographs of all the people, places and pets that had meant something to him. Most of the residents had one and volunteers would sit with them and look through the pictures trying to keep old memories alive. Sheila asked if she could have this and our not-so-unsentimental non-squirrel still has it.

Some months later, I had both Mum and Dad's ashes interred in her parents' grave in Littlehampton Cemetery. A memorial stone, in the form of an open book, was placed on the grave, with Mum's details on the left-hand page and Dad's on the right. At the bottom is inscribed:-

Love endures when diamonds blow away

CHAPTER FORTY-EIGHT

Epilogue
(1990-1999)

If this is going to be a potted history of the 20th century, as well as our parents' part in it, I need to include the happenings of the last decade; the bits they lived to witness and the bits that they did not. Of course, international news of 1990 was rather eclipsed by our family problems but at least our parents saw the *Hubble Telescope* being launched into space, Lech Walesa becoming President of Poland, Nelson Mandela being released from prison and the resignation of Britain's first female Prime Minister, Margaret Thatcher. However, by this time, all of that would have been of no interest to Dad and, in truth, of little interest to Mum.

The *Hubble Telescope* was named after the American astrologer Edwin Hubble and it was launched into orbit by the space shuttle *Atlantis* in April 1990. It is the only telescope ever designed to be serviced by astronauts and its observations have led to many breakthroughs in astrophysics.

Lech Walesa was the labour activist who came to prominence throughout the 1980's when he helped to form, and then to lead, communist Poland's first independent trade union, *Solidarity*. For these achievements, he received the Nobel Peace Prize in 1983. Communism collapsed in Poland in 1989, largely due to the efforts of Lech Walesa and *Solidarity*, but democratic elections to find a President were not held until 1990. Walesa won with a landslide majority and went on to guide Poland through its first free parliamentary elections in 1991.

As well as the re-unification of East and West Germany on 3rd October 1990, our parents also lived to see Lithunia declare its independence that year but I do not believe any of us appreciated that this would begin the break-up of the Soviet Union in 1991. In less than ten years, the "Mighty Russian Bear" would become fifteen independent nations, and within another decade, many of these would become members of the European Union. The much smaller Russia would become a primary source of oil and gas for Europe, but when privatisation of the state-owned industries was introduced in 1998, it created a chaotic situation that resulted in a near-collapse of the Russian economy. It was a period of excess that spawned a mob-mentality among the criminal element: the downside of the fall of communism. Gorbachev's 1985 *Glasnost* and *Perestroika* had led to this, and to the break-up of the USSR, but it had also brought democracy to the monolithic, communist state and a peaceful end to the Cold War, officially declared to have ceased in 1992.

I have mentioned Nelson Mandela's release from prison and his subsequent rise to become the first black President of South Africa, in Chapter 30. In addition, I have mentioned Margaret Thatcher several times but I have not recorded her political demise in November 1990. Our father was not a great fan of "Maggie", being a staunch Labour supporter all his life, but I think even he would have been sorry to see the way she was drummed out of office by members of her own party. (Of course technically he could have seen it, but the ways of the world were beyond his comprehension in 1990.)

The rot started when she insisted in introducing the very unpopular "Community Charge" in the late 1980's. In addition, her views regarding the European Community were not shared by others in her Cabinet. (They wanted more integration and she did not.) She was challenged as to her suitability to continue to lead the Conservative Party and lost the vote. She chose to resign believing that party unity, and the prospect of victory in the next general election, would be better served if she stepped down. Her tearful farewell from *10, Downing Street,* on 28th November 1990, brought sympathy from us all, supporters and non-supporters alike. She was succeeded by John Major and took her place in the House of Lords on 30th June 1992, as Baroness Thatcher of Kesteven. By then, however, she had made history several times over; history that our parents had lived to see. Not only was she the first female Prime Minister, and the first woman to lead a major political party in the UK, but her tenure was the longest since Lord Salisbury and the longest continuous period in office since Lord Liverpool.

Apart from these early events of the last decade of the century, our parents were destined to miss the rest of the news of the 1990's.

They would not see Queen Elizabeth's Christmas broadcast of 1992 when she spoke of her *"annus horribilis",* for not only had her favourite weekend retreat, Windsor Castle, gone up in flames but also the year had witnessed the divorce of her daughter, Princess Anne, (from Captain Mark Philips) and the separation of her sons, Princes Andrew and Charles, from their respective wives, Sarah Ferguson and Diana, Princess of Wales. Andrew and Sarah would go on to divorce in May 1996 and Charles and Diana would follow suit in August of the same year.

The fire at Windsor Castle did more than destroy 100 rooms and cause damage estimated at £60million. The subsequent debate on who should foot the bill, resulted in the Queen agreeing to pay income tax from April 1993; traditionally the sovereign had been exempt from taxes. In addition, the Queen agreed to pay "fringe royals" from her own money and in future only herself, the Duke of Edinburgh and the Queen Mother would be funded from the public purse. This news would have pleased

Dad no end!

More "royal" news occurred later in the decade. Diana, Princess of Wales, was probably the nation's most popular princess of all time, and the world's most photographed and photogenic "celebrity". The break-up with Prince Charles was exceedingly acrimonious and conducted in the full glare of publicity. Just one year after their divorce, on 31st August 1997, Diana was tragically killed in a car accident in France and a nation went into unprecedented mourning. Speculation exists to this day whether it was truly an accident.

To hear the news of Diana's divorce would have been bad enough for our mother, for she hated to hear of marriage break-ups, but to learn that this beautiful, vivacious, yet troubled, princess had died so young, leaving two young sons, would have saddened her greatly, as it did so many others around the globe.

So much news of this decade, like any other, might be said to fall into the category of "better not to know"! For instance, our parents would have been glad not to learn of the bombing of the *World Trade Center* in New York on Friday 26th February 1993. It was the gravest attack of international terrorism to occur directly on American soil in this century. A massive car-bomb had been left in the underground public parking garage and six people were killed and more than 1000 were injured but the terrorists had hoped to kill upwards of 35,000. Property damage was in excess of $500million. Five Pakistani nationals were later convicted of the bombing and each was jailed for 240 years and fined $250,000.

The most significant act of domestic terrorism on American soil occurred on 19th April 1995 when a bomb destroyed the Federal Building in Oklahoma City. It claimed the lives of 168 people and injured more than 680. Property damage was estimated to be $652million. American militia movement sympathiser Timothy McVeigh, with the assistance of Terry Nichols, was found to be responsible. McVeigh was executed by lethal injection in 2001 and Nichols is serving a life sentence. (Both of these terrorist incidents pale in comparison with the "9/11" terrorist attack but that occurred in 2001, a different century!)

And a very definite "better not to know" occurring around this time was the *"Rwandan Genocide"* of 1994. A civil war had raged in that country from 1990, between the Hutu people in the north and the Tutsi tribe in the south. An uneasy peace was brokered in 1993 but, after the assassination of the Tutsi leader Juvénal Habyariimana, in April 1994, a Tutsi rebel group calling themselves the *"Rwandan Patriotic Front" (RPF)*, invaded northern Rwanda from Uganda. The Hutu militia responded with the mass murder of an estimated 800,000 people in just 100 horrific days. The civil war resumed with yet more bloodshed but eventually the Tutsi *RPF* defeated the Hutu army and seized control of this battered and bloodied country.

Mum and Dad missed the "baby-boomers" coming into their own. Bill Clinton (born in 1946) became President of America in 1993 and Tony Blair (born in 1953) became Britain's Prime Minister in 1997, the youngest since Lord Liverpool in 1812. President Clinton would be impeached in 1998, over various allegations of sexual harassment and misconduct with female employees, but Tony Blair managed to hold onto power and see his *"New Labour Party"* win a record third term in office.

Our parents did not live to see the May 1994 opening of the *Channel Tunnel,* although they knew it was in the pipe-line (so to speak!) as the Treaty to build it had been signed in 1986. It was a joint Anglo-French project and work commenced on it in June 1988. In 1996, the American Society of Civil Engineers identified the *"Chunnel",* as it is affectionately known, as one of the seven wonders of the modern world. It is an undersea railway tunnel linking Folkestone (near Dover) with Coquilles (near Pas-de-Calais) in France and at its building peak, 15,000 people were employed daily in its construction. Ten people were killed on the project and it cost a staggering £4650million, 80% over budget. It is 31.4 miles long and 246 feet deep at its lowest level. 23.5 miles of the *Tunnel* is under the sea-bed making it the longest and deepest underwater tunnel in the world. For the first time in 13000 years, Britain was again linked to mainland Europe.

My parents also missed hearing about a fire in November 1996 which severely damaged the *Tunnel.* It started in a lorry carrying freight and the same problem happened again in September 2008. In December 2009, hundreds of passengers were stranded in the *Tunnel* when snow damaged electrical hardware. There were no reported deaths or serious injuries from these incidents, but they seriously damaged the public's perception of the "Chunnel" as a safe and reliable method of crossing the English Channel.

My parents did not see the birth of the *Euro* currency in 1999. This was adopted by 16 out of the 27 member states of the EU. The UK negotiated an exemption and currently still uses the pound-sterling.

They missed *OJ Simpson* being arrested, in 1994, for the double murder of his wife, Nicole Brown and her friend, Ronald Goldman. It was dubbed the "trial of the century" and, from start to finish, resembled something straight out of a *Hollywood* film studio. Sadly, it was not fiction. Controversially, Simpson was found not guilty but it was a sad chapter in the downward spiral of one of America's greatest football players.

No luck with a "not guilty" verdict for Fred and Rosemary West, of Gloucester in the UK. They were convicted in 1994 for the torture, rape and murder of at least twelve young women between 1967 and 1987. Their crimes went undetected until 1992 when Fred raped his 13-year-old daughter. Police enquiries into this incident eventually led to Fred's confession to the other murders. He hanged himself in his prison cell before he could be brought to trial but his wife was found guilty and sentenced to life imprisonment.

The century also spawned possibly the most prolific mass murderer of all time. From 1974 Dr Harold Shipman is thought to have murdered at least 400 of his patients with overdoses of morphine, although he claimed to have killed 508. His crimes went undetected until his arrest on 7th September 1998 after he attempted to forge the will of one of his victims. He chose to murder mainly elderly ladies who had substantial assets but few relatives. He was jailed for life in January 2000 but committed suicide on 13th January 2004.

The DNA fingerprinting and profiling developed by Alec Jeffreys, and used in a criminal trial for the first time in 1987, has now become a vital tool in forensic science and assists detective-work worldwide. Improvements in the technique are ongoing, one of the most important being the amplification of DNA by the Polymerase Chain Reaction (PCR) technique. This allows minute samples of DNA to be augmented, so even the tiniest specimen can now be analysed. It is commonly known as "Xeroxing" and with highly automated and sophisticated computer equipment, modern-day DNA profiling can process hundreds of samples each day.

It has recently been discovered that every living organism has its own DNA fingerprint, making it possible, for example, to say which tree produced a specific leaf. The possibilities that DNA profiling could eventually even draw a picture of a suspect, now do not seem so far-fetched. In 1994 Alec Jeffreys, the man who started it all, was knighted for his "Services to Science and Technology".

Forensic science generally has made enormous strides in the last decades, apart from DNA fingerprinting. For example electron microscopes, mass spectrometers, digital photography, image enhancement (courtesy of NASA), satellite navigation, sophisticated computer programmes, and forensic specialists in just about every discipline from pathology to psychology, podiatrics to dentistry, anthropology to toxicology, entomology to biology, graphology to geometry and everything in between, now all may play their part in identifying a criminal and then proving his guilt, or innocence.

Our parents missed the Olympic Games in Barcelona in 1992, and those in Atlanta in 1996, and thus they missed the making of a legend. Steven Redgrave had already won a gold medal in the *"Coxed Four"* of Britain's rowing team at Los Angeles in 1984 and in the *"Coxless Pair"* in the 1988 Olympics at Seoul. In '92 and '96 he added more gold medals, again for the *"Coxless Pair"*, and he went on to win another gold in the 2000 Olympics in Sydney. He is one of only four Olympians to have won a gold medal in five consecutive Games and is recognised as Britain's greatest Olympian. (This is despite being diagnosed with ulcerative colitis in 1902 and diabetes in 1997.) His tally of fourteen Olympic and World Championship gold medals is unsurpassed by any other rower in history (although later equalled by his long-time rowing partner Matthew Pinsett). He was knighted by the Queen in 2001.

Mum and Dad missed *"Mad Cow Disease"*, which hit Britain in 1996 and decimated the beef industry. *BSE*, or *bovine spongiform encephalopathy*, resulted in 4.4million cows being slaughtered, although only 179,000 have been found to have been infected with the disease. Since then, it has been identified in many other countries but the UK was the first, and the worst, to be affected. Cattle are herbivores, but they were fed protein supplements made out of the remains of other cattle, and it is believed that this caused the disease to spread. It is thought that the disease can be transmitted to humans who were unfortunate enough to eat the brain or spinal cord of infected animals. In humans, the illness is known as *Creutzfeldt-Jakob disease*. One hundred and sixty-four people have died of it in the UK so far with the number expected to rise because of the long incubation period.

I do not know what our countryman-father would have made of cows being fed meat products nor what he would have thought of a British scientist, Ian Wilmut, cloning a sheep in 1997. She was named *Dolly*, after the famous country and western singer, Dolly Parton, and she was the first mammal to be cloned with DNA taken from an adult cell. It was heralded as the most significant scientific breakthrough of the 1990's but triggered furious debate about the ethics of cloning. In the UK, and the USA now, the duplication of human embryos is allowed for research, aimed at developing new stem cell treatments, but cloning of humans is not permitted. It has opened the door to the possibility that many diseases will eventually be cured using stem cell treatment.

Also in 1997, a new sporting icon came to the fore when Tiger Woods won the prestigious *US Masters Golf Tournament* in Augusta, Georgia. At just 21 years of age, he was the youngest-ever winner. My parents missed that as well. They also missed the British colony of Hong Kong being handed back to China in the same year, with a huge firework display.

"Stars" of all kinds must have been in the ascendancy in 1997 for that was the year the *Hale-Bop Comet* was visible streaking across the sky. It was discovered by two independent observers, Alan Hale and Thomas Bopp, and it was probably the most-observed comet of the 20th century for it was visible to the naked eye for a record eighteen months. It was closest to the Earth on 1st April 1997 and will not appear again until 4530.

On 4th July 1997 NASA's unmanned "spacecraft of discovery", *Pathfinder*, arrived on the planet Mars, after a seven month journey through space. It consisted of a stationary "lander" and a surface "rover", called *Sojourner*. The "rover" was controlled by an Earth-based operator and as well as sending back numerous photographs, the extended mission included analyses of rock and soil. Communication was lost on 27th September, for unknown reasons.

Even a book, published in 1997, was destined to "hit the stratosphere" in sales, film rights and other spin-offs, for this was the year JK Rowling's first *"Harry Potter"* saga appeared on the shelves. This was followed in 1998 by the "most successful movie ever", *Titanic*. "Magic" years indeed that my parents did not live to see.

In 1998, the first element of an International Space Station (ISS) was launched. When completed it will have more than 100 components, including living and work areas, docking stations and laboratories. It will be 290feet long, have a wingspan of 396feet and be 143feet tall and it will weigh nearly a million pounds and support a crew of seven. Two Russians and an American were the first people to take up residence in November 2000. This is anticipated to be just the beginning of a continuous human presence. Co-operation in space is just one of the positive outcomes of the end of the Cold War.

During the 1990's the IRA had continued their bombing campaign of mainland Britain, targeting Lichfield City Railway Station and the Stock Exchange in 1990, Victoria Station in 1991 and London Bridge Station in 1992. Three mortar shells were fired at 10, Downing Street (the official residence of the Prime Minister) in 1991. Over the decade, they bombed a public house in Covent Garden, the Baltic Exchange at St Mary Axe, Canary Wharf and South Quay, all in London. They had targeted a gasworks in Warrington and the Arndale shopping Centre in Manchester, just to name the major incidents in mainland Britain. On 24th April 1993, a huge truck-bomb went off at Bishopsgate in the City of London, killing one person and injuring forty. It caused £1.6billion worth of damage to St Ethelburg's Church and Liverpool Street Station. The insurance claims were so enormous that the insurance underwriters, *Lloyds of London,* almost went bankrupt.

On Friday 10th April 1998, the *Good Friday Agreement* was signed in Belfast, aimed at bringing an end to *The Troubles.* It proposed devolved government for Northern Ireland: the creation of a *Human Rights and an Equality Commission*: the early release of terrorist prisoners in exchange for the de-commissioning of paramilitary weapons and far-reaching reforms of criminal justice and policing policies. That an agreement, between the British Government and all the warring, political parties in Northern Ireland, had finally been reached came as a huge relief to most people, although it came at a high price when the terrorist killers began to be released from prison. After the *"Agreement"*, the IRA scaled down their campaign somewhat but they did not formally give up their struggle for a united Ireland until 2005.

However, if we all thought the *Agreement* would bring an end to the bombs we were sadly mistaken. In 1997, there was disagreement within the IRA over policy and a splinter group broke away from the main organisation. They called themselves the *Real IRA* and they have carried on their bombing campaign in Britain and Ireland, north and south, into the new millennium. Their targets have included Hammersmith Bridge, Ealing Broadway Station, the BBC News Centre, Hendon Post-Office, the MI6 Building, and Belfast International Airport. However, their most infamous attack was at Omagh, in County Tyrone, on 15th August 1998. This killed 29 people and injured another 220 and was the single, most-deadliest strike of the *Troubles*. Thanks to the collaboration of the British and Irish Republican anti-terrorist squads, many of their leaders have been arrested but this organisation has vowed not to call a ceasefire until the British Government withdraws completely from Northern Ireland.

Social legislation continued in the 1990's. Although "Wages Councils" were abolished in 1994, the "National Minimum Wage Act" was introduced in 1998, aiming to ensure a minimum wage for all workers. In 1999, the "Employment Relations Act" introduced the statutory right to trade union recognition where supported by the majority of the workforce. But by far the most far-reaching, and controversial, piece of legislation was in 1998 with the UK's "Human Rights Act", incorporating the rights contained in the "European Convention of Human Rights". Although this outlaws discrimination in almost every facet of life, it is not a guarantee of equal treatment in all areas and therefore the UK will continue to issue its own anti-discriminatory laws well into the new millennium, including legislation on marital status, disability, age and gender re-assignment.

In 1999 Scotland inaugurated its own parliament, ending 300 years of rule from Westminster. But this was not the only UK parliamentary tradition to cease in this final year of the old millennium. "The House of Lords Act of 1999" removed the automatic right of most hereditary peers to sit and vote in the upper chamber of England's Parliament, a right that had been in existence since 1295. However, thanks to an amendment tabled by Lord Weatherall, just 92 heredity peers were allowed to remain until the House was fully reformed.

The number of members in the House of Lords is not fixed, but, as of July 2010, it had 722 members, compared to 650 in the House of Commons. Apart from 26 senior bishops in the Church of England (and the now 91 hereditary peers), the rest are so-called "life peers", ennobled by the Queen, at the suggestion of her Prime Minister, for services to industry, science, medicine and such-like, and, of course, to politics. The title is not able to be passed to their descendants. Very few "life peers" had existed until "The Life Peerage Act of 1958" came onto the statute books, permitting baronies for life, with no limit on numbers, to persons of either sex. Prior to this, women were not allowed in the Upper House and hereditary peeresses were not allowed to sit in the House of Lords until "The Peerage Act of 1963".

Over the centuries, the power and influence of the House of Lords had decreased; by 1999 it had no governmental power whatsoever, except to suggest amendments and thus delay a bill passed by the Commons. But, nevertheless, the old chamber had been a symbol of our traditions and our history, and a reminder of what had once made Britain "Great". One can only wonder what 600 unelected life peers are supposed to do, other than flaunt their titles and draw their expenses!

The year also saw the century's last full eclipse of the sun; the population in Britain will have to wait until 2090 for another one. Also, in this last year of the old century, NATO bombed Serbia to stop the repression and slaughter of ethnic Albanians in Kosovo. Thus, in one respect at least, the century was destined to end as it had begun, with problems in the Balkans.

And finally, yet importantly, in this, the last decade of the century, our parents missed the explosion of the *Internet*, without which this book (in this form, at least) would not have been written.

Of course, not only international news carried on but also did the saga of our family. After Mum's death, Uncle Tom was unable to return to his home in Littlehampton. He stayed with his son Derek and daughter-in-law Barbara until the last few months of his life when he had to go into a nursing home. He died on 16th July 1992, aged 91 years. Mum's other surviving brothers, Bill and Dick, also lived into their 90's, as did their wives Violet and Ethel. All Mum's brothers celebrated at least their Golden Wedding Anniversaries. Tom and Myrtle had missed their "diamond" by just eight months but Bill and Violet and Dick and Ethel celebrated theirs and Ethel and Dick even went on to celebrate their platinum (70 years).

Eventually Dad's surviving sister, Blanche, had to go into a nursing home, with severe dementia. I did try to visit a couple of times a year, although she did not have a clue who I was. I just wanted to make sure she was being cared for. The staff said she was no trouble at all; she was the sweetest old lady they could wish to have as a resident, and who lived only for the next meal! She had no other visitors apart from me and I always popped in uninvited and unexpected as part of my amateur sleuthing duties!

One day in 1998, I went to the nursing home only to be told she had died a few months earlier, aged 93 years, and that she had been buried in a "pauper's grave" at Worthing Cemetery. Over the years, my contact details had been lost apparently and I was upset to learn that, apart from a couple of staff, no one went to her funeral. In her younger days, Auntie Blanche could be difficult and argumentative but she always remembered us at Christmas and at birthdays and I would have liked to pay my last respects, as I know Dad would have wished me to do.

Sheila and Vernon returned to America in June 1992 and settled in Newport again. Later that year Russell went to a university in the American Mid-West to study Business Management. Eventually he moved to New York, became a Buddhist and currently he is studying traditional Indian medicine, *Ayurveda*, with the intention of becoming a practising physician.

I visited America in June 1993 to see Vernon graduate from high school with honours. He also went on to higher education and I went to see him graduate with a Master's Degree in bio-chemistry in 1998. He was in the top 10% of the "most outstanding graduates" and received an additional award for "*Excellence in Academics*". He is now an environmental chemist and, in 2003, he married Jennifer. Their daughter, Victoria, was born in 2004 and it is for Victoria that this book was conceived.

Sheila's biological mother, Phyllis, died in 1995, from a heart attack, aged 73 years. She had suffered greatly from arthritis in her final years, and to a lesser extent from an under-active thyroid gland, both problems she had inherited from her mother and also passed both onto her daughter, Sue. Sheila and her twin have missed the thyroid problem but they also suffer from arthritis.

This final chapter has concentrated on all the things Mum and Dad did not live to see but nevertheless the changes they had seen, in this final century of the old millennium, were remarkable, in technology, medicine, science, communications, politically and socially. Many advances were thanks to two world wars, the rise of socialism, the conquering of space, the emancipation of women, the independence of colonial nations and the recognition of the right of equality for all races.

There was a downside of course; they lived to see drug abuse become rampant and terrorism become a way of life. As crimes against children appeared to proliferate, youngsters no longer enjoyed the simple freedoms of city or countryside but stayed behind closed doors, glued to play-stations. "One-night-stands" had become commonplace, front doors were kept locked and families routinely disintegrated. All these things were alien concepts when our parents were born at the beginning of the century.

One can only wonder at what the next century holds, for good and ill. And will Victoria's daughter, or granddaughter, sit down in 2109 and write about her life and the century in which her mother/grandmother lived? Now wouldn't that be something?

ACKNOWLEDGEMENTS

It has taken me more than two years to complete this project and I would like to thank family and friends for their support throughout these many months. Also thanks for sharing your memories (and photographs) and allowing me to include them in this book, especially cousins Pam, Peggy, Brenda, Peter, Ivan and Clive and my sister-in-law, Iris. Also thanks to those who read the drafts and gave me such encouragement to continue. But most of my thanks go to my sister, Sheila Carpenter, without whom I would not even have begun this. Also for encouraging me to include less than flattering insights into her (at times) troubled past. She said the truth would set her free, but it takes a big and generous spirit to re-travel the painful journey for all to see.

My sources for the history were many and varied, although I am now more conscious of what, and whom, I have left out than what/whom I have included! Sometimes a comment on the radio, a sentence in a newspaper, or a television programme, would set me off on a quest to include some forgotten, or unusual, snippet. Unfortunately I am not able to give credit to all these original sources of inspiration because I did not think to make a note of most of them! Thus the history is an amalgam of information; the above, plus reference books, plus memories, plus, of course, the *Internet*. I have endeavoured to acknowledge you all below but I apologise for any omissions. Nevertheless, my grateful thanks to you all.

TIMELINES AND GENERAL INFORMATION
(The following sources have been used in various chapters throughout the book)
Wiki = en.wikipedia.org
20th century history timelines   ...history1900s.about.com
                                    ...www.chron.com/cs/CDA/plainstory.hts
ancestry.com
www.scaruffi.com
www.britsattheirbest,com
www.unionancestors.co.uk
WW11   ...www.headlinehistory,co.uk
        ...www.historyonthenet.com
        ...www.bbc.co.uk
        ...www.schoolsliason.org.uk
List of terrorist incidents GB   ...wiki
History of Northern Ireland   ...www.uk.filo.pl/Ireland
Provisional IRA campaign 1969-1997   ...wiki
Timeline of terrorist attacks   ...timelineofterrorism.com
Short history of immigration   ...news.bbc.co.uk
Capital offences in the UK   ...www.capitalpunishmentuk.org
Vietnam War   ...wiki
General history of UK ... *"History of England"* by John Burke, published by
                              "Book Club Associates" in 1974
Rural Sussex   ..."*A Time There Was*" by Phoebe Summers published on behalf of the Weald and Downland Museum, Singleton, by Alan Sutton Publishing Ltd.
Sussex..."*Black's Guide to Sussex and its Watering Places*",
                              published in 1902 by Adam and Charles Black
China (*I was inspired to include more of China's history than I originally intended from reading "Wild Swans" by Jung Chang, published by HarperCollins in 1991, and "The Last Emperor" by Edward Behr, published by Futura Publications in 1987. I used the following sources in various chapters for information about China included in this book.*)
        ....wiki

...history1900's.about.com
....www.talk talk.co.uk
...wsu.edu/-dee/MODCHINA/REV.HTM

CHAPTER ONE   *A New Century Dawns (1901-1902)*
Duncton..... www.gravelroots
Duncton Mills....Sussex Mills Trust
Petworth...www.old towns.co.uk
           ..."*The Shell Guides*", "Sussex" by John Godfrey (pub'd by M.Joseph)
           ..."*Illustrated Guide to Britain*", AA, published by Drive Publications Ltd
Petworth Park and House...The National Trust

CHAPTER TWO   *Food, Fire and Theft (1903-1908)*
Punishments for poaching...www.blakeston.stockton.sch.uk
Condoms...www.avert.org/condoms
Contraception....www.gale.edu
Herbal remedies...www.home-remedies-for-you.com

CHAPTER THREE   *A Rural Childhood (1909-1910)*
Free education from 1891...www.number10.gov.uk

CHAPTER FOUR   *A Tragedy (1911-1912)*
Puerperal Sepsis...."Family Health Encyclopedia"
                        by the British Medical Association,
                            published by Colour Library Books Ltd.
History of workhouses....www.workhouses.org.uk
Rules on Divorce...www.familyhistory.co.uk

CHAPTER FIVE   *Work and War (1913-1919)*
De Laval Milker ...www.old-engine.com
              ....http://library.think quest.org
First World War...www.teacheroz,com
              ....wiki
  (including all of the following:-
Posters
Analysis of WW1
Reasons for WW1
Conscription
Results:- Casualties + Division of land)
Battles...www.geocities.com

CHAPTER SIX   *India (1919-1926)*
East India Company ...wiki
British India and the Great Rebellion ...www.bbc.co.uk/history
History of the British in India...wiki
                   ...www.bbc.co.uk/history/british

CHAPTER SEVEN   *Sussex by the Sea (1905)*
Littlehampton History...."*Littlehampton Long Ago*" by H.J.F.Thompson,
                    published by J.P.Ltd West Street, Bognor in 1974
              ...."The Shell Guides" by John Godfrey
River Arun...wiki

CHAPTER EIGHT   *The Martin Clan (1905)*
Keir Hardie/General Elections 1906 + 1910...www.bbc.co.uk/historic

Birth of the Labour Party...www.workers power.com
Ford Motor Company ...wiki
Petrol pumps ... www.petroliana.co.uk
Filling stations ...wiki
History of tyres ... www.blackcircles.com
Automotive industry in UK ...wiki
Traffic circles ...www.alaskaroundabouts.com
John Loudon McAdam ...inventors.about.com
                    ...wiki
Tarmac ...www.tarmac.co,uk
        ...www.bbc.co.uk
Russian Revolution...wiki

CHAPTER NINE   *The Carefree Years   (1906-1912)*
Kellogs...wiki
The Boer War/Concentration Camps ...www.spartacus.schoolnet.co.uk
                                  ...wiki
Baden Powell Scout Camp at Brownsea Island....www.troop292nh.com
Crippen....wiki
Non-contributory Old Age Pension Act 1908 ....wiki
National Insurance Act 1911, Contributory Scheme ...www.redbook.i12.com
Boxer Rebellion ...wiki
                ...history1900's.about.com
Xinhai Revolution ...wiki
                  ...www.talk talk.co.uk
                  ...wsu.edu/-dee/MODCHINA/REV.HTM
Emperor Pu Yi...wiki
Scott's expedition to South Pole ...wiki
The first telephone...www.mkheritage.co.uk
                    ....wiki
Titanic ...wiki

CHAPTER TEN   *Love by Name and Love by Nature*
ancestry.com

CHAPTER ELEVEN   *On the Brink of Change   (1913-1918)*
First crossword puzzle ...history1900's.about.com
Albert Kahn ...wiki
            ...www.bbc.co.uk/programmes
            ...BBC television series *"The Wonderful World of Albert Kahn"*
Traffic Lights ...wiki
Warlordism in China ...wsu.edu/-dee/MODCHINA
Influenza pandemic ...wiki
Suffragette movement...www.historylearningsite.co.uk

CHAPTER TWELVE   *Out in the World   (1919-1923)*
Royal British Legion .... www.britishlegion.org.uk
Poppy Day origins ....warmemorials.net
History of Irish problems and Home Rule...wiki
                          ...www.wesleyjohnston.com
                          ...www.history/learningsite.co.uk
Albert Einstein ...wiki
Discovery of Tutankhamun's tomb ...history1900's.about.com

CHAPTER THIRTEEN   *The Roaring Twenties (1924-1929)*
Lewes Bonfire Society .... www.lewesbonfirecouncil.org.uk

Guy Fawkes .... wiki
General Elections of 1922/1924...wiki
General strike of 1926 ...wiki
"Roaring Twenties"...wiki
Early cinema heart-throbs...www.ehow.com
Birth of the BBC...wiki
Charles Lindbergh .... www.pbs.org.wgbh.amex/lindbergh
.... www.nasm.si.edu
Motorcycle helmets + law ...wiki
Chinese Civil War...wsu.edu/-dee/MODCHINA
...wiki
...wapedia.mobi
Northern Expedition (China) ...wiki
Dr Fleming + penicillin ...wiki
Wall Street Crash .... wiki
Great Depression .... wiki

CHAPTER FOURTEEN   *On the Move!*   *(1930-1933)*
Gandhi's Salt March ...wiki
Depression...wiki
Swing music ....library.thinkquest.org
....www.idfo.co.uk
FW Woolworths...business.timesonline.co.uk
Lindbergh kidnapping ...wiki
Dachau...wiki
Mao Tse Tung's Long March ...www.moreorless.au.com
....www.puhsd.k12.ca.us

CHAPTER FIFTEEN   *On the Brink*   *(1934-1936)*
Penguin Books ...wiki
Cat's eye ...wiki
Red telephone kiosks ...wiki
...www.thephoneybox.com
Hoover Dam ...wiki
Berlin Olympics 1936 ...wiki
Jarrow March ...wiki
John Maynard Keynes ...wiki
Queen Mary maiden sailing ...wiki
Spanish Civil War ...wiki
General Francisco Franco ...www.historylearning site.co.uk
Edward VIII abdication ...wiki
...news.bbc.co.uk
Stolen child...www.we3.org/welcome
Tommy Farr ...wiki

CHAPTER SIXTEEN   *Preparing for War*   *(1937-1939)*
The Second World War.... (see Timelines)
....wiki
Causes of WW2....wiki
Hindenburg accident ...wiki
Golden Gate Bridge ...wiki
Amelia Earhart ...bbc.news.co.uk
Japanese invasion of China 1937...wiki
Films at Saturday morning pictures...wiki
Comics+characters...wiki
Walls ice-cream bicycles ...www.canalmuseum

Barnardo's children's homes...www.barnardos.org.uk
Neville Chamberlain + Peace in our time ...wiki
...news.bbc.co.uk
Orson Welles + "War of the Worlds" ..wiki
Night of Broken Glass ...wiki
Kinder Transport Scheme ...www.childrenwhocheatedthenazis.co.uk
Anderson Shelters ...wiki
First commercial flight PanAm 1939 ...wiki
Voyage of the Damned ...wiki
Bletchley Park ....wiki
Colossus Computer ....wiki
"Gone with the Wind" ...wiki

CHAPTER SEVENTEEN   *The "Phoney War"   (1939)*
BEF...wiki
Phoney War...wiki
Vera Lynn ...www.historylearningsite.co.uk
ITMA ...ukonline.co.uk
"Road to ....." films ...wiki
Bing Crosby ...wiki
"White Christmas" ...wiki
Bob Hope ...wiki

CHAPTER EIGHTEEN   *Dunkirk   (1940)*
www.spartacus.schoolnet.co.uk

CHAPTER NINETEEN   *The Threat of Invasion Looms   (1940 post-Dunkirk)*
See Timelines

CHAPTER TWENTY   *The War Continues   (1940)*
Battle of Britain ....www.headlinehistory.co.uk
Rules on conscription ...www.historyonthenet,com
Dieppe Raid ...wiki

CHAPTER TWENTY-ONE   *The War Ends   (1940-1945)*
See Timelines
Dambusters + Guy Gibson ...wiki
....historylearningsite.co.uk
.....thedambusters.org.uk
Normandy Landings ...wiki
Attempts on Hitler's life ...wiki
...wikianswers.com
Casualties in the war, Europe and the Far East ...wiki
Chinese Civil War ...wiki
Results of the war ...wiki
Yalta Treaty results ...wiki
....spartacus.school.net
Lord Haw-Haw + William Joyce ...wiki
Pre-fabs ...wiki
Baby Boom ....wiki
Clement Attlee's Government:-
Nationalization/Welfare state ...www.guardian.co.uk
...www2.rgu.ac.uk
....opsi.gov.uk
...news.bbc.co.uk
National Parks ...wiki

CHAPTER TWENTY-TWO   *A New Arrival*   *(1946-June 1948)*
Winter 1947 ...www.metoffice.gov.uk
UK Floods March 1947 ....www.guardian.co.uk
Chuck Yeager...www.achievement.org
Independence of India ...wiki
MV Windrush ...wiki

CHAPTER TWENTY-THREE   *Double Trouble*   *(1ˢᵗ July 1948-1950)*
Murder in Arundel Park 1948 ...truecrimelibrary.com
                    ..."*Murder on my Mind*" by Fred Narborough,
                    published by Alan Wingate (Publishers) Ltd in 1958.
Vaccinations, whooping cough and measles ...whale.to/vaccines
                                ...www.net doctor.co.uk
Post-war conscription rules ...wiki
Emperor Pu Yi..."*The Last Emperor*" by Edward Behr,
                        pub'd by Futura Publications in 1987
Korean War ...wiki
            ...encarta.msn.com
McCarthyism ...wiki

CHAPTER TWENTY-FOUR   *Challenges and Change*   *(1951-1953)*
Festival of Britain ...wiki
Zebra crossings/Belisha beacons ...wiki
                    ...www.wigan.gov.uk
Enid Blyton ...wiki
Comet (de Havilland) ...wiki
                ....www.century-of-flight.net
                .....news.bbc.co.uk
BBC radio history ...www.radiorewind.co.uk
                ...www.whirligig-tv.co.uk
Teddy Boys ....wiki
            ....rockabilly.nl/general
Stalin's death + Khrushchev ...wiki
Polio ....www.britishpolio.org.uk

CHAPTER TWENTY-FIVE   *Family and Friendships*   *(1953-1954)*
Sealyham terriers ....wiki
De-rationing .....wiki
ITV.... wiki
First kidney transplant ...wiki
James Dean death.....wiki
Rosa Parkes ..... www.holidays.net
            ..... wiki
            ......historylearningsite.co.uk

CHAPTER TWENTY-SIX   *From Panto' To Politburo*   *(1955-1956)*
Sussex Bonfire Societies ...bonfire night.info/sussexbonfiresociety
History of Pantomime ......www.limelights.co.uk
Pressure cookers .....homecooking.about.com
Elvis Presley...www.history-of-rock.com
Grace Kelly marriage .....news.bbc.co.uk
Suez crisis ...wiki
        .....www.bbc.co.uk/history
Hungarian uprising 1956 ....wiki

CHAPTER TWENTY-SEVEN   *The Fifties End*   *(1957-1959)*

EEC ...wiki
Harold MacMillan/You've never had it so good...news.bbc.co.uk
11-plus exam...wiki
Munich air disaster...wiki
Sputniks 1 & 2.....kirjastoscifi
.........wiki
.........www.space.com/news
Laika...wiki
...www.space.com/news
NASA...wiki
Pasternik/Dr Zhivago ...wiki

CHAPTER TWENTY-EIGHT   *Saints and Sinners*   *(1960)*
LASER....wiki
.....www.thetech.org
The Pill....wiki
.....www.scf.usc.edu
....inventors.about.com
Swinging Sixties...wiki
Beatles ....wiki
Mods and Rockers...wiki
.......news.bbc.co.uk
Hippie movement ....wiki
.....www.oldhippie.jimgreenlee.com

CHAPTER TWENTY-NINE   *More Saints than Sinners*   *(1961)*
Adolf Eichmann...wiki
....www.jewishvirtuallibrary
Yuri Gargarin/First man in space...www.nasa.gov
..www.bbc.co.uk
Berlin Wall...news.bbc.co.u
......wiki
.....www.history.com
Thalidomide tragedy...wiki
.....www.helium.com

CHAPTER THIRTY   *Out in the Big Wide World*   *(1962-1965)*
Marilyn Monroe death ...wiki
....news.bbc.co.uk
Cuba Missile Crisis 1962.... www.johnclare.net
Winter 1963...www.metoffice.gov.uk
Kim Philby....www.spartacus.schoolnet.co.uk
Profumo Affair...wiki
Toynbee Hall...wiki
Royal Tournament (Earls Court) ..wiki
...royaltournament.org
Great Train Robbery 1963 ...howstuffworks.com
... wiki
Martin Luther King/I have a dream/March on Washington ...wiki
....usconstitution.net
Assassination of JFK.....wiki
.....news.bbc.co.uk
Cassius Clay/Mohammed Ali....wiki
.....news.bbc.co.uk
Imprisonment of Nelson Mandela....wiki
....nobel prize.org

Sharon Tate Murder/Charles Manson …bbc.onthisday.co.uk
....wiki
Troops to NI ....www.bbc.co.uk
Capital punishment in UK ...wiki
History of hanging ...capitalpunishment.org
....wiki
Ruth Ellis ..stephen-Stratford.co.uk
....wiki
Internet (ARPANET)/Licklider....wiki

CHAPTER THIRTY-THREE   *Black and White*   *(1970-1972)*
History of foundation of Israel ....wiki
Dawsons Field....wiki
.....news.bbc.co.uk
Ibrox Stadium disaster ...wiki
....news.bbc.co.uk
Angry Brigade/Bomb Squad ...www.guardian.co.uk
Discrimination laws ....www.brad.ac.uk
Decimal currency UK .....wiki
.....news.bbc.co.uk
London Bridge/Lake Havasu ....wiki
....roadtripamerica.com
School milk/Margaret Thatcher ...news.bbc.co.uk
"Talk of the Town"cabaret restaurant.....wiki
Bloody Sunday...www.historyb.com
....wiki
Parachute Regiment/IRA/12th Feb 1972 ....news.bbc,co.uk
....wiki
Bloody Friday ...wiki
....news.bbc.co.uk
BlackSeptemberhijackings/Deaths at Tel Aviv Airport/May1972 ....wiki
.....news.bbc.co.uk
Idi Amin/Asians expelled from Uganda/Arrival in UK ....wiki
....news.bbc.co.uk
....www.paralumun.com
Munich Olympics/Death of Israeli athletes ....wiki
....news.bbc.co.uk

Deaths of Duke & Duchess of Windsor....news.bbc.co.uk

CHAPTER THIRTY-FOUR   *All Change!*   *(1973-1975)*
EEC .....wiki
Vietnam War .....www.Vietnam-war.info/facts
....www.historyplace.com
....www.geocities.com
Skylab ....heasarc.gsfc.nasa.gov
....wiki
Mobile 'phones ...www.thephoneybox.com
Spiro Agnew ....wiki
Watergate scandal .....wiki
Richard Nixon....wiki
Terracotta Army .....wiki
History of IRA attacks ....wiki
Invasion of S.Vietnam by NVA ...wiki
US pulls out of Cambodia ....news.bbc.co.uk
Pol Pot/Khmer Rouge....wiki

...www.celebritymorgue.com
Referendum on Common Market....news.bbc.co.uk
Arthur Ashe/Wimbledon ...www.mademan.com
....news.bbc.co.uk
North Sea oil and gas ....www.abdn.ac.uk
...wiki

CHAPTER THIRTY-FIVE   *Home is Where the Heart is*   *(1976-1978)*
Concorde ...wiki
Nadia Comaneci/1976 Olympics ....www.infoplease/nadiacomaneci
Immigration/Racial Equality ....news.bbc.co.uk
Cultural revolution/Death of Mao....wiki
....news.bbc.co.uk
....www.historylearningsite.co.uk
Silver Jubilee of Elizabeth II .....wiki
Queen celebrates Silver Jubilee...news.bbc.co.uk
Vivienne Westwood ...dailymail.co.uk
Sid Vicious .....wiki
Punk Rock/Punk Fashion ....wiki
....www.fashion-era.com
Virginia Wade/Wimbledon....news.bbc.co.uk
Steve Biko ....news.bbc.co.uk
...africanhistory.about.com
Louise Brown/Test tube baby ...history1900's.about.com
...wiki
Pope John Paul II ....wiki
....news.bbc.co.uk
Jamestown Massacre .....www.infoplease.com

CHAPTER THIRTY-SIX   *Turbulent End to a Troubled Decade*   *(1979)*
Winter of Discontent ....libcom.org/history
....news.bbc.co.uk
IMF/Sterling devalued/Harold Wilson ......www.nationalarchives.gov.uk
Strikes UK .....www.eurofound
Death of Airey Neave.....news.bbc.co.uk
General Election 1979 ....wiki
Margaret Thatcher ....wiki
.....news.bbc.co.uk
Death of Mountbatten....news.bbc.co.uk
Antony Blunt .....news.bbc.co.uk
...wiki
....www.spartacus.schoolnet.co.uk
Three Mile Island accident ....wiki
Mother Teresa .....wiki
Ayatollah Khomeni.....www.bbc.co.uk
US hostages/Tehren Embassy siege....news.bbc.co.uk
Saddam Hussein/Iran-Iraq war....wiki
"Star Wars" movie ....wiki
"StarTrek" movie ..wiki
Film "Grease" ....wiki
1970's fashion ..wiki

CHAPTER THIRTY-SEVEN   *Golden Threads*   *(1980)*
US hostages (cont'd) ...news.bbc.co.uk
Siege at Iranian Embassy ,London ...news.bbc.co.uk
....wiki

Mount St Helen's eruption...news.bbc.co.uk
......pubs.usgs.gov
Rubik's Cube ..wiki
PacMan   ....wiki
Death of John Lennon ...wiki

CHAPTER THIRTY-EIGHT   *In Pursuit of Dreams*   *(1981)*
Peter Sutcliffe.....wiki
Reagan assassination attempt ....wiki
Brixton Riots www.20thcenturylondon.ork.uk
......news.bbc.co.uk
...www.new-diaspora.com
.... www.absoluteastronomy.com
AIDS www.kare11.com
IBM PC ....inventors.about.com
Charles and Diana marriage ....news.bbc.co.uk

CHAPTER THIRTY-NINE   *Memories*   *(1982-1983)*
Birth of Star Wars ....news.bbc.co.uk
....starwars.yahoo.com
....wiki
Falklands war .....news.bbc.co.uk
...wiki
Sun Myung's blessing ceremony ....www.newcovpub.com
....letusreason.org
Hyde Park & Regents Park bombs....news.bbc.co.uk
...wiki
Mary Rose ....news.bbc.co.uk
....wiki
HMS Victory/HMS Warrior....www.historicdockyard.co.uk
Cabbage Patch Kids ....wiki
Seat belt legislation ...wiki
Mallorca ....*Landscapes of Mallorca* by Valerie Crespi-Green
Dennis Nilsen ....wiki
US Embassy Beirut bomb....wiki
Terrorist bombing/Marine barracks/Beirut ....www.arlingtoncemetery.net
Hijacking of Flight TWA 847....wiki
Sally Ride ....wiki
Korean airliner shot down .....wiki
.....news.bbc.co.uk
Brinks Mat robbery ....wiki
Harrods bomb ....news.bbc.co.uk
...wiki

CHAPTER FORTY   *Skating into 1984*   *(1984)*
Torvill & Dean ...www.britannica.com
Robin Cousins/John Curry...wiki
GCHQ ....www.fas.org/irp/world/uk/chq
Miners strike....news.bbc.co.uk
......wiki
Yuppie....wiki
Libyan Embassy/Yvonne Fletcher ...news.bbc.co.uk
...wiki
Endeavour...wiki
Brighton bomb ...news.bbc.co.uk
....wiki

431

Assassination of Indira Gandhi ....news.bbc.co.uk
Golden Temple raid ....news.bbc.co.uk
Nehru....news.bbc.co.uk
Bhopal gas leak ...news.bbc.co.uk
　　　　　...history1900's.about.com

CHAPTER FORTY-ONE　　　*Going West*　　(1985-1986)
Bradford fire....news.bbc.co.uk
　　　　...wiki
Glasnost/Perestroika ...www.ehow.com
Ozone layer....wiki
Titanic wreck...news.bbc.co.uk
Printing strike....www.20thcenturylondon.org.uk
Challenger tragedy.....news.bbc.co.uk
MIR space station...www.infoplease.com
Air strike on Libya...news.bbc.co.uk
　　　　　....eightiesclub.tripod.com
　　　　　....wiki
Chernobyl....news.bbc.co.uk
Iran-Contra scandal...home.snu.edu

CHAPTER FORTY-TWO　　*A Traumatic Year*　(1987)
Terry Waite...edition.cnn.com
　　　　...wiki
DNA profiling...wiki
Alec Jeffreys...wiki
Colin Pitchfork....www.timesonline.co.uk
　　　　...wiki
Timothy Spencer...wiki
The Great Storm ....news.bbc.co.uk
Great storm of 1703...wiki
Black Monday ...wiki
Kings Cross fire...wiki

CHAPTER FORTY-THREE　　　*A Leap of Faith*　　(1988)
US shoots down Iranian airliner ....news.bbc.co.uk
Lockerbie bombing ....history1900's.about.com
　　　　...wiki
Newport ...."*The Complete Guide to Newport, RI*" by John T.Hopf

CHAPTER FORTY-FOUR　　　*Love Endures*　　(1989-1990)
Exxon Valdez oil spill ...wiki
　　　　　...www.ww4report.com
　　　　　....www.exxposeExxon.com
Hillsborough disaster...news.bbc.co.uk
Tiananmen Square massacre ...news.bbc.co.uk
　　　　　....wiki
Berlin Wall ....wiki
　　　　....www.jewishworldreview.com
Gulf War ...wiki

CHAPTER FORTY-FIVE　　*Be Not Afraid*　(1st January-14th January 1991)

CHAPTER FORTY-SIX　　*Come to Dust*　(15th January-8th October 1991)
Shakespeare's *Cymbelline* quote　　....www.amblesideonline.org

Gulf War_   ...wiki

CHAPTER FORTY-SEVEN   *When Diamonds Blow Away*
                        (9th October-28th November 1991)
"You'll Never Walk Alone" ... wiki
"Abide With Me" ... wiki

CHAPTER FORTY-EIGHT   *Epilogue*   *(1990's)*
Hubble Space Telescope ...wiki
Lech Walesa ....www.britannica.com
Release of Nelson Mandela ....news.bbc.co.uk
                         ....nobelprize.org
Resignation of Margaret Thatcher ....news.bbc.co.uk
                                ...wiki
Queen's Annus Horribilis speech ....news.bbc.co.uk
Andrew and Fergie separation....news.bbc.co.uk
Windsor Castle fire ...news.bbc.co.uk
Princess Diana car crash ...news.bbc.co.uk
Diana ....womenhistory.about.com
World Trade Centre bombing....www.adl.org
Oklahoma City bombing ...wiki
Rwanda genocide ...wiki
Baby Boomers...uktv.co.uk
Channel Tunnel ....wiki
Euro currency....wiki
OJ Simpson .... www.highbeam.com
Fred and Rosemary West ...wiki
Harold Shipman ....judicial-inc.biz
                ....news.bbc.co.uk
           ......www.trutv.com
DNA fingerprinting...wiki
                ...www.accessexcellence.org
AlecJeffreys ...wiki
Steven Redgrave...wiki
BSE ...wiki
Dolly ...edition.cnn.com
Tiger Woods ....www.highbeam.com
Hale Bopp Comet....wiki
Mars Pathfinder ...nssdc.gsfc.nasa.gov
Harry Potter ...wiki
ISS ..wiki
Good Friday Agreement ...www.nio.gov.uk
Real IRA ...wiki
Human Rights Act...www.yourrights.org.uk
House of Lords/Reform ...wiki
                ...www.parliament.the-stationery-office.co.uk

Lightning Source UK Ltd.
Milton Keynes UK

173025UK00008B/94/P